THE
FUTURE
CHURCH

ALSO BY JOHN L. ALLEN, JR.

Conclave

All the Pope's Men

The Rise of Benedict XVI

Opus Dei

A People of Hope

THE
FUTURE
CHURCH

HOW TEN TRENDS
ARE REVOLUTIONIZING THE
CATHOLIC CHURCH

JOHN L. ALLEN, JR.

IMAGE

NEW YORK

Copyright © 2009 by John L. Allen, Jr.

All rights reserved.
Published in the United States by Image, an imprint of the
Crown Publishing Group, a division of Random House, Inc., New York.
www.crownpublishing.com

IMAGE and the Image colophon are registered trademarks of Random House, Inc.

Originally published in hardcover in the United States by Doubleday Religion, an imprint of
the Crown Publishing Group, a division of Random House, Inc., New York, in 2009.

Library of Congress Cataloging-in-Publication Data

Allen, John L., 1965–
  The future church : how ten trends are revolutionizing the Catholic Church / John L. Allen, Jr. — 1st ed.
    p. cm.
  Includes bibliographical references (p.   ) and index.
  (alk. paper)
  1. Christian sociology—Catholic Church—Forecasting.   2. Catholic Church—Doctrines—
Forecasting.   3. Twenty-second century—Forecasts.   I. Title.
  BX1753.A39 2008
  282.09'051101—dc22

                                                                                    2008032650

ISBN 978-0-385-52039-3
eISBN 978-0-385-52953-2

Printed in the United States of America

Book design by Helene Berinsky
Cover design by Patti Ratchford
Cover photograph © Gary Yeowell / Getty Images

10 9 8 7 6 5 4 3 2 1

First Paperback Edition

CONTENTS

ACKNOWLEDGMENTS

I want to begin by acknowledging Trace Murphy, my editor at Doubleday, and Bill Barry, who was the publisher at the time this project took shape. Both are a writer's dream, literary professionals who care deeply about ideas as well as helping a book find its audience. They're extraordinarily good at what they do. Thanks are also due to everyone at the *National Catholic Reporter*, which has been my home in the print world for more than a decade. Tom Fox, Tom Roberts, Joe Feuerherd, Dennis Coday, Teresa Malcolm, Margot Patterson, Sr. Rita Larivee, Patty McCarty, Wally Reiter, Toni Ortiz, Arthur Jones, Rich Heffern, and all the other past and present members of the *NCR* cast have been marvelous friends and colleagues. I'm especially appreciative of their tolerance for my absences to do the reporting and writing this book required. In a similar spirit, I want to thank my friends and colleagues at CNN, especially my principal contacts over the years: Pamela Sellers, Maria Ebrahimji, and Gail Chalef. In moments of frustration I've sometimes joked that navigating the bureaucracy of CNN can make the Vatican seem like a well-oiled machine, and without Pam, Maria, and Gail, I would have been lost on any number of occasions. In terms of my colleagues in the Vatican press corps, if I started to tick off here the names of everyone to whom this book owes something, the list would never end. Suffice it to say that you know who you are, and I'm grateful.

Chapters of this book were read and critiqued by a number of people who deserve mention here: Cardinal Óscar Rodríguez-Maradiaga of Tegucigalpa,

Honduras; Cardinal Roger Mahony of Los Angeles; Archbishop John On-aiyekan of Abuja, Nigeria; Bryan Froehle; Philip Jenkins; George Weigel; Fr. Thomas Reese; Fr. Andrew Greeley; Fr. Daniel Madigan; Fr. Emmanuel Mbam; Russell Shaw; Rick McCord; Walter Grazer; Fr. Brian Johnstone; Fr. Edward Cleary; Fr. John Wauck; Pamela Schaeffer; and Tom Roberts. In every case, their reactions were extraordinarily helpful. Froehle in particular was generous with his time and expertise. Needless to say, the flaws in the book are of my own making, not theirs. My wife, Shannon, also read every line of this book at least twice, and along the way she fed me valuable ideas and resources. This book would never have seen the light of day without her support.

I also want to say thank you to those readers who sent me ideas, arguments, exhortations, and detailed reactions. That material was fundamental in shaping the decisions and the perspectives that run through the book. In a special way, I need to acknowledge a debt of gratitude to the audiences in various parts of the world with whom the ideas of this book were worked out during lectures, keynote speeches, workshops, and addresses I've given over the last couple of years. You will never know how much watching the reaction on your faces, listening to how hard you laughed at various points, and pondering the questions you had asked long after I had answered them on the spot have contributed to these pages.

A final note of thanks is in order for all those people in forty countries who have opened their lives, their minds, and their hearts to me over the course of the past decade, giving me an up-close-and-personal education in the contours and complexities of global Catholicism. In a special way, I want to think Cardinal Rodríguez and Archbishop Onaiyekan, each of whom opened his diocese and cleared his schedule for me in March 2007 to help test some of the ideas I'd developed about Catholicism in the global South against the realities on the ground. To both, a hearty *ad multos annos*.

A book freezes an author's thinking at a given moment in time. To follow the conversation beyond these pages, I invite readers who have not yet done so to sign up for my weekly Internet column, "All Things Catholic," and to check out my daily postings at this address: http://ncrcafe.org/node/507. I'll be keeping a close eye on the evolution of the trends described here.

This book is dedicated to my wife, Shannon, whose love constitutes the most powerful trend in my own life, and to our cherished pug, Ellis, a very catholic creature in terms of the universality of his affections. Both endured the long gestation of this book with grace, for which I will be forever grateful.

INTRODUCTION

In Thomas Friedman's enormously popular book about globalization, he summarized the essential message in four words: the world is flat. Globalization is knocking down one barrier to opportunity after another, creating a world in which smart, hungry go-getters in India, China, or Brazil can compete not just for the low-wage jobs Americans don't want, but for the high-tech, high-pay jobs they definitely do want. For that reason, Friedman's book came with a warning: Americans need to hustle in this century or they'll find themselves run over by this phenomenon.

This too is a book about globalization. Its subject is the oldest globalized institution on earth, the Roman Catholic Church. Its bottom line can also be expressed in a few words: the church is upside down. By that, I don't mean that the Church is topsy-turvy or out of whack. I mean that the issues, party lines, and ways of doing business that have dominated Catholicism in the forty-plus years since the close of the Second Vatican Council in 1965, that watershed moment in modern Catholic life, are being turned on their head by a series of new forces reshaping the global Church. This book comes with a warning too: Catholics in the twenty-first century won't just need hustle (though they certainly will need that), but above all they'll need imagination. They'll need the capacity to reconsider how they think about the Church, and what they do with their faith, because otherwise Catholicism won't rise to the occasion of these new challenges—it'll be steamrolled by them.

Consider the following ways in which the Catholic Church is upside down in the twenty-first century:

- A Church dominated in the twentieth century by the global North, meaning Europe and North America, today finds two thirds of its members living in Africa, Asia, and Latin America. Catholic leadership will come from all over the world in this century to a degree never before experienced.

- A Church whose watchword after the Second Vatican Council (1962–65) was *aggiornamento,* meaning an "updating designed to open up to the modern world," is today officially reaffirming all the things that make it different from modernity: its traditional markers of Catholic thought, speech, and practice. This politics of identity is in part a reaction against runaway secularization.

- A Church whose primary interreligious relationship for the last forty years has been with Judaism now finds itself struggling to come to terms with a newly assertive Islam, not just in the Middle East, Africa, and Asia, but in its own European backyard.

- A Church that has historically invested a large share of its pastoral energy in the young now has to cope, beginning in the North, with the most rapidly aging population in human history.

- A Church that has long relied on its clergy to deliver pastoral care and to provide leadership now has lay people doing both in record numbers and in a staggering variety of ways.

- A Church used to debating bioethical issues that have been around for millennia—abortion, birth control, and homosexuality—finds itself in a brave new world of cloning, genetic enhancements, and trans-species chimeras. Its moral teaching is struggling desperately to keep pace with scientific advances.

- A Church whose social teaching took shape in the early stages of the Industrial Revolution now faces a twenty-first-century globalized world, populated by strange entities such as multinational corporations (MNCs) and intergovernmental organizations (IGOs) that didn't exist when it crafted its vision of the just society.

- A Church whose social concern focuses almost exclusively on human beings finds itself in a world in which the welfare of the cosmos itself requires new theological and moral reflection.

- A Church whose diplomacy has always relied on the Great Catholic Power of the day is now moving in a multipolar world, in which most of the poles that matter aren't Catholic, and some aren't even Christian.

- A Church accustomed to thinking of the Christian "other" as the Orthodox, Anglicans, and Protestants today is watching Pentecostals march across the planet, shooting up from 5 to 20 percent of global Christianity in barely a quarter century—in part by siphoning off significant numbers of Catholics. The Catholic Church is itself being "Pentecostalized" through the Charismatic movement.

An old car commercial carried the tagline, "This isn't your grandfather's Buick." I would submit that what we're looking at today isn't your mom and dad's Catholic Church—and it may not even be your older sister's.

The aim of this book is to survey the most important currents shaping the Catholic Church today, and to look down the line at how they might play out during the rest of the twenty-first century. The word I'm using to describe these currents is "trend." To explain what I have in mind, let me quote the historian Arnold J. Toynbee from his book *Civilization on Trial*:

> The things that make good headlines are on the surface of the stream of life, and they distract us from the slower, impalpable, imponderable movements that work below the surface and penetrate to the depths. But it is really these deeper, slower movements that make history, and it is they that stand out huge in retrospect, when the sensational passing events have dwindled, in perspective, to their true proportions.

Those "slower, impalpable movements" are what I mean by "trends." (I lay out the six criteria I employed for what counts as a trend in the chapter on "Trends That Aren't.") In several cases, there are plenty of headlines associated with one or another aspect of the trends, but usually they're treated in isolation, as random events, rather than being seen as part of deeper historical patterns. I hope to put the pieces of the contemporary Catholic puzzle together, so we can see what the picture looks like.

Each of the examples of an upside-down Church given above corresponds to one of the ten trends surveyed in this book:

1. A World Church
2. Evangelical Catholicism

  3. Islam
  4. The New Demography
  5. Expanding Lay Roles
  6. The Biotech Revolution
  7. Globalization
  8. Ecology
  9. Multipolarism
 10. Pentecostalism

The ten chapters of the book correspond to the ten trends listed above. They are not listed in order of rank or priority, as if number one were more important than number ten. To be completely honest, the sequence simply reflects the order in which I wrote the chapters. No additional significance should be attached to why one trend is number two, for example, and another number eight.

The format in each chapter is to give the lay of the land first, examining what's driving the trend and what impact it's having on the Catholic Church, in a section called "What's Happening." I then move into more speculative territory, trying to anticipate what the trend could mean for the Church as the century unfolds. That part is called "What It Means." These are not really predictions, but possible lines of development that could still be redirected, blocked, or turned in the opposite direction by forces not yet on the radar screen. In each chapter, I offer four categories of outcomes: near-certain, probable, possible, and long shots. Not only does the degree of probability go down with each category, but the projections venture farther out in time. Near-certain consequences are usually short-term extensions of developments that we can already see happening. Long shots, if they happen at all, are usually far on the horizon. The arc of time under consideration here is the rest of the century, meaning roughly ninety years. Farther out than that, all bets are off.

The book's conclusion is intended as a stand-alone summary of what impact the trends will have in the century to come. I condense the likely profile of upside-down Catholicism into four points. They're styled as sociological notes of the Church in the twenty-first century, inspired by the theological notes in the Nicene Creed: "One, Holy, Catholic, and Apostolic." My notes are intended not as theological claims about the Church's inner essence, but rather as descriptive terms for what Catholicism will actually look and feel like in this century. The four notes are: "Global,

Uncompromising, Pentecostal, and Extroverted." Readers who just can't wait to arrive at the bottom line may want to read the conclusion first, then work backward.

Descriptive, Not Prescriptive

It's important to be clear at the outset about what this book is and what it's not. I'm a journalist, not a priest, theologian, or academic. My role is to document what's happening in Catholicism and to provide context for it, not tell readers what to think. This book is therefore an exercise in description, not prescription. I'm not trying to argue that these trends are the way Catholicism *ought* to go, or the issues it *ought* to face. I'm saying instead that they accurately express the way Catholicism *really is* going, and the issues it *really is* facing. I invite readers to bracket off the immediate instinct to debate whether any given trend is positive or negative, and to try to understand it first on its own terms. After that, I entrust the prescriptive debate to better minds than my own.

I stress this point because in writing about these trends, I find that many Catholics immediately want to challenge one or another of them on prescriptive grounds: "I don't think evangelical Catholicism is what Vatican Two had in mind," or "Ecology is just another word for pagan pantheism." I understand those reactions. Religion is about someone's ultimate concern, their deepest passion, and naturally Catholic blood boils when someone says the Church is moving in direction "x," if a given Catholic happens to regard "x" as obtuse, or heretical, or reactionary. In principle, that kind of argument is terrific. Part of the dynamism of Catholicism is that so many people help keep the Church alive by being passionate enough to push the Church to realize the best version of itself. To move immediately to forming opinions, however, is to miss the point of what I'm trying to do here. There will be time later to argue whether a given trend is a good idea or a bad one. For that sort of prescriptive debate to be useful, it first has to be based on solid analysis, and that's the work of this book.

In a similar vein, because this book is a work of journalism, it is not a statement of faith. I'm trying to describe the Church the way a sociologist might. I fully recognize that from a supernatural point of view, the lone trend that matters in Catholic life is God's will for the Church, which can always erupt in unpredictable ways. On this level, decisions about the Catholic future are forged not in dispassionate sociological analysis, but out of deep prayer and the spiritual effort to discern where the Holy Spirit is moving. Yet the Catholic understanding, put in its classic form in the thirteenth century by Saint Thomas Aquinas, is that grace builds on nature, it doesn't replace it. In other words, the descriptive observations about human realities in the Church offered here may not be the whole story, but they are nonetheless important preliminaries for spiritual reflection. They offer fruit for Catholic prayer, without any pretense of rendering it unnecessary.

In the interest of full disclosure, I should confess that I veer into prescriptive territory in the book's conclusion—not in terms of whether these trends are good or bad, but rather in urging Catholics to think and act in new ways in order to adapt successfully to this "upside-down" situation. This is one final point of resemblance between my book and Friedman's *The World Is Flat*. Friedman's list of drivers shaping a flat world is basically descriptive, but he's unabashedly enthusiastic about globalization. Similarly, I make no bones about my sympathy for Catholicism. I want to see the Church harness its resources to respond to the perils and promise of the twenty-first century, because I believe Catholicism has a potentially transformative contribution to offer that no other global actor can replicate. I don't pretend to know how to accomplish this, but I think I know how *not* to do it, which is to allow the Church's resources and energy to be consumed in stale internal debates. Tribalism will not be an adaptive behavior in the twenty-first-century Church.

I suppose I'm trying to strike a balance between leaving readers free to decide what to think, but at the same time encouraging them to think big.

Maybe a quick story will help explain the difference. Some time ago, I spent an afternoon discussing these trends with a couple hundred priests and pastoral workers in the Archdiocese of Seattle, at the invitation of Archbishop Alex Brunett. After I had finished, Brunett got up and told the crowd that in his opinion, an outlook he called "Trends Catholicism" offers a "hopeful vision for the future of the Church." I was a bit taken aback, since my intent was to describe trends, not to create one of my own. I wondered if I had gone off track someplace, and was now coming off as a prophet or reformer rather than a journalist. Upon reflection, however, I think I know what Archbishop Brunett meant. Reading about these trends won't tell you who's right or wrong in Church debates, but it does point to a broader horizon than the narrow set that is often seen as "issues in the Church." This book may not be prescriptive, but it is an invitation to perspective.

How Do I Know?

The ten trends described in this book are not like the Ten Commandments; they weren't revealed by God, and I didn't bring them down from a mountain carved on stone tablets. The Vatican does not issue an official set of Catholic Trends, and there's no international Catholic research agency that has established such a list. No international Catholic publication that I'm aware of puts out such a list either. So, it's a perfectly fair reaction to look at the list I provided above and ask: "How do you know?"

The truth is that compiling a list of trends in Catholicism is a subjective enterprise. My guess is that out of any ten Catholics you might pick at random and ask to name the most important forces shaping the future of the Church, not one of them would come up with exactly the same list presented here. That's part of the fun, since anyone is free to argue that some items on the list shouldn't be there, and that other things should be included that aren't. Yet I didn't just throw darts at a dart board, picking these ten forces at random. They're based on more than a decade of day-in, day-out analysis of the global Church. Let me briefly describe the three sources that have most influenced my decisions.

First is my experience of covering the Vatican and the global Church. Over the last decade, I've made reporting trips to forty countries on every continent, sometimes following the pope and sometimes on my own. I've had the opportunity to observe the Church in a variety of cultural, ethnic, socioeconomic, and political circumstances. Over time, that experience has given me a feel for what's circulating in the global Catholic bloodstream, as opposed to something likely to be a transitory and local affair. I certainly don't claim infallibility, but I've been lucky to be able to move around the Catholic world and to occupy a front-row seat for many of its recent dramas in a way that few other people have had the opportunity to do.

Second, I'm relying on thousands of hours of interviews with cardinals, bishops and priests, and even popes, as well as theologians, political activists, social workers, liturgical experts, leaders in ecumenical dialogue, and virtually every other species of life in the Catholic biosphere. Much of this conversation has come in and around the Vatican. Saint Peter's Square is to the Church what Times Square is to the world: stand there long enough, and you'll see virtually every Catholic alive. It's the crossroads of the global Church, and that has given me a unique opportunity to take the temperature of the Catholic Church in various parts of the world.

Third, I've drawn upon reactions from thousands of readers of my online Internet column, once called "The Word from Rome" and now rechristened as "All Things Catholic." I've developed this book a bit like open-source software, in that I've periodically put out bits and pieces of it and invited feedback. Though for the most part I never had the time to answer all those readers individually, they'll find traces of their contributions here and there. My column has a readership that reflects a wide cross-section of Catholic instincts and experiences, and this input was enormously helpful in pointing out gaps in my logic, lifting up things I'd never considered, and generally making this a much more thoughtful book.

None of this adds up to scientific certainty, but if I had to bet on ten issues that will be important for Catholicism in 2075, I'd feel pretty good about these selections.

Not the Usual Suspects

Some readers might want to take that bet, if for no other reason than because the items on the list are certainly not the subjects that usually come up in popular discussions of the Catholic Church. There's no trend concerning birth control, homosexuality, or abortion; nothing about women priests or the power of the pope; nothing about sex abuse by priests, clerical celibacy, democracy in the Church, or clefts between bishops and laity. (All these subjects are addressed throughout the book, but as pieces of a bigger picture.) In short, there's an obvious gap between the ten trends listed above and the topics generally touted in newspaper headlines and TV talk shows.

That discrepancy is discussed at greater length in the chapter on "Trends That Aren't," but suffice it to say here that the decision not to round up the usual Catholic suspects isn't an attempt to whitewash very real problems in the Church, nor is it based merely on the fact that some of these preoccupations in Europe and the United States are not live concerns for Africa, Latin America, and Asia, though that's certainly the case.

Instead, the decision not to style these topics as trends is shaped by two descriptive observations. First, whatever opinion one might hold on the merits of existing power structures in Catholicism or its teaching on sexual morality, there's little realistic basis to believe the official structures or doctrines of the Church will change significantly on these fronts in the period under consideration in this book, meaning the rest of the twenty-first century. For that reason, these are not forces likely to produce top-to-bottom transformation in the near future.

Second, without denying the importance of these hot-button issues, their centrality in day-to-day Catholic life is often exaggerated. In truth, a good deal of the most creative energy in the Church comes from individuals and groups least invested in internal debates, whether one would conventionally describe these circles as liberal, conservative, or somewhere in between. To take just one example, the Community of Sant'Egidio has to rank among today's most effective actors on the Catholic stage through its promotion of ecumenical and interreligious dialogue, conflict resolution, poverty relief, and opposition to the death penalty. The community takes no position, however, on matters such as gay marriage or clerical celibacy.

The HIV/AIDS epidemic offers another case in point. Most everyone knows that the Catholic Church is officially opposed to condoms as a solution to the crisis, but what people often fail to appreciate is that this position is more or less a footnote to the bigger story of Catholic mobilization. Today, the Vatican estimates that 27 percent of all AIDS patients worldwide are cared for by Catholic hospitals, hospices, and palliative care centers, representing by far the largest humanitarian response to the AIDS pandemic on earth. Discussion about whether the Catholic position on condoms ought to be revisited in light of AIDS is legitimate, and it goes on even at senior levels of the Church itself. Creating the impression that saying "no" to condoms is the dominant Catholic response to the crisis, however, falsifies reality. In fact, those Catholics most deeply involved with the AIDS issue probably spend the least time thinking about condoms—except, of course, when reporters and activists cajole them into doing so.

Such examples illustrate that trying to understand Catholicism primarily through the lens of the issues that make headlines results in only bits and pieces of the full picture coming into focus. No account of contemporary Catholicism can ignore its deep fissures surrounding such matters and they will repeatedly surface in this book. Nonetheless, we have to dig deeper to spot where things are truly heading.

Three Other Preliminaries

1. CONFLICTING IMPULSES

Even more than "How do you know?," far and away the most popular question I get when I talk about these trends is, "What does it mean?" People want to know whether the Church will become more conservative, or more liberal; more clerical, or more lay-led; more traditional or more avant-garde; more centralized or more diverse; and a whole series of other binary oppositions that interest one faction or another. Unfortunately, the right answer to almost all of those questions is "both," depending upon how you define the terms and which trend you're talking about.

Not all of these trends cut in the same direction, and in some ways they quite obviously work at cross-purposes. The rise of Southern Catholicism, the emergence of multipolarism, and the spread of Pentecostalism will all push Catholicism to provide greater scope for "inculturation," meaning allowing the faith to be shaped by the local culture in which it's expressed. Evangelical Catholicism, on the other hand, emphasizes traditional modes of language, dress, and behavior that by and large took shape in the West. To take another looming contradiction, evangelical Catholicism is driving the Church into what are perceived in the West as steadily more conservative positions on issues such as homosexuality and end-of-life care, yet new biotechnology debates over genetic engineering and GMOs (genetically modified organisms) will likely see Catholicism aligned as much with the secular left as with the right. In other words, the impulses unleashed by the trends are going to butt heads in a variety of fields, and it's hard to know right now exactly how things will shake out.

Anybody hoping for a straight, one-way line of development in the upside-down Church will be disappointed. Catholicism is too big and too complex not to contain conflicting tendencies. It's not really a question of which way the Church will go, but which *ways*—and sometimes that movement will be pulling in opposite directions.

The boundaries between one trend and the next are fluid, and they interact with one another across the board. In a sense, there's really only one trend here, globalization, which is producing reactions inside the Catholic Church as well as creating a whole new series of challenges outside. Yet each of these trends also has its own contours and its own inner logic. It makes more sense to treat them separately, noting along the way the places where the lines cross.

2. A QUESTION OF LANGUAGE

Academics are notorious for debating the fine points of language, and theologians are no exception. Today, some Catholic writers draw a distinction between "global Catholicism" and "world Catholicism." For those attached to this bit of nuance, the former is basically bad and the latter good. "Global Catholicism" is understood to be the Catholic equivalent of cultural globalization, meaning the eradication of local cultures and the imposition of a homogenized global system. "World Catholicism," on the other hand, refers to the planetary diversity of various languages, ethnicities, and traditions brought together under the Catholic umbrella, without eviscerating what makes them unique. I understand the distinction, but I'm not convinced that the words in themselves carry the meaning that these theologians suggest. In this book, I use "global Catholicism" and "world Catholicism" interchangeably. What I mean by both terms is the universal, planetary dimension of Catholicism, without intending to take any position about the proper balance between unity and diversity.

3. AMERICAN EYES

This is a book about world Catholicism, and Catholics from every corner of the globe tell their stories in these pages. Yet there's a sense in which this is world Catholicism as seen through American eyes. By that, I don't mean that the facts and figures have been skewed to serve American interests, nor that the selection of trends has been driven exclusively by an American sense of priorities. Were that the case, for example, the sexual abuse crisis would certainly be on the list. (I explain in the chapter "Trends That Aren't" why the crisis didn't make the cut.) But along the way, I pay special attention to what the mega-trends I'm describing will mean for the Catholic Church in the United States, both as a whole and for the various subgroups within it, as well as their implications for the American government and broader American culture.

This is not intended to suggest that every trajectory in the life of the Catholic Church ought to be measured by its potential impact on the United States. I like to remind American Catholics that we constitute 6 percent of the global Catholic population, which means that 94 percent of the Catholics in the world are not necessarily like us. If anything, the United States probably looms too large already on the global Catholic scene. Americans had eleven cardinals in the conclave that elected Pope Benedict XVI, for example, the same number as all of Africa, even though Africa has twice the

Catholic population. Brazil, the largest Catholic country on earth, only had three votes, which works out to one cardinal-elector for every 6 million American Catholics and for every 43 million Catholics in Brazil. Though Catholicism is not a democracy, that sort of discrepancy understandably strikes many Catholics around the world as unfair.

I look at the trends through American eyes firstly because that's likely to be the primary readership of the book, and I want American readers to be able to connect the dots between these broad forces and their own lives. Secondly, my experience living abroad suggests that sometimes Americans need help thinking in these terms. It sometimes comes more naturally for Catholics elsewhere to connect what's happening in Congo, or Colombia, or Cambodia to their own fate. A largely benign form of national parochialism is in some ways the original sin of much Catholic conversation in the United States. Pick up any random sample of recent titles on Catholicism in America, no matter what the political or theological stance, and in most cases the author's imagination seems to stop at the water's edge. The impression is that the future of American Catholicism is largely a domestic enterprise, with at most a fleeting connection with the rest of the Church.

I hope the American lens in this book will help Catholics in the United States to think in a more global key. As a matter of faith, doing so is implied in calling the Church "catholic"; as a matter of descriptive fact, it will be ever more difficult in the twenty-first century to consider issues in American Catholicism in isolation from the rest of the Church. In that sense, the choice to see through American eyes is a way of preparing readers for what's coming.

A WORLD CHURCH

Picture a warm Wednesday morning in Rome in the spring of 2050. Pope Victor IV, a Nigerian who took his name in honor of history's first African pope (Victor I, 186–197), is arriving for his weekly General Audience in a sun-splashed Saint Peter's Square. Though Victor takes pains to stress that he's the shepherd of the universal Church, not just a son of Africa, this doesn't stop television networks from supplying a soundtrack of pulsating traditional African music whenever he appears, or flashing images of gyrating tribal dancers. As the camera zooms in on the pope, TV commentators, as they invariably do, remark on how his immaculate white vestments set off his beaming black face. Most of these pundits have long since given up trying to reconcile Victor's earthy, exuberant personality with his uncompromising stance on hot-button issues such as abortion and gay marriage. After he denounced homosexuality as a "perversion" and a "disease" during a major address at the United Nations, many secular commentators in Europe and North America desperately tried to dislike him, but his infectious happiness has made doing so difficult. This simply is not the dour moral conservatism they expect from religious leaders.

Instead of the gentle papal wave of his predecessors, Victor pumps his fists and cries "Christ is Risen!" as he exits the pope-mobile and makes his way up the steps of the massive square, to the canopy where he will speak—and, if he holds to form, where he will also crack jokes, perform a few dance steps, and occasionally break into song. Since many Catholics in the audience are part of the Church's vast charismatic movement, they wave their arms in the air in a gesture of spontaneous praise. Some are quietly speaking in tongues, causing a babble of voices to rise from the square.

Journalists are hoping for comment from the pope on a recent proposal from the Vatican's Synod of Bishops for excommunication of Catholic executives responsible for companies that do not pay a living wage. Victor himself, a staunch critic of the inequities of global capitalism, had issued such a decree when he was the Cardinal-Archbishop of Lagos. A handful of Catholic CEOs in Nigeria, including a couple of members of the highly influential Knights of Malta, a group generally restricted to the Catholic jet set, actually found themselves turned away at the communion line. The idea of extending that policy to the universal Church drew a scathing editorial in the *Wall Street Journal* and some incendiary comments among Catholic neoconservatives, but it elicited widespread enthusiasm in the global South, where the vast majority of Victor's flock lives.

Today, however, the pope chooses to talk about something else, continuing a series of catechetical talks he began earlier in the year on witchcraft. He assures his listeners that Christus Victor, "Christ the Victor," is stronger than the spiritual "powers of this world," even though their power is real and dangerous. Lest this awaken Western stereotypes of primitive African religiosity, the pope engages in a brief theological tour de force, citing authorities from Justin Martyr and Saint Gregory of Nyssa through Saint Thomas Aquinas, grounding his teaching in classic Catholic tradition. As he finishes the audience, Victor descends to the first row of pilgrims, where, as he does each Wednesday, he performs brief prayers of exorcism for visitors who have reported episodes of demonic possession. As he exits the square, cries of *"viva il papa!"* rise up in a welter of tongues, including dozens of indigenous tribal languages from Africa, Asia, and Latin America.

At one point during the audience, a loud boom is heard over the square. It's later identified as a Roman bus backfiring, but one wag suggests it was actually the sound of Hilaire Belloc, the Anglo-French Catholic writer of the early twentieth century who famously asserted that "the Faith is Europe, and Europe is the Faith," rolling over in his grave.

The foregoing may seem like a scene from a papal potboiler. Yet each element is firmly grounded in current trajectories within the Catholic Church, so that while the details are fiction, the overall picture stands decidedly in the realm of fact.

At birth Christianity was not a product of Europe, but of Palestinian Judaism during the Hellenistic era. In terms of its aspirations, it was directed at the world. This universality, however, has been difficult to discern for much of Christianity's 2,000 years, since for most of that time it has seemed as tightly bound to European civilization as Hinduism is to India, or Shintoism to Japan. Where Europe went, Christianity went along for the ride, but where Europe did not venture, Christianity generally did not penetrate. Thus most of the Americas became Christian, but the great empires of Asia, such as Japan and China, largely eluded its grasp.

What makes the twentieth century unique is that this tight identification between the West and Christianity disintegrated. To consider the Catholic Church, at the beginning of the twentieth century, just 25 percent of the world's Catholic population lived outside Europe and North America. By century's end, however, 65.5 percent of the Catholic population was found in Africa, Asia, and Latin America. In a geographical sense, the twentieth century literally turned Catholicism "upside down." To paraphrase Belloc, today it would be more demographically and culturally accurate to say that "the South is the Faith, and the Faith is the South."

Of course, numbers by themselves don't tell the whole story. The preponderance of African, Asian, and Latin American Catholics at the grassroots does not mean they yet exercise an equivalent influence in Church affairs. Consider that the Italian cardinals cast nineteen votes in the 2005 conclave that elected Pope Benedict XVI, equivalent to the total number for Africa and Asia combined, despite the fact that there are just 55 million Catholics in Italy compared to 237 million in Africa and Asia. Given the slow pace of change in the official structures of Catholicism, it will be some time before the leadership ranks more accurately reflect the Church's demographic composition. Under any conceivable scenario, Catholic realignment does not augur a future in which the South simply replaces the North, but rather one in which ideas, movements, and controversies radiate out from multiple centers in both North and South.

More importantly, citing the baptismal rolls in a given region does not tell you much about the quality of the faith lived there. For more than five hundred years, Roman Catholicism enjoyed a near-monopoly in Latin America, with virtually every man, woman, and child counted as a member of the Catholic Church. Yet due to factors such as a chronic shortage of clergy and a pastoral model that did not prize the acquisition of an adult faith, the continent's Catholic homogeneity was something of an illusion—an illusion that is progressively being shattered by the growth of Pentecostal movements. It's also worth recalling that Rwanda, the site of the most horrifying genocide of the late twentieth century, is just over 50 percent Catholic (and 85 percent Christian), which means that the carnage was largely carried out by baptized Christians. Clearly, the religious affiliation of the country did not translate into Christ-like conduct.

Those cautions notwithstanding, there's no doubt that in the twenty-first century and beyond, Catholicism in the South is moving from being an object of history to a subject. Europe and the United States in this era of world Catholicism will not disappear, but the global South will provide a steadily growing share of leadership and vision. The late German Jesuit theologian Karl Rahner described this process as the emergence of a "World Church," which is the title I've elected to give the trend. Rahner believed that the Second Vatican Council (1962–65) launched a "qualitative leap" toward a new stage in Church history, in which the Church would no longer be dominated exclusively by European or Western cultural forms, functioning in other parts of the world like an "export firm." As a theological matter, Rahner said, Catholicism had always been a "World Church" in principle, but now that identity is being realized as a sociological fact. Rahner said that the significance of the shift to this World Church is on a par with the transition in the first century from Christianity as a sect within Palestinian Judaism to a broad-based religious movement in the Greco-Roman world. "A frontier has been crossed," Rahner wrote in 1979, "behind which it will never again be possible to return, even to the slightest degree." As we will see below, this is one of those rare cases in which a theologian's claim is open to empirical verification, and the numbers bear Rahner out.

This trend cuts across every issue in the life of the Catholic Church, from its doctrine to its modes of worship, from its political vision to its pastoral style. This chapter traces the shifts that are under way and looks down the line at how they might play out.

WHAT'S HAPPENING

The Numbers

A professor of mine once said he could write a history of the world in one sentence: "First the Agricultural Revolution happened, then the Industrial Revolution." In his estimation, those were the two historical forces with greatest consequence for shaping the modern world. Similarly, if I were asked to offer a history of Roman Catholicism in the twentieth century in one sentence, I would reply: "The center of gravity shifted from North to South." It would be a counterintuitive claim, since historians are accustomed to thinking of the great Catholic turning points of the past hundred years as the signing of the Lateran Pacts in 1929, resolving the famous "Roman question"; the pontificate of Pius XII from 1939 to 1958, which saw the Church through the Second World War and left controversy about the Church's reaction to the Holocaust; the Second Vatican Council, which launched an era of reform; and the pontificate of John Paul II (1978–2005), which exercised an enormous impact on the political and cultural debates of his day. All were indeed mammoth chapters in twentieth-century Church history. Yet in terms of both scope and scale, the eruption of the South towers over them all.

According to the invaluable work *Global Catholicism: Portrait of a World Church* by Bryan Froehle and Mary L. Gautier, in 1900, at the dawn of the twentieth century, there were roughly 266.5 million Catholics in the world, of whom over 200 million were in Europe and North America and just 66 million were scattered across the entire rest of the planet. Most of this remainder was in Latin America, some 53 million. The cultural and ethnic profile of the Church in 1900 was not terribly different from what it had been during the Council of Trent in the sixteenth century.

In 2000, by way of contrast, there were slightly under 1.1 billion Roman Catholics in the world, of whom just 350 million were Europeans and North Americans. The overwhelming majority, a staggering 720 million people, lived in Latin America, Africa, and Asia. Almost half the Catholic total, over 400 million people, lived in Latin America alone. Projecting forward to the year 2025, only one Catholic in five in the world will be a non-Hispanic Caucasian. This is the most rapid, and most sweeping, demographic transformation of Roman Catholicism in its two-thousand-year history.

These demographic trends are changing the Catholic map of the world. In the year 2000, these were the ten largest Catholic populations by country:

1. Brazil: 149 million
2. Mexico: 92 million
3. United States: 67 million
4. Philippines: 65 million
5. Italy: 56 million
6. France: 46 million
7. Colombia: 38 million
8. Spain: 38 million
9. Poland: 37 million
10. Argentina: 34 million

It's an arresting exercise to look down the line to the year 2050, drawing on population projections from the United Nations Population Division, and presuming that the Catholic percentage in each nation will remain more or less the same. This may overestimate the Catholic population in Latin America, where Catholicism is losing members both to Pentecostalism and to religious indifference, and in Europe, where secularization continues to eat away at Catholic faith and practice. It almost certainly underestimates the African totals, where growth in Catholicism is outpacing overall population growth. Nevertheless, based on the UN projections, here is the projected list of largest Catholic nations in 2050:

1. Brazil: 215 million
2. Mexico: 132 million
3. Philippines: 105 million
4. United States: 99 million
5. Democratic Republic of the Congo: 97 million
6. Uganda: 56 million
7. France: 49 million
8. Italy: 49 million
9. Nigeria: 47 million
10. Argentina: 46.1 million

For the first time, three African nations—the Democratic Republic of the Congo, Uganda, and Nigeria—will take their place among the largest Catholic nations in the world. Among the traditional Catholic powers these new African behemoths will dislodge are Spain and Poland, two cornerstones of the old European Christendom. Seven of the ten largest Catholic nations in the world will be south of the United States and Europe.

Africa offers the most striking illustration of what's happened in the past hundred years. During the twentieth century, the Catholic population of sub-Saharan Africa went from 1.9 million to more than 130 million—a staggering growth rate of 6,708 percent. Vocations are also booming. Bigard Memorial Seminary in southeastern Nigeria, with an enrollment of over 1,100, is said to be the largest Catholic seminary in the world. Its student population by itself is roughly one-fifth the total number of seminarians in the United States. Yet despite this phenomenal harvest, there is no surplus of priests in Africa, in large part because Africans are being baptized even more rapidly than they're being ordained.

Asia too saw impressive Catholic growth. Catholicism started the century as 1.2 percent of the Asian population, according to World Christian Database, and ended the century at 3 percent, meaning that the Church more than doubled its "market share." India's Catholic population grew from under 2 million to over 17 million, and should be at least 26 million by midcentury. From 1985 to 2005, the percentage of the population in South Korea which identifies itself as Catholic more than doubled, standing today at just over 11 percent, according to the 2005 census, meaning more than 5 million people. In 2000, there were more Catholic baptisms in the Philippines alone than in France, Spain, Italy, and Poland combined. In terms of Christianity as a whole, there were 350 million Christians in Asia in 2007 as compared to 372 million Buddhists. By 2010, there should be more Christians in Asia than Buddhists—a mind-bending reversal of normal impressions about the continent's preferred religion.

What all this means is that the global story of Catholicism today is growth, not decline. That's generally not the impression one picks up from casual conversation or TV sound bites in Europe or the United States, where talk of a "crisis" is the more usual fare. In 2003, David Brooks published an article in the *Atlantic Monthly* documenting global Christian expansion. Brooks was biting in his indictment of secular elites such as those who edit the magazine for which he was writing: "A great Niagara of religious fervor is cascading down around them," he wrote, "while they stand obtuse and dry in the little cave of their own parochialism."

Numerical growth by itself, of course, does not mean that everything in the Church is hunky-dory. As Pope Benedict XVI said in July 2007, "Statistics are not our divinity." Nevertheless, the remarkable Catholic Niagara of the twentieth century does suggest a baseline of vitality in the Church that too often escapes attention amid perceptions of drift and decline in Europe and other zones of the West.

The Causes of Catholic Growth

Peter Berger, a distinguished sociologist of religion, says that no important social phenomenon ever has just a single cause. That's certainly the case with the growth of Catholicism across the global South in the twentieth century. Believers, of course, interpret what happened as a work of the Holy Spirit. Church leaders also point to the hard work of Catholic missionaries at the retail level. Without negating the role of divine providence and direct missionary effort, social scientists also point to at least four other empirical factors: overall population growth; the transition from missionary to local churches; local circumstances that drove religious realignments; and the capacity of Christianity to embrace indigenous cultures.

1. POPULATION GROWTH

The twentieth century witnessed a population explosion across Africa, Asia, and Latin America, and Catholicism was one of the boats lifted highest by this tide. Global demographics are therefore the single most important factor in explaining the expansion of the Catholic population in the last century. Overall, the global population went from 2.5 billion in 1950 to 6.5 billion in 2005, while the Catholic population grew from 459 million to 1.1 billion—meaning that both grew by a factor of roughly 2.5 times, so that the overall expansion of the Catholic Church roughly kept pace with the global population. That total, however, glosses over wide regional differences. The Church suffered serious losses in the North, but grew dramatically in the South.

The population of Latin America and the Caribbean went from just over 60 million in 1900 to 167 million in 1950, and to 561 million by 2000. The Catholic share of the Latin American population actually declined over this period, from 97 percent to just over 80 percent today, but the raw number of Catholics soared to 449 million. In Africa, the total population went from 224 million in 1950 to 905 million in 2000, and in Asia it grew from 1.4 billion in 1950 to 3.6 billion in 2000; and in both instances the Catholic share of the population outpaced overall growth. The total number of African and Asian Catholics grew enormously, to 130 million and 107 million respectively by the year 2000.

As lower global fertility levels begin to kick in worldwide during the twenty-first century (a trend outlined in chapter four), the Catholic population will probably begin to decline along with the overall population. This century will therefore likely not witness the same explosive Catholic growth as the last.

2. LOCAL CONTROL

In many parts of the global South, the number of Western missionaries peaked around Vatican II in the mid-1960s and then began to decline. In part, this drop-off was related to post–Vatican II declines in the priesthood and religious life; in part, it was the result of a conscious Catholic policy of encouraging local control of the Church, promoting indigenous vocations and leadership. This transition to local control, many experts believe, contributed to Catholic expansion.

Froehle observes that when a church is dependent largely upon foreign missionaries, most incentives cut against rapid growth. Foreign personnel and money are relatively fixed, so bringing in rising numbers of converts puts greater strains on a limited set of resources. When the church is locally run, on the other hand, growth can become self-sustaining, as personnel and resources expand with overall membership. To put this simplistically, one million new Nigerian Catholics can't produce a single new Irish missionary, but they can produce lots of Nigerian priests. The more a church is seen as local, the greater its potential for long-term growth.

Pentecostal writer Allan Anderson argues that one factor fueling the expansion of Pentecostalism in the twentieth century was its "church-planting" approach to evangelization, which meant the quickest possible transition to indigenous leadership. Moreover, Anderson says, many of the largest and most successful forms of Pentecostalism in the global South were unrelated to Western missionary efforts, such as the Akurinu movement in East Africa or the Indian Pentecostal Church of God. The late-twentieth-century expansion of Protestant Christianity in China likewise began during the Cultural Revolution, at a time when it was virtually impossible for foreigners to even set foot on Chinese soil, let alone direct missionary enterprises. These observations tend to confirm Froehle's argument, that home-grown Christianity is best positioned for rapid expansion.

3. LOCAL CIRCUMSTANCES

Historical processes in Africa help explain why both Christianity and Islam prospered in the twentieth century. Though exact numbers are impossible, owing to imprecise and often politically skewed census methods, the best guess by most demographers is that there are close to 400 million Muslims and 400 million Christians in Africa today, each representing more than 40 percent of the total population. Jesuit Fr. Tom Michel, one of Catholicism's leading experts on Islam, has pointed out that Africa in the twentieth century was among the last places on earth where old tribal religions broke down, and the population chose from among the major faiths on offer, Islam and Christianity. The two achieved a rough stalemate, making them a bit like the Coke and Pepsi of global religion.

Similarly, Catholicism's gains in India reflect unique historical and social factors. Catholicism had its greatest missionary success among the Dalits, the permanent underclass of the Indian caste system, who often see choosing a non-Hindu religion as a means of rejecting oppression. Dalits account for somewhere between 60 and 75 percent of the total Catholic population of India. In South Korea, most experts believe that the dramatic expansion of Catholicism in the second half of the twentieth century is related in part to the leadership role played by Catholic activists in Korea's prodemocracy movement, especially Catholic layman Kim Dae-jung, who served as the country's president from 1998 to 2003 and who is known as the "Asian Mandela."

What these examples demonstrate is that no "one-size-fits-all" explanation for Catholic growth or decline is possible. In every part of the world, growth or decline is connected in part to local circumstances, and the future prospects for the Church will rise or fall as those circumstances evolve. For example, Catholicism could score significant missionary gains in China if the climate for religious liberty improves. There's already movement afoot; by one estimate, there are now substantially more Christians in China than Communists. (Roughly 50 million Chinese are formal party members, while best-guess estimates for all Chinese Christians, Protestants and Catholics together, is around 80 million.)

4. ABSORBING INDIGENOUS CULTURE

Gambian scholar Lamin Sanneh, a Catholic convert who teaches at Yale University, observes that Christianity had an important edge over Islam in some parts of Africa in its capacity to absorb the local language and culture, as opposed to Islam's need to "Arabize" its converts. This point too is counterintuitive, since critics have often accused Christianity of imposing European culture upon converts. To paraphrase von Clausewitz's famous remark about war, Christian evangelization has usually been seen as an extension of colonialism by other means.

In reality, Sanneh says, the explosion of Christianity was as much a reaction against colonialism as it was a product of it. Christianity, he found, grew where the local culture had preserved the indigenous name for God, as well as aspects of the native religion; Islam was successful where the indigenous religion had largely been obliterated. The capacity to "baptize" preexisting cultural traditions, and to insert them into a Christian context, has always been part of Christianity's missionary genius. The transition in Catholicism after Vatican II to celebrating Mass and the other sacraments in the local languages, according to experts such as Sanneh, was an enormous missionary asset in much of the global South.

Profile of Southern Catholicism

Skepticism is certainly in order about generalizations concerning 720 million people. Any bald claim about Catholicism across the global South will engender millions of exceptions. There is enormous variation between continents; Catholicism in sub-Saharan Africa is scarcely a half-century old, while the Church has more than 500 years of history in Latin America. There are also important contrasts within continents; the socially progressive, reform-oriented spirit of Brazilian Catholicism is distinct from the more clerical and devotional stamp of the Mexican church. Even within nations, there are differences—urban versus rural, indigenous versus European descent, and so on.

That said, the following five points are widespread enough to treat them as defining qualities.

1. MORALLY CONSERVATIVE, POLITICALLY LIBERAL

Western categories of "liberal" and "conservative" are often misleading in analyzing the South, because they presume a taxonomy that is not part of Southern culture. Nevertheless, "liberal" and "conservative" are familiar terms to European and American ears, and hence are most likely to roughly communicate something of Southern attitudes.

By Northern standards, Southern Catholics typically hold conservative attitudes on moral questions such as abortion, homosexuality, and the family. This dynamic is clear today within the Anglican Communion, where a minority of liberal Anglicans in the North, especially in the United States and Canada, is pressing ahead with the ordination of gay clergy and the blessing of same-sex unions, against a determined African majority that strongly opposes such measures. Today, there are some 38 million Anglicans in Africa, half the global total of 76 million.

A similar clash of cultures runs through Catholicism. One symbolic expression of this gap came in May 2003, when Nigerian Cardinal Francis Arinze, a senior Vatican official, delivered the commencement address at Georgetown University. Arinze inadvertently waded into America's culture wars, declaring:

> In many parts of the world, the family is under siege. It is opposed by an anti-life mentality as is seen in contraception, abortion, infanticide and euthanasia. It is scorned and banalized by pornography, desecrated by fornication and adultery, mocked by homosexuality, sabotaged by irregular unions and cut in two by divorce.

His apparent comparison of homosexuality to pornography and other social ills prompted a letter of protest signed by over seventy members of the faculty. For his part, Arinze expressed astonishment that anyone could take offense. Perhaps that is because, while America may be debating the gay rights issue, Nigeria certainly isn't. According to a 2006 Pew Global Survey, a whopping 98 percent of Nigerian Christians believe that homosexuality is "never justified."

Arinze is seen as a conservative on Church matters, but even Africans with more liberal views tend to share his instincts on sexual morality. The late Fr. John Mary Waliggo of Uganda, for example, was an influential African Catholic theologian and a member of his country's Human Rights Commission. He spoke admiringly of feminism and liberation theology, but he nevertheless defended his culture's staunch moral traditionalism.

"Things such as homosexuality are not just seen as sins, but as perversions," Waliggo said in a 2006 interview. "They're seen as hideous, they make you an outcast from your clan and village. If a man impregnates his sister, or if he has sex with another man, this is a kind of social sin which people believe will bring misery on the entire village, so he'd better just go away. This is what the people believe, and [as a theologian] you can't isolate yourself from society. . . . We've had too much armchair theology in the church. We want to be synthesizers and prophets of the people."

In Asia and Latin America, similar attitudes prevail. According to the 2006 Pew study, 72 percent of Indians, 78 percent of South Koreans, and 56 percent of Filipinos believe that homosexuality is "never justified." Even in sexually liberal Brazil, a strong 49 percent of the population agrees that homosexuality is "never justified," roughly the same percentage as in the United States. In Guatemala, 63 percent of the population takes that view. On the abortion issue, 79 percent of Brazilians, 85 percent of Guatemalans, 68 percent of Indians, and 97 percent of Filipinos are opposed to abortion, and solid majorities in almost every country want abortion to be against the civil law.

There are dissenting voices. Brazilian Catholic theologian Marco Fabri dos Anjos argued in 1999 that theologians must listen to victims in "exceptional situations," such as the oppressed and homosexuals. Anglican Archbishop Desmond Tutu of South Africa struck a tolerant note when asked about homosexuality during the 2007 World Social Forum in Nairobi, Kenya: "To penalize someone because of their sexual orientation is like what used to happen to us; to be penalized for something which we could do nothing [about]—our ethnicity, our race. I would find it quite unacceptable to condemn and persecute a minority that has already been persecuted," he said. In that light, it would be inaccurate to suggest that Southern Christians speak only with one voice. Yet it would be equally inaccurate to suggest that Anjos and Tutu represent anything other than a minority view.

When one leaves the ambit of personal morality and enters the terrain of economic, political, and military matters, however, Southern Catholic attitudes often strike Northern observers as remarkably "liberal." To be specific, Southern bishops, priests, religious, and laity often are:

- Skeptical of capitalism and globalization;
- Wary about the global influence of the United States;
- Pro-Palestinian and, by implication, sometimes critical of Israel;
- Pro–United Nations;
- Anti-war, and therefore overwhelmingly opposed to U.S. military action in Iraq and elsewhere;
- In favor of a robust role for the state in the economy;
- Quite "green," favoring strong protections for the environment.

In a 2002 issue of the journal *Theological Studies*, Dean Brackley, an American Jesuit who teaches in El Salvador, and Thomas Schubeck, a Jesuit from John Carroll University in Cleveland, surveyed moral theology in Latin America since the Second Vatican Council. While distinguishing various currents, Brackley and Schubeck found a "Latin consensus" on matters of economic justice. They described it this way: "The market is a useful, even necessary means for stimulating production and allocating resources. However, in the 'new economy,' overreliance on the market has aggravated social inequality, further concentrated wealth and income, and left millions mired in misery." The "Latin consensus" is not merely that too many people are poor; it is also that the free market, left to its own devices, necessarily produces a widening gap between wealth and poverty.

One example of this consensus in the Catholic hierarchy is the Archbishop of Tegucigalpa, Honduras, Cardinal Óscar Rodríguez-Maradiaga. A handsome, charismatic figure who plays the saxophone and pilots airplanes, Rodríguez has been an outspoken opponent of globalization, especially free trade agreements which he believes work to the disadvantage of the impoverished South. He has been a global leader in the campaign for debt relief. In a 2003 address to a group of Catholic charities in Rome, Rodríguez warned that globalization without solidarity amounts to "suicide for the poor and, therefore, for the majority of humanity."

Catholic bishops across the global South hold similar views. In a 127-page report issued in 2004, the Catholic bishops of Asia declared that "neoliberal economic globalization" destroys Asian families because it is the primary cause of poverty on the continent. In June 2005, a group of Catholic bishops from Eritrea, Ethiopia, Kenya, Malawi, Tanzania, Sudan, Uganda, Zambia, Somalia, and Djibouti declared that, "We are particularly horrified by the ravages of unbridled capitalism, which has taken away and stifled local ownership of economic initiatives and is leading to a dangerous gap between the rich few and the poor majority."

2. MIRACLES, HEALINGS, AND THE SUPERNATURAL

Attitudes toward the supernatural are perhaps the fundamental dividing line between the religious climates of the North and the South. In the North, even believing Christians are sometimes reluctant to talk too openly about the spiritual world. Claims of miraculous healings, of appearances of the Virgin Mary, or of demonic possession are sometimes greeted with skepticism, likely to be taken as indications of mental imbalance or emotional immaturity. (This is in some ways a description of elites rather than the grassroots, but it's pervasive nonetheless.) In the South, the spiritual realm is tangible, palpable, and constantly nearby—in some ways, more real than the physical world. Illness is as likely to be attributed to evil spirits as to physical causes, and this-worldly misfortune is seen in light of personal sin instead of bad luck.

As Anglican Kenyan theologian John Mbiti writes: "For African peoples, this is a religious universe. . . . The invisible world presses hard upon the visible: one speaks to the other, and Africans 'see' that invisible universe when they look at, hear or feel the visible and tangible world." Similar statements could be made about much of Asia and Latin America. A popular Korean Baptist minister, for example, is famed for raising seven people from the dead, three of them before their funerals! Statistics from the 2006 Pew survey again illustrate the point. While just 29 percent of Americans report that they have witnessed divine healings, 56 percent of Guatemalans, 71 percent of Kenyans, 62 percent of Nigerians, and 44 percent of Indians claim to have done so. Just 11 percent of Americans claim to have experienced or witnessed exorcisms, but 34 percent of Brazilians, 38 percent of Guatemalans, 61 percent of Kenyans, 57 percent of Nigerians, and 28 percent of Filipinos say they have had these experiences.

Given this appetite for the supernatural, one source of pastoral concern in the Catholic South is the border between "folk religion," often magic and witchcraft, and orthodox faith. In August 2006, the Catholic bishops of Southern Africa, which includes South Africa, Swaziland, and Botswana, issued a pastoral letter warning their priests not to moonlight as witch doctors and fortune tellers. Many in Southern Africa turn to *sangomas,* or traditional healers, to cure illness, ward off evil spirits, and even improve their sex lives, and some priests apparently have grafted that role onto their other pastoral tasks.

Interest in exorcism and demonic possession is also a defining feature of non-Western Christian cultures. Fr. Rufus Perea, a priest of the Mumbai archdiocese in India, has served as the president of the International Association of Exorcists, a Catholic body founded in 1993. In a 2000 interview, Perea said that the group's membership has swelled from just six in the early 1990s to hundreds. Perea also heads a companion association for lay people who cannot officially function as an exorcist, but who nevertheless offer informal prayers for deliverance.

3. PLURALISM, NOT SECULARISM

Much of Catholic life in the global North can be understood as a reaction to secularism, either attempting to meet it halfway (often the liberal impulse) or to fight it off (the conservative instinct). Outside of Europe and some elite pockets of the United States, however, secularism is not really a grassroots phenomenon. The social reality facing Catholicism in the global South is instead a highly competitive religious marketplace.

This contrast was on display during the Vatican's Synod on the Bible in 2008. Bishops from Europe and North America warned against a skeptical reading of Scripture based on secularism, while bishops from the South focused more on biblical literalism and fundamentalism, which many of their people imbibe from nearly ubiquitous Evangelical and Pentecostal movements. Alternatively, some bishops voiced concern with quasi-magical readings of the Bible informed by native religious traditions.

To put the point as simply as possible, the problem in the South usually isn't too much skepticism about religion, but too much credulity.

This fundamental cultural divide has consequences across the board, including the priorities of Church leaders and public perceptions of Catholicism. Southern Catholic leaders don't worry as much about defending the binding character of revealed truth, or the Church's hierarchical structures. Those things are largely uncontroversial in cultures in which robust religiosity is part of the air people breathe.

Instead, the task in the South is to accent what's distinctive about Catholicism vis-à-vis other religious alternatives, which, among other things, tends to alter the Church's cultural profile. Where the main rival to Catholicism is agnostic secularism, popular caricatures of Catholicism will style it as a conservative social institution, perhaps a little hide-bound. Where the alternative is Islam or Pentecostalism, however, Catholicism often appears comparatively moderate and sophisticated, arguably better able to engage modern science, politics, and economics than its competitors.

4. PROBLEMS OF GROWTH, NOT DECLINE

The biggest pastoral and administrative headache for many Southern Catholic leaders is managing growth, not contraction. For example, in 2005 I asked then-Archbishop Ndingi Mwana a'Nzeki of Nairobi, Kenya, to describe his most urgent challenges. He began by citing a problem that would be the wildest dream of many a Western bishop: "We have so many vocations." As a result, he explained, the infrastructure of Kenyan Catholicism for accommodating candidates for the priesthood is almost at the breaking point.

"Seminaries built for one hundred now have almost two hundred," he said. "They were built in the 1960s. Saint Thomas [in Nairobi], for example, opened in 1963 for fifty students, and now there are over one hundred. Another was built for one hundred, it now has many more."

Another challenge mentioned by Nzeki, and again one unfamiliar to most Western dioceses, is catechizing and forming the swelling numbers of Kenyans joining the Catholic Church. In that regard, he called for Western Catholics to volunteer to spend some time in his country, helping to educate new Catholics in the faith.

Monsignor Joseph Obunga, the former secretary general of the Uganda Bishops Conference, who died in April 2005, was blunt in asking for financial help from wealthy Catholic communities during a 2004 interview in Kampala.

"The bishops' conference here is struggling to make the seminaries run," Obunga said. "We need help. The support we give priests is very low, in the dioceses, also economically. . . . I would like to see more collaboration between the Americans, who have got money, and the Africans, who have got vocations. . . . The Church is one, universal, and Catholic, but we need to see those words put into action."

Africa is not alone. Even while Pentecostals eat away at a once-homogenous Catholic population in Honduras, the national seminary had an enrollment of 170 in 2007, an all-time high for a country where the total number of priests is slightly more than 400. Twenty years ago, there were fewer than 40 candidates. Bolivia saw the most remarkable increase; in 1972, the entire country had 49 seminarians, while in 2001 the number was 714, representing growth of 1,357 percent. Overall, seminary enrollments in Latin America have gone up 440 percent over the last quarter-century, according to statistics collected by the "Religion in Latin America" Web site created by Dominican Fr. Edward Cleary of Providence College. In North East India, a region of eight states centering on the city of Assam, there are now 1.5 million Catholics, just a century after missionaries first arrived. Local dioceses are today ordaining an average of fifty new priests every year, an impressive clip by global Catholic standards. Yet even where bishops are generating bumper crops of seminarians, this does not mean they have more priests than they need. In most cases, substantial increases in priests have not been enough to keep pace with the growth of the Catholic population. The worldwide priest-to-person ratio is one to 2,600, but in Latin America, for example, it's one to 8,000.

5. A STRONG POLITICAL ROLE

In non-Western nations, religious bodies are sometimes the only meaningful expressions of civil society—the only zones of life where protest can take shape, and where concern for the common good can be articulated. To take just one example, when the war-torn West African nation of Sierra Leone needed someone to head its National Election Commission who could be trusted across party lines to oversee the fairness of balloting, it turned to a former Sister of Saint Joseph of Cluny and a devout Catholic activist, Christiana Thorpe. Across the global South, Catholic leaders, including bishops and priests, play a directly political role that might be considered excessive by Western standards of church–state separation. Well-known recent examples include the role of the Polish Catholic Church in the collapse of Communism, and the pivotal contribution of Catholic leaders in the Philippines to the fall of the Marcos regime, broadly known as the "People's Power" movement.

A lesser-known story also illustrates the point, from the small African nation of Malawi.

In the early 1990s, Malawi was still under the eccentric rule of its dictator-for-life, a British- and U.S.-educated strongman named Hastings Kamuzu Banda, who had governed the country since independence from the United Kingdom in 1964. Though he's largely forgotten today, Banda was the quintessential African dictator of his era. He sashayed around in elegant three-piece English suits, with matching handkerchiefs and a homburg hat, along with a fly-whisk that symbolized his absolute authority over life and death. His unofficial motto was, "My word is the law."

In March 1992, the seven bishops of Malawi, led by Archbishop James Chiona of Blantyre, issued a dramatic pastoral letter titled "Living Our Faith," instructing that it be read aloud in all 130 parishes in the country. In it, the bishops denounced the vast disparity between rich and poor, as well as human rights abuses by both Banda's political party, the only one allowed under national law, and the government. They called for an end to injustice, corruption, and nepotism, and demanded recognition of free expression and political opposition. They also criticized substandard education and health systems. While none of this was new, it was the first time prominent Malawians had said it out loud and signed their names.

"Every human being, as a child of God, must be free and respected," the letter began. "We cannot turn a blind eye to our people's experiences of unfairness or injustice. These are our brothers and sisters who are in prison without knowing what they are charged with, or when their case will be heard." In a direct challenge to Banda's assertion that his word was law, the bishops said: "No one person can claim to have a monopoly on truth or wisdom."

The bishops managed to get 16,000 copies printed and distributed without Banda's intelligence services catching on. On the Sunday the letter was read out, attendance at Masses swelled. Reportedly, people wept, shouted gratitude, and danced in the aisles. Emboldened by the pastoral letter, grassroots opposition found its voice. In the country's largest city, Blantyre, poor squatters in illegal shantytowns—where cholera was rampant, and sewage flowed openly in the streets—stood up when security forces tried to run them out. Student protests broke out on university campuses. Opposition figures began returning. As news of the uprising circulated internationally, pressure grew for Western powers to take a stand. In 1994, donors froze all foreign aid to Malawi, forcing Banda to call free elections. In effect, his regime was over.

6. YOUTH AND OPTIMISM

The Catholic Church in many parts of the global South is remarkably young in at least two key senses: demographically and culturally.

According to the UN Population Division, 43 percent of the population of sub-Saharan Africa is under fourteen years old. That ratio is certainly reflected in the Church. In fact, the first thing that generally strikes a Western visitor to the typical African parish is the enormous number of children: quite often, kids are literally hanging from the rafters, and it can be difficult to determine sometimes if you're at a Catholic Mass or a day care center.

Aside from Latin America, where Catholicism has more than five hundred years of history, the Church in many other parts of the global South is also young historically. Although the faith has ancient roots in India, most of its growth there has come in the last half-century. In sub-Saharan Africa, Catholicism is almost entirely a product of the late twentieth century.

Taken together, these two forms of youth often give Catholicism in the South a remarkable degree of vigor, a sense of not being weighed down by the past, which can feel liberating to Catholics from Western cultures, perhaps especially Europe. This is an impossible point to quantify, but there's little doubt that being part of a growing Church with a substantial and constant influx of young people generally seeds hope about the future, while perceptions of decline can generate a sort of ecclesiastical ennui.

Americans can catch a glimpse of what this youthful current looks and feels like in the country's Southwest and West, where immigration has sent Catholic populations soaring in places such as Texas and California. These tend to be disproportionately young communities, often with a strikingly dynamic faith life. Often that energy is hidden from mainstream view because it percolates in Spanish, and because it's concentrated away from traditional centers of Catholic life on the East Coast, but it exists nonetheless.

WHAT IT MEANS

The late American cultural critic Neil Postman once famously argued that technological change is not additive, but ecological; that is, it doesn't just change one thing, it changes everything. Judging from its impact across a wide range of issues in Catholicism, the emergence of a World Church is exactly like that. It's not merely adding something new to the life of the Church, but rather driving a holistic transformation, turning it upside down in virtually every area. Though not exhaustive, this section offers a selection of potential consequences.

Near-Certain Consequences

1. LEADERSHIP FROM THE SOUTH

Centers of intellectual and pastoral energy in the South will have increasingly global importance in the century to come. The second half of the twentieth century already witnessed examples of their potential impact. Two influential, though hotly disputed, Catholic theological movements had their origins in the South: liberation theology, associated with Latin Americans such as Gustavo Gutierrez, Leonardo Boff, Ivone Gebara, and Jon Sobrino; and the theology of religious pluralism, pioneered in various ways by Asians such as Michael Amaldoss, Aloysius Pieris, and Tissa Balasuriya. Both are seen in the North as left-of-center, contradicting impressions of a uniformly conservative stamp to Southern Catholicism.

To be clear, Southern centers will not be the only places where leadership emerges. The North will still enjoy a disproportionate share of resources, giving it a bigger megaphone. Catholicism also has a firebreak which works to prevent any rising force from ever transforming the Church too quickly or too completely: Rome. That said, places such as Nairobi, Manila, and São

Paulo are nevertheless likely to be to the twenty-first century what Paris, Milan, and Leuven were to the Counter Reformation, meaning the laboratories in which creative new theological and pastoral approaches of the era take shape. Such is the nature of multipolar world Catholicism.

This will be so for at least five reasons.

First, Southern churchmen will rise to prominence in the Vatican and at other levels of the Church. Figures such as Cardinal Claudio Hummes of Brazil and Cardinal Ivan Dias of India in the Vatican, as well as the prominence of Rodríguez and Onaiyekan in international Catholic discussions, offer cases in point. Because dioceses in the global South tend to be smaller than in the North, the proportion of Southern bishops in the Church will steadily rise. Catholic writers and activists from the South will also be increasingly important, including such prominent Catholic women as Sr. Teresa Okure of Nigeria, Margaret Ogola and Teresia Mbari Hinga of Kenya; Agnes Brazal, Christina Astorga, and Henrietta da Ville of the Philippines; Claudia Montes de Oca Ayala of Bolivia; Sr. Evelyn Monteiro of India; Sr. Vilma Speranza Quintanilla Morán of El Salvador; and Sr. Filo Hirota of Japan.

Second, influential Southern theologians are well represented today in intellectual centers in the North, such as Sanneh at Yale, or Nigeria's Fr. James Chukwuma Okoye at the Catholic Theological Union in Chicago, or the Vietnamese-American theologian Peter Phan at Georgetown University. Third, increasing numbers of students from the South are studying at Northern universities, moving back and forth between both worlds, creating another channel through which Southern concerns reach a global audience. Fourth, the theological establishment in the affluent North is increasingly attentive to the ferment in the South. For example, Jesuit Fr. James Keenan at Boston College organized a 2006 global theological symposium in Padova, Italy (billed as "the first international cross-cultural conference for Catholic theological ethicists"), for which he raised $450,000 to cover the expenses of 140 theologians from Africa, Asia, Latin America, and Eastern Europe.

Fifth, the Southern voice will become more influential because at least some bishops in the North have come to see it as their role to ensure that this voice reaches their local communities. During a plenary session at the 2007 convention of the Catholic Theological Society of America, Auxiliary Bishop Richard Sklba of Milwaukee told the story of a young African seminarian who had approached him during the most intense period of the sexual abuse crisis in the United States, warning him against "ecclesial imperialism," meaning the assumption that America's answers were right for the entire Church. Sklba said he has been "haunted" by the comment. In a similar vein, Cardinal Roger Mahony of Los Angeles said, "In North America, sometimes we have this impression that our pastoral priorities are priorities for the universal church. They're not. It takes a great deal of patience and humility to listen to the rest of the Church."

2. A NEW SET OF ISSUES

As Catholics from the South set the global agenda, we will see new issues occupy the front burner in both grassroots conversation and official Catholic policy making. Two such matters of daily pastoral concern for Southern Catholics are polygamy and witchcraft.

Polygamy

Say "issues facing the family" to the typical bishop in the United States or Europe, and the automatic association is with the Western push for gay marriage. Across Africa, the Middle East, and parts of Asia, however, the biggest practical challenge vis-à-vis marriage often is polygamy (also referred to as "polygyny"). Though estimates diverge widely, sociologists believe that tens of millions of men and women worldwide are involved in polygamous marriages.

Some Protestant denominations have gone so far as to accept polygamy as a legitimate form of Christian marriage. In 1987, the Fifth General Assembly of the All-Africa Conference of Churches, the main Protestant ecumenical body, concluded that "the rather harsh attitude of the Church has been a painful but real cause of disintegration of some otherwise stable marriages and families." In 1988, the Lambeth Conference of the Anglican Communion decided to admit polygamists under certain circumstances in response to pressure from bishops in Kenya and Uganda.

Over the years, a few Catholic theologians have flirted with similar positions. Okoye from Nigeria wrote in a survey of contemporary African Catholic theology in the late 1990s that some theologians believe "the Church's strictures against polygyny are . . . the product of a Western mindset, and unbiblical." In general, however, that's not the mainstream Catholic view, in part because of a strong critique from Southern Catholic women. Okoye cites twenty-three female African Catholic theologians who have argued that since mutuality and equality are biblical ideals, Scripture should not be used to justify polygamous marriage. No body of Catholic bishops in the global South has recommended approval of polygamy. Speaking to the

Black Catholic Congress in the United States in July 2007, Onaiyekan said that on polygamy, "the Catholic Church is particularly firm and consistent, giving no room whatsoever for doubts and exceptions."

The issues raised by polygamy for the Catholic Church aren't so much theological as pastoral and canonical. For example, if a man or woman involved in a polygamous marriage wishes to convert, they must first bring their marriage into alignment with Church teaching. Yet sometimes there are good pastoral reasons for not doing so right away, such as letting children become older, or waiting until the other wives have found jobs or new living situations. The question becomes whether it's possible to deliver sacramental care to these converts in the meantime, and if not, how else their spiritual lives can be nourished.

Other practical questions abound. When a husband separates from his second or third wife, her prospects may be extremely limited. If she returns to her village, she may not be seen as a desirable marriage partner. If she drifts into a city, she may be subject to various forms of exploitation or abuse. Church leaders try to insist that the husband not simply cut his "extra" wives loose, but feel some ongoing responsibility to them, especially if child care is involved.

Cardinal Peter Turkson of Ghana made this argument at the 2005 Synod of Bishops in the Vatican:

> You can't just say to a man, "let the others go and stay with the first wife." There's a question of justice. You can ask the man to provide for her ongoing security, setting up a small business for her, for example. But then there's still her need for a sexual partner. You can't just say to everyone they should be celibate. . . . You don't want to expose them to prostitution and so on.

In the Catholicism of the twenty-first century, when moral theologians and Church leaders come together to talk about marriage, this is what they're likely to have in mind. That may strike some Catholics in the United States and Europe as irrelevant to their concerns; if so, it's a sensation that Catholics from other parts of the world know all too well.

Witchcraft

While Northerners may see magic and witchcraft in largely benign terms as a form of New Age spirituality, across the South the working assumption is that magic and witchcraft are real but demonic, so the proper response is spiritual combat. The famed Methodist Yoruba scholar Bolaji Idowu has written, "In Africa, it is idle to begin with the question whether witches exist or not. . . . To Africans of every category, witchcraft is an urgent reality."

It's also a matter of life and death. In Nigeria, an elderly woman was beheaded in 2007 after she was accused of placing a member of another tribe under a curse. In turn, her murder triggered a spate of interethnic killing that left eighty dead. Secretive cults on Nigeria's one hundred university campuses, with names such as Black Axes and Pyrates, often practice *juju*, or black magic, to terrify their rivals, and violent struggles between these cults have left hundreds dead in recent years. In 2007, a gang of villagers in Kenya beat an eighty-one-year-old man to death, suspecting him of having murdered his three grandsons through witchcraft.

It's not just Africa. In the state of Chiapas in southern Mexico in 2005, a mob severely beat six people, suspecting them of casting spells. Police intervened and saved the six from death. Another indigenous man in Chiapas was not so lucky in April 2003, when a similar mob stoned him and hacked him to death with machetes following accusations that he was a witch. In Kokrajhar in India, five members of two families were killed in August 2006, accused of issuing curses that had caused several locals to come down with viral fever and jaundice. One elderly couple was hacked to death using machetes and spears. According to an Associated Press report, more than 150 people in the region were killed over accusations of witchcraft during the period 2001 to 2006.

In February 2007, the Catholic University of East Africa in Nairobi, Kenya, held a three-day symposium on the pastoral challenge of witchcraft. Experts warned that witchcraft was "destroying" the Catholic Church in Africa, in part because skeptical, Western-educated clergy are not responding adequately to people's spiritual needs.

"It is important for the Church to understand the fears of the people, and not to attribute them to superstition," said Michael Katola, a lecturer in pastoral theology. "Witchcraft is a reality; it is not a superstition. Many communities in Kenya know these powers exist." Katola warned that inadequate pastoral responses are driving some Africans into Pentecostalism.

"Many of our Christians seek deliverance, healing, and exorcism from other denominations because priests do not realize they have redemptive powers," he said. "If we don't believe in the existence of witchcraft as Satanism, then we cannot deal with it."

Sr. Bibiana Munini Ngundo said that the Catholic Church has not paid sufficient attention to "integral healing," leading people to put their trust in diviners and magicians. Fr. Clement Majawa of Malawi listed fourteen categories of witchcraft practiced in Africa and argued that the Church's denial "only escalates the problem."

"Since Christ in the gospels encountered the devil, it is proper for Christians to accept the reality of witchcraft," Majawa said.

It does not tax the imagination to picture a future pope from the global South issuing an encyclical presenting Jesus Christ as the definitive answer to the "spirits of this world." As Okoye points out, the implicit Christology of many Africans is that of "Christus Victor," whose resurrection invested him with definitive power to vanquish the dark forces in the spiritual world, to break spells, and to reverse curses. A document from the Vatican along these lines would arguably stand a better chance of finding an audience at the global Catholic grassroots than virtually any other subject that Western theological elites might desire a future pope to address.

3. A SHIFT FROM *AD INTRA* TO *AD EXTRA*

In traditional Catholic argot, *ad intra* refers to the internal life of the Church, while *ad extra* means its engagement with broader religious and social questions outside the Church. A distinguishing feature of Catholic life in the global South is its predominantly *ad extra* focus. Theologians, bishops, and lay activists tend to be more concerned with how the Church tackles questions such as the relationship with Islam or the alleviation of poverty, rather than "insider Catholic baseball" such as women's ordination to the priesthood or how power is distributed in the Church.

Phan made the point with respect to Asia in a presentation at the 2007 convention of the Catholic Theological Society of America. Surveying Asian theology, Phan said, one will find a "conspicuous absence of the issues that have preoccupied Western theologians." Examples cited by Phan include "papal primacy, infallibility, the Roman Curia, episcopal collegiality, the ordination of women, celibacy, and institutional reform." Instead, Phan said, the Asian focus quickly moves "from *ad intra* to *ad extra*, from self-absorption into mission."

One window onto the general absence of *ad intra* concerns was offered by the 2006 international conference organized by Boston College's Keenan in Padova, Italy. Some participants from the United States and Europe criticized what they saw as an overemphasis on sexuality in official Catholic moral teaching, as well as an "authoritarian, top-down Church government."

(This *ad intra* critique was intended, at least in part, to enhance the credibility of the Church's *ad extra* witness.) When Southerners took the floor, the result was often more outward-looking. A sampling of Southern voices:

- Redemptorist Fr. Vimal Tirimanna of Sri Lanka discussed the efforts of Christians, Sikhs, Buddhists, and Muslims to oppose stringent anti-conversion laws recently floated in his country under the pressure of what he called "religious extremists." Sri Lanka is a majority Buddhist nation that has fought a long-running Hindu rebellion in the South, leading to an upsurge in Buddhist nationalism. Rumors of proselytism by Christians in recent years have led to attacks on churches by angry Buddhist mobs.

- Salesian Fr. Ronaldo Zacharias of Brazil explained that given the explosive social conditions in the cities of his country, the rich are increasingly fleeing into the countryside, constructing their own "paradises." The resulting decline in civil society in major urban areas has opened the door to organized crime, which Zacharias said sometimes exercises greater real power in the cities than the elected authorities. He described the country's political class as largely a refuge of "robbers and thieves."

- Elisee Rutagambwa, a Rwandan theologian writing his dissertation at Boston College, addressed the 1994 Rwandan genocide. He described the cruel irony that perpetrators of the crimes detained by the International Criminal Court for Rwanda enjoy decent housing, eat three times a day, and receive Western-style health care, including antiretroviral medications for those who are HIV-positive, while the survivors have largely returned to the poverty and neglect that they suffered prior to the outbreak of violence.

- Jesuit Fr. Tony Mifsud, a Maltese priest who has been living and teaching theology in Chile since 1974, said that when theologians from the South are asked to list their priorities, internal Catholic debates rarely come up. Mifsud said this *ad extra* emphasis is mostly a matter of pastoral realities. "Direct experience is more significant in setting the agenda, and the experience of poverty hits you hard," he said.

4. TURBOCHARGING ORTHODOXY ON SEX

In broad terms, Southern Catholics are robustly orthodox. They're not interested in metaphorical interpretations of the Resurrection or the Eucharist, they have no problem with belief in miracles, and they don't get hung up over whether liturgical texts say "man" or "person." One consequence of this orthodox tide will be to push Catholicism into a more traditional position on two questions that often define the "culture wars" in the West—abortion and homosexuality. Combined with the rise of evangelical Catholicism, to be discussed in the next chapter, this reality means that prospects for reconsideration of traditional Catholic teaching on these points are virtually zero.

The rise of the global South will likely embolden more "hawkish" Northern bishops, such as those bishops in the United States who have said they would deny communion to pro-choice Catholic politicians. It's worth recalling that when Pope Benedict XVI said during a press conference aboard the papal plane in May 2007 that pro-choice Catholic legislators should not receive communion, he was responding to a question about statements from Catholic bishops in Mexico to the effect that legislators who voted to liberalize abortion in Mexico City had excommunicated themselves.

Nigeria's Onaiyekan puts the Southern view of sexual morality this way:

The virulent and strong currents [in the North] that have tried, and almost succeeded, to push a non-traditional view of sexuality—on homosexuality, abortion, and so on—are actually quite circumscribed, even if they're in circles that are very powerful. It's not only the Africans who are complaining, but it's the Asians too, and the Latin Americans. We are the mainstream, not them. The onus lies upon them to explain why they are doing something new. It's a very heavy onus to explain how it is that for 2,000 years the Church somehow did not understand what Jesus meant.

Even on the question of contraception, where one might expect the Southern Church to take a more liberal stance because of HIV/AIDS, the moral line is often strikingly traditional.

For example, Archbishop Nzeki of Nairobi in 2006 urged the government to reject condoms in AIDS prevention efforts. "When condoms are provided, chances of promiscuity increase since a majority of our people end up engaging in casual sex," he said. In the same year, the bishops' conference of Tanzania called a school science syllabus "sinful" because it included condoms as one way to prevent HIV/AIDS. In June 2004, Bishop Rafael Llano Cifuentes, president of the Brazilian Bishops Commission for Family and

Life, claimed that "using a condom to stop AIDS is like trying to put out a fire with petrol." In 1996, Catholic leaders in Honduras blocked efforts to distribute condoms at polling stations during national elections. Thus when Benedict XVI asserted that condoms actually make the problem of AIDS worse at the beginning of his March 2009 trip to Africa, it triggered a firestorm of protest in the West, especially in Europe, but virtually no reaction at all in most of the global South. In effect, the pope simply gave voice to what most Southern bishops had been saying all along.

5. SUPPORT FOR THE LEFT ON ECONOMIC JUSTICE AND WAR

Southern leaders are sometimes dubious, however, about the way Northern conservatives champion their stands on homosexuality and abortion but not on questions of economic and social justice.

"As Africans, we are often surprised by the extent to which our brothers and sisters in the North will sometimes follow only half of the gospel," Onaiyekan said in a 2007 interview in Abuja. "Some Christians will oppose abortion but support war. How can you say no to the killing of a fetus, but yes to the killing of an adult?"

While allowing for important exceptions, the preponderance of Southern Catholic opinion aligns with the Western left on matters of international economic structures, the proper role of the state in promoting an equitable distribution of resources, the role of international bodies such as the United Nations, the moral legitimacy of war, the death penalty, and support for the Palestinians in the Middle East. The increased visibility and impact of leadership from the South will likely move the Church into more aggressive stands on these questions. Some professional alarmists may fret that the real "clash of civilizations" in the future will not run between Islam and the West, but between North and South.

One reason that Catholic positions on these matters have been less visible in the West is that official doctrine regards abortion and homosexuality as moral absolutes, whereas other matters leave room for prudential judgment. This distinction, however, is one to which many Southern Catholics are less sensitive. The Catholic bishops of Zimbabwe, for example, unambiguously told their country's aging dictator, Robert Mugabe, at Easter in 2007 that he either had to go or face "open revolt." The bishops did not say they wished to offer some considerations to illuminate the public conscience, which is the formula that might have been used in the United States or Europe. They simply told Mugabe, "Pack your bags."

6. URBAN MINISTRY

Just as the twelfth and thirteenth centuries bred new forms of religious life in Europe to respond to urbanization, most notably mendicant orders such as the Dominicans and the Franciscans, so too new forms of ministry will evolve in the twenty-first century to evangelize the swelling urban centers in the global South. In 2008, the world reached a momentous milestone: for the first time, a majority of its population, some 3.3 billion people, lived in urban areas. By 2030, that number will be 5 billion. At that point, 81 percent of city dwellers on earth will live in developing nations, most in the global South. The UN has termed the coming thousand years "the Urban Millennium."

New urban ministries in the South are likely to be predominantly lay-led, owing in part to chronic shortages of priests, with an emphasis on forming community as an antidote to the breakdown of traditional rural social networks. While parishes will still be important, the focus of much Catholic urban ministry in the twenty-first century is likely to be smaller and more mobile pastoral centers staffed by lay leaders. In many ways, Catholicism is likely to steal a page from the Pentecostal playbook; in Brazil, a popular saying goes that in the shantytowns, the only two things that work are organized crime and the Pentecostal churches. Such a mode of ministry accents personal morality, engaging forms of worship, spiritual experience, and fellowship.

7. DIVERSITY AND UNIFORMITY

Inevitably, the global character of Catholicism will push it in the direction of what theologians call "inculturation," meaning expressing the faith differently according to the argot and customs of local cultures. Celebrating the Catholic Mass, for example, is a different experience in Nigeria than in India, and the issues that occupy the pastoral attention of Church leaders also vary. Multiply the number of cultures in which the Church is a living force, and its internal diversity increases.

Yet as these centrifugal energies grow, so too will an equal-and-opposite centripetal force, reflecting alarm that the unity of the Church not be lost amid the welter of different cultural idioms. The more inculturated the Church becomes, the stronger the determination will grow that it also protect its own distinctive culture transcending variations of language and geography. In many cases, Catholic leaders in the global South will support a degree of uniformity, based on Roman patterns, as a way of helping their people understand what's distinctive about Catholicism compared to other religious alternatives.

In one sign of the times, Latin is staging a comeback as a liturgical language at international Catholic events such as World Youth Days, Eucharistic Congresses, the World Meeting of Families, and so on—not primarily for theological reasons, but because Catholics who speak different languages and come from different regions can share the "Agnus Dei," and the "Pater Noster," without feeling like someone else's culture or language is being privileged at the expense of their own.

For a Church that prizes balance, there are two extremes to be avoided: call them the "Microsoft option" and the "CNN option." The 2007 edition of Microsoft Office is currently available in thirty-seven languages, but it's the exact same product in each case—the same design, the same functions, the same programming. A user creating a Power Point file in Hindi and someone doing so in Finnish are having precisely the same experience, making any suggestion of inculturation an illusion. Meanwhile, CNN has a family of twelve channels around the world, such as CNN+ in Spain, CNN TÜRK in Turkey, and CNN-IBN in India. Often the only thing these channels share is the CNN brand; the content is enormously different, and without the network logo, most viewers would have no idea they're related. In that situation, any claim to core unity is false.

Catholicism tries to fall somewhere in between, practicing unity on the essentials and diversity for the rest. Getting that balance right will be a major twenty-first century headache.

Probable Consequences

1. PERMANENT TENSIONS WITH THE UNITED STATES

The contours of the relationship between the global Catholic Church and the United States will depend to some extent upon who's in power at a given moment in the White House. The early months of 2009, for example, witnessed a striking difference in tone between the Vatican and conservative sectors of opinion in American Catholicism, including some of American bishops, with regard to U.S. president Barack Obama—with the Vatican, in this instance, taking a more moderate and approving stance.

Under Obama, the rise of the global South in Catholicism probably augurs a better relationship for the administration with the Vatican and the global Church than with American Catholics, some of whom evaluate Obama almost exclusively through the prism of his policies on abortion and other "life issues."

Peoples. Slovenian Cardinal Jozef Tomko, then the head of the Vatican office that issued the document, said that such transfers were damaging to the Church in the South. India, Tomko said, doesn't have enough priests to take care of its 17 million Catholics, yet at that time there were 39 priests from India working in one Italian diocese alone. Overall, Tomko claimed, there were 1,800 foreign priests in Italy, with more than 800 working in direct pastoral care.

"Many new dioceses could be created in mission territories with such a number of diocesan priests!" Tomko complained.

South–North movement of priests promises to be a growing source of friction for other reasons as well. In some cases, more liberal congregations in the North are uncomfortable with what they perceive as the conservatism of foreign priests. Sometimes the difficulties are more practical. Fr. Cletus Onyegbule, a Nigerian working in the Diocese of Allentown in Pennsylvania, said in 2006 that when he first began delivering homilies in America, his congregation always looked askance at him whenever he described something as "important." Only later did he discover, he said laughingly, that many thought he was saying "impotent."

Redistribution of priests is equally controversial among Southern bishops, some of whom feel it's the latest chapter in a long history of Northern colonial plunder. Onaiyekan of Nigeria put it this way in a 2006 interview: "What we don't want is to get into a *Gastarbeiter* situation, where a European priest feels overwhelmed having to say three Masses on Sunday, and so he wants a black man to say them. Surely this is not where the Church wants to go, getting poor people to do jobs that the rich don't want to do, as today happens in other walks of life."

As with general immigration patterns, such laments will likely do little to alter the underlying economic and social forces that induce priests to relocate. In the near-term future, the North will still be more affluent than the South, and the South will still generate more new priests than the North. In such a situation, a northward migration of priests is to some extent inevitable.

4. A TOUGHER ECUMENICAL AND INTERRELIGIOUS LINE

In the immediate post–Vatican II period, the architects of Catholicism's relationships with other churches and other religions were Europeans who carried a sense of historic guilt for sins of the past, from the Crusades to the Wars of Religion, and in particular they were haunted by the Holocaust. Their approach was dominated by the need for an examination of conscience and a spirit of reconciliation. Tomorrow's trailblazers, on the other hand, will be Africans, Latin Americans, and Asians, who are more likely to regard themselves as victims rather than perpetrators of religious intolerance. In the Middle East and parts of Africa and Asia today, Catholics suffer under aggressive forms of Islamicization, while Catholics in India are reeling from militant Hindu nationalism. In Latin America, Catholics often see themselves as targets of aggressive proselytism from Pentecostal and Evangelical movements.

In such contexts, self-defense rather than deference becomes the leitmotif of ecumenical and interfaith relations. For example, the Christian Association of Nigeria is an ecumenical body to which the Catholic Church belongs, formed as a self-defense league when anti-Christian violence by Islamic radicals broke out in the late 1970s. The group's general secretary, S. L. S. Salifu, summed up the spirit of much Southern opinion in 2007 when asked if the pugnacious spirit of his organization is consistent with Jesus' admonition to turn the other cheek.

"Of course it is," Salifu said. "You can't turn the other cheek if you're dead."

None of this means that ecumenical and interreligious dialogue is headed for extinction under Southern leadership. On the contrary, the Catholic bishops of Asia have pioneered a flourishing "triple dialogue" with the cultures and religions of Asia and with the continent's poor. In much of Africa and the Middle East, relations among Christians are close, in part because they face a common threat vis-à-vis radical Islam. Anglican–Catholic relationships in Africa may be stronger than anywhere else on earth, as both share a sense of revulsion about liberal moral tendencies among their coreligionists in the North. In Latin America, Catholics and Pentecostals are making common cause against the stirrings of secularization, especially in the legislative arena.

Demographic shifts in Catholicism are nevertheless reorienting the ecumenical and interfaith outreach of the Catholic Church in two important ways.

First, reconciliation and mutual theological understanding are yielding pride of place to reciprocity and religious freedom. If the top post–Vatican II question was how Catholicism can be reformed to make space for a positive view of others, the question more likely to drive the twenty-first century is how other religions, and the societies they shape, can be reformed to make space for Christianity. Second, the monopoly of "dialogue" as virtually the only way Catholicism relates to other Christians and other religions is giving way to more complex forms of engagement. Dialogue will remain important, but the twenty-first century is also seeing a comeback of apologetics, meaning a principled defense of the faith, and proclamation, meaning explicit efforts to invite others to conversion. Both are a reflection of the fact that many Southern Catholics are less inclined to tiptoe around the sensitivities of others, because they don't feel responsible for creating those sensitivities in the first place.

The key question may be whether the humility and passion for unity of post–Vatican II ecumenism, which were undeniably historic achievements, can be creatively combined with today's greater Southern willingness to push back when the other side doesn't play fair. Such a blend may be precisely what it means to think in a global key.

Possible Consequences

1. A THIRD-WORLD POPE

Of all the implications of an era of World Catholicism, none excites the media or public opinion like the prospect of a "third-world pope." For many observers, the sociological transformation of the Church will not seem fully real until a pontiff with a black or brown face sits upon the Throne of Peter. Over time, the election of a pope from the South is all but inevitable. A Latin American was actually the runner-up in the conclave in 2005 that elected Pope Benedict XVI: Jesuit Cardinal Jorge Mario Bergoglio of Buenos Aires, Argentina.

I classify it here as "possible" because I have no way of knowing whether it will happen in the twenty-first century, the twenty-second, or the twenty-fifth.

In itself, the election of a pope from the developing world would tell us little about the character of that man's papacy. The Nigerian Arinze would be a very different pope from Rodríguez of Honduras, who in turn would be very different from Ivan Dias of India—to take just three names that were mentioned prominently in 2005. At the level of symbolism, however, a pope from the South could be tremendously important. An African, for example, would not merely put a "face" on the epochal shifts within Catholicism, but he could also prove a formidable challenge both to racism in many parts of the world as well as to the broad neglect that usually envelops the suffering of Africa.

2. "SEAMLESS GARMENT" CATHOLICISM

The late Cardinal Joseph Bernardin of Chicago created one of the most oft-quoted, and controversial, formulas in Catholic public life in the United States in a lecture at Fordham University in 1984. He called for a "consistent ethic of life," spanning issues such as abortion and euthanasia as well as poverty reduction, health care, and antiwar activism. Bernardin used the metaphor of a "seamless garment," a reference to John 19:23 and the seamless robe of Christ which the soldiers who executed him did not tear apart. In American Catholic practice, however, things have not worked out that way. The seamless garment image has become loathsome to many Catholic conservatives, who feel that it gives cover to leftist Catholics to blur the Church's uncompromising stand on abortion or homosexuality.

If there is any hope of transforming this situation, it may be an impulse from the South, where a combination of traditionalism in matters of sexual morality and personal lifestyles, along with a progressive outlook on social and economic questions, comes naturally. Bernardin's vindication may come not from the force of theological argument, but from the impact of Catholic demographics.

In the short term, the Southern voice in Catholicism likely will be only selectively heard in the North. Over time, however, such deafness will become steadily more difficult to sustain. In the Church of the twenty-first century, it will be increasingly tough to be a Catholic in favor of gay marriage or the legalization of abortion, and it will be equally hard to remain a Catholic and support military actions such as the war in Iraq or the economic disparities generated by globalization.

3. RECONSIDERATION OF PRIESTLY CELIBACY

In principle celibacy is not a doctrinal question, yet the debate is largely frozen in place because it has become a lightning rod for deeper divisions in the Church, from the identity of the priesthood to the authority of tradition. This polarization, however, is characteristic of the North. In the South, bishops and theologians often approach the question more practically. Struggling with severe priest shortages, their basic concern is how to deliver pastoral care, especially in isolated rural areas or in the peripheries of cities.

At the 2005 Synod on the Eucharist, several Southern bishops mentioned areas in the developing world, including Latin America and the Pacific Islands, where isolated communities strung out over vast distances often go without priests for long periods of time. Bishop Roberto Camilleri Azzopardo of Comayaga, Honduras, for example, reported having one priest for every 16,000 Catholics in his diocese. Privately, several bishops suggested that the Church might consider the ordination of *viri probati*, meaning tested married men, to serve these communities. Led largely by bishops from the North, the synod instead reaffirmed the discipline of celibacy.

It's possible, however, that a future Southern pope, or a future synod more influenced by voices from the South, may revisit the issue. Sometime in the twenty-first century, limited experiments with the *viri probati* might be approved. It's improbable that the Catholic Church will ever simply abandon priestly celibacy, and under almost any scenario one can imagine, celibacy will remain the norm for members of religious orders. Nevertheless, pragmatic Southern leadership may be willing to consider limited exceptions to accommodate specific pastoral needs.

A brief footnote is in order. It's an article of faith among some liberal Western Catholics that celibacy is impractical in the developing world, especially in Africa, and that many priests simply flaunt the discipline. Establishing the truth of these perceptions is almost impossible. There are certainly cases: in May 2009, for example, Archbishop Paulin Pomodimo of Bangui, the lone archdiocese in the Central African Republic, resigned after a Vatican investigation confirmed reports that several of his priests had been living in what amounted to common law marriages with women and the children they had fathered. Local clergy fired back that white priests and religious in the country were guilty of "ecclesiastical neocolonialism," since, they charged, some white priests and bishops were engaged in the same behavior.

To date, however, there have been no reliable sociological surveys to determine how widespread such cases are, and Church authorities are notoriously reluctant to address the question. One gets different answers depending upon who you ask: Western missionaries tend to report that there is blatant disregard of celibacy, while local priests and bishops usually deny it. An Irish missionary who's been in Kenya for twenty years, for example, told me in 2006 that he's heard of several cases of local priests who are sexually active, including one who lives openly with a girlfriend and three children. On the other hand, a Nigerian priest of the Abuja archdiocese who lived in Belgium and Italy for twelve years said in 2007 that he believes priests are more likely to violate their vows of celibacy in Europe. Frankly, he said, European priests are less inclined to take Church strictures seriously across a range of matters, not just celibacy. One Nigerian priest currently studying in Canada put the point this way: "The sexual abuse scandals are not wonderful testimonies of celibacy well-lived in the West." Virtually every African priest and bishop with whom I spoke on the subject said that he finds Northern impressions of uncontrollable African sexuality deeply offensive.

In the abstract, there seems little a priori reason to believe that celibacy is any less practical in the South than the North. The argument Southern bishops and priests make who want to relax the rule is not that Southern clergy are incapable of upholding it, but rather that given their pastoral challenges, some flexibility is in order.

4. PRIEST REDISTRIBUTION

If Roman Catholicism were a multinational corporation, it would not take a systems analyst long to realize that there is a serious mismatch between the Church's market and its allocation of resources. Two thirds of the Catholics today are in Africa, Asia, and Latin America, but just slightly over one third of the Catholic priests. If the Church responded to corporate logic, it would implement a scheme for the redistribution of its priests to where its business is growing.

As noted above, however, Catholicism is doing precisely the opposite. The tendency is for priests from the South to relocate to the North. As Philip Jenkins has written, "Viewed in a global perspective, such a policy can be described at best as painfully short-sighted, at worst as suicidal for Catholic fortunes."

That impression has certainly occurred to bishops in the South.

During the 2005 Synod on the Eucharist, Bishop Lucio Andrice Muandula of Xai-Xai in Mozambique said, "It comes naturally to me to ask to what extent an ecclesial community without the Sacrament of the Eucharist can reach that dynamism of life which allows it to change into a missionary community." He was prepared to draw the obvious conclusion: "One must insist on the equal redistribution of priests in the world."

In the short term, it is difficult to imagine bishops in Europe or the United States shipping off large numbers of their priests to the South, and it's also an open question how pastorally helpful it would be, given the difficulties of adjusting to different languages and cultures. Yet under Southern leadership, Catholicism will probably move gradually to arrest the northward flow of priests, and will encourage some movement in the opposite direction. At a minimum, Church authorities will become stricter about allowing local bishops in the North to "poach" clergy from dioceses in the developing world.

5. A BOOST FOR CATHOLIC LIBERALISM FROM INDIA

In the 1980s and '90s, liberal Catholics in the North generally looked to three centers of Church life for inspiration: Chicago in the United States, under Bernardin; Milan in Italy, under Cardinal Carlo Maria Martini; and Westminster in England, under Cardinal Basil Hume. As those figures have passed from the scene, and as the rise of the global South implies flagging interest in internal reform movements, the question for traditional Catholic liberals is where their new center of imagination may be found.

One possible answer is India. India's Catholic population should be around 26 million in 2050, placing India among the top twenty Catholic nations, roughly on a par with Germany. Those numbers should give India an amplified voice in global Catholic conversation.

On several contentious theological issues, including religious pluralism, inculturation, and ecclesiology, Indian Catholic thinkers such as Michael Amaladoss, Felix Wilfred, and Aloysius Pieris (a Sri Lankan but part of the Indian discussion) express attitudes regarded in the West as left of center. The overrepresentation of "untouchables," or Dalits, also means that Indian Catholics are especially attentive to poverty, discrimination, and structural injustice.

To be sure, not every Indian bishop, priest, or theologian would accept these progressive views. Nevertheless, they represent something of a mainstream consensus, which suggests that more liberal Catholics in the North may increasingly look to India for strategic alliances. In the case of the United States, this tendency will be augmented by the fact that most Indian theologians and activists are fluent in English.

Long-Shot Consequences

1. THE FIRST COUNCIL OF MANILA

To date there have been twenty-one Ecumenical Councils, meaning gatherings of Catholic bishops from around the world. The first seven were held in various locations within the Greek world, the remainder in Western Europe. The last one to meet outside Rome was the sixteenth-century Council of Trent, which launched the Catholic Counter-Reformation. As the center of gravity shifts southward, it is not inconceivable that a future Ecumenical Council could be held in the developing world: a Council of Manila, perhaps, or a Council of Nairobi. Arguably, such a council could be justified by the need to chart a new course for the Church in response to its new, and historically unprecedented, sociological and cultural contours.

I rate this scenario as a long shot for two reasons. First, Vatican II brought together 2,865 bishops. Today, the total number of bishops, archbishops, and cardinals in the Catholic Church is more than 5,600. The logistics of assembling such a throng would be daunting. Second, if an ecumenical council were to be called, the odds-on favorite for venue would be Rome, understood as the crossroads of the universal Church.

Still, the vision of all the bishops of the Catholic world traveling south in order to chart the Church's future is beguiling. As the example of Vatican II reminds us, there doesn't have to be a consensus for such an event to happen. Pope John XXIII did not consult widely prior to calling a council, and it's just possible that a future Southern pope might feel the same way about a Council of Manila.

2. A FIRE SALE AT THE VATICAN

In 1963, Pope Paul VI laid his tiara, the three-tiered jeweled crown that was traditionally the symbol of the pope's authority as a monarch, upon the altar in Saint Peter's Basilica, symbolically renouncing all claims to temporal power. Paul's intention was to sell the tiara and give the proceeds to the poor, but Cardinal Francis Spellman of New York persuaded the pope to donate it to the Catholics of the United States, vowing to take the papal crown on a tour of the country and to donate all the proceeds to poverty relief. The tiara is today on permanent display in the Basilica of the National Shrine of the Immaculate Conception in Washington, D.C.

The spirit of simplicity behind Pope Paul's act is one that resonates deeply with many Catholics in the global South, who worry about perceptions of the wealth of the Church in the midst of poverty. Jesuit Cardinal Jorge Mario Bergoglio of Argentina, for example, sold off the chauffer-driven limousine that came with his position and takes public transportation.

Cardinal Gracias of Mumbai, India, says that simplicity of lifestyle is an important theme for bishops from the South, even at home.

"We've got to become simpler ourselves," Gracias said in a 2006 interview. "In India, we have lots of big edifices, in the form of churches, office buildings, parish houses, and so on. Today it's a little embarrassing. When we construct our places today, we're very conscious of that. Also our dress habits, food habits, our manner of travel, all should be as simple as possible."

The Catholic Church will not, of course, sell off Saint Peter's Basilica in the twenty-first century. It's possible, however, that a future pope from Asia or Latin America might be inclined to selectively auction off some items from the Vatican Museums, or some trappings of the papal office, in order to help the poor. Such a pope might also feel sufficiently uncomfortable in such surroundings that he would decide to relocate the papal residence into more modest quarters in another part of Vatican City, converting the Apostolic Palace into a tourist destination—a museum of papal history, perhaps—or even a relief center for needy Romans. Such a gesture could capture the imagination of the world.

3. CATHOLIC–ANGLICAN UNITY IN THE SOUTH

At the moment, ecumenical progress between the Catholic Church and Anglicanism seems hopelessly stalled. Differences over the validity of Anglican ordinations and the primacy of the pope remain unresolved, and new disputes over the ordination of women and homosexuality have widened the gap. Looking at things that way, however, assumes a Northern frame of reference. In the South, Catholics and Anglicans are much more united.

In part, this is because the largest concentration of Anglicans in the South is in Africa, where Catholics and Anglicans usually feel a strong sense of common cause vis-à-vis Islam and, to some extent, Pentecostalism. Seen from a Southern point of view, debates over sexual morality are less of a wedge between Catholicism and Anglicanism than between Northern and Southern Christianity. If by mid-century the Southern currents in both Anglicanism and Catholicism are more influential in setting the tone, this could radically alter the ecumenical dynamics between the two traditions. Even if structural reunion remains out of reach, the prospects for practical cooperation and interaction would be much greater.

EVANGELICAL CATHOLICISM

Anyone who regards the statement, "I'm a card-carrying Catholic," as a mere metaphor has obviously never met Marian Mulhall. A communications executive in Ireland, Mulhall decided in 2005 to combine her professional skills with her commitment to the Church. Her goal is to support priests, but first she had to develop a moneymaker. Mulhall thus began pitching the "Catholic Identity Card." For roughly forty-five dollars, a Catholic can obtain a credit card–size piece of plastic bearing the holder's name, a picture of Pope Benedict XVI, a holographic icon showing the hands of a priest breaking the Eucharistic host, and a phrase in bold letters stating: "I am a Catholic. In the event of an accident or emergency, please contact a priest."

Mulhall explains the appeal this way: "It should be carried with you always. In doing so it makes a clear statement that you are a Catholic, that you make no apologies for being a Catholic, and that in fact you are proud to be a Catholic."

It says a great deal about contemporary Ireland that the thought would even occur to anyone that a card might be necessary to identify the bearer as Catholic. Just a generation ago, Ireland was still an overwhelmingly Catholic society, with rates of weekly Mass attendance in excess of 80 percent. Marketing a card to remind people they're Catholic would have been akin to selling them a card to remind them they're Irish, and since the British would never let them forget it, one cannot imagine the sales potential would have been terribly strong.

In sociological terms the Catholic identity card is a by-product of Western secularization and growing cultural pluralism. Even in Ireland, Catholics no longer live in homogenous neighborhoods, schools, and families. Across the Western world, Catholicism has gone from being a culture-shaping majority to perceiving itself as an embattled cultural minority, and is responding as embattled minorities always do: With a "politics of identity" based on reaffirming traditional beliefs and practices, sharpening the borders between itself and the surrounding culture. It's akin to the response of ancient Judaism when faced with the challenge of maintaining its identity in the diaspora: "Building a fence around the law."

The Catholic identity card is the tip of the iceberg. Signs of fence-building in today's Catholic Church are everywhere:

- Catholic liturgies are becoming steadily more traditional, with a preference for Roman-sounding phrases and older practices such as taking communion on the tongue rather than in the hand.

- Catholic universities, hospitals, and charitable organizations are under strong pressure to prove that they haven't "gone secular"—and this pressure doesn't always, or even generally, come from Rome. The May 2009 controversy about U.S. president Barack Obama's commencement address at the University of Notre Dame offers a clear example. The Vatican sat out the controversy, and the most ferocious criticism came not from U.S. bishops but from pro-life groups and grassroots activists concerned about the implications for Notre Dame's Catholic identity.

- Priests, brothers, and nuns are under scrutiny for alleged deviations from their traditional ways of life. In 2009 alone, American nuns were facing two separate Vatican-sponsored investigations along these lines.

- Pope Benedict XVI's decision to revive the old Latin Mass, and his broader insistence on reading the Second Vatican Council in continuity with earlier layers of Catholic tradition, aims at projecting a more classical sense of Catholic identity.

This thrust toward revival of traditional markers of Catholic thought, speech, and practice—which one can sense in Catholicism today both from the top down and the bottom up—is part of what's described in this chapter as "evangelical Catholicism." (The root term "evangelical" comes from the

Greek word for the Gospel, and the verb "to evangelize" means "to spread the Gospel.")

To understand why "evangelical" is the best way to describe this trend, it's useful to review how the term arose in Protestant usage. In the eighteenth and nineteenth centuries, Christianity was challenged to the core by the rise of empirical science, especially modern biblical scholarship, and by increasingly secular models of social life. In response, Protestantism spawned three responses that cross denominational borders, and that still define the basic options today:

- Mainline liberalism, which sees the relationship between church and culture as a two-way street, adjusting teachings and structures in order to be relevant to the modern world.

- Evangelicalism, which sees the church's problem not as a crisis of teaching but as a crisis of nerve. The antidote is bold proclamation of timeless truths, using the tools and argot of the new cultural milieu.

- Pentecostalism, which is equally determined to challenge modernity on its own turf, but emphasizing spiritual experience rather than doctrine.

To put the differences into a sound bite, mainline liberals want to reach a détente with modernity; evangelicals want to convert it; and Pentecostals want to set it on fire.

All three instincts have clear analogues inside Catholicism. In terms of the official structures and leadership of the Church, what we might call mainline Catholic liberalism enjoyed a heyday from the late 1960s through the mid-1980s. Beginning with the election of Pope John Paul II in 1978, however, Catholicism has become steadily more evangelical—uncompromising and unabashedly itself, more interested in evangelizing culture than accommodating it.

The defining features of evangelical Catholicism are:

- A clear embrace of traditional Catholic thought, speech, and practice, the usual word for which is "orthodoxy";

- Eagerness to proclaim one's Catholic identity to the world, emphasizing its implications for culture, society, and politics;

- Faith seen as a matter of personal choice rather than cultural inheritance.

Evangelical Catholics are not at all identical to their Protestant counterparts, and some Protestants resent it when Catholics borrow the term. Both groups, however, share an underlying religious psychology that, despite theological differences, often makes them more like one another than like other members of their denominations. Among those who've spotted an evangelical Catholic impulse, though they define it differently, are David O'Brien of the College of the Holy Cross, Deacon Keith Fournier in his 1990 book *Evangelical Catholics*, and William Portier of the University of Dayton in a 2004 piece in the theological journal *Communio* titled "Here Come the Evangelical Catholics."

From the outside, it's tempting to simply label all this "conservative." That's not entirely wrong, as the impulse does often have a conservative feel, from defending the authority of the pope to preferring that priests wear Roman collars and that churches "look like churches," rather than meeting halls or neomodernist abstractions. Yet labeling such attitudes "conservative" can obscure as much as it reveals, for two reasons.

First, there are many younger Catholics these days eager to take part in Eucharistic adoration, and who axiomatically accept Church teaching on abortion, but who are also strongly pro-environment, antiwar, and pro–poverty relief—understanding all of that as an expression of their Catholic identity. The key point about evangelical Catholics, especially the younger breed, is not that they're politically liberal or conservative. It's that their formative experience wasn't growing up in a rigid, stifling Church, but rather a rootless secular culture. Their hunger for identity is better understood in terms of generational dynamics, not ideology.

Second, from a historical point of view, evangelical Catholicism isn't "conservative" because these days there's precious little cultural Catholicism left to conserve. For the same reason, it's not traditionalist, even though it places a premium upon tradition. In truth, evangelical Catholicism is every bit as creative a response to modernity as liberal Catholicism. Evangelicals take religious freedom and the separation of church and state for granted. Many evangelical Catholics actually welcome secularization, because it forces religion to become a conscious choice, which they regard as the only truly Christian option. As the late Cardinal Jean-Marie Lustiger of Paris, the quintessential evangelical Catholic, put it, "We're really just at the dawn of Christianity."

Pope Benedict XVI is a good illustration of the point. The usual media shorthand for his outlook is "conservative," sometimes even "archconservative." Yet the pope's aim is not conservation of some *status quo ante*—he doesn't harbor any illusions about re-creating the homogenous Catholic culture of his Bavarian youth, and he's not nostalgic for the return of the Papal States. Borrowing a term from Arnold Toynbee, Benedict XVI's vision of Christianity in the secular West is as a "creative minority." Toynbee believed that when a civilization goes into crisis, its prospects for recovery are dependent upon its creative minorities—subgroups which, because of their passion and vision, exercise influence beyond their numbers. For that to work, these creative minorities must have a solid sense of their own identity and a strong degree of internal cohesion—precisely Benedict's program for the Catholic Church. Call that what you will, but "conservative" hardly seems the right term.

Evangelical Catholicism is, in one sense, a stepchild of secularization, but it is also a conscious and carefully crafted strategy to resist the perceived evils of secularization. It's an attempt to ensure that the weakening of religious faith and practice in the secular world is not reproduced inside the Church. The evangelical Catholic impulse is designed to ensure that Catholicism does not end up, in a memorable phrase from the French Catholic philosopher Jacques Maritain, "kneeling before the world." Without a doubt, evangelical Catholicism is the most consequential trend at the policy-setting level of the Catholic Church today. Observers hoping to understand why decisions are being made the way they are in the Vatican, or by national bishops' conferences, must come to terms with it.

Dating the current ascendance of evangelical Catholicism to John Paul II is not to suggest the impulse was born yesterday. It has deeper roots, in some ways reaching back to the late nineteenth century and the pontificate of Leo XIII, who decisively broke with papal nostalgia for the European ancien régime and began to work out how the enduring principles of Catholicism could be creatively expressed in the new world then taking shape. Among other things, the modern tradition of Catholic social teaching has its origins in this ferment. Thirty years of bishops' appointments by John Paul II and Benedict XVI, however, have ensured that a broadly evangelical outlook is shared by much of the Church's leadership class.

At the grassroots, one can cite multiple eruptions of evangelical Catholic energy, from the Communion and Liberation meetings in Rimini, Italy, which annually draw more than 700,000 Catholics committed to challenging secularism, to World Youth Day, an international Catholic youth festival centered on the pope that routinely draws crowds in excess of a million, and which is one part liturgy and one part rock-and-roll festival. The expansion of evangelical-tinged Catholic media and an ever-growing host of Catholic blogs reflect the trend, as does the proliferation of Catholic schools and colleges marked by evangelical fervor. In his 2004 *Communio* article, Portier argued that a disproportionate share of undergraduate and graduate theology students and parish ministers come from the evangelical camp.

Evangelicals may not drive other views out of the Church anytime soon—in fact, one could make a good historical case that there will always be liberals, evangelicals, and Pentecostals in the Church, with their influence waxing and waning. Evangelical Catholicism is clearly, however, much more than a top-down phenomenon radiating out from Rome.

Today's reality is comparable to something Nelson Mandela once said of globalization. Debating the desirability of globalization, Mandela said, is like debating the desirability of winter—whether you like it or not, it's on the way. Evangelical Catholicism is a bit like that. Whatever one makes of either its theological merits or its sales potential in today's spiritual supermarket—and there's ample debate on both points—emblems of evangelical momentum such as Mulhall's Catholic identity card feel less like the dying ripple of a wave that has already crested, and more like harbingers of things to come.

WHAT'S HAPPENING

Oceans of ink have been spilled trying to define "secularization," but common sense understands it as a general weakening of traditional religious faith, affiliation, and practice, along with a strong distinction between church and state, which arose in modernity in response to forces such as the Enlightenment and empirical science. As a grassroots phenomenon, secularization is largely confined to Europe, where it has become a de facto marker of cultural identity. As sociologists and policy analysts like to say, secularization today is part of the European "package," sort of like TNT and CNN come with basic cable.

Given that Europe represents a diminishing share of the Catholic population, it might be tempting for some Catholic leaders simply to write it off, investing time and treasure elsewhere. Yet that's unlikely for at least three reasons. First, the Vatican is a European institution, so European cultural trends exercise a disproportionate impact on the day-to-day concerns of Vatican officials. Second, it's an article of faith in many quarters that when Europe sneezes, the rest of the world catches a cold. One reason Catholicism has fought tooth-and-nail battles against the Socialist government of Prime Minister José Luis Rodríguez Zapatero in Spain, for example, is the conviction that Spanish trends eventually radiate out and shape culture in Latin America, where half of all Catholics today live. Third, secularization has a disproportionate global following among academics, artists, policy makers, and journalists, so it carries a big cultural club even when it doesn't correspond to popular sentiment. The United States is a good example; famed sociologist Peter Berger says that America is a nation of (Asian) Indians, who are intensely religious, ruled over by Swedes, who certainly aren't.

For these reasons, concern about the fate of Europe looms large among senior policy-makers in the Catholic Church. After the conclave of April 2005 that elected Pope Benedict XVI, many cardinals said they felt he was the right man to tackle the crisis of faith in contemporary Europe—suggesting that Europe was their top "voting issue." Europe's crisis of faith is certainly real. Consider the results of a 2002 Pew Global Attitudes Project, which asked people around the world to say how important religion was to them. The following are the percentages in various nations who said it was "very important":

- Indonesia 95 percent
- Nigeria 92 percent
- India 92 percent
- Philippines 88 percent
- Guatemala 80 percent
- United States 59 percent
- Poland 36 percent
- Great Britain 33 percent
- Italy 27 percent
- Germany 21 percent
- Russia 14 percent
- France 11 percent
- Czech Republic 11 percent

The European nations at the bottom of the list include the birthplace of the English Reformation, the headquarters of Roman Catholicism, the land of Luther, the "eldest daughter of the Church," the home of Russian Orthodoxy, and the heartland of the Bohemian Reformation. These low levels of religious intensity in the historical cradles of Christian civilization speak volumes about the transformation that's taken place. Among many Catholic commentators, it has become common today to refer to a European "ecclesiastical winter."

Scholar David Voas of the University of Manchester reports that the cultural deck in Great Britain today, to take just one European nation as an example, is decisively stacked against religion. Survey data reveal that two religious parents stand only a 47 percent chance of raising a religious child, while one religious parent has just half that prospect, 24 percent. The odds that a child of two parents who don't attend services and aren't affiliated with a religion will turn out to be religious are slightly over 3 percent—in essence, statistically insignificant. Voas draws the obvious conclusion: "In Britain, institutional religion now has a half-life of one generation, to borrow the terminology of radioactive decay."

A Snapshot of Secularization

Secularization is not a straight-line transition from faith to disbelief that works at a uniform rate, or with predictable outcomes. It's more like a transition from a socially dominant religious system to a bewildering variety of impulses, movements, and currents, often pulling in different directions, and with little apparent regard for internal coherence.

For one thing, the decision not to affiliate with a church doesn't necessarily mean defection from religion. Sociologist Grace Davie coined the term "believing without belonging" to explain the notable pocket of Europeans who say they believe in God, or who pray, and yet say they have no religious affiliation. More than two thirds of Europeans still say that religion is at least "somewhat important" in their lives. According to Austrian sociologist Paul Zulehner, there are really only three European zones where atheism, meaning the positive conviction that God does not exist, is held by a strong majority: the Czech Republic, the former East Germany, and Estonia. Beyond those three places, majorities of Europeans are still "spiritual" or "religious," even though they don't subscribe to the traditional religious options.

Conversely, there are also pockets of Europeans who say they belong to a church, but who don't necessarily believe in God, go to church, pray, or regard religion as important. This phenomenon of "belonging without believing" is especially strong in Eastern Europe, where national identity is closely tied to being Orthodox.

Davie has also identified a current of "vicarious religion," meaning people who don't belong to a church and who don't practice a faith, but who for various reasons want religion to hang around. She points to the example of Sweden in 1994, when a ferry sank on the way from Tallinn, Estonia, to Stockholm. Most of the 894 people killed were Swedish, and without any prompting from officialdom, ultra-secular Swedes spontaneously flocked to local churches. For another case, she cites England after the death of Princess Diana, when "everyone knew" there had to be a funeral in Westminster Abbey. In moments of crisis, even otherwise secular people instinctively wanted churches to perform their traditional roles.

Complicating the situation further is the spread of what French sociologists call *bricolage*, or Anglo-Saxons "patchwork religion," referring to the tendency to assemble one's own religion rather than taking one off the shelf from the traditional churches. In Catholic parlance, this is known as "cafeteria Catholicism." The result is sometimes a syncretistic blend of difficult-to-reconcile ideas. According to the European Values Survey, for example, 25 percent of Europeans say they believe in reincarnation, including Catholics and Protestants, even though reincarnation contradicts orthodox Christian doctrine. Some self-identified Christians actually tell pollsters that they believe in Heaven but not in an afterlife.

British sociologist Eileen Barker says that "unless we use guns," the future holds increasing levels of diversification. Forces driving it include the mass media and the Internet, which expose people to a wide range of spiritual options; cultural emphasis upon the individual and personal choice; escalating geographical and social mobility; and changing job structures, which mean that people will have new life experiences inducing them to consider new options.

The Cost for Catholicism

Survey data on religious affiliation offer one window onto the impact of secularization on the Catholic Church. Consider these four historically Catholic European nations: France, Belgium, Austria, and Hungary. According to 2007 data from the Pew Forum on Religion and Public Life, only 40.5 percent of the French, 39.9 percent of the Belgians, 63.9 percent of Austrians, and 45.1 percent of Hungarians today call themselves Catholic. In three of the four, Catholics are now a minority, and the trend is sharply downward in Austria as well. Other Catholic nations seem in comparatively better shape. In Ireland, Catholics are 84.5 percent, in Italy 80.4 percent, and in Spain, 70.3 percent. Yet all represent steep declines from the beginning of the twentieth century, when 95 percent or more in each nation was Catholic.

Vocations to the priesthood offer another measure. In 1950, Europe had 249,127 priests, but by 2000 the number had dropped to 208,659, a 15 percent loss. In 2004 the total was down to 199,978. Church observers say the real European figure is actually considerably lower, since the continent's totals are buoyed by a large number of foreign priests. While Europe had 64 percent of all Catholic seminarians in the world in 1950, today it has just 24 percent, according to *Global Catholicism* by Froehle and Gautier.

Mass attendance is also down. A 2006 report by the Germany-based research group World Views found that the highest level of church attendance in Europe comes in Poland, where 56.7 percent of the population attends services weekly. Poland is the only nation in Europe where a majority goes to church at least once a week. Germany, evenly divided between Protestants and Catholics, has an attendance rate of 8.2 percent. In France, fully 60 percent of people report that they "almost never" attend religious services, while the share that attends services at least once a week is less than 10 percent. In Ireland, a 2006 survey by RTE, the state broadcast network, found that 48 percent attend Mass at least once a week, a healthy number by European standards, but significantly down from 81 percent just a generation ago.

Even in Italy, where levels of faith and practice remain relatively high, close inspection reveals underlying weakness. In 2003, a study of youth in Rome, the pope's own backyard, was published under the title *Il Volto Giovane della Ricerca di Dio* ("The Young Face of the Search for God"). Commissioned by Cardinal Camillo Ruini, at the time the pope's Vicar for Rome, sociologist Mario Pollo conducted 120 interviews with Roman "adolescents" (age sixteen to eighteen) and "youth" (age twenty-two to twenty-six). The results do not paint a rosy picture. While solid majorities believe in God, their concept of divinity often has little to do with Christian revelation. Some saw God as a ray of light, some as a force of nature, some as an abstract idea such as love. Some 40 percent of adolescents said they believe God is the same for all religions. Three quarters of adolescents said Jesus is a man of great values, but not the Son of God. Many expressed hostility toward the institutional Church. "I'm sure of one thing," one young man said. "If I needed something, I wouldn't go to them."

How to explain all this is a matter of fierce debate. Some Catholics fault the institutional Church for failures to continue the reform course set by the

Second Vatican Council, arguing that Catholicism has made itself unattractive and irrelevant. Others say that post–Vatican II confusion led the Church to drop its guard, so that rather than "throwing open the windows," as Pope John XXIII put it, in order to let the Gospel loose in the world, the reverse happened: the world crept into the Church. Whatever one makes of these arguments, there's no question that secularization poses a deep crisis for Catholicism.

Catholic Perceptions: A Secular Inquisition

While quantitative measures and analytical studies are useful, sometimes they're not the best way of understanding how religious leaders make policy. Often it's not reality itself, but perceptions of reality, that are most decisive. At senior levels of the Catholic Church today there's a growing perception that a tipping point has been reached, and that Western secularization is crossing the line from indifference to outright hostility toward religion. This impression was cemented in part by two high-profile recent clashes between the Church and Europe's secular elites.

One came with the failure of Christian leaders in Europe, led by Pope John Paul II, to persuade the European Union to make a reference to God, the so-called *invocatio Dei*, in its 474-page constitutional document. At present, the draft is in political limbo, after defeats in referenda in both France and the Netherlands in 2005. Its brief preamble is styled as an enumeration of the underlying values of the EU, and the lone reference to religion comes with a statement that the "cultural, religious and humanist inheritance of Europe" has emphasized "the central role of the human person and his or her inviolable and inalienable rights." As anodyne as that may sound, it was an improvement over an earlier draft, which had cited Greco-Roman antiquity and the Enlightenment, but not Christianity, as sources of European culture—a historical lacuna that embarrassed even some determined secularists.

In the wrangling that followed, some EU nations, such as Poland, Ireland, and Italy, proposed inserting a "God clause" into the text, but in the end the effort failed. That result came despite the fact that from 2002 forward, John Paul II had no higher European priority than urging a specific reference to God, and to the continent's Christian roots, in the preamble. The bitterness generated by the defeat can be glimpsed from a tough speech given by Pope Benedict XVI to European politicians and bishops in March 2007, when he accused Europe of lapsing into an "apostasy of itself."

A second episode came in 2004 with the nomination of Rocco Buttiglione, an Italian politician and confidant of John Paul II, as the European Commissioner of Justice. During hearings before the European Parliament, Buttiglione was asked about his views on homosexuality, on family and gender relations, and on stem cell research. In each case, he struck a conservative Catholic stance, though he was careful to distinguish his private moral views from his role as a public official. On homosexuality, for example, Buttiglione said: "Many things perhaps considered immoral do not have to be prohibited . . . I can think that homosexuality is a sin, but this does not influence politics as long as I don't say that homosexuality is a crime."

Eventually the entire slate of ministers had to be withdrawn when it became clear that Buttiglione could not be confirmed. The episode jarred Catholic sentiment, since it appeared to mark a new litmus test for public office in Europe: "Orthodox Catholics need not apply." In the wake of the Buttiglione case, Italian Catholic writer Vittorio Messori quipped that there are now only three categories of people against whom one can discriminate in Europe with impunity: hunters, smokers, and Catholics.

Cardinal Renato Martino, president of the Pontifical Council for Justice and Peace, fumed. "It looks like a new Inquisition. It is a lay Inquisition, but it is so nasty," he told reporters. "You can freely insult and attack Catholics, and nobody will say anything."

Catholic activists and leaders not only find themselves coming up short in political and cultural debates, but in some cases their very presence in those debates seems increasingly unwelcome. The climate has led some Catholics to complain of "fanatical" and "intolerant" forms of secularization that, to them, seem determined to muzzle any religious voice. Pope John Paul II in 2005 warned of an "exaggerated secularism" that leads to "restrictions on religious liberty." Unlike Newtonian physics, in the realm of politics and culture sometimes it's not just actions, but perceived actions, that produce equal and opposite reactions. This perceived animosity of secular elites has reinforced the drive toward evangelical Catholicism.

The Rise of Evangelical Catholicism

The years immediately following the Second Vatican Council (1962–65) were dominated by a spirit of outreach and collaboration with the secular world, which critics sometimes derided as assimilation. The election of Pope John Paul II in 1978 marked a decisive shift in favor of a more robust evangelical challenge. The following four examples illustrate how the evangelical press for affirmation of traditional Catholic identity is unfolding in different areas of the Church's life.

1. THE LITURGY WARS

It's rare to be able to date the birth of a trend with any precision, but within the realm of Catholic liturgy, meaning the rites and rituals of the Church, one good candidate for the public debut of the evangelical instinct is September 20, 1997. On that day, the Vatican's Congregation for Divine Worship and the Discipline of the Sacraments, then led by a Chilean cardinal named Jorge Medina Estevez, wrote to the U.S. bishops to reject their proposed English translation of the rite for ordination. That act was the opening shot of what came to be known as the "liturgy wars."

In short order, the Vatican also rejected a translation of the Old Testament Psalms and a proposed version of the Lectionary, the collection of Scripture readings for use at the Mass. All relied on an approach to translation known as "dynamic equivalency," premised on trying to make texts accessible to modern ears. As part of that effort, dynamic equivalency is favorably inclined to "inclusive language," meaning avoiding gender-specific terms where possible.

In March 2001, the Vatican issued a new set of principles for translation titled *Liturgiam Authenticam,* which amounted to a sweeping rejection of the dynamic equivalency approach. The Vatican also created a body of bishops from across the English-speaking world to advise it on matters of liturgical translation, called the Vox Clara Commission, under the leadership of Australian Cardinal George Pell, one of the leading critics of modern translations.

Cumulatively, the effect has been to shift the Church toward much more traditional language, even when it involves word choices and sentence structures unfamiliar in twenty-first-century spoken English. As *Liturgiam Authenticam* put it, "Translations must be freed from exaggerated dependence on modern modes of expression and in general from psychologizing language. Even forms of speech deemed slightly archaic may on occasion be appropriate to the liturgical vocabulary." To take perhaps the sharpest example, in the Latin text of the Mass the priest says to the congregation, *Dominus vobiscum,* to which they respond, *et cum spirit tuo.* In the post–Vatican II translation, that exchange was rendered as, "the Lord be with you," followed by, "and also with you." Under the principles of *Liturgiam Authenticam,* however, the response will become, "and also with your spirit." Defenders argue that's what the Latin says; critics say it won't make much sense to the average person in the pew.

Similar trends apply in other areas of Catholic worship, such as music and liturgical architecture. While use of pop music and "folk choirs" were once the rage, today the recovery of polyphony and Gregorian chant is encouraged. When new churches are built today, they are not the modernist structures of the Paul VI era. They're more likely to draw inspiration from the Baroque or Gothic periods, reflecting traditional Catholic aesthetics.

Revival of the pre-Vatican Tridentine Mass in Latin is also part of this picture. In 1984, Pope John Paul II gave permission, known as an "indult," for celebration of the old Mass with the authorization of the local bishop. In 2007, Pope Benedict XVI broadened that permission through a *motu proprio*, meaning an exercise of his legal authority. It allows all priests to celebrate the old Mass privately except during Holy Week, and publicly whenever a "stable group" of Catholics ask for it, without having to ask the bishop's permission. Though the vast majority of Catholics will probably still attend the new Mass in the vernacular language, Benedict's hope is that over time, the old Mass will exert a gravitational pull on the new, drawing it toward greater sobriety and reverence.

2. CATHOLIC EDUCATION

In 2004, Karol Markosky, at the time a twenty-two-year-old senior at Iona College in New Rochelle, New York, returned from spring break and noticed something different about the college's classrooms. It took her a moment to put her finger on it: there were crucifixes on the walls. She later told a reporter that her first thought upon seeing the crucifix was, "Oh, so we really are a Catholic college!"

In point of fact, Iona College had always been a Catholic college, founded by the Congregation of Christian Brothers in 1940. Yet like many small Catholic liberal arts colleges in the 1960s and 1970s, Iona gradually became less focused on its religious identity, or at least its external markers. No one really knows when the crucifixes came off the walls, although one theory is that they were removed during a renovation and nobody made an issue out of putting them back. No one, that is, until an alumnus from Iona's class of 1956 was invited to a session about the mission of the college in 2004. Asking to remain anonymous, the alumnus offered to pay for crucifixes and having them installed. Some people feared blowback from a diverse student body, but twenty-one-year-old Andy Cardot, a non-Catholic who went to

Iona to play football, seemed unfazed: "I don't see any problem with it," he told a reporter. "They're not forcing anything on you."

Questions about what makes a Catholic college Catholic are hardly new, but they received a fresh lease on life in 1990, when Pope John Paul II issued his apostolic constitution *Ex Corde Ecclesiae,* "From the Heart of the Church." The document aimed to reassert the Catholic identity of church-affiliated Catholic colleges and universities, lest they gradually follow the path blazed by institutions such as Harvard and Princeton, which once had a religious identity but gradually had shed it like an old layer of skin. Most controversially, *Ex Corde* stipulated that local bishops should oversee the theology taught at Catholic institutions within their territory, and gave them a legal instrument with which to do so—a *mandatum.* The idea was that just as a driver needs a license to get behind the wheel of a car, so a theologian should have a *mandatum* from the bishop before he or she teaches.

After a decade of back-and-forth wrangling, the U.S. bishops finally agreed to implement the *mandatum.* Then the sexual abuse crisis exploded, and the issue largely faded from view. When it resurfaced, focus shifted to a broader analysis of how Catholic identity shapes every aspect of an institution's mission—admissions, student life, curriculum, personnel, even physical plant and athletics. Under the leadership of Canadian Archbishop Michael Miller, who served from 2003 to 2007 as Secretary of the Congregation for Catholic Education, the Vatican began to push Catholic colleges to develop a system of assessment for measuring Catholic identity, the same way institutions measure student outcomes and professional development of faculty. Miller's vision was of an objective and quantifiable system, used not to punish underperforming institutions but as a stimulus to improvement.

Just ask Holy Cross Fr. John Jenkins, president of the University of Notre Dame, about how agonizing these questions can be. When Jenkins took over in 2005, he inherited bitter debates over a gay film festival and *The Vagina Monologues,* a play about female sexuality and violence against women that includes sketches on lesbian relationships, orgasms, and rape. Supporters see both as examples of Notre Dame's commitment to open discussion and academic freedom, while critics regard them as proof of confusion about what the university stands for.

In January 2006, Jenkins announced he would be reviewing the university's sponsorship of both productions. He invited the university community to have their two cents, and by all accounts, he carefully pondered what he heard. His initial statements, in which he said he found *The Vagina Mono-*

logues inconsistent with Catholic teaching, raised hopes among critics that the play would be scrubbed. Instead, Jenkins eventually announced that the play and film series could continue, but without fund-raising or publicity that might imply approval, and with accompanying discussions that clearly presented a Catholic viewpoint. Critics found the moves insufficient, and some called for Jenkins's resignation.

That drumbeat grew even more intense in the early months of 2009, when Jenkins and Notre Dame invited U.S. president Barack Obama to deliver the university's commencement address and awarded him an honorary doctorate. Jenkins justified the decision as a way of opening a dialogue with the president, but critics blasted Notre Dame for conferring an honorary degree upon a public figure whose stands on abortion and other "life issues" are clearly at odds with Catholic teaching. As the dust settled, those critics included approximately eighty American bishops. The Obama–Notre Dame controversy provided a classic instance of the contrast between the mainline liberal instinct and evangelical Catholicism: For the former, the invitation to Obama was about respectful engagement with well-intentioned secular leaders, exploring possible areas of common ground. For the latter, this was a failure to stand up for core Catholic values, a critical lack of evangelical nerve. It's an open question what the future might hold for Jenkins or the university he leads, but the controversies make one point crystal clear: tensions over Catholic identity are now a defining feature of the landscape for Church-affiliated schools and colleges.

3. PRIESTLY IDENTITY

In October 2006, Cardinal Francis Arinze of the Congregation for Divine Worship and the Discipline of the Sacraments wrote to Bishop William Skylstad, president of the United States Conference of Catholic Bishops, to inform him that lay Eucharistic ministers must not purify the sacred vessels (meaning the chalices which contain the Body and Blood of Christ) after communion has been distributed at Mass. Skylstad promptly dispatched a letter to the American bishops informing them of the ruling, and urging their compliance.

A decade earlier, in December 1997, the Vatican issued a document with a similar spirit, stipulating that lay people may not govern parishes, use titles such as "coordinator" or "chaplain," deliver homilies, make decisions on parish councils in the absence of a priest, wear stoles or other liturgical garb, or receive training in seminaries alongside future priests. (Some items were

later tweaked for the United States, such as allowing laity to enroll in seminary courses or to use the term "chaplain," which is sometimes an official
job category in hospital or university systems.)

Rome has also drawn the line on anything that might suggest the assumption of ecclesiastical authority by laity. In 2002, the Midwestern
province of the Capuchins elected a nonordained friar, Brother Bob Smith
of Milwaukee, as their provincial, a result that was confirmed by the Capuchin leadership in Rome. The election was annulled by the Vatican. In
2000, the Vatican told the United States bishops that they could not appoint
a woman religious, Mercy Sr. Sharon Euart, as general secretary of their
conference. (In normal Catholic parlance it's a bit odd to think of brothers
and sisters as laity, but under Catholic doctrine, one is either fish or fowl,
meaning ordained or not. In that strict sense, religious brothers and nuns
remain laity.)

Critics often derided these moves as pointless bureaucratic meddling.
But from the point of view of Church officials, and Catholics who shared
their concerns, something profoundly important was at stake: the identity
of the ordained priest.

The diagnosis is that an overly "horizontal" view of the Church has led
to the notion that the functions performed by a priest can just as well be
done by someone else, and that the common priesthood of all baptized
people is what's truly fundamental. Such an understanding was encouraged
by some currents in post–Vatican II theology, especially Fr. Edward Schille-
beeckx, a Belgian Dominican, who argued that in early Christianity the
priesthood emerged "from below" out of the social dynamics of Christian
communities, and only gradually acquired a cultic function modeled on the
ancient Israelite priesthood. Such ideas were what then-cardinal Joseph
Ratzinger had in mind in 1998 when he warned against a "functionalist"
understanding of the priesthood rather than something "ontological" and
"sacramental."

The priesthood sets off alarms over identity for two reasons. First,
some worry that if the Church does not maintain a clear distinction between the priesthood and the laity, then confusion will follow about the tasks
a priest is ordained to perform, above all celebration of the Mass and the
other sacraments. In other words, as goes our theology of the priesthood,
so go the sacraments, and ultimately the Church as the mediator of those
sacraments. Second, and perhaps more practically, if anyone's going to
communicate a strong sense of identity to the typical Catholic in the pew,

it'll be the parish priest. But for that to work, the priest must first have a strong sense of Catholic identity himself.

As a result, reinforcing traditional markers of priestly identity has become a front-burner matter. A 2005 document from the Vatican banning the admission of homosexuals to Catholic seminaries, and thus banning them as priests, is the most recent expression. The strong defense of priestly celibacy in Catholicism today also needs to be seen against this backdrop. Regardless of historical or doctrinal debates, celibacy is the most visible way the Catholic Church has of underscoring the difference between priests and everyone else, and in a time when this distinction is thought to be in peril, any change in the discipline is unlikely.

Some Catholics fear that this emphasis will lead the Church back to clericalism, meaning an exaggerated deference to clergy that regards laity as a lower order of life. Archbishop Timothy Dolan of New York, who served as rector of the North American College in Rome prior to being made a bishop, insists it does not have to play out this way. In remarks to his seminarians, Dolan once said: "Clericalism speaks of privilege, prerogatives, special treatment, being served rather than serving; it prefers sacristies to streets, and is usually more concerned with cuff links and cassocks than care of souls." Lest there be any misunderstanding, Dolan said explicitly: "I call you to priestliness, not clericalism."

4. THEOLOGICAL CLARITY: CHRISTOLOGY AND ECCLESIOLOGY

Evangelical Catholicism has strong theological implications, especially in two areas: Christology, meaning the Church's teaching about Jesus Christ; and ecclesiology, meaning teaching about the Church itself. Put in a nutshell, twenty-first-century Catholicism will reject interpretations of Jesus as a humanitarian leader, a moral sage, a political revolutionary, or a founder of a religious movement on par with Buddha or Muhammad, strongly reasserting Jesus' identity as the living Son of God and the lone Savior of the world. With equal emphasis, it will insist that the Catholic Church, with its hierarchical structure and sacramental system, is the community called into being by Christ—in short, the "one true Church."

The charter for this aspect of evangelical Catholicism was a September 2000 document from the Congregation for the Doctrine of the Faith, headed by then-cardinal Joseph Ratzinger, titled *Dominus Iesus*. While allowing that followers of other religions can be saved in a mysterious fashion, and only through the grace of Christ, *Dominus Iesus* insisted they are nevertheless in a "gravely deficient situation" in comparison to Christians, who alone "have the fullness of the means of salvation."

The last two high-profile Vatican censures of a theologian during Ratzinger's term at the Congregation for the Doctrine of the Faith, and his first such case as pope, involved writers working in the area of Christology. All were Jesuits: Fr. Jacques Dupuis, a Belgian who spent almost three decades in India; Fr. Roger Haight, an American; and Fr. Jon Sobrino, a Basque who lives and writes in El Salvador. All three cases involved setting limits to claims that Christ and the Holy Spirit are active in non-Christian religions. These were also the concerns underlying a critical December 2007 notice from the Committee on Doctrine of the U.S. bishops' conference about Vietnamese-American theologian Fr. Peter Phan, whose 2004 book *Being Religious Interreligiously* was faulted for fudging Catholic teaching on "Jesus Christ as the unique and universal savior of all humankind" and "the Church as the unique and universal instrument of salvation." In other words, the core objections were to Phan's Christology and ecclesiology. Concern for proper Christology was also the motive force behind Benedict XVI's first book as pope, *Jesus of Nazareth*, released in April 2007. Its aim was to defend the reliability of the gospel accounts, and to argue that the gospels present Christ as God Himself.

The same agenda is clear in ecclesiology. In July 2007, the Congregation for the Doctrine of the Faith put out an interpretation of the famous Vatican II statement that the Church of Christ "subsists in" the Catholic Church, rather than simply "is" the Catholic Church. Ecumenists had long taken this phrasing as a recognition that no existing church, including Catholicism, can claim to be the one true Church, but the congregation rejected that reading. Instead, the congregation said, the phrase was intended to show that all the elements instituted by Christ endure in the Catholic Church.

What's to Become of Catholic Liberalism?

Given that evangelicals are running the table in terms of the Church's internal battles, some liberal Catholics may wonder if there's any future for them. Some of the more pugnacious elements among evangelicals enjoy stoking those anxieties, suggesting that Catholic liberals are an aging cohort stuck in the 1960s and about to go the way of the dodo bird. In reality, rumors of the death of liberal Catholicism are almost certainly exaggerated, for three reasons.

First, just as the evangelical impulse is one way of responding to modernity, so too is religious liberalism. Most sociologists say that complex religious institutions are always likely to contain both and several others (such as the Pentecostal instinct, emphasizing experience over belief). Only sects have the luxury of rigid consistency. In that sense, "liberalism" is one of the basic structural options within any great religious tradition. In the same way that there will always be liberal Jews, Muslims, Hindus, and so on—though their numbers and influence may wax or wane—there will always be liberal Catholics.

Second, most sociological evidence suggests that in Catholicism today, liberalism is hardly on the brink of extinction. Richard Gaillardetz, a prominent lay theologian at the University of Toledo, argued in 2007 that in the United States liberal Catholicism is less an ideology than a "pastoral phenomenon . . . alive in parishes that have a flourishing catechumenate, vibrant liturgies, thoughtful and relevant preaching, and multiple lay ministerial opportunities," as well as "in a growing number of intentional Christian communities that are determined to keep alive a vision of the church that they associate with Vatican Two." Looking around, observers such as Gaillardetz say that the moderate-to-liberal camp represents a disproportionate share of the church's workforce in the trenches, meaning priests, deacons, religious, and laity, as well as among professional theologians.

In the global North, the evangelical camp actually seems a distinct minority within the overall Catholic population (meaning the share of the population that identifies itself as Catholic, regardless of how intense their faith or practice may be). In 2005, sociologist Dean Hoge published a survey about how American Catholics define what it means to be Catholic. At the top of their list was belief in the resurrection of Jesus, the Eucharist and the other sacraments, and helping the poor. Other traditional markers of identity were sidelined: only 29 percent said a celibate male clergy was important, and just 42 percent said that about the teaching authority of the Vatican. Seventy-six percent said one could be a good Catholic without going to Mass on Sunday, and 75 percent said the same about following Church teaching on birth control. This is not just an aging cohort that will soon vanish, some stereotypes to the contrary. On several points, younger Catholics are actually more likely to hold what is popularly seen as a "liberal" position. Only 43 percent of Catholics twenty-six or younger, for example, agree that the Catholic church has "more truth" than other religions, as compared to 61 percent of Catholics sixty-five and older.

Third, in real life the opposition between the "evangelical" and "liberal" positions is not nearly as sharp as the shorthand treatment in this chapter can make it sound. Terms such as "evangelical" and "liberal" are ideal types rather than airtight ways of categorizing flesh-and-blood people, and most Catholics reflect elements of both, and many others, in their own thinking.

All that said, there's little question that in the Catholicism of the near-term future, the liberal camp is unlikely to make much headway in terms of setting policy. On issue after issue, whether it's women priests or birth control, the tide is running decisively in the opposite direction. Moreover, evangelicals are disproportionately represented among those Catholics most likely to actually practice their faith, such as those who show up for Mass at least once a week. Given those realities, some progressive Catholics believe that their future lies in engaging social and political questions outside the church—shifting to *ad extra* rather than *ad intra* causes. Social Service Sr. Simone Campbell, executive director of the Catholic social justice lobby Network, said the call of the hour is "mission."

"This mission is discovered by touching the anguish of the world, listening to the crying needs around us, and being willing to respond in new ways," she said.

In a lecture delivered a decade ago, Jesuit Fr. Thomas Reese laid out seven survival strategies for reform-minded Catholics in an era increasingly closed to their agenda:

- Schism
- Prophetic criticism and demands for reform
- Public conformity but private independence
- Silence
- Christian witness in the world
- Doing what you can within existing structures
- Laying the intellectual foundations for change

While one can debate the merits of each choice, perhaps the relevant sociological observation, Reese said in 2007, is that Catholic liberals today can be found doing all of the above. Catholic liberalism is in for some years in the wilderness, but there's little reason to believe it's going away.

WHAT IT MEANS

Though evangelical Catholicism is strongest in the global North, identity questions surface in their own way in the South as well. Across much of Africa, Catholicism is less than a century old, so attachment to external markers of identity helps to shape a young and still fluid sense of what it means to be Christian. In Asia, where Catholicism amounts to 3 percent of the population, pressure to assimilate to the spiritual vision of the great Asian religions is a constant fact of life, feeding its own form of concern for Catholic distinctiveness. The growth of Pentecostalism in Latin America is also driving some Church leaders to emphasize what makes Catholics different. Refracted through local circumstances, therefore, the dynamics outlined here apply to much of the Catholic world.

Near-Certain Consequences

1. NEW ENERGY AND (PERHAPS) NEW GROWTH

As an empirical matter, both in the United States and around the world, the religious movements that have grown most dramatically over the last half-century are those with clear boundaries between themselves and the prevailing culture. In their book *A Theory of Religion*, Rodney Stark and William Bainbridge called this "high-tension religion." Low-tension groups, according to Stark and Bainbridge, are usually dissolved into the "cauldron of secularism."

In the United States, the relative success of high-tension groups is incontestable. According to a study by Glenmary Research Center, the churches that posted the most dramatic gains from 1990 to 2000 were the Church of Jesus Christ of Latter-day Saints (the Mormons), the conservative Christian Churches and the Churches of Christ, and the Assemblies of God, followed by the Catholic Church. Globally, the same pattern holds. The two most dynamic worldwide religious movements today, Shi'a Islam and Pentecostal Christianity, are both classic instances of high-tension religion.

Sociologists debate to what extent the "high-tension" nature of these groups by itself explains their growth, or whether factors such as population flows in given areas and success at meeting basic social and spiritual needs are more important. Broadly speaking, however, groups that assert a clear identity seem to have a better shot at expansion and revival. That might seem a counterintuitive result, because when groups become stricter they may alienate some members and in the short run get smaller, not bigger. But several sociologists of religion argue that in the long run, this attrition can work to resolve what they call the "free rider" problem. High-tension groups screen out members with low levels of commitment, enhancing the participation levels of those who remain. This, in turn, drives more effective recruiting and retention. The trick seems to be finding the right level of strictness, because otherwise demands escalate until the group hits a point of diminishing returns.

Within Catholicism, Stark and another colleague, Roger Finke, published research in the mid-1990s suggesting that conservative dioceses in the United States tend to generate larger numbers of vocations to the priesthood. Comparing ten dioceses identified by a cross-section of church experts as either "traditional" or "progressive," they found that traditional dioceses outperformed progressive ones by a factor of about three to one. Once again, there are a variety of ways of explaining these results, but the basic pattern seems clear.

As Catholicism shifts to a stronger assertion of its identity, it's reasonable to expect an initially smaller but more committed membership, which will produce new energy and could lead over time to new growth. The extent to which this occurs in any given location will depend upon local circumstances, including the degree of competition in the local religious marketplace. (Catholicism, after all, isn't the only competitor embracing a "high-tension" strategy.)

To say that evangelical Catholicism is likely to produce energy and growth is not, of course, to say it's a good idea. Critics may argue that it's too little, too late to deal effectively with secularization, or that growth could be achieved in other ways. They might also claim that apart from its implications for membership, the version of Catholic identity on the rise today is objectionable on other grounds. Predicting growth is also not to claim that Church leaders are promoting Catholic identity for the sole motive of boosting membership. Rather, it's merely to observe that from a sociological point of view, the evangelical Catholic movement is one way of coping with the losses imposed by secularization, and there's a track record to suggest it might work.

2. WORST OF TIMES, BEST OF TIMES FOR REFORMERS

Liberal reform movements in the twenty-first century will find themselves in a "catacomb period." Catholics who support gay marriage or the ordination of women to the priesthood will not be able to hold those views openly and maintain official roles in the Church. Groups such as We Are Church, the Women's Ordination Conference, Call to Action, and the like, will find it impossible to meet on Church property, to advertise in Church publications, and to attract official representatives of the Church to their discussions. Members of these groups will not be approved by bishops as speakers in official Church venues, and even when a bishop might be willing to sign off, other forces in the Church will mobilize to oppose their presence. Even groups that deliberately attempt to steer clear of doctrinal questions, such as Voice of the Faithful, will have much the same experience. To a significant extent, this is already the case.

For this reason, organized Catholic reform movements are likely to decline over the twenty-first century in terms of both membership and influence. Most Catholics will not want to devote their time and treasure to causes that carry little prospect of success. From time to time, some crisis or particularly intense battle will give birth to a new movement, but it is likely to suffer the fate of those that have gone before it: an intense period of activism, followed by gradual atrophy and decline.

The foregoing, however, describes the situation facing reform movements *inside* the Catholic Church. Externally, there may be a burgeoning audience in the twenty-first century for the Catholic reform message.

The mass media will probably give increasing voice to reformers, because they can articulate alternative Catholic points of view steadily more difficult to find within officialdom. Leaders of groups such as We Are Church or Call to Action may not talk to bishops very much, but they'll be popular with *Nightline* and *Hardball*. Some political forces in the secular culture (from both left and right, depending upon the issue) will be attracted to supporting Catholic reform movements, as a way of reminding legislators and policy makers that the bishops and the Vatican do not speak for a unified bloc of Catholic opinion. Their motive will not be to change the Church but rather to diminish its political effectiveness, so the lack of response from Church authorities will not weaken their resolve. If anything, the harder the bishops push, the more the reformers will push back.

The twenty-first century for Catholic reformers thus shapes up as a time for the catacombs internally, but for high chic outside.

3. AN *AD EXTRA* SHIFT FOR CATHOLIC LIBERALS

For Catholic liberals who don't want to be at odds with Church leaders, evangelical Catholicism is likely to push them into a steadily more *ad extra* posture—more engaged on issues such as combating global poverty, ending war, abolishing the death penalty, and protecting the environment than with matters such as clerical celibacy or hierarchical authority. They can organize, advocate, and teach about the former with the support of Church authorities, which they certainly cannot do on the latter. Ironically, the Catholic identity impulse, which is by intent and design an *ad intra* phenomenon, will likely have the effect of producing a boom period of *ad extra* Catholic activism.

One model is provided by the Community of Sant'Egidio in Italy, which was founded amid Europe's liberalizing energies of 1968 by progressive Catholics who didn't want to leave the Church. Rather than fighting battles inside Catholicism, Sant'Egidio opted to concern itself with the Church's mission *ad extra*: concern for the poor, anti–death penalty activism, peacemaking and conflict resolution, as well as ecumenical and interfaith dialogue. Unlike most other progressive movements that have gone into decline, Sant'Egidio has prospered. In the twenty-first century, movements such as Sant'Egidio are the future of liberal Catholic activism.

Liberal energies will also be pulled in the *ad extra* direction because of leadership from the global South. To some extent, this dynamic was clear in the reception of Latin American liberation theology in the Catholic North in the 1970s and 1980s, though it got bogged down in the politics of the era. As a more pragmatic and pastoral way of expressing the same values frames the agenda, much energy in the North will again be swept along with it—especially among those who feel they're losing on other issues.

4. PERCEPTIONS OF CATHOLICISM AS "FAR-RIGHT"

Catholic social teaching is notoriously difficult to characterize as either "liberal" or "conservative" in terms of secular politics. The Catholic Church is officially against abortion and opposed to gay marriage, which aligns it with the political right; but the Church is also against the death penalty, against war, and for poverty relief, positions more at home on the left.

Yet given the way "sex sells" in popular culture, it tends to be statements on sexual morality by the hierarchy that define public perceptions of the Church, especially in Europe and the United States. As those positions become more sharply defined under the influence of evangelical Catholicism, the Church is likely to be perceived in the media and in some secular circles as a basically "far-right" institution. This is an especially live possibility in the United States, given the passing from the scene of traditional leaders of the "religious right" in the Protestant world, such as the Rev. Jerry Falwell. In effect, the evangelical wing of the U.S. bishops has become the new voice of the religious right in American politics.

Secular think tanks, political action committees, and media outlets will be happy to augment these impressions, since every cause needs an enemy. For example, the liberal Political Research Associates issued a report after the 2004 election which concluded, "The Church hierarchy will increasingly direct resources into political activism that will further the Catholic wing of the Christian Right." There was no mention of the bishops' statements in opposition to the Iraq war, or in favor of universal health coverage. The same report warned, without citing evidence, of a "growing international alliance comprised of Mormon institutions, the U.S. Christian Right, the Vatican, and certain elements within theocratic Islam," focused on combating any liberalization of "reproductive rights."

The effect of this drumbeat in the global North is likely to be a growing imbalance between the full range of Catholic concerns and the Church's public profile. If the Church wishes its stances on other matters to be heard, it will have to find ever more creative ways to get them across.

5. CHURCH–STATE CLASHES

Identity pressures on matters such as abortion and homosexuality, combined with the Southern tendency to wade into political debates without pulling punches, will produce a Catholicism in the twenty-first century more inclined to take tough positions, and less shy about saying so. In the North, this will expose Catholicism to greater criticism about purported violations of church–state separation.

One consequence may be increased pressure for a review of the financial privileges enjoyed by the Catholic Church under civil laws. On November 1, 2004, one day ahead of the American presidential election between George Bush and John Kerry, U.S. Representative Charles Rangel, a liberal Democrat, published an opinion piece in the *New York Observer* stating that, "By injecting themselves in partisan politics, the bishops have raised a red flag that could cast a shadow on the tax-exempt status of all religious institutions."

Similar pressures are growing in Europe. In 2006, the Executive Commission of the European Union ordered Spain to stop exempting the Catholic Church from sales tax. Though that move was not tied to any specific political intervention by the Church, European observers said the subtext was growing hostility between the EU and the leadership of the Catholic Church.

Nor is this sort of veiled threat heard only from the left; conservative organizations in the United States, for example, appealed for a review of the tax-exempt status of the Archdiocese of Los Angeles in 2006 after Cardinal Roger Mahony took outspoken positions in favor of immigration reform.

Another form financial pressure may take is Catholic withdrawal from state-funded social service programs that conflict with Church teaching. Catholic Charities in Boston, for example, was forced to stop providing adoption services in April 2006 after it failed to win an exemption from a state law that required adoption agencies that receive public funding to provide services to same-sex couples. At roughly the same time, the Archdiocese of San Francisco announced that it would reconsider its participation in a similar program. In February 2007, the English government announced that private adoption agencies that refuse to serve gay couples would no longer receive reimbursements for their services, resulting in the loss of over $9 million in annual payments to Catholic charities in England.

6. NO DISSENT ON THE CHURCH'S PAYROLL

Newspapers, journals, and other publications officially sponsored by a diocese or a religious order within the Catholic Church have always occupied a nebulous middle ground between journalism and evangelization. Some Catholic publications see their role as emulating the best standards of Western journalism, gauging their work by secular standards of balance, openness to all points of view, factual accuracy, and capacity to stir reader interest. Other publications see themselves more as a fifth evangelist than as the fourth estate, unabashedly promoting the official Catholic view. Both are defensible models, but in the twenty-first century, the former will be increasingly difficult to realize in any official Catholic venue.

The resignation of Jesuit Fr. Thomas Reese as editor of *America* magazine shortly after the election of Pope Benedict XVI in April 2005 illustrates the point. Reese stepped down under pressure after the Congregation for the Doctrine of the Faith made it clear that the magazine needed a change in editorial direction. That capped five years of behind-the-scenes maneuvering involving Reese and *America*, the American bishops, the Jesuit order, and Rome. Leave the balance to CNN and *Le Monde*, Rome said; if Catholics pick up a publication sponsored by the Church, they have the right to see Church teaching presented faithfully and sympathetically.

The same principle will apply to pastors, theologians, chancery officials, and anyone else who ever speaks publicly in the name of the Catholic Church: if they want to criticize the Church, they should not expect to do it on the Church's dime.

7. BISHOPS AS TEACHERS-IN-CHIEF

According to traditional Catholic theology, the three aspects of a bishop's responsibility are the *munus docendi* (teaching), the *munus sanctificandi* (sanctifying), and the *munus regendi* (governing). While all three are essential, in different historical periods one or another often looms especially large. Pre–Vatican II, within largely intact and intensely devotional Catholic cultures, teaching and sanctifying often seemed fairly routine, so that governing was the major challenge, understood especially as building up the Church's institutional presence. In the old days in the American Church, the joke used to be that the more debt a bishop carried for building schools, hospitals, and parishes, the better a job he was presumed to be doing.

In this age of identity, the function of teaching is likely to be the *munus* that is seen as most critical. Bishops will make their careers in the Church not on the basis of how much physical plant they're able to erect, but rather how boldly and courageously they defend the Church's traditional teachings. From the point of view of the Vatican and evangelical Catholics at the grassroots, a bishop's reputation will be based on his engagement in public debates and his success in shaping a local Catholic culture strongly imbued with a sense of identity, not his administrative skills or financial prowess. This shift may have a self-reinforcing impact on evangelical Catholicism; concern for Catholic identity will drive bishops to become more aggressive teachers, and as they do so, that teaching will further accelerate the spread of the evangelical instinct.

Probable Consequences

1. MIGRATION OF CATHOLIC LIBERALS

As identity pressures tighten, an increasing number of liberals who work for parishes and dioceses will either elect to move on voluntarily, or will find themselves out of a job. The same thing will be true for bishops' conferences, Catholic hospitals, Catholic schools, and so on, though the process will be uneven. Among Catholic colleges and universities, it will be seminaries and institutes directly licensed by the Vatican where the identity pressures are most keenly felt. It's less likely that institutions such as Georgetown or Boston College will experience a similar constriction of diversity in theological or political outlook.

While some conservatives may be tempted to mumble "good riddance" about the prospects of liberals exiting the official structures of the Church, there are three potential consequences worth pondering.

For one thing, Church authorities may be able to shield future priests from serious contact with alternative views in seminaries, but they certainly can't prevent them from cropping up once those freshly ordained priests fan out into parishes, university chaplaincies, and other pastoral assignments. Seminarians may not have to read Charles Curran or Leonardo Boff as part of their classwork, but they'll find their ideas, often in second- and third-hand form, out in the field. Arguably, a narrow sense of Catholic identity in seminary formation may leave priests ill-equipped to defend that identity once they step back into a milieu more defined by secular culture. Ensuring that seminarians are confronted with a healthy diversity of perspectives, therefore, could be seen as a service to Catholic identity rather than a threat to it.

Second, this migration could end up enhancing Catholicism's left wing in terms of its capacity to engage broader social and cultural debates. If liberals are more likely to work in secular or ecumenical settings, to know the argot of modernity, and to know how to move the levers of social power outside the Catholic Church, they will arguably be in a better position to wield influence. Professional migration outside the Church may enhance the capacity of the Catholic left to build coalitions, and to argue persuasively with those who are not formed by the Catholic tradition. Ironically, evangelical Catholicism could end up giving a boost to the social capital of Catholic liberalism.

Third, by indirectly providing moderate and liberal Catholics with incentives to seek refuge outside the official structures of the Church, the bishops lose a degree of leverage. A liberal priest who holds a job with the diocese or bishops' conference, or a liberal theologian who teaches in a seminary, generally feels a stake in maintaining a good working relationship with ecclesiastical authorities that may be lost when they move into non-Catholic settings.

2. DOUBTS ABOUT DIALOGUE

While a number of forces will propel Catholicism toward greater ecumenical and interreligious engagement in the twenty-first century, including the rise of Islam, multipolarism in international affairs, and Pentecostalism, the sort of dialogue Catholicism is likely to practice will be different. There will be great caution about anything that smacks of syncretism, or a "lowest common denominator" approach that might compromise Catholic distinctiveness. Apologetics, meaning a defense of the faith, will take a place alongside dialogue as a central mode in which Catholicism responds to other Christian traditions and other religions.

The rising apologetic tide is clear from the success in Italy of *Il Timone*, a monthly magazine and Internet site devoted to "countering the attacks of those who dispute Catholic truth." It's produced by journalists and intellectuals who define themselves as a "national team of apologists," and who say they're "Catholics without adjectives, just Catholics." In the United States, the *Handbook of Christian Apologetics* by Peter Kreeft and Ronald K. Tacelli is still selling strong a decade and a half after its initial release. As evangelical Catholicism takes hold, the attitude of a growing sector of Catholic opinion will feel sympathy for Ronald Knox, an early-twentieth-century English Catholic writer, who said that the only clear result of the study of comparative religions is to make people "comparatively religious."

3. A NEW LANGUAGE FOR REFORM

The "politics of identity" mean that theological debate in Catholicism will face increasing scrutiny from Church authorities, especially in the global North where identity pressures are the strongest. Theologians who advocate new approaches in Church teaching or practice will have to phrase those proposals in the language of Catholic identity if they are to have any hope of being heard.

Ironically, one model of this kind of astute phraseology was offered by a Lutheran scholar, Michael Root, at the 1997 convention of the Catholic Theological Society of America. Root's aim was to convince the Catholic Church to recognize some validity to ordained ministry in Protestant denominations such as his own. On the surface, such a proposal would seem to contradict the evangelical Catholic emphasis on the unique status of the Catholic Church, but in this regard Root's case was ingenious. By citing official documents, he demonstrated that Catholic teaching holds the following points:

- The one church of Christ is "present and at work" in other Christian bodies, such as the Anglican Communion and Lutheranism;
- These "ecclesial communities" are instruments of salvation for their members;
- They have preserved the "basic truths" of the gospel.

At the same time, Root observed, Catholicism also holds that these bodies lack valid ordained ministries—meaning, in effect, that they don't have real bishops. (He recalled one droll English Catholic wit who defined the Archbishop of Canterbury as a "dubiously baptized layman.") Root then drew the obvious conclusion: if the three points given above are true, then the Catholic Church must believe that bishops are not essential to ecclesial communion, to the presence of the Church, to the means of grace that lead to salvation, or to the teaching office. Otherwise, he suggested, it would be impossible to explain the presence of those qualities in communities that don't have bishops. Root's contention was that recognizing some measure of validity to Lutheran and Anglican priests and bishops is essential to defending the *Roman Catholic* theology of the bishop's office.

Since both Lutherans and Anglicans have ordained women as priests and bishops, to say nothing of practicing homosexuals, it's unlikely that a Catholic Church driven by identity concerns will move to recognize those ministries as valid anytime soon. Nevertheless, Root's argument illustrates the kind of theological discourse that will be increasingly essential in the twenty-first century. Arguments will either be rooted in a strong sense of Catholic identity, or they will go nowhere. This is a point that applies not just to formal academic theology, but to conversations within the Church of any sort.

4. GREATER TRIBALISM

Catholicism in the North, and perhaps particularly in the United States, is marked by serious internal divisions. This situation is conventionally described as a split between left and right. In reality, however, the situation is more complex. A more accurate description of the present lay of the land would be "tribalism," referring to the various Catholic subcultures that dot the landscape: liturgical traditionalists, *communio* Catholics, progressive reformers, charismatics, peace and justice activists, and so on.

While strong internal diversity in a large Church is both inevitable and desirable, many regard the present situation as dysfunctional. Members tend to read their own publications, attend their own conferences, worship with the like-minded, and generally have little interaction with the competing tribes. Catholics of differing temperaments and perspectives often are engaged in completely separate conversations, with few common points of reference. The trends described in this chapter seem likely to exacerbate these lines of division.

I rate increased tribalism as "probable" rather than "near-certain," however, because to some extent it will depend upon how the chieftains of the various tribes respond. One intriguing signal in this regard came at the 2007 convention of the Catholic Theological Society of America from the outgoing president, Daniel Finn. He called upon the CTSA to stop issuing public statements critical of the Vatican and of the bishops, in part because doing so had divided the theological community, driving away more conservative scholars.

"They felt no longer welcome, out of a sense that they're on the margins of a group that pokes fun at Vatican shortcomings and puts the CTSA name on statements they do not endorse. They feel it's not their group," Finn said. "Our Church is wracked by divisions caused by ideological simplicities on all sides, and we need broader dialogue than we have today. In the CTSA, all theologians should feel respected, and a majority should not employ the mechanics of majoritarian democracy to produce statements that the minority would find offensive and leave."

In this era of identity pressures, perhaps influential Catholics such as Finn will recognize the potential for greater acrimony and take steps to counteract it. It's difficult at present to see that happening on a widespread scale, but in principle it's possible.

5. A PRO-AMERICAN IMPULSE IN VATICAN DIPLOMACY

The previous chapter illustrated how the rise of the global South is likely to exacerbate tensions between the Catholic Church and American foreign policy. Evangelical Catholicism, however, is supplying a more pro-American impulse, which is being felt especially at the senior levels of the Church. Since the mid-1990s, the spread of what Vatican officials regard as intolerant secularism in Europe has bred increasing disenchantment with the EU. Meanwhile, the religious vitality of the United States, including the strong role that "faith and values" issues play in American politics, has convinced many senior figures in Catholicism that the United States will be the Church's best partner on the global stage.

This shift hardly means there will be no future conflicts between the Vatican and the White House. What it does suggest is a growing Vatican determination not to let those conflicts fester into enduring opposition, and to distinguish its own diplomacy from the anti-Americanism of the European political left. Post-9/11, this tendency has been given new impetus by the rise of Islamic radicalism. While the Vatican and the United States may differ over strategy, the power and determination of the United States is seen as critical to defending Christian interests in the Muslim world, especially religious freedom for Christian minorities. The new fondness in Rome for the United States had something of a "coming out party" during Pope Benedict XVI's trip to the United States in April 2008, when Benedict repeatedly praised the religious vitality of America, in comparison to Europe, and the American version of church–state separation.

Ironically, this pro-American impulse may end up irritating some Catholic conservatives in the States because it can imply giving even liberal American leaders the benefit of the doubt. By the standards of the European secular left, many American Democrats come across as relatively moderate and respectful of the Church. That's a large part of the reason the Vatican has been warmer to Obama than some American Catholics.

Possible Consequences

1. BISHOPS IN THE DOCK

As Europe, Canada, Australia, New Zealand, and regions of the United States move increasingly toward recognition of homosexuals as a protected class in society, the Catholic Church will face mounting pressure related to its restrictive positions on homosexuality. It's possible that the stance of the Church on issues such as gay marriage, adoption by homosexuals, and differential treatment of homosexuals in hiring and military recruitment may actually be criminalized, leading to prosecution of bishops and other church officials under the categories of "hate speech" and "human rights violations."

Such a scenario is not just idle speculation. In 2004, a Pentecostal pastor was convicted in Sweden under laws against hate speech for declaring that homosexuality is "a deep, cancerous tumor on all of society." The country's supreme court later set aside the conviction, under provisions in the European Convention on Human Rights concerning freedom of religion. Swedish prosecutors, however, have vowed to revisit the issue. In British Columbia, Canada, in 2005, a local branch of the Knights of Columbus was taken before a regional human rights tribunal for refusing to rent a hall to a lesbian couple for a wedding reception. Their right to refuse the rental was eventually upheld, but the Knights were ordered to pay each woman $1,000 for offense to their "dignity, feelings, and self-respect."

In France in 2004, a new federal law added "anti-gay comments" to a class of prohibited speech that already includes racist and anti-Semitic insults. Though no religious figure has yet been prosecuted, French Catholic leaders have expressed concern that the law might prevent bishops from opposing gay marriage. As mentioned above, in 2007 the English government determined that any adoption agency that does not allow gay couples to adopt is in violation of English law. Though at present this simply means that the government will not pay those agencies for their services, it is a short step from that to prosecuting agencies, and the bishops responsible for them, for refusing to serve same-sex applicants.

Some priests today, especially those shaped by an evangelical Catholic outlook, view the idea of going to prison for defending traditional positions on issues such as gay marriage somewhat the way priests in Eastern Europe once looked at the possible consequences of defying the Soviets, or the way that Chinese priests do today for spurning the official government-sponsored Catholic association: nothing to be desired, but have your affairs in order just in case.

"Many young priests I know expect that the prospect of one of us spending some time in jail for teaching the faith is not a distant or unlikely proposition. It is a plausible reality to be prepared for," said Fr. Raymond de Souza of Canada, a noted commentator on Church affairs, in June 2007.

Homosexuality is not the only hot-button issue that could provoke a legal response from civil authorities. In the spring of 2007, when an Australian archbishop suggested that Catholic politicians who vote in favor of embryonic stem cell research are out of step with Church teaching and should not come forward for communion, the speaker of the regional parliament announced that he would convene an investigation to see if the archbishop's words constituted a "threat" punishable under Australian law.

Exactly what all this augurs is difficult to say. There may be a silver lining for Catholicism, since historically the Church has usually been at its best when it's powerless. The sight of bishops in the dock to defend their beliefs may inspire sympathy in some quarters. On the other hand, supporters of gay rights or embryonic stem cell research usually assert that the Church eventually will be forced to adjust to new social realities. Lacking a crystal ball it's difficult to say, but in the meantime more frequent collisions between the irresistible force of secular tolerance and the immovable object of religious commitment to traditional morality seem a safe bet.

2. FASTING AND ABSTINENCE

In pre–Vatican II Catholicism, one of the most visible ways in which Catholics distinguished themselves from the surrounding culture was by the discipline of fasting and abstinence, including fasting from midnight until the reception of the Eucharist on Sunday (now truncated to one hour) and abstaining from meat every Friday in honor of the death of Christ on the Cross on Good Friday (now restricted to the Fridays of Lent). As one Catholic scholar has noted, these observances were once as much a marker of Catholic identity as abstaining from pork is of Judaism.

Although no one ever prohibited the earlier customs, they largely went out of fashion, seen as reflecting an external piety that often masked an absence of genuine internal faith. In the identity-driven Catholicism of the twenty-first century, it's entirely possible that fasting and abstinence will once again come to characterize Catholic life, and not because these disciplines are imposed from on high, but because they express a longing for distinctiveness that characterizes a growing swath of the Catholic population.

In 2004, Eamon Duffy of Cambridge University laid out this argument in the London *Tablet*, generally perceived as left-of-center on many issues in the Church. He wrote that after Vatican II, much in Catholicism that was "profound and life-giving was lost" due to "a spirit of philistine dismissal of 'tradition' as nothing more than the dead hand of the past." He called the abandonment of these disciplines not "a simple change in devotional habit," but "the signal of a radical discontinuity in the tradition and a decisive shift in theological perception."

Duffy advocated a return to the discipline of fasting and abstinence, not on the basis of orders from Rome, but based on a genuine "sense of the faithful" that Catholics need to reconnect to their tradition, rediscovering within it "some of the supports which helped our fathers and mothers to live the gospel."

3. A REVIVAL IN RELIGIOUS LIFE (OR TWO?)

The numerical decline in religious life in the global North following the Second Vatican Council has been dramatic. In the United States, for example, there were 185,000 religious women in more than 500 orders in 1965. By 2000, the number of sisters had dropped to 103,560, and nearly 60 percent were over 70 years old. The number of those under 50 was fewer than 6,000.

What is far less clear is how to explain the drop-off, a debate that, inevitably, becomes swept up in the ideological crossfire in Northern Catholicism. Thus Kenneth Briggs, in his 2006 book *Double Crossed: Uncovering the Catholic Church's Betrayal of American Nuns,* argues that the reforms unleashed by Vatican II would have brought about a renewal of religious life had it not been for the fact that Church authorities artificially crushed it. Other voices blame the reforms themselves for introducing a period of confusion that led many men and women religious to question the value of their vocations. If the laity are just as holy as we are, and we're being encouraged to go out into the world anyway, then what's the point of taking vows of poverty, chastity, and obedience?

Without any pretense of settling that question, two facts about religious life in the early twenty-first century seem clear. First, the most impressive growth in both men's and women's communities is coming from the global South. Ask any religious superior these days where their vocations are coming from, and they are likely to cite whatever Southern nation or region in which that order has a beachhead. Second, in the North the religious orders that are growing, at least from the outside, appear most traditional in terms of both external piety and theological outlook.

In a Catholicism shaped by the politics of identity, many religious orders will rediscover precisely those elements that mark them as distinct—wearing habits, for example; engaging in more sustained periods of both individual and common prayer; and less immersion in secular pursuits. This option for a more high-tension style of religious life could in theory produce a revival in religious orders, at least in terms of head counts.

On the other hand, any attentive observer of the contemporary Catholic scene also knows that many religious orders in the global North today have a center of gravity considerably to the left of diocesan bodies of priests, or of other Catholic institutions. The leaders of religious orders tend to favor collegial and participatory modes of government, and they often foster a greater liberty for theological innovation than many diocesan priests or lay employees of bishops might enjoy. For that reason, some religious orders may be fairly resistant to the momentum of evangelical Catholicism. If so, this option may create a high-tension model of religious life in another sense—in this case, tension not with the broader culture, but within the Church.

Such an option may not be a prescription for larger numbers of vocations, but it could mean that institutions and parishes run by religious orders become the "harbors in the storm" for more liberal Catholics who feel increasingly uncomfortable in other Catholic venues. Liberal Catholics may seek out schools and parishes staffed by religious orders in greater numbers, and they may become more willing to provide financial and logistical support to their various works. Thus it's possible that both "conservative" and "liberal" orders, and elements within those orders, may find the twenty-first century to be a boom period—the former in terms of vocations and energy, the latter as the refuge of choice for an increasingly beleaguered wing of the Church.

4. SPACE FOR NON-DOCTRINAL REFORM

In the wake of the sexual abuse crisis in the United States and elsewhere, a host of voices insisted that the Catholic Church needs a better system of governance on matters such as personnel and finance. Bishops making these decisions by themselves, or drawing upon a hand-picked group of advisors likely to rubber-stamp virtually any proposed move, seemed a significant part of what had gone wrong. In response, these analysts proposed more collaborative modes of administration drawing upon the professional expertise of laity, and greater accountability measures, especially in how the Church's money is spent.

Despite movement in some areas, these calls for greater collaboration and accountability have only been partially realized, in part because they run into the brick wall of identity concerns. For example, there is still no mechanism in Catholicism, aside from direct papal intervention, to remove a bishop who has failed in his administrative responsibilities. Reluctance to explore alternatives is undoubtedly linked to the fact that in the present climate, anything that appears to weaken a bishop's authority is suspect.

As the twenty-first century unfolds, however, bishops and other Church leaders may feel less of this sort of anxiety. As markers of Catholic identity become ever more set in stone, bishops may perceive less risk in talking about reforms that do not, at least in principle, concern matters of doctrine or ecclesiastical authority. As time goes on, this trajectory could result in more developed systems of collaboration and accountability, understood not as harbingers of a root-and-branch overhaul of Catholic ecclesiology, but as reasonable gestures of good government within the traditional hierarchical system.

5. A SMALLER MARKET FOR THE MOVEMENTS?

New movements in Catholicism such as Opus Dei, the Neocatechumenate, Communion and Liberation, and so on often foster a stronger sense of Catholic identity than a typical parish or school, since those institutions have to accommodate a broader cross-section of theological and political outlooks. Evangelical Catholics sometimes complain that their desire for deep prayer and devotion, or their fidelity to Church teaching, has actually been unwelcome in some Catholic parishes or schools. In that sense, the movements have sometimes offered an "oasis" for Catholics seeking a more robust version of Catholic identity.

In a future shaped to a greater degree by evangelical Catholicism, this hunger for a thick Catholic identity will be satisfied to a greater degree by mainstream parishes and schools. It will no longer be as necessary, therefore, to join a movement in order to feel like one is taking a strongly counter-cultural stand. The mere act of remaining Catholic in a time of sharpening tension between the Church and the surrounding culture will often do the trick. Under that scenario, the movements could become a victim of their own success. As the entire Church becomes more like the movements, their specific appeal may recede.

By the same token, many Catholics will continue to see in the movements a particularly committed way of expressing their identity, guaranteeing that while they may not experience the same rapid growth they saw in the twentieth century, the movements are nevertheless here to stay.

Long-Shot Consequences

1. SCHISM IN THE NORTH

Formally speaking, a schism requires a bishop to lead a group of Catholics in creating a parallel ecclesiastical structure, with valid but illicit ministers and sacraments. That's what makes the traditionalist Society of St. Pius X, founded by rebel Swiss Archbishop Marcel Lefebvre, a schismatic body (though its supporters deny it), and it's what makes the Married Priests Now! movement of Zambian Archbishop Emmanuel Milingo a schism (though its adherents deny any intention of creating a new "sect"). In both cases, a bishop recognized as valid by the Catholic Church has broken away, taking a piece of the Church with him. Catholic theology and canon law constrain Rome to recognize the priests of both groups as validly ordained, hence the sacraments they administer as also valid, though they are seen as "illicit" and Catholics who follow them are, objectively speaking, sinning against the Church. (What the subjective intent of such Catholics may be is another matter.)

From time to time, frustrated liberals predict such a schism on a more massive scale in Europe and North America, noting that in both regions, polls suggest a majority of Catholics differ with official Church teaching on a number of controversial points—birth control, clerical celibacy, the ordination of women, and so on. At present, a formal schism along these lines has to be rated as an extreme long shot, because there does not appear to be a Catholic bishop with a sufficient following who would be prepared to lead such a formal break. In the meantime, the various "informal schisms" in the Catholic Church in the global North are likely to grow, with a number of Catholics regarding themselves as in a form of internal exile.

To some extent, the tribalization of Catholicism in the North described above insulates the Church against formal schisms. Since liberal Catholics already have a network of parallel institutions—schools, publications, conferences, and organizations—the need for a parallel ecclesiastical structure is reduced. A tipping point might come if such Catholics were somehow denied the sacraments, but it is difficult to imagine that happening on a scale widespread or systematic enough to produce a twenty-first-century form of the Protestant Reformation.

2. TWO-PARTY ECUMENISM

Despite enormous gains in the twentieth century, the ecumenical movement has not eliminated denominational boundaries among the various Christian confessions. The Lutherans have not come into communion with Rome, nor have the Orthodox and the Anglicans formed a single unit. The basic divisions in the Christian world that resulted from the great schism of the eleventh century, sealing the break between Eastern and Western Christianity, and the sixteenth century, with the Protestant Reformation, still characterize Christianity today.

Underneath those enduring denominational boundaries, however, runs another fault line in Christianity that today is arguably even more basic. Perhaps a good way to capture it, at least in the global North, is to borrow language from Judaism, distinguishing between "orthodox" and "reform" Christians. In the former camp would be evangelical Catholics, the bulk of Eastern Orthodox, most Pentecostals, and Evangelicals within traditional Protestant denominations. In the latter are liberal Catholics, a handful of progressive Orthodox believers, and the bulk of "establishment" Protestants and Anglicans.

Because orthodox Christians emphasize doctrinal boundaries, the prospects for formal ecumenical reunion among the members of this camp are so remote as to be scarcely worth considering. The Eastern Orthodox see papal primacy as a threat to their autonomy, while identity-based Catholics see a robust conception of papal jurisdiction as an essential "note" of the Church. Those ecclesiological differences will certainly endure. It's just on the cusp of thinkability, however, that non-Catholic orthodox Christians might be willing to acknowledge the Pope as their de facto leader and spokesman on social and cultural issues, pooling resources in the fight against the dictatorship of relativism.

What might such an informal alliance look like?

To date, Catholicism has not become a formal member of the World Council of Churches, the main ecumenical body for mainline Protestant groups—in part out of fears that Catholicism would end up dominating the council because of its numerical strength, but also because the more liberal center of gravity within the WCC on some issues creates tension with the Vatican. What the future might spawn, however, is a sort of orthodox alternative to the WCC, in which the Vatican plays a leadership role in organizing those Christians who do not presently feel represented by the WCC or other ecumenical groups. Whether this orthodox alternative develops into a formal association with offices and a staff, or remains at the level of an informal network of contacts and alliances, it could become an important alternative in articulating the ecumenical aspirations and vision of global Christianity.

The ecumenism of the twenty-first century, at least in the North, could thereby become an ecumenism largely driven by ideological and theological kinship rather than by denominational affiliation, leading to two parallel ecumenical movements for the orthodox and reform expressions of Christianity. Call it a form of "two-party ecumenism."

3. MILLIONS OF CATHOLIC AMISH?

A defining feature of evangelical Catholicism is its deliberately counter-cultural ethos, with "culture" in the North meaning post-modern secularism. Depending on the context, this instinct can either seem conservative or liberal. When what's being rejected is the sexual revolution, or the majoritarian mode of establishing truth implied by democracy, it seems conservative; when it's the profit motive of capitalism, the values of consumer society, and the realpolitik of military might, it seems liberal. But in both cases, it's a deliberate choice to be different.

The question is, how different? One trajectory evangelical Catholicism in the twenty-first century could take is pushing an increasing number of Catholics toward a sweeping rejection of contemporary modes of life. In part, this could mean a choice to unplug from the hyperconnected world of data streams and 24/7 connectivity, fostering a more contemplative mode of life with a preferential option for silence. In part, it could mean an effort to build alternative communities organized on the principle of solidarity and the common destination of goods—both core elements of Catholic social doctrine, and both of which stand at odds with the working assumptions of capitalist cultures.

Such a radical form of Catholic identity might reject not merely the sexual morality or official agnosticism of post-modernity, but the whole kit and caboodle. Imagine the Catholic Worker movement, for example, or the communities created by Jean Vanier and L'Arche, becoming the normative Catholic approach to life. If that were to happen, the world of the twenty-first century would look and feel appreciably different. A few thousand Catholics living like Amish would be a curiosity; millions, however, would be a revolution.

ISLAM

On any list of moments most pope-watchers never thought they'd live to see, the image of Benedict XVI standing in Istanbul's Blue Mosque on November 30, 2006, alongside Grand Mufti Mustafa Cagrici, engaged in a moment of shared silent prayer, would probably finish close to the top. Not only was this the pope who recently had rattled Muslim cages by quoting a fourteenth-century Byzantine emperor to the effect that Muhammad brought "things only evil and inhuman," such as "his command to spread by the sword the faith he preached," but in his former guise as the Vatican's doctrinal czar, then-cardinal Joseph Ratzinger hadn't exactly been crazy about interreligious prayer. He had once called it "a concession to that relativism which negates the very meaning of truth."

Yet here was this quintessential pope of Catholic identity, standing reverently before the *mihrab,* a niche indicating the direction of Mecca, and praying with a Muslim cleric—on live television, no less, broadcast on CNN, Al-Jazeera, and scores of other international networks. Those who knew Benedict's history could but rub their eyes. To add yet another level of irony, Cagrici was one of thirty-eight Muslim scholars who had signed an open letter to Benedict XVI, essentially accusing him of misunderstanding Islam.

Reaction in the press corps reflected this incredulity. Before Benedict XVI said, "thank you for this moment of prayer" on his way out, reporters had begun frantically debating whether what had happened should be described as "prayer" or "meditation." One veteran journalist insisted that it had to be prayer because the pope's lips were moving, while another shot back that for all we knew he was reciting his shopping list. Facing the urgent need to file stories and do broadcasts, no one really had time to ponder why moving lips should be considered a hallmark of prayer in the first place. A knot of reporters clustered around a TV playback monitor, doing frame-by-frame analysis to see if Benedict's lips actually had moved. (For the record, they seemed to.) Afterward, Church spokespersons attempted to play things down, insisting that popes pray all the time, so what's the big deal? The spin missed the point that it wasn't the act, but the context, that had created the drama.

So, what made such a remarkable turn of events possible? The short answer is that 9/11 happened, and then 9/12.

The terrorist attacks of September 11, 2001, produced a sea change in interfaith priorities inside Catholicism. Senior Catholic officials who had given Islam little thought before were suddenly consumed with the subject, especially with Islamic radicalism. Then came Pope Benedict's infamous lecture on September 12, 2006—what Catholics might call "9/12"—at the University of Regensburg in Germany, with the incendiary quotation about Muhammad cited earlier, and the global firestorm that followed. Whatever the other fallout from Regensburg, it reinforced the conviction that Islam *matters*. Benedict's remarkable bit of damage control in Turkey two months later was a clear sign of that realization.

The questions raised by Islam—the hopes it generates, as well as the fears it elicits—are destined to cut across a steadily expanding range of issues in the twenty-first century. In effect, Islam has replaced Judaism as the most important interfaith relationship for the Catholic Church, and Catholicism has become a lead actor in the global drama surrounding the so-called "clash of civilizations."

At one level, the eruption of Islam into global Catholic consciousness is a reflection of simple arithmetic. There are 2.3 billion Christians and 1.6 billion Muslims in the world, representing more than 50 percent of the human family. By definition, the relationship matters. Moreover, Islam represents competition for converts, social influence, and political power in parts of the world such as sub-Saharan Africa, Indonesia and the Philippines, and the Indian subcontinent, where Christians and Muslims rub shoulders and sometimes cross swords. New zones of conflict may also erupt, especially in China, the world's last great untapped missionary "market." A similar challenge is increasingly being felt in Europe itself, where rising Islamic immigration and falling European birth rates pose the question for some of whether the cradle of Christendom could undergo a metamorphosis, in an image popularized by British writer Bat Ye'or and by the late Italian journalist Oriana Fallaci, into "Eurabia," meaning an outpost of Arab and Islamic civilization.

The fate of Christianity in the Middle East is also at stake, including what Christians regard as the "Holy Land"—Israel and the Palestinian Territories, the land where Christ lived and the early Church took shape. When the British mandate in Palestine ended in 1948 and the State of Israel was born, Christians represented 20 percent of the population. Today they're around 2 percent, and dropping. Across the Arab world, as recently as 1975 there were an estimated 25 million Christians, while today that number is 12 million. Daniel Pipes, writing in the *Middle East Quarterly* in winter 2001, predicted that within a relatively brief arc of time, Christians "will effectively disappear from the region as a cultural and political force." Little has happened in the eight years since to revise that forecast. The causes of the dramatic Christian exodus are debated, but inevitably the fate of this shrinking Christian presence—which ought to represent a natural bridge between the two religions—is bound up with currents in the broader global relationship between Christians and Muslims.

Terrorism carried out by Muslim extremists is inducing anguished reflection within Catholicism, especially on the legitimate use of armed force. The Vatican opposed the U.S.-led invasion of Iraq in 2003 but appeared to countenance the earlier incursion in Afghanistan following 9/11—leading some critics to suggest incoherence. The debate pits Christian realism against Christian hope in a uniquely high-stakes fashion. The religious zeal of many Muslims also holds up an uncomfortable mirror for Western Christians, revealing the extent to which their own spiritual force may have been sapped by secularization.

All this puts the accent on potential perils. Yet many Catholic analysts also see great promise, beginning with Pope Benedict XVI, who has sketched a vision of a great Catholic–Muslim alliance against forms of secularism in the West hostile to religious faith and to a robust role for religion in public affairs. Part of that alliance would include joint efforts in the cultural, social, and political spheres, in defense of shared values such as the sanctity of human life and the defense of the traditional family. Though Benedict got off to a troubled start in making this pitch to Muslims with his Regensburg address, there are signs that his message may be slowly getting through. When Western public opinion blasted the pope in March 2009 after he claimed at the beginning of a trip to Cameroon that condoms make the problem of AIDS worse, the deputy imam of the country's largest mosque, Sheikh Mohama Oussani Waziri, declared that his only regret was that the pope had not invited Muslims to join his challenge to received secular wisdom.

Whether Christians and Muslims can meet one another in constructive cooperation, or whether their relationship is destined to be one of conflict and rivalry—and the reality seems likely to be a mixture of both—their interaction will be a major driver of world history in the twenty-first century.

WHAT'S HAPPENING

Global Islam

The World Christian Database put the number of Muslims in the world in 2007 at 1.6 billion, while Christians totaled 2.3 billion. This makes Christians 33 percent of the global population and Muslims 21 percent, meaning that together Christians and Muslims represent well over half of the human family. The two largest branches of Islam are Sunni and Shi'ite, with Sunnis representing around 80 percent of the total.

Muslims sometimes claim that while the raw total of Christians may be larger, the number of practicing Muslims is greater. That may be the case, though it's impossible to establish with statistical precision. Given high levels of Christian practice in the global South, it's not clear that Muslim religiosity is necessarily more intense. Contrary to Western stereotypes, there are also nominal Muslims. In Indonesia, for example, the world's largest Muslim nation, strict anti-Communist policies in the 1960s meant that anyone lacking a religious affiliation was suspect, so millions of Indonesians declared themselves Muslim, sometimes without real conviction. In northern Nigeria, several minority tribes accepted Islam because it was the religious option of the dominant Hausa tribe. Many never embraced the faith, and those tribes are today a source of a growing number of converts to Christian Pentecostalism. The same point sometimes applies to the West. In Italy, for example, estimates for attendance at mosques are roughly the same as comparable figures for Catholic Mass attendance.

Worldwide, Islam adds roughly 23 million adherents a year, according to the World Christian Database, and this growth is mostly demographic. Islam adds roughly one million new followers per year through conversion. (That's one million net, representing the balance of new converts over defections.) Recent declines in birth rates in Islamic states suggest that even this modest rate of growth may not be sustained. Christianity adds about 30 million new members a year, a higher absolute total but a lower rate of growth—1.38 percent for Christianity, 1.84 percent for Islam. As Philip Jenkins notes, those nations with the fastest rate of population growth and the youngest demographic profile today are evenly distributed between Christian- and Muslim-dominated societies. Barring some "x factor," one hundred years from now Christianity will still be the largest religion in the world. Fears of the world being overrun by Islam—such as those expressed by Samuel Huntington, who predicted in *The Clash of Civilizations* that "in the long run . . . Muhammad wins out"—are most likely overheated.

One underappreciated point is that a substantial majority of Muslims are not Arab. According to the *CIA World Factbook*, these are the world's ten largest Muslim nations as of 2007:

1.	Indonesia	202,071,531
2.	Pakistan	159,799,666
3.	India	151,402,064
4.	Bangladesh	124,872,121
5.	Egypt	72,301,532
6.	Turkey	71,016,329
7.	Nigeria	67,515,582
8.	Iran	64,089,570
9.	Morocco	33,318,331
10.	Algeria	32,999,883

Only three of the ten have substantial Arab populations. Overall, less than 20 percent of the world's Muslim population is Arab. This is an important point for the future of Christian–Muslim relations: many Muslims see the Christian world through the lens of Europe and the United States, and Christians usually see Islam through the prism of Arab nations. Contrary to those stereotypes, most Christians are not Europeans or North Americans, and most Muslims are not Arabs.

Islam in Europe

Rising Muslim immigration in Europe has set off special alarms across the Catholic world, raising the specter in some quarters of a demographic reversal of the Battle of Lepanto in 1571, which preserved Christendom from the Ottoman threat. In his book *The Cube and the Cathedral*, American Catholic writer George Weigel imagines a future in which the muezzin calls Muslims to prayer from Saint Peter's Basilica, and the Cathedral of Notre Dame in Paris has been turned into "Hagia Sophia on the Seine—a great Christian church become an Islamic museum." Weigel is exaggerating to make a point, but his image nevertheless captures real fears held by many people.

Given the struggles facing institutional Christianity in Europe, combined with the very real dangers of Islamic radicalism—the Paris riots, the London bombings, the murder of Theo van Gogh in Holland—the case for panic is depressingly easy to make. Some Christian leaders, however, are more sanguine about how things might shake out in the long run. Realistically, they argue, Europe hasn't been Christian for some time, so protecting the continent's "Christian identity" may be an anachronism. In that context, they believe the arrival of a large pool of new Europeans who share some basic spiritual and moral values with Christians may prove to be a boon, if a growing number of Muslims enter the middle class and make their peace with pluralism.

No one knows exactly how many Muslims are in Europe today, in part because some are undocumented, and in part because several European censuses do not inquire about religious orientation. Drawing upon various sources, the U.S. National Intelligence Council estimates that the Muslim population in the European Union rose from 5 million in 1985 to 15 million in 2005, representing 200 percent growth. The largest Muslim community in the EU zone is in France, with 5 million Muslims, or 8.3 percent of a population of 60.4 million. Germany is in second place with 3.5 million Muslims, or 4.3 percent of its population, and the United Kingdom has 1.6 million, or 2.7 percent of its population.

By 2025, the National Intelligence Council projects a Muslim population in the EU of 28 million; by 2050 it anticipates 40 million, which would represent 15 percent of a population of roughly 500 million Europeans. (That estimate does not include the possibility of Turkey's admission to the EU.) In some nations, the Muslim share may be higher. By mid-century, Muslims could be 25 percent of the population in France and Germany. In

Europe as a whole, however, some experts believe that the Muslim total will level off at around 15 percent. Philip Jenkins says that the best parallel may be to the Catholic population in the United States, which rose to 25 percent of the country quickly in the late nineteenth and early twentieth centuries, and has subsequently remained stable. Among other things, declining fertility rates in the Middle East and North Africa suggest that current levels of Islamic immigration may not continue.

Aside from fears of jihadist violence, today's Catholic anxiety about Muslim immigration in Europe is also related to politics. So far, swelling Muslim populations have benefited the secular left in most countries, on the basis of support for multiculturalism, strong social welfare systems, and the Palestinians. Yet there's also a rising chorus on the European left today critical of accommodation of Muslims, insisting that the secular values of the Enlightenment must be defended against what they see as religious extremists. In 2006, twelve left-leaning intellectuals put out a manifesto suggesting that the real fault line in Europe runs between "theocrats and democrats," a taxonomy that seems to lump Muslims and observant Christians together. Many analysts believe the natural home of a European Muslim middle class will ultimately be center-right parties that defend traditional morality and a strong role for religion in public life. To some extent this future is now in Germany, where, as ironic as it may sound, a small but growing number of Muslims are becoming Christian Democrats.

That this is not mere fantasy is suggested by the Philippines, where the current ruling party is known as the "Christian Muslim Democrats," a fusion of center-right parties of both Christian and Muslim inspiration. A historic peace deal in 1996 granting broad autonomy to the majority Muslim Mindanao region prompted many Filipino Muslims to reject armed insurgency, accepting peaceful insertion into the political system. Some experts see the experience as proof that antagonism can be converted into partnership under the right conditions.

Whether Christians and Muslims in Europe learn to think of themselves as allies, experts say, depends on how things develop on both sides. Muslims need to rein in the radicals, but Christians also need to be "open-minded," according to Rev. Johan Candelin of Finland, a pastor in the Swedish Lutheran Church and head of the Religious Liberty Commission for the World Evangelical Alliance, a body that represents 420 million evangelical Christians in 128 nations.

"Far from all Christians," Candelin conceded, "are open-minded."

Sunnis and Shi'ites

Islam has no central authority and no uniform doctrinal system, so borders of theological debate and spiritual practice are fluid. In a 2007 essay for Harvard's *Nieman Reports,* prominent Muslim intellectual Tariq Ramadan complained that Western perceptions of Islam routinely fail to acknowledge the internal complexity that's taken for granted inside Christianity. Ramadan complained that no matter what Muslims say, many Westerners presume they all have a basically similar theological and political stance. Ramadan underscores the absurdity of such an impression with a Catholic comparison: "Who could claim," he asks, "that the liberation theologian Leonardo Boff is nothing but the prettified face of Monsignor Marcel Lefebvre?" (The latter reference is to a traditionalist French archbishop who split with Rome over the reforms of Vatican II; in many ways, the far-left Boff and far-right Lefebvre represent matter and antimatter in the Catholic universe.) As Ramadan rightly says, "One could only smile at such a fantasy-like approach" to Catholic complexities.

What follows is a brief, and highly simplified, presentation of the two leading branches of the Islamic family, which can only hint at the variety Ramadan describes.

1. SUNNI ISLAM

The word "Sunni" comes from the Arabic term *sunnah,* meaning "tradition"—referring to the words and actions of Muhammad collected in written form and considered by Muslims to be authoritative. Following the death of Muhammad in 632, the forerunners of today's Sunnis accepted Abu Bakr as his rightful successor rather than Muhammad's blood relatives, following the tribal custom of selecting the leader of the community on the basis of a consensus of elders.

Beginning in the ninth century, Sunnis fostered different strains of interpretation of Islamic practice, called *madhhabs,* which encompass diverse options, from mystical and reformist to literal and traditionalist. No matter which *madhhab* Sunnis follow, they pray at the same mosques and perceive themselves to be part of the same community. Diversity within the Sunni universe is staggering—ranging from puritanical Wahhabi Islam or the Taliban at one extreme, to reformers such as Ramadan and his democratic, pluralistic "European Islam" at the other.

In general, Sunnis believe in a direct approach to God through the Qur'an without need of clerical intermediaries. Sunnis over the centuries have come to reject images of Muhammad, and visual iconography generally, as an invitation to idol worship. In most Sunni communities, groups of socially prominent "lay people" administer the mosque, including its finances, and hire and fire those who lead the prayer and preach. In that sense, Sunni Islam is somewhat analogous to low-church Congregationalist Protestantism, deemphasizing formal ministers and centralized structures in favor of broad participation.

2. SHI'A ISLAM

Shi'ites regard the blood relatives of Muhammad, first of all his cousin and son-in-law Ali, and then his heirs through the Prophet's daughter Fatima, as his legitimate successors. ("Shi'a" is Arabic for "group" or "faction.") There are an estimated 130 to 190 million Shi'ite Muslims in the world, representing somewhere between 10 and 20 percent of the global Muslim total. Most are concentrated in the Persian Gulf region. Ninety percent of Iran's population of 70 million is Shi'ite. Shi'ites are also a majority in Iraq and Azerbaijan and a plurality in Lebanon, and there are significant Shi'a populations in Afghanistan, Syria, Kuwait, Bahrain, Qatar, and several Central Asian nations, as well as India and Pakistan.

The seminal event in Shi'a history is the martyrdom in 680 of Ali's son Hussein in Karbala, Iraq, during an uprising against the caliph. Hussein's death came to be regarded as an act of sacrifice analogous to the death of Christ on the Cross, and ritual commemoration of it is the core of the Shi'a experience. On the Feast of Ashoura, celebrated on the tenth day of the Islamic month of Muharram, images of Hussein are carried in elaborate processions. Shi'ites cry and listen to poems, while some make a small cut in their scalp to recall Hussein's sacrifice and others practice self-flagellation. "Passion plays" reenact the martyrdom of Hussein.

Shi'ites cherish a set of spiritual figures analogous to Catholic saints in the "Twelve Imams" (or "Seven Imams," depending upon which strain one follows) who came after Muhammad. While in Sunni Islam an "imam" is simply the leader of the prayer, in Shi'ism the term is restricted to these few successors of Muhammad. They are even sometimes seen as quasi-divine mediators between the human world and the divine realm, and Shi'ites celebrate feast days and pilgrimages in their honor. Shi'ite clergy are regarded as deputies of the Twelfth Imam, the *Mahdi,* who will one day return, so in the absence of the imam, a strong accent on clerical authority has developed.

Sufism

Experts caution that Sufism is not a branch of Islam analogous to the Sunnis and the Shi'ites, but I present it here simply to illustrate the diversity in the Islamic world. Most Sufis are Sunnis, though Shi'a also has a strong mystical and ascetical tradition.

Sufism is a grab-bag term that covers a wide variety of mystical and Gnostic practices as well as diverse forms of popular devotion—virtually everything that can't neatly be accounted for in the categories of Islamic law, or Shariah. Sufism emerged in the Middle East around the eighth century, and the term has been broadened into a diverse range of beliefs and practices aimed at purity of heart and an ethic of love. Many Muslims, both Sunnis and Shi'ites, actually regard Sufis as exotic, if not heretical. The World Christian Database puts the total number of Sufis at 237 million, though other experts regard that as little more than a wild guess, since Sufis are scattered, not centrally organized, and notoriously difficult to count.

Sufis have been termed "Muslim Buddhists" because of their emphasis upon the need to overcome dualisms, including the self. Like Buddhists, Sufis tend to organize into "brotherhoods" under a Master. Some Muslims regard the Sufis as pantheists, incompatible with strict monotheism. Some writers have styled the Sufis as an essentially apolitical form of Islam, uninterested in political power or Shariah; a popular Sufi saying is, "If you can't change the kings, then change yourself." Others, however, say that's absurd, noting that the political role of Sufi brotherhoods in Africa, for example, is very significant. In British India, the Sufi leaders were much courted by the colonizers because their charismatic authority was a useful way of controlling their followers. Even in independent Pakistan, the authority of the *sajada nishin* (literally, "the one who sits on the prayer rug"), a Sufi leader, has an important role in politics. It's also worth noting that the Taliban in Afghanistan developed out of a South Asian strain of Sufism.

Perhaps the best-known expression of Sufi Islam in the West is the "Whirling Dervishes." They are technically known as the Mevlevis, after Mevlana ("Our Master") Rumi, a medieval mystical poet who has recently become extraordinarily popular in the West. Their worship, which involves a graceful whirling dance leading to spiritual ecstasy, is known as *sema*, which literally means "listening."

Radical Islam

The West has invented a variety of terms for radical Islam—jihadism, Islamism, and so on—which can suggest that it's an organized group with definable boundaries and a common set of doctrines. In reality, no such coherence exists. With precious few exceptions, those figures and movements commonly regarded as "radical" would not identify themselves in those terms. Most simply think of themselves as faithful Muslims, or as part of some specific social or spiritual movement—Wahhabis, perhaps, or the Taliban, and so on. Moreover, speculation about what percentage of Muslims is "radical" is all but pointless. By most accounts, the share of the Muslim population supportive of violence and terrorism is extremely low, but sympathy for some of the ideals and frustrations that motivate the terrorists is more widespread. Little more that's empirically useful can be said.

Headcounts, however, are not always the most reliable way of assessing social and political impact. It would require a peculiar kind of intellectual blindness to simply dismiss Islamic radicalism—admittedly difficult to define or to measure—as a marginal movement with no relationship to "true" Islam. However suspect it may be theologically, on the ground Islamic radicalism is a powerful reality with which mainstream Muslims, and the world, must come to terms.

The birth of modern Islamic radicalism is conventionally dated to 1928, when an Egyptian schoolteacher named Hassan al-Banna founded the Muslim Brotherhood. Al-Banna was a Sufi, and he intended his organization to be a vehicle of moral and social reform. By the end of World War II, however, the Muslim Brotherhood was radicalized, becoming an armed movement that carried out attacks against the British and fought alongside the Palestinians. In 1948, the Egyptian government banned the group, and al-Banna himself was gunned down while getting into a taxi. Most Egyptians believe his murder was planned, or at least condoned, by the government. Radical movements are often deeply hostile to the ruling class in most majority Muslim states, who are perceived as corrupt and unjust, merely passing themselves off as Islamic.

Out of that Egyptian milieu stepped Sayyid Qutb, a poet who joined the Muslim Brotherhood and who created the intellectual basis for Islamic radicalism during the 1950s and 1960s, until he was hanged by the Nasser government in 1966. Ironically, the crucible in which Qutb's radicalism was forged was the United States. He spent 1948–50 attending Wilson Teachers College, the Colorado State College of Education (today the University of Northern Colorado), and Stanford University. Based on that experience, Qutb penned his famous tract, "The America I Have Seen."

A particular zone of disgust for Qutb was what he saw as the sexual licentiousness of American culture (and this, bear in mind, was the early 1950s). Qutb said that "providing full opportunities for the development and perfection of human characteristics requires strong safeguards for the peace and stability of the family." Qutb summed up his diagnosis this way: "I fear that a balance may not exist between America's material greatness and the quality of its people. And I fear that the wheel of life will have turned, and the book of life will have closed, and America will have added nothing, or next to nothing, to the account of morals that distinguishes man from object, and indeed, mankind from animals."

Another stream feeding Islamic radicalism is the Wahhabi movement in Saudi Arabia, founded by the eighteenth-century preacher and reformer Muhammad ibn Abd al-Wahab, who wanted to forge a "pure" form of Islam. Muhammad ibn Saud, a local sheikh, saw the movement as a means for extending political control over the peninsula. After the collapse of the Ottoman Empire, one of ibn Saud's descendants, Abd al-Aziz ibn Saud, established the Kingdom of Saudi Arabia in 1922 and made Wahhabi Islam the official creed. Shortly thereafter massive oil reserves were discovered, and the Saudis saw this wealth as a blessing intended to spread Wahhabism throughout the world.

The Muslim Brotherhood and Wahhabism intersected in the 1960s, when the Saudis welcomed the brotherhood after it had been disbanded under Egypt's President Nasser. While most Wahhabis are neither terrorists nor radicals, the stringent Islamic doctrine of Wahhabism proved a natural seedbed for jihadist energies. (The teams that carried out the terrorist strikes of September 11, 2001, were Wahhabis.) Islamic radicals were further emboldened by the Iranian Revolution of 1979, the first modern occasion when Muslims successfully overthrew a Western-backed secular regime.

The point of this brief and inevitably superficial overview is to suggest that radical Islam is not merely a few malcontents, but a tradition with a significant base of support in Muslim opinion, including access to considerable financial resources. Despite the fanaticism and violence bred by Islamic radicalism, there's also a protest against Western modernity at its core that's not entirely alien to the moral critique offered by some Christian thinkers, including Pope Benedict XVI. If they could set aside their prejudices, at least some of the spiritual sons and daughters of Sayyid Qutb might eventually recognize a potential ally in evangelical Catholicism—and therein lies perhaps the last, best hope for meaningful Muslim–Christian dialogue.

Trends in Contemporary Islam

1. THE "SHI'A SURGE"

Some Sunni elites have long regarded Shi'ites as the great unwashed of the Muslim world, a plebian and marginal subculture, though that perception rests on shaky historical foundations. The great Persian literary, mystical, and artistic traditions are fundamentally Shi'a, and the powerful Shah of Iran was hardly an emblem of the downtrodden. If anything, many experts say the ancient Persians preserved a higher literary and artistic culture than the Arabs.

In any event, Shi'a Islam is today enjoying a revival. In April 2007, the Center on Islam, Democracy and the Future of the Muslim World, sponsored by the Hudson Institute in Washington, D.C., published a report on what it called a "growing trend" of conversions to Shi'a across the Islamic world. Among forces driving the trend, according to the report: Iranian-sponsored missionary activity; the appeal in some circles of Iranian president Mahmoud Ahmadinejad; the fact that Iraq is likely to emerge as the first modern Arab state led by Shi'ites; and the rising star of the Shi'a political and paramilitary movement Hezbollah in light of its success in the July–August 2006 war with Israel, coupled with the appeal of its charismatic leader, Hassan Nasrallah. While that analysis may reflect a typical bias in policy circles to discount specifically religious considerations in favor of politics, nonetheless the evangelical momentum of Shi'a Islam seems real.

Though precise numbers are elusive, conversions to Shi'a are occurring, according to the report, in Egypt, Jordan, Syria, Sudan, Algeria, Morocco, and other parts of the Muslim world. In Jordan in 2006, several hundred Sunni families were said to have become Shi'ites. In Algeria in November 2006, several Shi'ites were dismissed by the Minister of Education for allegedly conducting Shi'a missionary work in schools. Reports from Morocco indicate that Sunnis working abroad, especially in Spain and Belgium, have been proselytized by Shi'ites and have taken their new faith home. In Sudan, the main council of Sunni organizations has reported that whole villages have converted to Shi'a, and that Shi'a mosques are proliferating.

The "Shi'a surge" in Syria is especially noteworthy. The *New York Times* reported in April 2007 that one analyst now puts the Shi'a at 6 to 8 percent of the country's population of 19 million, between 1.1 and 1.5 million people. A recent study carried out by Sunni religious authorities in Syria covering the period 1985–2006 acknowledges significant growth in the Shi'a population but insists that conversions were from the minority sect of Alawis rather than Sunnis. A Sunni scholar in Syria, Wahbah al-Zuhayli, has accused the report of grossly underestimating Shi'a expansion.

2. SUNNI–SHI'ITE CONFLICT

Sunni–Shi'ite rivalry runs deep in Muslim history. Shi'ites often claim that under the Sunni Abbasid dynasty in Baghdad, their members were beheaded, buried alive, even placed alive in the walls of government buildings. Sunnis claim they were treated equally mercilessly under the Safavids in Iran.

Over the centuries, Sunnis have charged that Shi'a is heretical for a variety of reasons: that its emphasis on Ali turns him into a god, denying the uniqueness of Allah; that the doctrine of the infallibility of the Twelve Imams turns them into rivals of Muhammad; that the Shi'ites have "added to the Qur'an," forging Hadith, meaning oral traditions, to justify their doctrines; that Shi'ite holy days and pilgrimages corrupt the purity of the faith; that the Shi'ites practice "dissimulation," meaning strategically hiding their faith in order to escape persecution, and hence cannot be trusted (a charge, some historians of religions have noted, not entirely unlike polemics directed over the years at Jesuits); and that the Shi'ites are morally suspect because they permit temporary marriages.

Alongside this history of conflict, however, is also one of détente. Experts say the story of Sunni–Shi'a relations is one of alternating periods of *taqarub*, or rapprochement, and *takfir*, meaning mutual excommunication. On July 6, 1959, the head of the Al-Azhar mosque in Cairo, widely recognized as the most authoritative institution in the Sunni Muslim world, issued a fatwa recognizing the main "Twelver" branch of Shi'a as religiously legitimate. Throughout the second half of the twentieth century, activists motivated by dreams of a pan-Muslim alliance have played down the Sunni–Shi'ite breach. The Muslim Brotherhood insists that intra-Muslim divisions must be suppressed for the sake of fighting the common enemy of Israel and the United States. Ecumenical efforts continue, as symbolized by a conference on Dialogue for Islamic Schools of Thought in Doha, Qatar, in

January 2007, attended by over 200 scholars from 44 Islamic nations, including both Sunnis and Shi'ites.

Nonetheless, it doesn't take much for old wounds to reopen. Many members of the Sunni minority in Iraq saw the execution of Saddam Hussein as a bloody act of Shi'a retribution, a perception fueled by video showing executioners chanting "Muqtada, Muqtada, Muqtada," a reference to Shi'ite cleric Muqtada al-Sadr, whose Mahdi Army militia is held responsible for attacks on Sunnis. Similarly, many Sunnis saw the efforts of Hezbollah to topple the government of Lebanese prime minister Fouad Siniora, a Sunni, as another Shi'ite power grab. One illustration of mounting resentment came in a four-hour anti-Shi'a tirade recorded by militant Islamist leader Abu Musab al-Zarqawi two months before his death in June 2006. Scholar Nibras Kazimi speculated in 2006 that "Zarqawi's most enduring legacy may be the transformation of anti-Shi'ism into a central tenet of the jihadist worldview." Other experts, however, say that such sectarian rivalries should not be exaggerated. They note that Ayman al-Zawahiri, Osama bin Laden's main lieutenant, is more careful to stress a sense of common cause with the Shi'ites.

3. A CRISIS OF AUTHORITY

Richard W. Bulliet observed in a 2002 essay in the *Wilson Quarterly* that Muslims have traditionally looked for leadership to the *ulama* class, meaning jurists with specialized training in an established Islamic school, and often with some formal grant of authority from the state—muftis, sheikhs, and so on. As long as nationalism remained a popular force, these imams and muftis continued to hold authority. Today, however, the weakening of the nation-state, along with frustration over perceived corruption and authoritarianism in many Islamic governments, has discredited these establishment figures.

Leadership has increasingly been provided by radical figures who generally lack formal religious training, such as Osama bin Laden, Ayman al-Zawahiri, and Abu Musab al-Zarqawi. Bin Laden is an engineer, Zawahiri a surgeon. Even Sayyid Qutb, the father of Islamic radicalism, was a schoolteacher. Yet because they have no ties to the state, they are perceived to be more credible in many circles. Their skill in manipulating the mass media, especially television and the Internet, has amplified their voice, as has widespread literacy in the Islamic world.

The crisis of authority is also a problem *within* radical Islam. Al-Zarqawi's rift with his mentor, Abu Muhammad al-Maqdisi, illustrates the point; al-Maqdisi criticized al-Zarqawi for targeting fellow Muslims, but couldn't bring him to heel. This suggests that the Islamic world in the twenty-first century will continue to struggle with authority—who wields it, how it's recognized, and how to deny it to someone who asserts it illegitimately.

Some say that what Islam needs today is a Reformation, a reference to the Protestant Reformation in Europe in the sixteenth century. In light of the crisis of authority, however, Jesuit Fr. Daniel Madigan, an expert on Islam at Georgetown University, says this has things exactly backwards. Islam has already had its Reformation, Madigan argues, and what it needs now is a Counter-Reformation. Here's how Madigan puts it:

> The elements of the Reformation were a rejection of traditional structures of authority and a personalized, individualized reading of scripture without the acquired wisdom of the tradition to guide it. This was made possible by printing and dissemination of the Bible, which enabled the newly literate middle classes to decide for themselves what the text meant or did not mean, whatever the priest or bishop might be preaching or practicing. That's the Reformation for you, and that's precisely what has taken place among Muslims in the last century—religious printing started in the late nineteenth century, literacy grew, and the ulama were discredited as flunkies of corrupt regimes. So, bin Laden or al-Zarqawi or any Pakistani in Britain can sit around with his mates and decide authoritatively what he should do. That's your Reformation. What we need is a Council of Trent, perhaps. Reform the clergy and get them trained properly so that they can bring the acquired wisdom of the tradition to bear on the actual situation, instead of leaving it to the loose cannons.

4. NEO-SUFISM

Experts on Islam often complain that relatively marginal radical groups have an outsize media profile in the West, under the logic of "if it bleeds, it leads," while far more widespread moderate and reform-oriented movements fly largely below radar. The various forms of neo-Sufism across the Islamic world today make the point.

The concept of "neo-Sufism" is elastic. At one level, it can refer to a revival in Sufi spiritual and mystical practices. In Indonesia, for example, a growing number of young university students and affluent housewives are attracted to Sufi prayer services, especially Thursday-night gatherings when followers chant the ninety-nine names of God. Since music in worship is frowned upon in Sunni Islam, such forms of devotion are often experienced as liberating. In that sense, neo-Sufism draws upon the legacy of Sufism without its trappings, such as Masters and brotherhoods.

Neo-Sufism as an organized social force, however, can be defined as a competitor to radical Islam in terms of shaping the Islamic reaction to modernity. The crucial difference is that radicals want to seize political power, while neo-Sufis generally want to change people's souls. The most widespread forms of neo-Sufism have arisen in Turkey, under the inspiration of Said Nursi in the early twentieth century, and later his disciple, Fethullah Gülen.

Nursi is author of the *Risale-i Nur,* the "Message of Light," a 6,000-page commentary on the Qur'an. He rejected political and military solutions to secularism, instead concentrating on Qur'anic study in light of the natural sciences. Nursi was a champion of interfaith dialogue well ahead of his time, defending the rights of Armenians and Greeks in Turkey. In 1950, he sent a collection of his works to Pope Pius XII in Rome, and in 1953 he met with Patriarch Athenagoras of Constantinople. A conservative estimate for the size of his "Nurcu movement" today is five to six million, with some claiming as many as nine million.

Like Nursi, Fethullah Gülen believes in an Islam that is faithful to its traditions but open to the best of modernity. Gülen particularly stresses education, though his schools are not Islamic but secular institutions grounded in religious values. His "Gülen movement" is a mini-empire estimated to be worth $25 billion, with its own TV stations, a news agency, a bank, 35 newspapers and magazines in various languages, unions, student associations, more than 600 schools (including several in the United States, concentrated in New Jersey and Texas), and six universities in 75 countries, including Virginia International University in Fairfax, Virginia. Gülen is also a strong believer in interfaith dialogue who met Pope John Paul II in 1998. His movement runs interreligious centers around the world, including the Interfaith Dialogue Center in Paterson, New Jersey. For Catholics, it may be helpful to think of the "Gülen movement" as a sort of Islamic analogue to Opus Dei, the Catholic body founded by the Spanish priest Saint Josemaría Escrivá in the late 1920s. Both are attempts to blend a deep fidelity to religious identity with openness to modernity; both have spawned mini-empires of schools, media outlets, youth centers, and other institutions; and both tend to attract highly articulate young professionals and intellectuals who exercise influence within their faith communities beyond their numbers.

A 2005 conference at Rice University estimated Gülen's following at six million. If so, the adherents of Nursi and Gülen together could number as many as 15 million people, which would represent a bloc larger than some global religions. The total Jewish population in the world in 2006, for example, was estimated at 14 million. Jesuit Fr. Thomas Michel, a former Vatican official and an expert on Islam, claims that the moderate movements launched by Nursi and Gülen "point the direction the worldwide Islamic community is heading far more accurately than do the increasingly isolated circles of those who are involved in terrorist fringe organizations."

5. MUSLIM DEMOCRATS

If there is a single figure who best symbolizes hope for a democratic evolution in Islam, it may well be Tariq Ramadan, a Swiss-born Muslim intellectual and the grandson of Hassan al-Banna, founder of the Muslim Brotherhood. Named by *Time* magazine as one of "100 Innovators for the 21st Century," Ramadan advocates a "European Islam," religious enough to offset secularization, yet pluralistic enough to combat radicalism. Critics accuse Ramadan of saying one thing to elite Western audiences and another to young radicals, charging that he equivocates on anti-Semitism and the use of violence. Admirers style him "the Muslim Martin Luther." Whatever one makes of him, Ramadan illustrates the emergence of a new generation of Muslim intellectuals and activists who support a synthesis of democracy with distinctively Islamic concepts. Bassam Tibi, a Syrian-born political scientist in Germany, has a similar outlook. He coined the phrase "Euro-Islam" to refer to a new branch of Islam he believes is emerging, one that combines fidelity to Qur'anic principles with values such as democracy, human rights, the separation of church and state, and gender equity.

Ramadan and Tibi work in the West, but there are also Muslim reformers inside majority Islamic states. Mohamed Talbi has been referred to as "the Tunisian Sakharov" for his insistence on democratic governance, transparency, and the rule of law. Sudanese scholar Abdullahi An-Na'im has made the case for interpreting the Qur'an in ways consistent with basic freedoms, such as religious identity and gender equity. Nurcholish Madjid, an Indonesian Muslim intellectual who died in 2005, made a career out of insisting that for Islam to be victorious in the global struggle of ideas, it needs to embrace tolerance, democracy, and pluralism.

To be sure, one should not underestimate the depth of resistance to such ideas. To take one example, moderate Sudanese scholar Mahmoud Mohamed Taha was hanged in Khartoum for protesting against Shariah laws. Nevertheless, Muslim writers such as Reza Aslan, an Iranian living in the United States, believe that reform will carry the day.

"The vast majority of the more than one billion Muslims in the world readily accept the fundamental principles of democracy," Aslan wrote in 2005's *No god but God.* "Ideals such as constitutionalism, government accountability, pluralism and human rights are widely accepted throughout the Muslim world." He quotes Abdolkarim Soroush, a political philosopher in Iran: "We no longer claim that a genuinely religious government *can* be democratic. We claim that it cannot be otherwise."

An additional factor that may push Islam toward reform is demographics. Fertility rates are dropping more rapidly in the Middle East today than anywhere on earth. In the short term, this may exacerbate radicalism; fewer children mean more women competing for jobs, and male-dominated traditionalists may try even harder to keep them at home. Over the long run, however, as author Phillip Longman observes, aging societies tend to be peaceful ones. They can't afford to maintain large armies and also pay for pensions and health care. As children become scarce, parents are also less inclined to encourage them to risk life and limb. As Europe aged in the 1970s, the appeal of radical movements such as the Red Brigades and the IRA diminished, and something similar may happen in the Middle East.

Christian–Muslim Tensions

The rise of radical Islam has produced deep scars in many Christian communities, especially in the Middle East, North Africa, and parts of Asia. Despite the fact that these antique Christian churches have roots that predate the arrival of Islam, many radicals see them as a beachhead for Western influence. At their most extreme, the tensions are producing new Christian martyrs. For example, on March 27, 1996, Muslim radicals kidnapped seven Trappist monks from their monastery in the Atlas Mountains near Algiers. After two months, the Groupe Islamique Armée announced that the monks' throats had been cut. The bodies were never recovered; the severed heads were buried at the monastery in Tibhirine.

To take another prominent case, an Italian missionary named Fr. Andrea Santoro was gunned down in February 2006 by a sixteen-year-old Muslim in the small Turkish city of Trabzon. The boy's father said he had a history of mental illness, but Bishop Luigi Padovese, the region's apostolic vicar and Santoro's superior, said a "rising tide" of anti-Christian propaganda also had played a role. As one example, he cited a rural Turkish newspaper that in 2006 carried an article with the headline A PRIEST SIGHTED. It reported that local children had seen a priest in the vicinity of their town, but had chased him away to great applause. The article quoted a local politician: "Priests who arrive in our area want to re-establish the Christian Greek-Orthodox state that was here before. There are spies among these priests, working for the West."

Even when anti-Christian sentiment does not lead to martyrdom, it can result in severe hardships. Lina Joy, for example, converted from Islam to Christianity in Malaysia in 1998. She applied to change religious affiliation on her identity card but was rebuffed by civil courts, on the grounds that it's up to Islamic authorities to decide who is no longer a Muslim. This is not just a matter of words on paper; unless her non-Muslim status was recognized, Joy was barred from marrying her Christian fiancé. Publicity surrounding the case brought death threats, and Joy was eventually forced to go into hiding.

Christians living in some predominantly Muslim areas say harassment has become so routine that it almost goes unnoticed. To take just a thirty-day period of time, June 2007, four episodes illustrate what's happening on the ground:

- Fr. Manuel Musalam, leader of the small Latin Rite Catholic community in the Gaza Strip, appealed for international protection after Hamas gunmen torched and looted his church along with the nearby Rosary Sisters School. He said that every cross in both the church and the school had been destroyed, and every copy of the Bible burned, in addition to the school's computers and other equipment being destroyed.

- A Hamas leader in Gaza warned Christians to "get ready" for Islamic rule, stating that "missionary activity" will no longer be tolerated, and those suspected of trying to convert Muslims to Christianity will be "harshly punished." The consumption of alcohol will be prohibited, he said, and Christian women will be expected to cover themselves in public.

- Chaldean Fr. Ragheed Ganni, age thirty-four, the pastor of Holy Spirit Church in the Nur district of Mosul, Iraq, and subdeacons Basman Yousef Daoud, Ghasan Bidawid, and Wadid Hanna were forced out of their car and shot to death after celebrating Mass on Saturday, June 2.

- The third Italian Catholic priest in the Philippines to be kidnapped in the last ten years, Fr. Giancarlo Bossi, a member of the Pontifical Institute for Foreign Missions, was hauled away from his parish by militants linked to the Moro Islamic Liberation Front, which has waged a bloody war for the independence of Mindanao since 1978. (Bossi was released a month later.)

Collectively, such realities have fueled the push for a more challenging Catholic stance toward Islam. In particular, the issue of reciprocity—that Christian minorities should receive the same protection that Muslim immigrants receive in the West—is becoming a top Catholic priority. In 2006, for example, Bishop Rino Fisichella, rector of Rome's Lateran University and a papal confidant, said it's time to "drop the diplomatic silence" about anti-Christian persecution and called on the UN and other bodies to "remind the societies and governments of countries with a Muslim majority of their responsibilities."

Saudi Arabia offers perhaps the classic case in point. In the 1990s, the Saudi government spent $25 million to build the largest mosque in Europe, in Rome, with the support of John Paul II. Meanwhile in Saudi Arabia, the Qur'an is officially the country's constitution, with public religious expression other than Wahhabism prohibited. This ban is backed up by the *mutawaa,* or religious police. Christians cannot build churches in the country, an area three times the size of Texas, and they cannot worship in public or private. In 2005, the *mutawaa* conducted four raids of Christian "house churches," according to the Center for Religious Freedom. Christians cannot import Bibles or wear religious symbols, and clergy cannot wear religious dress. A handful of Capuchin priests charged with pastoral care of several hundred thousand Catholics, mostly Filipino, Lebanese, and Indian guest workers, cannot minister openly.

Without suggesting equivalence to Christian martyrdom, it's important to observe that Muslims too sometimes experience limits on their religious freedom in predominantly Christian societies. Debates over legal bans on head scarves in France offer one well-known example. Candelin of the World

Evangelical Alliance also cites the case of Turkish Muslims in Greece, who face limits from the Greek government on their ability to appoint muftis and teachers, to assemble, and to form legally recognized associations. It's also worth noting that more priests and religious are killed each year in majority Christian nations such as Colombia and Brazil than in predominantly Muslim states, suggesting that recent Christian martyrdom is not exclusively, or even principally, related to Islamic extremism.

A Test Case: Nigeria

Imam Sani Isah of the Waff Road Mosque in Kaduna, the capital of the Muslim-dominated north in Nigeria, says that his country is Saudi Arabia and the Vatican rolled into one. It's a volatile mix of tens of millions of highly motivated Muslims, and a roughly equal number of devout Christians. Lessons about Christian–Muslim coexistence in Nigeria may have broad global implications, especially for a future in which growth for both traditions will come largely in the global South.

Serious Muslim–Christian violence broke out for the first time in 1978. The pretext came with a Pentecostal revival in the northern city of Kafanchan, when a Muslim woman grabbed a microphone to shout anti-Christian slogans. Violence ensued, triggering anti-Christian outbreaks in Kaduna and elsewhere. Since then, uneasy calm punctuated by periods of extreme violence has been the story line. Some examples:

- Waves of violence in Kaduna in 1987 and 1992 left hundreds dead and caused an informal religious partition of the city.

- Clashes between Muslim and Christian tribes across the country from September 2001 to May 2004 are estimated to have cost at least 1,800 lives and some 160,000 cattle.

- Controversies over Shariah in several northern Nigerian states triggered violence that left 1,000 dead in Kaduna in 2000, and 2,000 dead in Jos in 2001.

- In summer 2002, thousands of people died during clashes in Plateau state, with an estimated 100,000 people displaced and 88 localities almost entirely destroyed.

- Violence broke out in November 2002 when a newspaper columnist satirically suggested that Muhammad might have taken a wife from among the contestants in the Miss World pageant. Hundreds died and dozens of churches and mosques were destroyed.

- In 2004, 630 Muslims were slaughtered by armed Christians in Yelaw-Shenda, followed by 200 Christians killed in Kano as a reprisal.

- In February 2006, violence followed the Danish cartoon controversy. More than 150 people were killed after a group of Christians was massacred by angry Muslim militants, triggering several anti-Muslim outbreaks.

Nigerians insist that while these episodes have garnered the most media attention, they aren't the whole story. In the Yoruba lands of the Southwest, for example, Christians and Muslims can be found happily intermarried, sharing the same extended families. Further, observers say, violence billed as "religious" is often really a matter of tribes clashing over concrete issues such as water or land use. Even in the north, there are encouraging signals. In Kaduna, Imam Muhammad Ashafa and Pastor James Wuye have established the Interfaith Mediation Centre, where they train pairs of imams and pastors to fan out wherever violence begins to stir. (Wuye lost his right hand battling Muslims when he led Christian militias in the 1990s). Their efforts have been credited with preventing bloodshed.

Yet there is also a troubling footnote. Many Nigerian Christians, as well as some Muslims, believe a fragile peace has been achieved in part because Christians answered violence from the Muslim side with violence of their own. Without this capacity of Christians to push back, these observers say, Muslim leaders might never have agreed to negotiate a truce. Even Imam Sani Isah ruefully concedes that's probably correct. Nigerian Christians thus know peaceful coexistence with Muslims is possible, because most have Muslim neighbors, colleagues, and friends. At the same time, experience has taught them that in dealing with religious zealots and bullies, sometimes strength has to be answered with strength.

Catholic–Muslim Relations under John Paul II and Benedict XVI

John Paul II was a great pioneer of Catholic outreach to the Islamic world, meeting with Muslims more than sixty times, including a pop star–style rally with Muslim youth in Casablanca in August 1985. On that occasion he said, "We believe in the same God, the one God, the living God, the God who created the world and brings his creatures to their perfection." Later, John Paul made history by becoming the first pope to enter a mosque, which he did at the Grand Umayyad Mosque in Damascus in May 2001. Under John Paul II, the Vatican established five standing dialogues with Muslim groups:

- The Muslim-Catholic Liaison Committee, created in 1995, which brings together Vatican officials and representatives of various Muslim organizations such as the World Muslim Congress, the World Muslim League, the International Islamic Committee for Da'wah and Humanitarian Relief, the International Islamic Forum for Dialogue, and the Islamic Economic Social and Cultural Organization of the Organization of the Islamic Conference. This meeting usually ends with a joint communiqué; in 2004, for example, the group denounced bombings against Catholic churches in Iraq.

- An annual session with Al-Azhar University in Cairo, launched in 1998. Al-Azhar is widely considered one of the most authoritative institutions in the Islamic world; some have called it "the Muslim Vatican." The Muslim representatives proposed that the meeting take place each year on February 24, the anniversary of a visit to Al-Azhar by Pope John Paul II in 2000.

- A Coordinating Committee with the World Islamic Call Society, based in Libya. The committee includes six Muslims and six Catholics, meeting annually in Rome or Tripoli.

- A biannual colloquium with the Islamic Culture and Relations Organization of the Ministry of Culture and Islamic Guidance in Iran, held in either Rome or Tehran.

- An agreement on April 25, 2002, for a standing dialogue with the Ministry of Religious Affairs in Turkey.

The relatively "dovish" approach under John Paul and his key advisors on Islam, such as English Archbishop Michael Fitzgerald, was never universally popular among senior Catholic leaders. Post-9/11, pressure grew for a reevaluation, and one figure laying the groundwork was then-cardinal Joseph Ratzinger. As a result, Islam has become one of the few areas of substantive contrast between the papacies of John Paul and Benedict XVI.

Prior to his election to the papacy, Ratzinger had a profile as more of a hawk. In 1996, he gave a book-length interview to journalist Peter Seewald, published in English in 1997 as *Salt of the Earth*. In it, he expressed doubt as to whether Islam could be reconciled with Western-style democratic pluralism. Ratzinger also irked some Muslims by his opposition to Turkey's candidacy to join the European Union. In an August 2004 interview with *Le Figaro*, Ratzinger said that Turkey is "in permanent contrast to Europe," and that it should look to play a leadership role in a network of Islamic states. (During his 2006 trip to Turkey, Benedict said that the Vatican would not oppose Turkey's candidacy if human rights guarantees are met, especially religious freedom.)

As pope, Benedict XVI has indeed taken a more challenging line. He seems to believe that John Paul's efforts to build bridges with Muslims were essential, but that, those bridges having been built, it's now time to walk across them. That means dialogue must press beyond the tea and cookies stage, beyond the mere capacity to be polite to one another, and into discussion of real issues. That's an exercise fraught with the potential for conflict, as Benedict's Regensburg lecture illustrates. Benedict's "stump speech" with Muslim audiences always includes a clear challenge to reject violence and terrorism, as well as the need to integrate faith and reason.

Paradoxically, however, Benedict XVI has arguably scored his greatest interfaith success with Muslims, and his own ambivalence about the theological premises of interreligious dialogue has helped elevate the relationship with Islam to the top tier of Catholic concerns.

First, the fundamental "clash of civilizations" Benedict XVI sees in the world today runs not between Islam and the West, but between belief and unbelief—between a culture that values the supernatural and recognizes a role for religion in public life, and one that does not. In the struggle against a "dictatorship of relativism," Benedict has said, Muslims should be natural allies. The real threat to Christianity as Benedict sees it comes not from Islam, but from secularism. Thus when Benedict prods Islam toward reform, he sees himself not as a Crusader, but as a friend speaking from within a shared space of common religious concern.

Second, Benedict XVI has described his vision of the relationship between Christianity and other faiths in terms of "intercultural," rather than "interreligious," dialogue. In a preface to a 2008 book by Italian philosopher and politician Marcello Pera, Benedict asserted that interreligious dialogue, "strictly speaking, is impossible," because it means setting aside one's own religious identity. Yet "intercultural dialogue," the pope wrote, is "urgent and necessary"—by which he meant, in part, a search for common ground on how religious values can shape political and social life. In other words, Benedict's approach to interfaith relations puts the accent less on theological reflection and more on what the religions can do together in the world. That has the practical effect of elevating Islam, with its 1.6 billion adherents and enormous impact on global affairs, to a clear pride of place. Even Benedict's travel schedule reflects a new emphasis on Islam: when John Paul II visited the Holy Land in 2000, he spent just twenty-four hours in Jordan and devoted most of his energy in Israel to relations with Judaism. In 2009, Benedict spent almost four days in Jordan, whose Hashemite monarchy sees itself as a leader of Islam's moderate center. In Jerusalem, Benedict added a visit to the Dome of the Rock alongside repeating John Paul's stop at the Western Wall.

WHAT IT MEANS

Reactions to Islam will play out differently for various Catholic constituencies. For "hawks," it will be a matter of apologetics, evangelization, and pushing the issue of religious freedom; for "doves," it will mean dialogue, academic exchange, and efforts to address the roots of Islamic radicalism in social injustices. In some ways, these reactions bear comparison to differences within Catholicism during the Cold War, when one wing of the Church believed in engagement with the Soviet world and another in confrontation. Then and now, the difference between "hawks" and "doves" is often not a matter of opposing camps, but opposing instincts in the same people. Most Catholics today probably feel the tug of both outlooks, and aren't quite sure how to reconcile them. Officially, Church leaders will try to hold both impulses in a creative tension; in practice, they'll often butt heads.

Near-Certain Consequences

1. EXPANSION IN ISLAMIC STUDIES

The most obvious consequence of the rise of Islam is that more Catholics are interested in it. The twenty-first century will see swelling Catholic interest in Islamic theology, history, and cultures. Arabic and Persian will become more popular foreign languages, especially for future Church diplomats and academics. Islamic Studies will be a growth industry in Catholic intellectual and pastoral activity. Catholic institutions will seek Muslim scholars, and students will seek opportunities to study abroad in Muslim nations. Journals devoted to Islamic topics will become increasingly common. More dissertations and scholarly articles will be written on Islamic topics, as well as popular articles and documentaries in Catholic media. Some of this will be informational, and some of it apologetic.

Instances of the trend are not difficult to find.

In Rome, the Pontifical Gregorian University created the Institute for the Study of Religions and Cultures in 2006, addressed to the undergraduate and graduate population—which includes a substantial percentage of the future priests and bishops of the Catholic Church. Though the program offers concentrations in Judaism, Hinduism, Buddhism, and Christianity, as well as Islam, the driving force behind the project and its first president was an expert in Islam, Jesuit Fr. Daniel Madigan. In a symbolically fitting touch, the first graduate student to enroll and to graduate with a master's degree was a Muslim woman from Turkey.

The Pontifical Institute for Arabic and Islamic Studies in Rome, perhaps the Catholic Church's most prestigious academy for the study of Islam and Islamic cultures, is also experiencing growth—not in the absolute number of students, according to a 2007 interview with Fr. Miguel Ángel Ayuso Guixot, a Spanish Comboni missionary who serves as rector, but in the number of countries these students represent. There are roughly fifty students in the institute's graduate programs, Ayuso said, who will become responsible for dialogue programs with Muslims in their home communities, dioceses, and countries.

Examples of interest in the broader Catholic world include Georgetown's Center for Muslim-Christian Understanding, founded in 1993 and renamed the Prince Alwaleed Bin Talal Center for Muslim-Christian Understanding in 2005 after it received a $20 million gift from the Saudi prince. Georgetown is also currently the only Catholic university in the United States to have its own Muslim chaplain.

Another example came in 2005, with the launch of a new international journal called *Oasis* by Cardinal Angelo Scola of Venice. The publication is directed at countries with an Islamic majority and is designed to promote dialogue with Christian minorities in those countries. It's published in four editions: English-Arabic, English-Urdu, French-Arabic, and Italian-Arabic.

In June 2006, Scola convened a summit in Cairo of Catholic bishops and other leading figures from Africa, the Middle East, and Europe to discuss human rights and democracy in Christianity and Islam.

2. GREAT COMMISSION CATHOLICS

Facing a self-confident Islam, two modes of Catholic interfaith relations will gather strength in the twenty-first century: apologetics and evangelization.

Cardinal Avery Dulles brought out a revised edition of his 1971 book *A History of Apologetics* in 2005 to respond to growing interest in defense of the Christian faith vis-à-vis Islam. Dulles makes the point that Christianity's original experts on Islam were writers from the seventh through the fourteenth centuries who articulated a defense of Christianity in light of Islamic objections. They include John Damascene, Peter the Venerable, Raymond Martini, Raymond Lull, Ricoldus de Monte Croce, Dionysius the Carthusian, Cardinal Juan Torquemada, Cardinal Nicholas of Cusa, and even the Florentine reformer Savonarola (of "bonfire of the vanities" fame). In the twenty-first century, such writers will be back in vogue.

What might a twenty-first-century Catholic apologetics with regard to Islam look like?

To take just one example, a growing number of Catholic pamphlets and Web sites are devoted to debunking the "Gospel of Barnabas," a supposedly suppressed early Christian gospel that has Jesus predicting the coming of Muhammad. Though the fourth-century *Codex Sinaiticus* contains an "Epistle of Barnabas," the text circulated among Muslims today is regarded by most scholars as a fifteenth-century fabrication intended to provide scriptural basis for Islamic claims. Nevertheless, it is widely regarded in Muslim circles as authentic; some of the protestors who poured into the streets following Benedict XVI's Regensburg address carried signs citing the Gospel of Barnabas as proof that the Pope should be more respectful of Muhammad. (Whether efforts to debunk the Gospel of Barnabas will succeed is another matter, especially in a world in which official Church spokespersons have not even persuaded millions of Westerners to disregard bogus claims made in popular entertainment such as *The Da Vinci Code*. Some believe that official efforts to discredit texts regarded as suppressed may have the paradoxical effect of bolstering their credibility among people already inclined to view those institutions with suspicion.)

The twenty-first century will also see subtle, but persistent, attempts among some Catholics to reawaken the Church's missionary efforts among Muslims. Far more explicit campaigns are already well under way among Protestant Evangelicals and Pentecostals, who call themselves "Great Commission Christians," referring to the commission given by Christ after his resurrection: "Go forth and make disciples of all the nations." The most determined movement in "Great Commission Christianity" today focuses upon what its architects call the "10–40 window," meaning a swath of the globe between 10 degrees latitude north of the equator and 40 degrees south of the equator. It includes North Africa and the Middle East, India, and China, representing the part of the world with the lowest percentage of Christians. Of the 56 countries in the 10–40 window, 44 are majority Muslim states.

While Catholic evangelization will not be quite so explicit, evangelization and proclamation will nevertheless receive proportionately greater emphasis, leading to the emergence of what we might call "Great Commission Catholics." They will take pains to avoid impressions of coercion or manipulation, since complaints about a lack of religious freedom in the Muslim world loom large in Christian apologetics. Nonetheless, alongside existing forms of dialogue and socio-political cooperation—and, no doubt, sometimes complicating those efforts—some evangelical Catholics will make plans to convert Muslims.

A 2003 booklet published by *Catholic Answers* under the title "Islam—A Catholic Perspective," gave this advice to Catholics: "Love is a keynote of Christianity that Islam lacks. In the words of one Muslim convert to Christianity, 'Christianity is a religion of love; Islam is a religion of fear.' Muslims do not have the kind of loving, intimate relationship with God that Christians do. Show that to them, talk about it—about how much you love God and want them to share in the feeling of God's love—and that will help show them the light of the gospel."

3. RELIGIOUS FREEDOM

The press for greater religious freedom in the Islamic world will unfold both on the level of formal diplomatic efforts from the Vatican and from local bishops, as well as informal grassroots initiatives from Catholic activists, think tanks, and NGOs. The Egyptian-born politician and journalist Magdi Allam, now a prominent Catholic convert in Italy and a member of the

European Parliament, has proposed the creation of a worldwide "Permanent Observatory" to monitor religious freedom. Allam is heir to Oriana Fallaci as Italy's leading hawk on Islam. He's close to the Communion and Liberation movement and has the ear of senior Vatican officials.

Experts on Muslim–Christian dialogue have recommended a six-point program for advancing the issue of religious freedom:

- Acknowledge that Christians have had, and in some places continue to have, their own struggles with religious freedom;
- Don't make reciprocity seem like special pleading for Christians, but rather a principled stand in favor of freedom for all religions—including Muslims in the West;
- Make it clear that this is not a crusade against Islam;
- Recall areas where Catholics and Muslims are natural allies, such as resistance to secularization;
- Speak directly to Muslim governments that are responsible for repressive policies, not just to clerics and theologians;
- Make religious freedom part of a broader message about civil and political liberties across the board.

It's important, such experts say, to accent positive experiences. Fr. Tom Michel, a former Vatican official and expert on Islam, offered the example of former cardinal Salvatore Pappalardo of Palermo, Italy. When Muslims in Palermo needed a place to worship, Michel said, Pappalardo gave them an unused church. Michel also said that religious freedom should not be phrased as a problem just in the Islamic world. "The situation is just as bad, or worse, in places like India," he said, warning that an exclusive focus on Islam feeds suspicion that "reciprocity" is a smokescreen for Western interests. Mohammad Fadel, an Egyptian scholar at the University of Toronto, said that Catholicism should avoid awakening "old paradigms" in the Muslim world, one of which involves "outside powers using minority religious communities as a pretext for interfering in internal affairs," such as the British did with the Copts in Egypt.

It's also important, experts say, to highlight positive developments in religious freedom in the Islamic world. For example, 2008 saw the opening of the first Catholic church in Qatar, on the Arabian peninsula. Our Lady of the Rosary parish, consecrated by a special delegate of the pope during a public ceremony attended by more than 10,000 people, was built on land donated by Qatar's Sheikh Hamad Bin Khalifa Al-Thani. During Pope Benedict's May 2009 trip to Jordan, he blessed the cornerstones for several new Catholic institutions, including two parishes at the site of the baptism of Jesus in the Jordan River and a new Catholic university. Jordan in many ways is a model of respect for its Christian minority; while Christians represent just 3 percent of the population, 8 percent of the seats in parliament are set aside for Christian representatives. Lifting up such examples, many observers believe, provides a more balanced impression of the diversity across majority Muslim societies.

Catholic willingness to push back against perceived Muslim intransigence will become bolder. In the June 2007 issue of *Oasis*, for example, Archbishop Ruggero Franceschini of Izmir in Turkey complained in strikingly open terms about the way Christianity is presented in Turkish schools: "The objective is to negate Christianity, or to undermine its worth by means of inferences which are both simplistic and groundless. This is dished out to the students with a garnish of hatred and violence which may have no effect on some, while for others it nourishes opposition which is both extreme and venomous. Thus, nationalists and Islamists have a free rein in manipulating opposition, which may be latent or unprofessed." Franceschini issued a call to arms: "Pressure from outside is needed to remove this fundamentalist, nationalistic obstacle, in order to allow other Churches to be recognized and accepted."

4. GROWING EMPHASIS ON SHI'A ISLAM

Traditionally, Catholic–Muslim dialogue has focused on the Sunni world. If the "Shi'a surge" continues, however, Catholicism may find itself increasingly reaching out to Shi'ite leaders. In this historically decisive moment, the Catholic Church may be the global institution with the best prospects of nudging Shi'ites toward reconciling their intense religious commitment with peace and pluralism.

As Catholics and Shi'ites get to know one another better, they will be struck by several parallels in the two traditions. Iranian writer Vali Nasr, author of the 2006 book *The Shia Revival*, argues that the divide between Sunni and Shi'a bears comparison to that between Protestants and Catholics, with Shi'a being the branch closer to Catholicism. Among the points of contact are: a strong emphasis on clerical authority; an approach to the Qur'an accenting both scripture and tradition; a deep mystical streak; devotion to a holy family (in the case of Shi'ites, the blood relatives of Muhammad) and to saints (the Twelve Imams); a theology of sacrifice and atonement through the death of Hussein; belief in free will (as opposed to the Sunni doctrine of predestination); holy days, pilgrimages, and healing shrines; intercessory prayer; and strongly emotional forms of popular devotion, especially the festival of Ashoura commemorating Hussein's death.

Nasr compares a Shi'ite who goes to the shrine of Hussein in Karbala, Iraq, to a Catholic who makes a pilgrimage to the shrine of Our Lady of Guadalupe in Mexico. Other similarities to Marian traditions in Catholicism are also not hard to find. On the outskirts of the Iranian holy city of Qom, for example, is the small mosque of Jamkaran, where Shi'ites believe that the Twelfth Imam once appeared and offered prayers. Nasr writes that it plays a role in Shi'a spirituality similar to that of Fatima in Catholicism, where Mary is believed to have appeared six times to three child visionaries in 1917. Over the last decade devotion to Jamkaran has been flourishing, especially among young Shi'ites, who flock to the site to pray in the mosque and to work in a vast kitchen dedicated to serving the poor.

Fellow Iranian writer Reza Aslan says that rational interpretation of Islamic law by Shi'ite clergy potentially creates a flexibility sometimes lacking in Sunni Islam, which is often shackled to a more literal reading of the Qur'an. Aslan believes Shi'a-influenced societies may be more amenable to experimentation with democracy, human rights, and pluralism, provided they're grounded in religious reasoning—as, for example, in Catholic social theory.

Catholicism and Shi'a have even struggled with some of the same doctrinal disputes. Just as the Vatican found itself at odds with liberation theology in the 1970s and 1980s, so Shi'ite authorities were divided over the "Red Shi'a" movement launched by Iranian writer Ali Shariati, who died in 1977. Like the liberation theologians, Shariati—who had studied sociology in Paris—drew on Marxism to generate a form of Shi'ism attentive to poverty and oppression. In another parallel with liberation theology, Shariati questioned the authority of the Shi'ite clerical elite, whom he accused of perverting Shi'a Islam into a "counterrevolutionary doctrine."

In October 2005, Benedictine Fr. Mark Serna, a veteran of Catholic–Shi'ite exchange, wrote: "In distinction to Muslims in the Sunni tradition, Shi'ite Muslims are very natural dialogue partners with Roman Catholics and monastics. There are many areas of mutuality: a profound contemplative and mystical tradition; veneration of saints, especially of Mary, the

Mother of Jesus; notions of infallibility and authority; high emphasis on rational inquiry into matters of faith; belief and praxis; and philosophical and theological study."

Outreach to Shi'ites doesn't mean silence about anti-Christian persecution, or reducing contacts with Sunnis. It does suggest, however, efforts to forge ties with Shi'ite leaders, activists, and movements, and to resist the Western tendency to see all Shi'ites through the prism of radical Iraqi cleric Muqtada al-Sadr, or Iran's Revolutionary Guard. For example, Catholics could promote exchanges with Shi'ite institutions in Najaf, Iraq, sometimes seen as a more moderate point of reference alongside Qom for leadership in the Shi'a world. Rising oil revenues in Iran mean Qom is flush, while instability in Iraq has devastated Najaf. (Four senior clerics in Najaf were shot or stabbed to death over two months in the summer of 2007 alone.) These are not either/or choices, and outreach to Najaf does not imply cutting ties with Qom, where Christian scholars are commonly invited for academic exchanges. There is also a standing Catholic–Shi'ite dialogue sponsored by Ampleforth Abbey in York, England; the Heythrop Centre for Christianity and Inter-religious Dialogue at the University of London; and the Imam Khomeini Education and Research Institute in Qom.

5. COMBATING THE "ROOTS OF TERRORISM"

During a December 2004 conference on religious freedom in Rome organized by the United States Embassy to the Holy See, Madigan articulated the view of an influential sector of Catholic opinion on Islam. Referring to terrorist strikes, Madigan said, "They are not simply irrational acts. They have causes that must be understood in their complexity, if we hold out any hope of dealing with them." For observers such as Madigan, one of these causes is underdevelopment and injustice in the Muslim world. If that's the diagnosis, then the cure is to remove the injustices.

John Paul II shared this outlook.

"History shows that the recruitment of terrorists is more easily achieved in areas where human rights are trampled upon and where injustice is a part of daily life," he said in 2002. Responding to terrorism means "new and creative political, diplomatic and economic initiatives aimed at relieving the scandalous situations of gross injustice, oppression and marginalization which continue to oppress countless members of the human family." John Paul added: "The international community can no longer overlook the underlying causes that lead young people especially to despair of humanity, of life itself, and of the future, and to fall prey to the temptations of violence, hatred and desire for revenge at any cost."

That view is sometimes unpopular among Catholics who see it as a form of moral equivocation with regard to violence. Nonetheless, concern for the "roots of terrorism" is widespread among Vatican diplomats and many Catholic bishops, especially in the global South, and it dovetails with the interests of Catholic activists and organizations working on issues of global justice. Three issues seem destined to rise in importance in Catholic politics:

- Peace-making, especially in the Israeli–Palestinian conflict and throughout the Middle East and North Africa.
- Reform in international economic structures, working alongside Muslim governments and activists. In March 2009 *L'Osservatore Romano*, the Vatican newspaper, suggested that principles of Islamic finance could offer the West a model for restructuring the global economy.
- Attention to the marginalization of immigrant groups in the West, especially Muslim immigrants in Europe.

Probable Consequences

1. THE IMPORTANCE OF NIGERIA

As the focus in global Catholic attention shifts to Islam, Nigeria may well emerge as a central point of reference. Nigerian Christians know both the lights and the shadows of living side by side with Muslims, and they will likely put a very different stamp on the global relationship. Nigerian Catholics do not bear the weight of guilt for historical wrongs perpetrated by the West against Muslims; if anything, they perceive themselves as the victims of aggressive "Islamicization." As a result, there's a greater willingness among Nigerian Catholic leaders to assert their interests, and to insist that dialogue must be a two-way street.

Archbishop John Onaiyekan of Abuja believes that a central weakness of the Church's approach to Islam is that it has been overly dependent on Catholics from the Middle East, most of whom grew up in tiny Christian communities surrounded by an overwhelming Muslim majority. In such a context, Onaiyekan says, these Catholics developed fairly minimal expectations of their Muslim neighbors—"As long as they aren't killing us," as he put it, "everything's okay." In his view, that's setting the bar far too low. Catholics must insist that Muslims accept religious freedom as a matter of principle, he said, not merely as a grudging gesture of second-class citizenship. In the spring of 2007, Onaiyekan took part in a dialogue with leadership of the National Mosque in Abuja where one of the Muslim leaders argued that Christians should not feel threatened by Shariah because they too would have rights in Shariah courts. "That's not a right we want," Onaiyekan shot back. "It's not a right we accept."

That spirit, which reflects a situation of rough social equality, is likely to inform Catholic attitudes in the twenty-first century to a greater degree. The rising importance of Africa in global Catholicism also means that African instincts on many questions, including relations with Islam, will be more influential.

2. RISING THEOLOGICAL INTEREST: CHURCH–STATE SEPARATION

No question is being driven to the top of the theological agenda by the rise of Islam with greater urgency than what Christians call church–state relations, meaning the proper relationship between religious communities and the civil authorities. Debate over Shariah pivots on precisely this point: To what extent should the state enforce religious precepts, especially when many citizens don't share them? Western voices often say that abandoning the idea of civil enforcement of Islamic law is the price Muslims must pay for admission to a pluralistic world, while Muslims often insist that Westerners will never understand Islam until they grasp its fundamental drive toward governing all the affairs of the *ummah,* meaning the Islamic community, according to the principles of the Qur'an.

Trying to reconcile these two positions will be perhaps the primordial challenge in Muslim–Christian relations in the twenty-first century, and in this regard some experts believe the United States could play an important role.

There are roughly four million Muslims in the country, yet most observers believe American Islamic communities by and large have not developed the extremist subcultures familiar in England and France. Though it's impossible to say for sure why not, one possible factor is the impact of the culture of religious pluralism in the United States, in which religious communities have flourished without entanglement with the state. American Catholic legal analyst Kevin Seamus Hasson, president of the Becket Fund for Religious Liberty, lays out the argument this way: At the Second Vatican Council, American Catholics led the way for the universal Church toward a new understanding of religious freedom, enshrined in the declaration *Dignitatis humanae.* Perhaps American Muslims can make an analogous contribution to the global Islamic debate. Since Catholics have walked this path before, Hasson says, they may be in a special position to encourage American Muslims to find their voice.

Imam Shamsi Ali of New York's Islamic Cultural Center thinks Hasson has it right.

"Aside from a small minority, most Muslims have bought into the American approach," he said in 2007. "We don't have to formalize Islam publicly. We live Shariah here better than Muslims in many other places where it's supposedly the law."

3. RISING THEOLOGICAL INTEREST: "JUST WAR"

Church leaders and theologians will be challenged in the twenty-first century to develop a theology of armed force that does justice to the reality of the threat posed by Islamic radicalism, but at the same time sets limits to morally dubious conflicts justified in the name of that threat. Under John Paul II, the older repertoire of the "just war" tradition, which presumed a context of two states locked in conflict, was supplemented by the new language of "humanitarian intervention," which presumed a situation of an aggrieved minority requiring international assistance. Neither seems fully adequate to the new realities of the twenty-first century, in which the primary actors are mobile and transnational terrorist networks.

To date, Catholic reflection has been strongest as a *via negativa,* marking out what cannot be done. Tobias Winright of St. Louis University, for example, says that Catholic social doctrine has developed a set of apparently exceptionless norms *in bello,* referring to the conduct of war. He cited bans on targeting noncombatants, the use of torture, arbitrary imprisonment, and "indiscriminate" bombings of whole cities or widely dispersed areas. What seems to be missing is an equally clear and practical set of concepts about what can be done that would be both effective and moral. Ideally, such reflection could be carried out with Christian and Muslim scholars together, each drawing on the resources of their own traditions, groping toward a consensus that could enjoy the broad acceptance of reasonable people on both sides.

4. TENSIONS IN JEWISH–CATHOLIC RELATIONS

The centrality of Islam to the Catholic imagination will likely be a mixed bag in terms of relations with Jews. Islamic-inspired terrorism is creating a new sympathy for Israel, which may balance a perceived pro-Palestinian tilt in Vatican diplomacy and in international Catholic opinion. As Catholicism seeks better understanding of the Islamic world, some Church figures will turn for insight to Jewish leaders and thinkers, who have a long experience, if not always a positive one, of living side-by-side with Muslims. Efforts to promote the religious freedom of Christians in the Islamic world may also be of benefit to Jewish communities.

On the other hand, the focus on Islam will amplify the voice of local Catholic churches in the Muslim world, and because these churches are mostly ethnically Arab, they tend to be strongly critical of Israel and of alleged Jewish influence on American foreign policy. Especially among the Catholic left in Europe, efforts to combat the "roots of terrorism" will often translate into political sympathy for Muslims against Western interests, including Israel.

All of this occurs amid five broad shifts in Catholic attitudes toward Judaism.

First, "evangelical Catholicism" implies a reassertion of traditional Catholic beliefs and practices, coupled with robust public proclamation of Catholic identity. As a result, Church leaders are increasingly less inclined to down-play aspects of Catholic identity that might awaken Jewish sensitivities. For example, while Catholicism will not engage in organized campaigns of proselytism, Church leaders are less timid about asserting that Christ is the lone savior of the world and that his message is meant for all, including the Jews. Concern for Jewish reaction did not stop Benedict XVI from reviving the old Latin Mass, including a controversial Good Friday prayer for the conversion of Jews (though that prayer was redacted), and it's unlikely to stop the Vatican from eventually declaring Pope Pius XII a saint. The point of these gestures is not to irritate Jewish opinion; but concern for Jewish opinion (or anyone else's) is less likely these days to stop the Church from being itself.

Second, a generational shift is under way. The European pioneers of Catholic–Jewish relations, for whom the living memory of the Holocaust is a powerful motivating force, are passing from the scene. The new cohort re-mains committed to the cause, but its leaders may not feel the same sense of personal moral obligation. Catholic leaders from the global South don't carry the same sense of historical responsibility for the Holocaust, which they are more likely to see as a dark chapter of Western, rather than Chris-tian, history.

Third, the demographic shift in Catholicism away from Europe and, to a lesser extent, North America, means that increasingly leadership will be coming from regions where Catholic–Jewish relations yield pride of place to dialogue with other traditions, especially Islam and the religions of Asia. Catholic leaders from Africa, Asia, and Latin America are less likely to have personal experience of Judaism, and they preside over local churches where Judaism is not an important sociological presence. Their interfaith priorities lie elsewhere.

Fourth, Benedict XVI's preference for intercultural rather than interreligious dialogue, placing the accent on social and political cooperation rather than strictly theological encounter, may also drive Catholic–Jewish ties down the list of concerns. Judaism may be Christianity's most important relationship theologically, but it doesn't pack the same cultural punch around the world as does Islam, say, or Hinduism.

Fifth, there is a growing sense among some Catholic leaders, albeit one they're usually reluctant to voice out loud, that overtures from the Catholic side are not always matched by a similar spirit among some Jews. When Benedict XVI visited Israel in 2009, for example, his speech at the Yad Vashem Holocaust memorial drew strident criticism from some Jewish commentators because it failed to condemn Christian anti-Semitism and because the pope did not express regret for lifting the excommunication of a Holocaust-denying bishop—even though Benedict had made both points repeatedly on other occasions. As Cardinal Walter Kasper, the Vatican's top official for relations with Jews, put it after the Yad Vashem controversy: "There seems to be an attitude of, 'That's good, but it's not enough.' "

For all these reasons, the twenty-first century will likely see an evolution in Jewish–Catholic relations, away from the experience of the Holocaust and European anti-Semitism as the primary focal points of conversation. Leaders in relations with Judaism will find themselves pressed to develop a new logic for the relationship and a new agenda for theological, cultural, and political interaction.

5. PARTNERSHIPS WITH MUSLIMS IN THE "CULTURE WARS"

One area where Catholics and Muslims will certainly find themselves in agreement comes with the culture wars, especially abortion and homosexuality. The Vatican and Islamic nations collaborated on these issues during United Nations conferences in Cairo in 1994 on population, and Beijing in 1995 on women. In Cairo, the Vatican and a bloc of both Islamic and Latin

American states lobbied successfully to delete a reference to "sexual rights" in the final document, and to avoid a reference to "other unions" besides marriage. In Beijing in 1995, a conference on women ended with a proclamation that women should be able to "control all aspects of their health, in particular their own fertility," but once again stopped short of new legal recognition of either abortion or homosexuality. The joint efforts of the Vatican and Islamic nations in this regard were dubbed an "unholy alliance" by critics.

As the twenty-first century develops, these issues are hardly likely to recede in importance, especially the question of legal protection for homosexuality. These debates will create opportunities for Muslims and Catholics to collaborate. To take just two small examples, in early November 2006, Jewish, Muslim, and Christian clerics joined forces in Jerusalem to block a scheduled Gay Pride parade. In 1996, the late Cardinal Maurice Otunga, archbishop of Nairobi, and the senior Muslim cleric in Kenya burned condoms together in a public park, as a way of expressing common cause against a proposed "safe sex" program in Kenya schools.

More broadly, the Catholic Church and Islamic leaders in the West are likely to find themselves shoulder-to-shoulder in defending the right of religious communities to express themselves in public debates. In this sense, the growing secularization of the West, above all Europe, may actually prove to be a positive force in interfaith relationships. In 1996, Boston College philosophy professor Peter Kreeft published a book making the case for just such an interreligious partnership. In that pre-9/11 age, Kreeft gave his book the provocative title of *Ecumenical Jihad*. He argued that the Vatican–Islamic alliance at Cairo and Beijing was "a greater victory with Islam than the Battle of Lepanto was against it."

6. CHRISTIAN ATHEISTS

Conventional wisdom has it that "there are no atheists in foxholes." In truth, atheists can be found even in foxholes, but often they're atheists whose deepest yearning is to be wrong. In just that spirit, among people who believe that Western civilization today is locked in mortal combat with radical Islam, there's a growing contingent of what we might call "Christian atheists," meaning nonbelievers nonetheless committed to a strong defense of Christian culture. Examples include the German philosopher Jurgen Habermas and the late Italian journalist and intellectual Oriana Fallaci.

Habermas describes himself as a secular atheist, yet in a 2004 essay he declared: "Christianity, and nothing else, is the ultimate foundation of liberty, conscience, human rights, and democracy, the benchmarks of Western civilization. To this day, we have no other options [to Christianity]. We continue to nourish ourselves from this source. Everything else is idle postmodern chatter."

Likewise, Fallaci's credentials as a nonbeliever were never in doubt. She once defined Christianity as "a beautiful fable," and wrote: "I'm tired of having to repeat, in writing and also orally, that I'm an atheist. In addition to being a secularist, I'm also profoundly anti-clerical. Priests don't sit well with me." Yet a colleague of Fallaci and a fellow nonbeliever, Italian journalist Vittorio Feltri, summed up her position during a panel devoted to Fallaci at the 2007 meeting of the Catholic movement Communion and Liberation in Rimini, Italy: "All of us have been shaped by a Christian culture. Facing a threat from the outside, and we all know where it comes from, we have to rally around our culture, which is the culture of Christianity, even if in the end we can't bring ourselves to believe in God, except perhaps, every now and then, at night. This was Fallaci's argument, and I share it from the first word to the very last."

Bishop Rino Fisichella, rector of Rome's Lateran University and an intimate of Pope Benedict XVI, befriended Fallaci and gave her a deathbed blessing. He explained why he did so during the Rimini panel: "I held Oriana Fallaci's hand as a priest, as a bishop, asking the Lord to look upon her with great mercy, if for no other reason than that she suffered so greatly, because she was so alone, and because in her last years, radically and with deep conviction, she defended the idea that this country belongs to the West. She defended like few others the profoundly Christian roots of the civilization to which we all belong, including the faith that, let's not forget, God forever offers to us as a great gift. We have to remember this woman for what she did, for what she said and wrote. She was a great woman, a great Italian, who deserves to be viewed with respect, and who now belongs to the history books."

This budding détente between institutional Christianity and some of its sharpest Enlightenment-inspired critics, motivated by a deep sense of shared peril, is likely to gain strength as long as radical Islam is perceived as a serious threat.

Possible Consequences

1. REVIVAL OF CHRISTIAN IDENTITY IN EUROPE

Paradoxically, concerns about Islamic immigration may help revive the flagging spiritual energies of European Christianity. Philip Jenkins believes that the specter of a rising Islamic tide is fueling a rediscovery of traditional markers of English identity such as St. George's Day. Similar stirrings can be glimpsed elsewhere. In 2007, Christian books were selling at all-time high levels in Holland, and a "prayer-in-the-workplace" movement has been surprisingly popular. Crucifixes have been reintroduced to Catholic schools in the country, and school Masses, which were formerly empty, are now well attended. In the same year, *Der Spiegel* ran a story about religious revival in Germany headlined RELIGION, BORN AGAIN.

It would be a mistake, experts warn, to overinterpret these developments. A good deal of it is informed by the politics of Muslim immigration rather than a genuine spiritual awakening. Such sentiment could also fuel the growth of far-right movements; in England, for example, the revival of St. George's Day has been enthusiastically embraced by the right-wing British National Party. Despite those caveats, it's possible that as Islamic immigration continues to redefine the sociology of Europe, it will have the contradictory effect of, at the same time, making the continent more sensitive to religious pluralism, and at the same time prompting Europeans to take a new, and more appreciative, look at their Christian roots.

2. CATHOLIC–FEMINIST ALLIANCES

As counterintuitive as it may seem, during the twenty-first century Catholics and feminists may end up making common cause in demanding that Islamic societies show greater respect for women. Already, when it comes to human rights issues for women in many Islamic societies—the right to vote, for example, or to pursue an education, the right to equal treatment under the law, or the protection of women who have abandoned Islam—the Catholic Church and feminist organizations often find themselves on the same side of the fence.

In 2002, for example, Cardinal Anthony Olubunmi Okogie of Nigeria became something of a hero in feminist circles when he volunteered to take the place of a Muslim woman, Safiya Hussaini, who had been sentenced to death by stoning by a Shariah court for the crime of adultery. (The ruling was eventually reversed and Hussaini relocated to Italy.) In other such cases, such as that of Lina Joy in Malaysia, Catholic and feminist leaders have joined forces. In 2007, the German diocese of Hildesheim offered a model legal contract they recommended that Catholic women demand their Muslim fiancés sign before marriage, to protect their rights on matters such as financial autonomy, custody of children, and the bias in favor of men in divorce cases. The contract reflected critiques that many secular European feminist groups had also issued, and it won praise from several feminist leaders in Germany.

To be sure, this alliance is fragile. The prime concern for Catholic leaders is usually religious freedom, while for Western feminists it often includes "reproductive rights." Nevertheless, this marriage of convenience offers an intriguing example of how sometimes a change in context, rather than a change of heart, is all it takes to reconfigure political allegiances.

3. ANGLICAN–MUSLIM DIALOGUE

The Anglican Communion could emerge as an important axis for Muslim–Christian conversation in the twenty-first century. Anglicanism is the center of Christianity's most anguished, and most public, debates over questions of authority. Somewhat like Islam, the Anglican Communion has a few symbolic points of reference, especially the Archbishop of Canterbury, but no real central authority. Both traditions struggle to rule out aberrations in doctrine or discipline as illegitimate, because always the question arises: "Who says?"

Trends generating the crisis of authority in the two communities are, of course, wildly different. For Anglicans, the issue is homosexual bishops and the blessing of homosexual unions, while for Muslims it's terrorism. But the underlying issue of authority is much the same: both traditions have a problem saying, "That's not who we are."

Prospects for fruitful Anglican–Muslim exchange may be enhanced by the fact that it tends to be African Anglicans calling for stronger authority in opposition to what they see as heterodox stances in the North. African Anglicans could lead an exchange with Muslims around the same issues. Whether confessional rivalries and identity pressures on both sides would permit such a development to take place is difficult to say, but it's an intriguing possibility.

4. SUPPORT FOR INDIA

In light of the rise of radical Islam, many Western voices these days are calling for greater strategic partnerships with India. Writer Christopher Hitchens, for example, has proposed "a strong, open alliance with India on all fronts, from the military to the political and economic, backed by an extensive cultural exchange program, to demonstrate solidarity with the other great multiethnic democracy under attack from Muslim fascism." One of former president George W. Bush's few foreign policy breakthroughs was reversing decades of tension between the United States and India, forging a new partnership that saw India contribute troops to the U.S.-led campaign in Afghanistan.

Though Catholics are less than 2 percent of the Indian population, while Muslims are 13 percent, by 2050 Indian Catholics should still number around 26 million, placing India among the top twenty Catholic nations on earth. Given that, the Catholic community in India could become an important voice in the global Church with regard to Islam. Some experts say, however, that for this to happen, Indian Catholics themselves will need to take a stronger interest in Christian–Muslim relations. At present, local observers say, most Indian Catholic theological energy is directed at relationships with the great religious traditions of East Asia, principally Hinduism and Buddhism, leaving relatively little time and energy for any concentration on Islam.

Long-Shot Consequences

1. A WILD CARD: BLOWING UP SAINT PETER'S

From time to time, Italian police sources announce heightened security measures around Saint Peter's Square in light of reports that radical Islamic terrorists might be considering a strike against the symbolic heart of Western Christianity. Other rumored targets have included Westminster Abbey in England, Santiago de Compostela in Spain, the Duomo in Milan, Italy, and Notre Dame in Paris. To date nothing of the sort has happened, but no one can rule it out.

If Islamic-inspired terrorists blew the dome off St. Peter's, the consequence could be an immediate radicalization of Christian opinion, and could even lead to the formation of armed cells of Christians ready to take the fight to Muslims. Lest that scenario be dismissed as fantasy, it's worth recalling that this is exactly what happened in Nigeria. After a series of Muslim-led riots in the 1980s, bands of Christian youth organized themselves into militias. Although members took pledges to act only in self-defense, leaders admit that the zero-sum logic of combat quickly led them to take the offensive. James Wuye, the Nigerian pastor and ex-militia leader, admitted that his group once blew up a bridge in a Christian area and blamed it on Muslims in order to have a pretext for an attack. A strike at a cherished Christian symbol could produce this reaction on a mass scale, armed with much more lethal weaponry.

Nor is an attack on a Christian building the only such scenario. It's also possible that Islamic radicals might try to kill the pope, and once again this is more than speculation. In 1995, a group led by the Kuwaiti radical Ramzi Yousef, one of the architects of the 1993 World Trade Center bombings, planned to assassinate Pope John Paul II while he was in Manila for World Youth Day. On January 15, 1995, a suicide bomber was supposed to dress up as a priest while John Paul II passed in his motorcade. The plot fell apart after a fire broke out in the apartment of one of the terrorists, where police found maps with routes plotting the papal motorcade, a rosary, a photograph of the pope, Bibles, and clerical garb including robes and Roman collars.

If such a plot should eventually succeed, all bets would be off in terms of where the Catholic–Muslim relationship might go.

2. A NORTH–SOUTH CLASH OF CIVILIZATIONS

Let's suppose for a moment that those who predict a Muslim democracy movement are right, and that at some point in the twenty-first century Islamic radicalism declines. If Islam makes its peace with pluralism, what then?

One possible scenario is that impoverished Southern Christians and impoverished Southern Muslims might conclude that their poverty unites them more than their religion divides them. In that case, the real "clash of civilizations" in the post-modern world might turn out to pivot on the North–South divide, not the one between the West and Islam. Politically, Southern Christians and Southern Muslims already have much in common. They tend to be anti-American, anti-globalization, and pro-Palestinian, and they also share a dislike of Northern secularization and what both regard as a weak sense of personal morality. Both tend to see themselves as the victim of structural economic injustice and neocolonialism. All that could make for a powerful Southern coalition.

If things develop in this direction, the "rise of Islam" that matters in the twenty-first century would no longer be radical terrorists, but mainstream political activists working in concert with hundreds of millions of aggrieved Southern Christians, pushing a sweeping reform of international economic and political systems. Ironically, the demise of the Islamic radicals could produce a global realignment far more radical than anything they dared dream.

3. A NEW THEOLOGICAL EVALUATION OF ISLAM

The post–World War II period saw a remarkable evolution in Catholic attitudes toward Judaism. Once Jews were seen as the people who had spurned Christ, and Christianity was seen as the revelation that had superseded Judaism. Today, Catholics typically regard Jews as "elder brothers in the faith" whose covenant with God remains eternally valid. While that shift has not solved all the theological and political problems between the two communities, it's a dramatic change in a brief arc of time.

In one sense, the situation with Islam is far more complicated. Christianity emerged out of Judaism and regards Jewish scripture and law as part of its own tradition, a stance it does not take with regard to Islam. Historically, many Christian writers have regarded Islam as a Christian heresy; others have taken Islam as a "scourge of God," a form of divine chastisement for Christians who lost their way.

It's possible, however, that if Catholic–Muslim theological dialogue deepens, and if Catholics and Muslims forge partnerships against secularization and what Benedict XVI calls the "dictatorship of relativism," a more positive theological evaluation might emerge. During his trip to the Middle East in 2009, Benedict XVI recalled that he was among the cofounders of the Foundation for Interreligious and Intercultural Research and Dialogue, a Swiss institute that promotes "trilateral" dialogue among Jews, Muslims, and Christians—in effect, a recognition that Christianity has ties with both the two faiths that run deeper than other interreligious relationships.

What might a new theological evaluation of Islam look like?

Muslims could come to be seen as "younger brothers in the faith," whose revelation in the Qur'an and in various oral traditions is not regarded as of the same order as the Old and New Testaments, but nonetheless enjoys a status different from the sacred texts of other religions. Muhammad could come to be seen as a legitimate "prophet," not in the precise sense that Islamic theology attaches to the term, but in the broader Christian view of prophets as religious and moral reformers. (Imagine what impact it might have on Christian–Muslim relations, for example, if popes were to use the formula "the prophet Muhammad.") At the moment, such an evolution is difficult to anticipate, but a century is a long time. Before World War II, recent innovations in Jewish–Catholic relations would have been difficult to predict.

From a Catholic point of view, there's an additional incentive for moving in this direction that does not apply in the same way to Jews. Though all three monotheistic religions in a sense sprang from a Middle Eastern matrix, both Christianity and Judaism grew up in the West. Whatever problems Jews have had with Christians, it is generally not because Jews conflate Christianity with the Western powers. Because Islam has developed largely outside the West, however, both its leaders and its "street" struggle to make distinctions between Christianity as a religious system and Western nations as a political force. A deeper degree of theological understanding might make this distinction more clear.

THE NEW DEMOGRAPHY

Back in the mid-1980s, I worked at George Mason University in northern Virginia as an events planner. At the time, interdisciplinary studies were all the rage, and so the university decided to try an experiment in exchange across departmental boundaries. Each year they would ask everyone in the university community to read the same book, and then to come together for conversation about the issues it raised. While I never quite understood who picked the books or what criteria they used (as a lowly member of the non-teaching staff, I didn't have to), it nonetheless struck me as a largely commendable effort to cajole people out of the ghettoes of hyperspecialization.

One year, the title was *The Handmaid's Tale* by Canadian novelist Margaret Atwood, which I dutifully purchased and read. The story envisions a near-term future in which the United States has collapsed following a nuclear war, and in its stead, in Massachusetts of all places, a far-right theocracy has arisen called the Republic of Gilead. The resulting society is a feminist's nightmare: women are strictly controlled, unable to have jobs or money and assigned to highly segregated classes. At the top of the female pecking order are the chaste, childless "Wives" of senior government officials and other VIPs; then come the housekeeping "Marthas"; and finally the reproductive "Handmaids," the few women still fertile after fallout from the nuclear blast, who copulate with their masters (in as chaste a manner as possible, under the circumstances), and then turn their precious offspring over to be raised by the "morally fit" Wives. The book was later made into a fairly bland movie starring Natasha Richardson and Robert Duvall.

At the time, I regarded the novel as an entertaining bit of feminist agit-prop, a hyperbolic cautionary tale about what a society run by the Phyllis Schlaflys and Jerry Falwells of the world might look like. Today many elements of the novel still seem overwrought, but its identification of "fertility panic" as one of the deep currents that would shape the future of Western societies turned out to be stunningly prescient. (In fact, if we set *The Handmaid's Tale* alongside other contemporary novels such as P. D. James's *The Children of Men*, there's actually a budding genre of low-fertility dystopias.) Even in the absence of a nuclear war, fertility rates have never before fallen so low, so fast, and as comprehensively as they did in the late twentieth century, creating widespread alarm about a "birth dearth." It turns out that the century's major demographic crusade, the much-ballyhooed effort to stem global overpopulation, succeeded beyond anyone's wildest dreams.

Demographers tell us that the Total Fertility Rate needed to maintain a stable population is 2.1 children for each woman who has completed her childbearing years. That's the number of children it takes for a woman to replace herself with a female who will live to the age of childbearing, taking into account that slightly more boys than girls are born, and that not all children survive. Among statisticians, the number 2.1 is considered "replacement level." The most authoritative source for monitoring fertility rates is the United Nations Population Division (which is not, by the way, affiliated with the United Nations Population Fund, accused by critics of advocating abortion and contraception—the Population Division just crunches numbers). The Population Division reports that over the period 1950–55, the global fertility rate averaged 5.02, well above replacement level. The rate has gone down in every subsequent five-year period, reaching 2.65 today, meaning that it's been cut almost in half.

That number, it should be stressed, is a global average that masks considerable diversity. In general, fertility rates are higher in developing countries, especially in Africa, and substantially lower in affluent nations in the North as well as some countries in Asia and Latin America. Projecting current trends as far out as 2040, the Population Division foresees a fertility rate well below replacement level worldwide, which should "bottom out" at around 1.85. The future is now, however, for 42.8 percent of the world's population, which as of 2004 was already living in nations whose fertility rate had dropped below replacement level.

Let's take a couple of examples.

Not long ago, the official family planning motto for Singapore, reflecting fears of runaway population growth, was, "Stop at Two!" Since it has the fourth-highest level of population density on earth, behind Monaco, Macau, and Hong Kong, Singapore is especially sensitive to population swings. Today, with a fertility rate of 1.3, Singapore's new catchphrase is instead "Three or More!" Stung by fears of a rapidly aging society and a consequent loss of economic competitiveness, the state now runs its own matchmaking service to try to promote marriage and child-rearing, complete with carefully choreographed seven-minute encounters between potential mates.

Or consider the case of Turkey, where pro-Islamist prime minister Recep Tayyip Erdogan has lambasted widespread use of contraception as "straight-out treason to the state," and has informed the Turks that "Allah wills" more babies. Despite his fervor, Turkey's fertility rate is at 2.31, and the UN Population Division expects it to drop below replacement level by 2020—another sense in which, whether Europeans like it or not, Turkey is drawing ever closer to Europe.

Experts call this the "Second Demographic Transition." The first came with a dramatic drop in infant mortality toward the end of the eighteenth century, which fueled the modern population explosion. Western Europe, for example, doubled its population from 60 million in 1750 to 120 million in 1850. Such unprecedented growth gave rise, among other things, to the modern science of demographics: for the first time, academics started wondering what makes population levels rise and fall. To be honest, they were mostly interested in what makes them rise, since that's what was happening at the time. In his *Essay on the Principle of Population*, Thomas Malthus predicted that population would increase relentlessly in geometric fashion, producing mass famine and eventual anarchy. Things in the field of futurology, alas, have not improved measurably since his day.

Contrary to Malthus's expectations, today's transition cuts sharply in the opposite direction, toward enduring levels of lower fertility. An alternative, and more popular, name for what's happening is "The New Demography." Whatever we call it, it means that sometime in the twenty-first century the world will begin depopulating, a phenomenon that has already hit Western Europe and Japan. (The United States, for reasons to be explored later, is likely to be something of an exception.) How far and how fast population will drop remains to be seen. The UN's "low scenario," which assumes that fertility rates will stabilize at 1.85 and stay there, puts the global population in 2300 at 2.3 billion, which would be a stunning decline by more than three quarters from where population levels are estimated to peak in the second half of the twenty-first century, around 9 billion.

Such dramatic implosion is improbable, and what actually transpires will be influenced by a host of economic, political, and cultural factors, most of which are impossible to anticipate. Fertility rates are not mechanical; they're shaped by human choices. What we can say for sure is this: by now, declining fertility has been around long enough to make some population contraction, especially in the developed world, a mathematical certainty. Ultra-Catholic Italy, for example, produced a million live births in 1960; today the annual average is just over 500,000. With a current fertility rate of 1.28, Italy is projected by the UN to lose almost a fifth of its current population of 57 million by 2050, a drop-off to rival the impact of the medieval Black Plague.

This topsy-turvy demographic picture is part of what's turning the Catholic Church upside down in the twenty-first century.

WHAT'S HAPPENING

In the first half of the twenty-first century, population will grow across most of the global South (dramatically in some places, above all sub-Saharan Africa) and will fall in most of the North (again, dramatically in some places, above all Europe and Japan). More than 95 percent of the world's population increase will happen in developing countries, nearly all in rapidly expanding urban areas. In the short term, meaning the next thirty-five years or so, this promises a stark contrast between a young South and an old North. One index of the difference is that half of the world's population today is under the age of twenty-four, but 90 percent of those under twenty-four live in the global South. This demographic reality promises to exacerbate differences that already divide North from South, such as race, class, and worldview.

But at mid-century, something else will happen.

After leveling out at 9 billion sometime around 2050, the population of the planet will begin to fall, and will do so with increasing momentum throughout the rest of the century. It will do so because fertility is falling in much of the South today too, but the downward slope in the South began later and from a higher point of departure, so it's taking a bit longer for the bottom to fall out. In the 2004 edition of its population estimates, the United Nations Population Division described declining fertility as "almost a universal phenomenon."

What might happen farther down the road, say after 2100, is anybody's guess. Some expect that fertility rates will return to replacement levels and that the global population will hold steady or experience mild growth, while others think the drop-off will remain prolonged and severe. What we know for sure is that by the time today's twenty-year-olds reach retirement age, the population of the world will be contracting. The decline will be most aggravated in Europe and parts of Asia, including China, which could lose 20 to 30 percent of its population every generation beginning around mid-century.

Declining fertility, coupled with the aging of the "baby boom" generation, means the elderly will be the fastest-growing segment of the global population, leading to substantial increases in the median age in most countries.

In its 2005 report *Taking Care: Ethical Caregiving in Our Aging Society,* the President's Council on Bioethics reached this sobering conclusion: "In the years ahead, the age structure of most advanced industrial societies will be unlike anything previously seen in human history, with both the average age of the population and the absolute number of old people increasing dramatically." While the North will get old first (one might be tempted to call us "prematurely gray"), the rest of the world will eventually catch up. By mid-century both Mexico and China will actually be more "gray" than the United States.

Causes

Identifying the cause of this slide in fertility is the $64,000 question among demographers, sociologists, and cultural theorists of all stripes. In a 2004 analysis, the United Nations Population Division cited the following factors: "Increased infant and child survival, greater access to education and health services especially for women, expanded access and use of effective contraception methods combined with changes in individual and parental aspirations, increased women empowerment and participation in the market economy."

While all of the above no doubt play a role, it still begs the question of what underlying force is responsible for this constellation of trends. Perhaps the most persuasive sound bite comes from Ben Wattenberg, author of *Fewer* and America's leading amateur demographer: "Capitalism is the best contraception."

What Wattenberg means is that by encouraging transitions from the countryside to the city, and from agriculture to manufacturing, the Industrial Revolution fundamentally altered the economics of the human family, transforming children into a liability instead of an asset. On the farm, children pay for themselves through increased production. In cities, kids become a net drain on resources. Phillip Longman, another writer on demographic trends, cites a 2001 study from the U.S. Department of Agriculture which calculated the cost of raising a middle-class child from birth to age seventeen in the United States today, taking account both of direct expenditures and the opportunity cost of the mother's lost wages, bypassed promotions, and so on. The total? A staggering *$1.03 million*. That's before the parents have spent a cent on college tuition, which today averages almost $10,000 a year for a state university and $24,000 in a private institution. Under those circumstances, it's not hard to figure out why many Americans limit the number of children they have.

By vastly increasing the supply of consumer goods, capitalist systems also encourage people to spend more of their wealth on consumption rather than child-rearing. Wattenberg tells the story of Hungary, where a popular saying in the 1960s put the choice for young couples in stark terms: *kichi vod kochi*, which means, "kid or car." The American equivalent might be found in Enid Charles's classic 1934 book, *The Twilight of Parenthood*, in which she wrote that, "Statistics clearly show that the choice between a Ford and a baby is usually made in favor of the Ford." One sociological study in Brazil found that birthrates in the country fell across the country region by region in tandem with the introduction of television, which exposed Brazilians to a consumer-driven lifestyle, especially in the popular *telenovellas*, or soap operas. One can't push such a finding too far, given the danger of a post hoc fallacy; it may be that the advent of TV, rather than actually causing anything, was simply a measure of rising affluence. Still, as a rough indicator, it's interesting.

Further, the need for income in a market economy encourages more women to enter the workplace, making it difficult to have children and creating incentives for smaller families. Finally, capitalist systems provide parents with no direct "payoff" for their investment of raising children. All of us benefit if Mr. and Mrs. Smith raise the child who cures cancer, but

Mr. and Mrs. Smith don't receive any payout for doing so. Three other twentieth-century innovations—easily available contraception, the growing social acceptability of divorce, and pensions that provide for security in old age without a large family—sealed the deal. Ironically, it turns out Marx may have been right all along when he predicted that capitalism would sow the seeds of its own decline, though not exactly for the reasons he thought.

Fertility Anxiety

As is always the case with rapid social change, the decline in fertility has induced considerable anxiety. Social conservatives see it as the ultimate reductio ad absurdum of a "pleasure principle" morality that separates sexual gratification from reproduction, leading to a sort of collective cultural suicide. Economists fret about how economic growth can be sustained, since from the beginning of the Industrial Revolution, boom cycles have always coincided with expanding populations that create a growing base of producers and consumers. Who will invest in, manufacture, and purchase the widgets of the future, when the consumer base for widgets and everything else is steadily shrinking? This is not merely speculation; one prominent Japanese economist has called his country's downturn in the 1990s "the world's first low birthrate recession," attributable to a declining consumer base and an excessive savings rate characteristic of an aging population. Meanwhile, military strategists worry about how a declining population will be able to sustain defense expenditures and to field armies, and whether volatility in population will trigger realignments in power relationships. Virtually everyone wonders how an increasingly "gray" society will be able to afford pensions and health care. In 2000, the cost of long-term institutional care in the United States was $137 billion, and in 2040 that figure could be $346 billion.

Granted, some of this hand-wringing is informed by an ideological agenda. Cultural conservatives, including many Catholics, are inclined to emphasize the downside of declining fertility because it bolsters their case against contraception, abortion, divorce, and a catalogue of other perceived social ills. Military hawks are always prowling for the next threat to justify high levels of defense spending, and fear of being outbred by potential enemies is a time-honored rhetorical instrument. If the truth be told, this may be largely an empty threat. Since the "other" right now is Islamic radicalism, it's worth noting that the sharpest drops in fertility anywhere on the planet today are in the Middle East. Demographer Youssef Courbage believes that the fertility rate for the region will fall to 2.08 in 2020, below replacement level. In 100 years, Philip Jenkins predicts, the most successful grassroots movement in the Middle East may not be Hamas or Hezbollah, but the AARP!

Some analysts think lower global fertility will bring blessings. Writing in the *New Statesman* in 2002, Anthony Browne augured that declining populations "will involve a gradual but significant redistribution from the owners of capital to the owners of labor." Companies will be compelled, Browne theorized, to train the unskilled, and to accommodate both mothers and the elderly in order to keep them working. Workers will be able to command higher salaries for their labor. In other words, Browne sees a "demographic dividend" for the working class. It's a plausible scenario, though it overlooks the fact that declining population may mean declining economic growth, which could make jobs harder to find. As swelling populations of retirees spend down their savings, the amount of capital available for investment and job creation could dwindle.

However one interprets the data, frisson about fertility is undeniably a sign of the times. Few forces have greater potential to alter the course of history than sharp fluctuations in population, both in terms of raw numbers and also distribution. As Auguste Comte once said, "Demography is destiny." Empires rise and fall, social systems mutate and disintegrate, on the basis of such currents. Religions also expand and contract. Sociologist Rodney Stark argues that early Christianity grew because Christians had higher fertility rates than pagans and were less inclined to infanticide. In the West, we are already living in an older, shrinking society, and that reality presents challenges all across the board, from education to medicine, from investment and savings to politics and pop culture.

The Global Picture

1. EUROPE

If declining fertility is a by-product of modernity, it's no surprise that it crested first in Europe. In 1957, when the European Union was founded, every one of the twenty-seven nations that are now EU members had fertility rates above 2.1. Today, not one of them does. All told, between now and 2050, Europe both East and West is projected by the United Nations Population Division to drop from 728 million people to 590 million, a loss of 131 million people. Yet as the failure of Malthus's projection reminds us, fertility rates do not follow laws of geometric inevitability. Europe could still stage a recovery and mitigate the dramatic demographic contraction sketched here. As of this writing, there was some evidence that such a recovery might be stirring, at least in some parts of the continent. Revisions in 2008 to UN population projections found a greater than expected rebound in European fertility levels, though they remain below the replacement rate.

A piece in *The Economist* on June 16, 2007, found that demographically speaking, there are really two Europes. One stretches from the Mediterranean through Central and Eastern Europe, and is characterized by fertility rates of 1.5 or below. These countries are caught in a "fertility trap," meaning that below-replacement fertility has become the new family pattern, resulting in a widespread embrace of one-child and childless families. The other Europe runs from Scandinavia to France, and has fertility rates around 1.8, much closer to replacement, and trending upward in some places. France, Denmark, and Ireland today have the highest fertility rates in the EU. In these countries, older women are having children at rates almost high enough to compensate for lower fertility among younger women. If these trends hold, somewhere around mid-century France will surpass Germany as Europe's largest nation. Great Britain's population will rise 15 percent by 2050.

What accounts for the difference? Conventional theories don't seem to work. The high-fertility tier includes thoroughly secularized nations such as France, and less secularized ones such as Ireland. It includes nations that dole out generous benefits to families with children, such as Sweden and France, and ones that do not, such as Great Britain.

The Economist suggested an explanation that, if true, would amount to an enormous historical irony. It's those nations that have most thoroughly rejected the traditional norm of two-parent monogamous marriage, it hypothesized, that are reproducing at the highest levels. In Northern Europe and France, the social stigma once attached to birth outside of marriage is almost completely gone. France removed the category of "illegitimacy" from its official documents in 2005, and in Sweden today, 55 percent of all births are out of wedlock. By affirming birth wherever and however it occurs, the article suggested, these nations have managed to boost fertility to a degree that countries where the older stigma still holds sway have not. In other words, an ethic of "anything goes" may trump Catholicism in today's Europe as a way to prod people to have more kids. Who would have thought it?

None of this means that Europe is out of the woods. Even the most generous projection shows Europe losing population; its share of the global total, according to *The Economist*, will fall from 21 percent to 7 percent by 2050. Yet the data does suggest that alarmist predictions about Europe's "cultural suicide" may have been overdrawn.

2. THE UNITED STATES

The American population is expected to grow steadily throughout the twenty-first century, reaching 400 million in 2050, up from just over 300 million at the time of this writing, leaving it the third-largest country on earth after India and China. In part, this growth will be due to the higher-than-average fertility rate of 2.3 among the country's growing Hispanic minority. White Americans have a fertility rate of 1.8. The last year in which white, non-Hispanic American women had enough children to replace themselves was 1971. Hispanics are 15 percent of the population today but will be 21 percent by 2030. Hispanics in the United States have a median age of 27, which means their population is not aging as rapidly. The median age for whites is almost 40.

American population growth will also be fueled by immigration, again with Hispanics making the largest contribution. Due to its comparatively open immigration policy, the United States accepts by far the largest number of legal immigrants in the world. Between 1991 and 2000, the United States admitted 9.1 million legal immigrants, which, according to one estimate, was more than the entire rest of the world combined. Given bitter debates over immigration, it's not clear whether such high levels will be maintained, but under any scenario it seems likely that the United States will have more immigrants than Europe. As Europe's population drops, that of the United States will rise, and at some point around mid-century the United States will overtake Western Europe in terms of total population.

Whether levels of Hispanic immigration will continue throughout the twenty-first century at their presently high levels is another question. Declining fertility and rising median ages in Mexico mean that the waves of immigrants that have swelled the Hispanic population in the United States are likely to ebb sometime in the twenty-first century. In the United States itself, the Hispanic fertility rate is declining. It went from 2.96 in 1990 to 2.73 in 2000, according to the Centers for Disease Control and Prevention; the Census Bureau puts the figure at 2.3 for 2004. The Hispanic elderly population is also growing. The U.S. Census Bureau estimates that the share of elders who are Hispanic will rise from 4 percent to 16 percent by 2050.

3. ASIA

Fertility rates in the traditional regional powerhouses of Japan and China have imploded. With a rate of 1.3 children per woman, Japan is already beginning to experience population loss, and over the next 40 years stands to lose as much as a quarter of its 128 million people. South Korea likewise had a remarkably low 2004 fertility rate of 1.23, and Singapore 1.35. The UN expects Korea to lose three and a half million people by 2050.

Perhaps even more startling is the situation in China, long seen as "exhibit A" in the case for global overpopulation. A rigid one-child policy, combined with the explosion of the Chinese middle class, has caused one of the most dramatic fertility declines on the planet. China had a fertility rate of 6.1 as recently as 1960, while today the UN number is 1.8, and many Chinese demographers peg it lower still, at 1.3. Because of momentum, population losses will not begin until mid-century, but could then become massive. The Chinese situation is further complicated by the fact that under the one-child policy, parents had a strong preference for male children, aborting girls at a much higher rate. The ratio of male to female births in China is now 117 to 100, which would mean that 17 percent of Chinese men won't be able to find women to marry unless they import them. China will age as much in one generation as Europe has in the last 100 years, prompting the observation that it will be the first Asian nation to get old before it gets rich.

4. LATIN AMERICA

The UN Population Division predicts that the population of Latin America and the Caribbean will rise from 561 million in 2005 to 782 million in 2050. That increase, however, glosses over the fact that several countries once regarded as "poster children" for overpopulation now find themselves on the other side of the equation, especially Brazil and Mexico— coincidentally the two largest Catholic countries on earth, representing almost 20 percent of the entire Catholic population worldwide. Brazil went from a fertility rate of 6.15 in 1960 to 2.1 today, while Mexico fell from 7.0 to 2.03, below replacement level. By 2050, Mexico will actually be older than the United States, with a median age of 43 as compared to 41.

Argentina today has a fertility rate of 2.25 and is predicted to drop below replacement level by 2015. Chile as of 2007 stood at 2.0, already below replacement level. Colombia had a comparatively robust rate of 2.46, but it too is falling and will reach replacement level around 2025. The percentage of the total population between 15 and 59 years of age in Uruguay in 2007 was already lower than in the United States, meaning that it is an older society.

5. AFRICA

Africa offers the most stark contrast to the overall thrust of the New Demography, because it's the continent least marked by declining fertility. The total fertility rate for the entire continent fell from 6.6 in 1950 to 5.2 in 2002, a much smaller decrease than anywhere else in the world. The fertility rate for sub-Saharan Africa is 5.6, easily the highest of any zone on the planet. In North Africa the rate is 3.5, considerably lower but still well above the replacement level of 2.1 Of the ten nations with the highest fertility rates in the world, eight are in Africa.

As a clear example of the difference, the World Bank in a 2004 report compared Nigeria and Japan. In 2004, the two countries had roughly similar populations, 137 million in Nigeria and 128 million in Japan. By 2050, Nigeria will be at 205 million, while Japan will have dropped to between 120 and 112 million.

According to the Population Resource Center, Northern Africa will grow by 68 percent between now and 2050, while sub-Saharan Africa will grow by a remarkable 132 percent, from about 700 million people to 1.6 billion. That is to say, sub-Saharan Africa will add more than the entire present population of the United States, twice, in the next 43 years.

On the other hand, continent-wide totals mask marked differences country by country. Niger has a fertility rate of 7.91, but according to the 2004 World Bank Database, the number is 3.1 in Botswana, 2.7 in South Africa, and 2.0 in Mauritius, actually below replacement level. In general, Southern Africa has seen the sharpest declines, while regions of West and Central Africa have experienced little or no drop-off. Explaining these contrasts is difficult, although many experts point to differing levels of economic development, as well as differences in the availability of family planning programs.

6. THE MIDDLE EAST

The short-term demographic forecast for the Middle East is for explosive growth. Overall, the region's population is expected to more than double by 2050, to reach 649 million people. Yasser Arafat once declared that "the womb of the Arab woman is my best weapon," and on the surface these numbers would seem to prove him right. In 2000, the American Jewish Committee published projections indicating that the population of Israel in 2050 would be around 9 million, which means that in the Middle East, Israelis will be outnumbered roughly 72 to 1.

Yet short-term growth conceals an underlying force that cuts in the opposite direction, which is that fertility rates are falling faster in the Middle East than anywhere else on earth. They are coming down from a high level, but they're coming down dramatically. Iran offers perhaps the clearest example, where the fertility rate since 1950 has fallen by two thirds, and now stands at 2.0, below replacement level. Between now and 2050, the median age in Iran will rise by roughly 20 years, from 20.6 to 40.2. Within ten years, the absolute number of children under the age of four will begin to fall, while the number of Iranians over 65 will soar. In the future, population growth in Iran will be almost entirely due to increases in the number of people who survive to old age, not growth in the number of children. By 2030, Iran will have more people over 65 than children under 14.

Similar trends are unfolding in Egypt, Lebanon, Syria, Saudi Arabia, Jordan, Iraq, and Algeria. In Egypt, for example, the number of children will begin dropping by 2017 and will continue to fall all the way to 2050. Turkey's fertility rate today is 2.32, and by 2050, the age structure of Turkey will be older than that of the United States. The median age in these nations will increase 15 to 20 years by the middle half of the twenty-first century.

Although TV images of vast crowds of Muslim youth today seem to belie these claims, the truth is that these are the children of the 1980s, which was the Middle Eastern "baby boom," and they are being followed by a "baby bust." As noted in chapter three, over the long term these trends may dampen Islamic radicalism, as aging societies tend to be more focused on prosaic questions such as funding pensions and health care. Scarcity of children may also mean that the current glorification of martyrdom goes out of fashion.

Graying

Perhaps the most visible hallmark of the New Demography is a dramatic surge in the world's elderly population, a reality that is already clear in advanced nations. In the United States, the median age was 30 in 1950, but it will reach 41 by 2050. In Europe it will be 47.1, and in Japan a staggering 52.3. Fully a third of all Japanese will be over 60 within a decade, creating a potentially serious shortage of elder-care facilities and personnel. One leading Japanese politician has actually proposed exporting retirees to the Philippines in order to relieve the pressure.

By the end of the twenty-first century, the share of the population over 60 will rise from 10 to 22 percent, giving the entire planet a median age similar to that of Western Europe today. In 2050, there will be almost two billion people over the age of 60.

As the President's Council on Bioethics stated in 2005, we are on the brink of becoming a "mass geriatric society." According to the U.S. Census Bureau, Americans aged 14 and under presently outnumber those 65 and above by almost two to one, 60.5 million to 34.7. By 2050, that ratio will have swung strongly in the opposite direction. There will be 75.9 million Americans above 65, as opposed to 59.7 million under 14, meaning the elderly will outnumber the youngest in the country by more than 16 million. The population of "old olds," meaning those above 85, will also increase fourfold.

The grayest state in the Union in the year 2005, according to the Census Bureau, was Maine, which had a median age of 41.2. By 2050, that will be roughly the median age for the entire nation. Within a half-century, America won't have to remember the *Maine*; we will *be* Maine.

The graying of the planet will be even more rapid elsewhere. It took the United States fifty years, from 1950 to 2000, to increase its median age by five years, from 30 to 35. In the first fifty years of the twenty-first century, by way of contrast, Algeria will go from a median age of 21.7 to 40, a jump of almost 18 years in the same span of time. In Egypt, by 2050 the elderly population will be growing twice as fast as the working-age population. In China, the ratio of elders to young people will swell by a factor of four, with 26 percent of the population 60 or older by 2040, meaning some 360 million people. Demographers describe China as facing a 4-2-1 problem: Each young adult will potentially be caring for two parents, plus four grandparents. Brazil is aging at a rate 2.1 times that of the United States and 3.1 times faster than Holland. By 2050, according to the UN numbers, one quarter of Brazil's population will be over 60, a total of 63 million people.

Pensions and Health Care

Of all the implications of the New Demography, none is as much of an absolute certainty as increasing strains on retirement benefits and health care around the world. As the percentage of the population above 60 grows with each passing year, so too will the amount of resources societies will have to allocate to paying pensions and to funding health care systems, especially elder care. The difficulties of doing so will be compounded by the fact that there aren't as many workers in their productive years moving through the system to fund allocations for the elderly.

In the United States, dire warnings surface periodically about the prospect of the Social Security system "going broke." Despite the mythology many Americans carry in their heads that they have a Social Security "account" somewhere, in reality their payments are simply absorbed into the general budget to pay benefits to today's retirees. When their time comes, the workers of tomorrow will fund their benefits. It's what's known as a "pay as you go" system.

There are serious challenges ahead. In 1955, America had nine workers for every retiree. Today the ratio is 3.3 to 1, and it will fall to 2 to 1 by 2035. In that same span of time, Social Security payments will rise from 4.5 percent of gross domestic product to 7 percent. If nothing changes, by 2017 the Social Security system will be taking in less than it pays out, and by 2041, the "trust fund," meaning set-aside allocations to fund future payments, will be exhausted. This is hardly a problem unique to America, which, as we have seen, actually has a growing population relative to other developed nations. In 2002, shortfalls in the German pension system caused the country's deficits to exceed European Union limits, triggering a crisis in European equity markets. Nor is this just a first-world concern. Shortfalls in Brazil's pension system set off panic in international financial markets in 1998, and as of this writing the structural problems in the system are still largely unaddressed. In 2005, the Brazilian pension fund carried a deficit of $18.6 billion, a figure sure to worsen as Brazil's over-60 population swells from 16 million to 63 million in 2050.

In theory, the pension problem could be solved by one of two strategies: raising taxes or cutting benefits. Both are notoriously unpopular politically. In 2006 alone, Europe witnessed major strikes in both Britain and France over proposed government plans to cut benefits, and in both cases the governments were forced to back down. In the United States, talk of cutting Social Security has long been seen as the "third rail" of American politics, the surest possible way to doom a candidacy. Absent a deus ex machina solution of some sort, tension around retirement systems is destined to grow dramatically.

The pension problem, however, pales in comparison to health care. According to the Congressional Budget Office in the United States, under current conditions the cost of Medicare and Medicaid will rise from 4.3 percent of the gross domestic product in 2000 to a staggering 21 percent in 2050. By 2020, estimates are that 157 million Americans will have some form of chronic illness, up from 125 million in 2000. Medicare expenditures are expanding by 9 percent annually and Medicaid by 8 percent. Unless something changes, those two programs alone will eat up a larger share of the country's output than the entire federal government does today. In other words, without significant tax hikes or astronomic rates of economic expansion, all the federal government would be able to do in 2050 is pay for health care—no roads, no schools, no armies, nothing else.

These problems will be compounded dramatically as the population ages. In the late 1990s, the average health care expenditure in the United States for someone aged 65 to 69 was $5,684, compared to $9,414 among persons aged 75 to 79, and $16,465 among persons aged 85 or older. It doesn't take a math genius to realize that as the population 80 and above in the country grows from 10.6 million in 2005 to 28.7 million in 2050, the total outlay for health care will skyrocket. This, by the way, doesn't begin to address how much assisted living facilities and retirement homes cost. In 2007, the total cost of nursing home care in the United States was projected to be $66 trillion, a 12 percent jump over 2006. That figure, by the way, reflects considerable belt-tightening by nursing homes in a competitive industry rather than real costs, since the cost of liability insurance and personnel for nursing homes is rising much more rapidly than what they actually charge.

Immigration

In theory, the global population imbalances of the coming half-century could easily, and profitably, be solved by massive relocations of people from the South to the North. All those under-twenty-four-year-olds in the South who are unemployed or underemployed could replace shrinking populations of younger workers in Europe and Asia, maintaining the "dependency ratios" in the host societies and generating remittances for their home countries that would promote economic development.

Political science tells us, however, that it's precisely when countries most need immigrants that immigration tends to become a tough sell. Periods of declining population unleash fears about national identity, so further dilution of that identity through immigration runs into stiff resistance. In addition, the levels of immigration that would be needed in Europe today to offset population loss are almost unimaginable. In order to maintain its current population, Europe would have to increase its intake of legal immigrants each year from 376,000 to more than 1.9 million. If Europe wanted to maintain its current workforce of people aged 15 to 64, it would have to welcome 3.2 million immigrants every year. To venture even farther into the fantastic, if Europe wanted to maintain a constant dependency ratio, meaning the ratio of working-age people to those over 65 and under 15, it would have to admit 27 million immigrants annually. Under any scenario, that's unlikely to happen.

Further, immigration is arguably a Band-Aid solution, because immigrants often arrive with a third or more of their working years behind them, and then begin to draw on the host country's social services as well as its health care resources. In the long run, they don't add nearly as much to a society as do newborn children. The bottom line is that declining fertility, along with rapid aging and population loss, above all in the affluent North, is destined to be one of the trends of our time, no matter what politicians decide to do about immigration laws.

WHAT IT MEANS

At one level, the New Demography will unleash new currents in global diplomacy, in international economics, and within societies struggling to cope with rapid demographic change. Roman Catholicism, as one of the few institutions on earth with a truly global reach, will be called upon to help the broader culture negotiate these transitions. At the same time, the Church will also be feeling the impact of these shifts in its internal life, which will create new headaches but also new moments of opportunity.

Near-Certain Consequences

1. NETWORKS OF CARE IN CHURCHES

Under any conceivable future scenario, the elderly will receive less in retirement benefits and less in both public and private assistance to meet the costs of health care, as there will be fewer younger workers to pay into the pool at a time of rapidly rising costs. Need for charitable assistance will therefore increase dramatically, putting significant strains on Catholic charitable organizations and social service providers.

Traditionally, much elder care has been delivered within the family structure, but the imbalance between a mushrooming population of seniors and declining numbers of young adults will mean that an increasing portion of the elderly don't have that option. By 2020, 1.2 million Americans aged 65 or older will have no living children, siblings, or spouse. The number of isolated elders is likely to be even greater in other Western societies. The Institute for Health and Aging in the United States reports that in 1990, for every person over 85 years of age, there were 21 people between the ages of 50 and 64. In 2030, for every person over 85, there will be only six people between 50 and 64, a massive contraction in the pool of potential caregivers.

Given these realities, parishes and dioceses will find themselves under increasing pressure to act as an alternative support system, matching churchgoers who have the time and resources with elderly who need assistance. That assistance won't just be financial. Many elders will also need emotional support, including basic companionship and contact with younger members of the community. Forward-thinking parishes and dioceses are studying ways today to institutionalize and augment the informal networks of assistance that have always been part of Catholic culture.

One example would be organizing teams of volunteers who could provide a break for families caring for elderly members at home, allowing caregivers to run errands, have a night out on the town, or just get away for a few hours. Parallel to that, parishes could offer workshops and support services for home-based caregivers on issues such as navigating the complexities of health care systems, strategies for coping with Alzheimer's and Parkinson's, and managing their own emotional welfare to avoid burnout.

2. PARISH NURSING

One key figure in these networks of care is likely to be the parish nurse. In the United States, the Parish Nurse Resource Center in St. Louis, Missouri, reports that there are 4,000 nurses today working either full- or part-time in American Catholic parishes, with an additional 6,000 serving other Christian bodies, most prominently the Lutherans, the United Church of Christ, and the Baptists. This suggests that at present, fewer than 20 percent of American parishes have a nurse on staff. As the century develops, a substantial number of Catholic parishes that today don't have a parish nurse will feel the need for one.

The resource center says there are also growing programs for parish nurses in Canada, the United Kingdom, South Africa, Swaziland, Australia, New Zealand, and South Korea. Five universities in Korea offer concentrations specifically for parish nurses.

Because these nurses do not work under the direct supervision of a doctor, they generally cannot perform invasive procedures such as administering injections. Instead, they take blood pressure readings, monitor medications, check general health levels, and answer questions about health care. Many run support groups for parishioners who are caring for ailing family members, as well as for those who have lost a loved one. The nurse also can act as an advocate for elders as they navigate through health care systems.

Though it's too early to have much hard data about the impact of parish nursing, a study conducted by Avera Health, which serves a five-state area of the American Midwest, reported in 1999 that in one church the parish nurse screened 452 people, of whom 24 percent had blood pressure levels that were too high; in another, the nurse screened 117 people, of whom 41 percent had elevated blood pressure. In at least some cases, flagging those problems early may have prevented the development of more serious conditions.

By no means are parish nurses focused exclusively, or even primarily, on the elderly. Many spend a great deal of their time working with low-income and immigrant populations. Given their demographics, most Catholic parishes in the future will likely come to think of a nurse the way they do today of youth ministers, directors of religious education, and even parish secretaries—as an essential part of the parish team.

Filling that slot, however, may not be easy. According to the American Association of Colleges of Nursing, 30 states currently face a shortage, and by 2020, 44 states plus the District of Columbia will not be able to field enough nurses to meet demand. Similar trends obtain elsewhere; according to the World Health Organization, ten years ago Poland was graduating more than 10,000 new nurses annually, while today the number is 3,000. The reasons are fairly simple: the increasing complexity of the job, difficult working conditions, insufficient student assistance, and low salaries.

This point suggests that perhaps the Catholic Church should worry a bit less about the priest shortage, which tends to occupy a considerable degree of its time and attention, and more about the nurse shortage, both at the policy level and in terms of its own staffing needs.

3. THE DEMOGRAPHIC DIMENSION OF SOCIAL JUSTICE

Leaders within the Church who work on public policy questions—bishops, theologians, social action directors, lobbyists, and activists of all sorts—will find that "elder equity" is perhaps the dominant domestic policy issue of the future. Assuring that societies make adequate provision for their elderly, and that available resources are distributed fairly across lines of race, class, and gender, will be a towering challenge.

The risks of a rising number of elderly people living without adequate support systems, and without even minimal resources to provide for basic safety and comfort, was illustrated in shocking fashion in France in 2003, when a summer heat wave caused a stunning total of 11,000 deaths. Most victims were elderly people living alone, who couldn't afford air-conditioning and who had no one to check in on them to be sure they weren't in danger. Given that 16 percent of the population of France is already over 65, these dangers will only grow. The same pattern is unfolding almost everywhere, with greatest intensity in the rapidly aging countries of the developed world.

Inevitably, the impact will fall disproportionately upon women, the poor, and those who are non-white. As Boston College theologian Lisa Sowle Cahill notes, retirement incomes for women average only 55 percent of those of men, and for older African American or Hispanic women, poverty is the rule rather than the exception. Such affronts to human decency will command both a moral and a practical response from the Catholic Church.

4. MAKING INTERGENERATIONAL PEACE

At the same time, the Church will need to be attentive to a corollary possibility, which is that as a rapidly growing percentage of social resources is diverted to the elderly, mostly through entitlement programs, young adults and families may feel victimized. Some social theorists worry about a crisis of "intergenerational solidarity," with young workers squeezed to support a ballooning population of elderly retirees, eating up more and more of their income through payroll taxes and other measures. Compounding the resentment such a situation could create is the likelihood that soaring budgets for pensions and elder care will make new investment in programs of interest to young people, such as child care or parental leave programs, more difficult. This is a special risk if older people simply vote their class interests. The nightmare scenario is that in such a world, the young could end up hating the old.

Aware of these dangers, Catholic thinkers and activists will be pressed to identify strategies that could ameliorate these intergenerational tensions. As one example, Singapore gives adult children significant financial incentives to live with their parents, such as tax rebates and preferential housing choices. The government also provides generous contributions to pensions and health care for adult children who stay home to care for elderly parents. The idea is to reduce the strain on elder care facilities, while also reducing some of the financial tensions between generations. To take another model, in 1988 the Community of Sant'Egidio launched a program to help Italian elderly stay in their own homes rather than entering a nursing home, coordinating with family members, doctors, hospitals, and social services. In addition to promoting the autonomy of the elderly, such an approach keeps the cost of full-time residential care to a minimum, easing the burden on younger taxpayers.

Given its traditional concern with the welfare of the family, the Catholic Church will feel compelled to try to make the case for policies that protect the human dignity of the elderly, while at the same time ensuring that society doesn't cut off its nose to spite its face—in other words, that having children and forming families does not become virtually impossible because young people are working almost exclusively to fund programs for older people. As one of the few institutions in society that routinely brings the elderly and the young together, the Church has a unique capacity to help negotiate the generational conflict that future decades are sure to witness.

5. A CRISIS IN CHURCH PENSIONS

Under the weight of a rapidly swelling population of elderly people in the developed North, the Catholic Church is certain to face its own difficulties in meeting pension and health care commitments. Because the Church makes moral judgments about the behavior of other institutions, it will face pressure to have its own house in order, and that may be easier said than done.

In the United States, Church-run pension plans are exempt from the requirements of ERISA, the federal Employee Retirement Income Security Act, which establishes disclosure standards and conflict of interest restrictions.

The same First Amendment exemption also means that Church-run pension plans are not covered by the Pension Benefit Guaranty Corporation, a federal agency that acts as a safety net when private pensions come up short. Church personnel also do not enjoy the same legal protections with regard to health care benefits as employees in other sectors. In 2006, the *New York Times* highlighted the case of Mary Rosati, a onetime novice with the Sisters of the Visitation of Holy Mary in Toledo, Ohio. Rosati claimed she was dismissed by the order after she was diagnosed with breast cancer, an accusation the order denied. Rosati sued, but a U.S. District Court held that her removal was beyond the reach of the court because of the First Amendment. In the future, however, it's not a foregone conclusion that this "ministerial exemption" will always be upheld. Even if it is, that doesn't solve the moral question of the Church's responsibility to its own personnel.

It will be difficult for the Catholic Church to urge justice for the elderly in the broader society if it is not seen to do justice to its own retirees. Bishops, religious superiors, financial officers, and other responsible parties in the Church will face sharply increased pressure to ensure that pension and health care obligations are adequately funded, occupying an increasing share of the Church's resources.

6. GROWTH IN ELDER MINISTRY

Under Pope John Paul II, the Catholic Church made an enormous investment in youth ministry, meaning outreach to Catholics from grade school through their young adult years. Such a commitment makes great sense. In a time of declining vocations, it's a way of inviting young people to consider the priesthood and religious life. In an era of increasing secularization, it's a way of trying to counteract the values young people absorb from the broader culture. In the global South, the option for youth is also a natural demographic choice, given the relative youthfulness of most societies.

The demographic trends described in this chapter, however, suggest that in the North, the growth industry of the future is likely to be ministry to elders. What youth ministry was to the John Paul years, elder ministry will be to the twenty-first century.

In the United States, the Catholic Church will have 6.8 million additional members over the age of 65 by 2030, by far the most substantial expansion of any subgroup in the Church. Inevitably, these trends mean that the Church will be pressed to invest an increasing share of its resources in ministry to the elderly. Ministries that will expand rapidly include:

- Chaplains in nursing homes, assisted living facilities, and hospitals;
- Ministry to shut-ins, including the need for Eucharistic Ministers who can take the sacrament to elderly parishioners;
- Demand for funerals and anointing of the sick;
- Pastoral programs to help people deal with bereavement and loss;
- Catholic nursing homes, hospitals, and day care centers.

There are encouraging models. Blessed Trinity Catholic Church in Ocala, Florida, for example, has developed a comprehensive program of elder ministry. The parish's office of elder care services offers a professional nursing staff, health monitoring and medication management, nutrition programs, staff and volunteers who are trained in the care of elders with Alzheimer's and other forms of dementia, and a comprehensive set of referrals to other health care providers. Blessed Trinity offers adult day care, meaning supervision and assistance to physically and/or mentally frail older adults. The program is styled in part as an alternative to nursing homes for families who want to care for elders at home. One note of caution is that the program is "pay-as-you-go," charging on an hourly, daily, weekly, and monthly basis. The Church will want to take care that its services also reach impoverished seniors.

In at least a few cases, Church-run nursing homes, assisted living centers, and retirement homes may become the functional equivalent of small parishes, with burgeoning populations and even full-time resident pastoral care. Matching retired priests with nursing homes and assisted living facilities, negotiating a discount for the priest, may also be one way dioceses can trim their own expenditures.

7. INCREASE IN LATE VOCATIONS

Flat or declining numbers of young people in Northern nations, coupled with the general difficulties experienced by the Church in attracting vocations, suggests that an increasing share of tomorrow's priests will enter the priesthood later in life, in some cases as a "second career." Data published by the United States Conference of Catholic Bishops, collected and analyzed by the Center for Applied Research in the Apostolate at Georgetown University, shows that men aged 50 and above represented 9 percent of ordinations in the country in 1999, and 13 percent in 2006. It seems likely that more than half of all new priests in 2050 will be over 40.

At present, it seems a jump ball as to whether bishops will welcome this trend, or merely tolerate it.

On the one hand, bishops eager to get more priests into the field may see the boom in late vocations as a godsend. Given that today's elderly are generally healthier for longer periods of time, a man ordained at 50 may be able to render 25 years or more of service. He's also arguably more likely to relate to an aging congregation. Further, the diocese does not have to carry the expense of an undergraduate or graduate education. These late vocations often come with professional background and experience that makes them more effective pastors and administrators, and the Church didn't have to pay for it.

On the other hand, many bishops are ambivalent about late vocations for at least three reasons. First, the number of productive years a priest will provide before the bishop has to start paying for his retirement and health care is reduced. Second, candidates with careers in business, law, education, or other fields are sometimes more difficult to form. They have their own experience in managing personnel and running systems, and many are accustomed to corporate standards of performance and accountability that may not harmonize easily with diocesan culture. Third, some bishops are reluctant to embrace late vocations because it can seem like surrender on attracting younger men. Most bishops prefer to devote the lion's share of their resources to promoting vocations among high school- and college-aged candidates, accepting later vocations with gratitude but rarely actively soliciting them.

In the long run, however, bishops may not have a great deal of choice. As the rest of the world grays at an accelerating rate, late vocations will become the global norm. This shift could change the sociology of the priesthood, especially in the direction of greater pressure to adopt policies and practices modeled on institutions in the secular world with which these priests will be increasingly familiar.

Probable Consequences

1. A EUROPEAN–AMERICAN SPLIT ON IMMIGRATION

In the twenty-first century, European and American bishops are likely to move in opposite directions in terms of their attitudes on immigration, in part because of varying demographic patterns. Two high-profile recent interventions from cardinals on immigration issues offer vignettes of things to come.

Cardinal Giacomo Biffi of Bologna, Italy, now retired, issued a pastoral letter in September 2000 that caused a sensation. In a nutshell, Biffi suggested that the Italian government should give preferential treatment to immigrants from traditionally Catholic nations such as the Philippines, Eritrea, and Latin American countries, in order to defend Italy's Catholic identity. Though Biffi did not say so out loud, it was understood that he meant the government should limit Muslim immigrants from Albania and North Africa. He called increases in immigration from non-Catholic cultures "one of the most serious and biggest assaults on Christianity that history remembers." Biffi's analysis drew sympathetic reactions from several senior Catholic figures. The Vatican's then-secretary of state, Cardinal Angelo Sodano, said that "the ideas of Cardinal Biffi are wise, very wise." Cardinal Camillo Ruini, at the time the president of the Italian bishops' conference, said that Biffi had a legitimate point.

Contrast that with Cardinal Roger Mahony of Los Angeles, who in 2006 spoke out strongly in opposition to a measure proposed in the U.S. House of Representatives that would have criminalized several forms of assistance to illegal immigrants—including, at least potentially, giving them a sandwich in a Catholic soup kitchen, or new clothes from a Catholic charity center. In January of that year, Mahony launched an education campaign about the measure throughout the archdiocese. On Ash Wednesday, Mahony denounced the bill from the pulpit as "blameful" and "vicious," and threatened to organize civil disobedience if it became law. Mahony became a staple on TV talk shows and in the op-ed pages, and many observers credited him with helping to drive massive turnout at a March 25 demonstration in downtown Los Angeles in opposition to the measure. Other American bishops joined Mahony in calling for pathways to legalization for a substantial number of the country's estimated 11 million illegal immigrants. Though the American bishops didn't get the reform they wanted, the punitive dimensions of the House bill never became law.

What this contrast illustrates is that American bishops are generally more pro-immigration than their European counterparts, in part because most new immigrants in the United States are Catholic, while in Europe a higher percentage are Muslims. In general, this means that pro-immigration leadership at the senior levels of Catholicism in the twenty-first century is more likely to come from the United States than from Europe.

One possible unintended consequence may be a gradual softening of the anti-American sentiment of some Catholic leaders across the global South, or at least a growing capacity to distinguish the positions of the American government from those of the Catholic Church. Southern bishops, especially in Latin America and Africa, are concerned about the fate of their migrant co-nationals in the North, and they will find in coming decades that the American bishops are more likely to support pro-immigrant policies.

2. PRO-AMERICAN DRIFT IN VATICAN DIPLOMACY

As outlined in chapter two, the postwar tendency of the Holy See to regard Europe as its most natural partner in global affairs has been eroded under the impact of secularization and disenchantment with the EU. The demographic realities of the next century will not do much to boost Europe's stock with the Vatican. Europe will be a shrinking, aging society, increasingly focused on its internal difficulties and with a declining capacity to project influence internationally. The United States, by way of contrast, will continue to grow throughout the century, adding almost 100 million people over the course of the century. The percentage of its population that is Catholic will steadily rise under the impact of Hispanic immigration and disproportionately high Hispanic birthrates. To put the trajectory simplistically: Europe will become smaller and less Catholic, the United States will get bigger and more Catholic.

This line of demographic development will likely reinforce a tendency in Vatican diplomacy toward a more "America-friendly" stance. It will certainly be of cold comfort to Church officials that some European nations have arrested their declines in fertility by chucking the traditional Christian model of the family out the window. Virtually alone in the affluent North, the United States has avoided the deepest inroads of secularization while managing to stay demographically vital.

Such an inclination in favor of the United States will collide with a host of other opposing forces, primarily the rise of the global South in Catholicism and the anti-American political instincts of some Southern Catholic leaders. The Vatican's traditional European biases toward America are also not going to vanish overnight. Yet in this complex cocktail of opposing forces, the New Demography adds a splash of pro-American flavor.

3. A (DOCTRINAL) BOOST FOR CONSERVATIVES

In the doctrinal arena, the New Demography will likely have its most direct impact on questions that touch human reproduction and population, such as birth control, abortion, and homosexuality. In broad terms, today's demographic realities seem likely to strengthen the conservative position within the Catholic Church. This camp believes that it's those parts of the world where contraception and abortion have become most widespread that are in the grip of a demographic winter, and that this correlation confirms the wisdom of the traditional Catholic position.

In fact, some Catholic commentators have argued that today's low fertility rates offer the closest thing one will ever find to empirical proof for a papal encyclical, in this case Paul VI's 1968 *Humanae vitae,* which reiterated the traditional ban on birth control. This marks a sea change from a quarter-century ago, when the warnings of demographers about overpopulation were invoked by liberal reformers to support their views on the same cluster of issues. In the Catholic pro-life movement today, the books cited throughout this chapter by Ben Wattenberg and Phillip Longman, who see the data as empirical confirmation of the Church's teaching, have become required reading.

To be sure, demographic trends by themselves will not resolve the culture wars inside Catholicism. But in these battles, the overall global trend toward declining fertility at least means that conservatives will not have to face the accusation of moral indifference to overpopulation that dogged them for much of the twentieth century. That in itself marks a gain for their position.

4. A (DEMOGRAPHIC) BOOST FOR CONSERVATIVES

There is another sense in which, over time, demography will likely reinforce the conservative camp within the Church. To put the point crudely, conservatives are likely to outbreed everyone else. Since large families have always been a mark of Catholic distinctiveness, it's reasonable to assume that having children at levels above the replacement rate will also figure in the Catholic "politics of identity" of the twenty-first century.

A connection between religious commitment and high fertility is not mere speculation. The state of Utah, for example, where almost 70 percent of the population is made up of registered members of the Church of Jesus Christ of Latter-day Saints (Mormons), has the country's highest fertility rate, the youngest median age of first marriage, and the highest percentage of married households, according to U.S. Census Bureau figures.

Within the Catholic world, anecdotal evidence also suggests a linkage between conservative doctrinal positions and fertility. In research for my 2005 book on Opus Dei, I routinely met large families among the lay members of the group, which prides itself on fidelity to the official teaching of the Catholic Church. When I visited the Chicago home of supernumeraries Doug and Shirley Hinderer in September 2004, for example, I met their nine children. While in London, I visited two supernumerary households: Jim and Theresa Burbidge, who have five children, and John and Jane Philips, who have ten.

In some parishes, one can spot the more conservative parishioners these days not so much by who takes Communion on the tongue or who lines up for confession before Mass, but rather by who has a large brood of kids. Not only does this swell the general ranks of conservatives, but it means the parents of those kids are more likely to be involved in the Church than 25- to 44-year-old Catholics without children.

5. "GRAY THEOLOGY"

In her 2005 book *Theological Bioethics,* Boston College theologian Lisa Sowle Cahill analyzes Western approaches to aging, decline, and death in terms of three contemporary trends: individualism, meaning self-determination; the medicalization of social problems, such as the proper balance between independence and dependence; and the refusal to accept that life has limits, resulting in frustration and despair when science, technology, and money fail to take away the suffering that is inevitably part of life. One task for a contemporary theology of aging, she writes, is to develop an alternative Catholic understanding of death and dying, one more rooted in community, in spirituality and moral discipline, and in an acceptance of the finitude of life rooted in faith about the life to come.

David Tracy has written that renewed attention to Christian doctrines of eschatology, referring to teaching about death, judgment, and the afterlife, may cajole the broader culture into taking the "third age" in life more seriously, according the elderly greater respect, and valuing the contributions of their wisdom and life experience. In that sense, Tracy suggests, a renewed interest in eschatology could offer valuable resources for bringing theological wisdom to bear on contemporary demographic realities. Such efforts to construct a "gray theology" will become increasingly urgent, especially in the global North.

6. RESISTANCE TO EUTHANASIA

The possibility of elderly persons feeling pressured into euthanasia—either to spare their families the burden of taking care of them, or because they don't have families or anyone else to provide care—will grow dramatically as society ages.

As noted above, by 2020, 1.2 million Americans aged 65 or older will have no living children, siblings, or spouse. Moreover, today's caregivers are much more likely to work outside the home, which means they either have to pay for supplementary care during the day or sacrifice years of work and income to deliver the care themselves. In some cases, caring for an elderly relative may actually compete with raising a family of one's own; according to the President's Council on Bioethics, American women today spend as much time caring for adult family members as they do in caring for children. Caregivers are also increasingly likely to be elderly themselves, meaning the provision of care puts significant strains on their own health. Even for those families lucky enough to be able to afford to pay for home health care, there's a shrinking pool of available workers. All of these realities increase the possibility that dependent elderly persons will come to see staying alive as imposing an unfair burden upon their younger family members or upon society at large.

In such a context, Church groups with a strong commitment to a pro-life message will be called upon to ensure that elders in such situations have options. Among other things, this implies that if the Catholic Church's advocacy on euthanasia is to be credible, it will have to do more than lobby against liberalizing legislation. It will also have to mobilize its own resources to help ensure that the social conditions that prompt people to consider euthanasia. Though abortion and embryonic stem cell research may be the dominant pro-life issues today, euthanasia may well emerge as the flagship pro-life cause of tomorrow.

Possible Consequences

1. SHIFTS IN ECUMENICAL DIALOGUE WITH THE ORTHODOX

The New Demography may add another chapter to the challenges facing ecumenism in the decades to come, particularly with regard to the Orthodox churches. Simply put, many Catholics may look at population projections for nations that are the heartland of Orthodoxy and ask themselves, "Why bother?"

Outside of Macao and Hong Kong, the lowest fertility rates in the world today are in Eastern Europe and Russia. Unlike Catholicism, Methodism, Anglicanism, and other Christian denominations, Orthodoxy has historically never been a missionary tradition, and hence has never put down significant roots in the global South, except for the presence of a small Orthodox diaspora. Orthodoxy, therefore, cannot look to Africa or Asia to offset its losses in Eastern Europe.

Today, Orthodoxy numbers roughly 250 million adherents, divided among fifteen independent churches and their subdivisions, almost all of which are defined along national lines. The Russian Orthodox Church is the largest. As Russia's population falls from 143 million in 2005 to a projected 111 million in 2050, the Russian Orthodox Church will suffer proportional losses. Reflecting those realities, Philip Jenkins has written that falling birthrates may prove to be more devastating to the Orthodox than Muslim or Communist persecutions ever were. By 2030, all Orthodox believers together will likely represent less than 3 percent of the earth's population.

Granted, the Catholic Church is not Microsoft, and the numerical bottom line does not always drive its thinking. Catholicism has invested considerable resources in dialogues with the Assyrian Church of the East, for example, and the Armenian Apostolic Church, which are all out of proportion to their numerical significance. Further, recent popes have expressed a preferential option for the Orthodox, in part because the split between East and West is the primordial schism, and in part because Orthodox traditionalism on doctrinal and liturgical questions coheres well with evangelical Catholicism. Nevertheless, declining population numbers in the Orthodox world may cool enthusiasm for ecumenical relations on the Catholic side, as well as render any progress somewhat less significant.

What will demographic decline mean for Orthodox attitudes?

Population erosion could engender ever more tenacious assertions of traditional Orthodox identity, making ecumenical progress even more difficult. On the other hand, those same trends may induce realists in the Orthodox camp to conclude that the future of Orthodoxy as a stand-alone enterprise is limited, and that their best prospects for survival lie in some sort of federation with Roman Catholicism. In reality, both of these things are likely to happen at the same time, meaning that it will be the competition between these two views in the Orthodox world that largely determines which way ecumenical relations develop.

2. PRESSURE FOR A NEW LOOK AT STEM CELLS

Pressure may grow at the Catholic grassroots in the future for reconsideration of the Church's condemnation of embryonic stem cell research, driven by the rapidly expanding elderly population in the Church, coupled with the fact that embryonic stem cell research is often touted as a possible source of new remedies for Parkinson's, Alzheimer's, and other neurological disorders that disproportionately strike elderly people. The emergence of a bloc of 13.3 million American Catholics over the age of 65 by the year 2030, and even greater numbers of elderly Catholics in Europe, could be a powerful constituency within the Church for a more positive position. Obviously, demographics do not determine what Catholicism teaches, but the composition of the Church may have some effect in shaping its sense of priorities and its willingness to take a new look at difficult questions.

The spread of Alzheimer's disease may be the strongest force pushing the Church in this direction. Worldwide, the Alzheimer's Association estimated the number of cases in 2007 at 26 million. In the United States, it was somewhere around 4.5 million. Projections for 2050 anticipate a rise between three and four times above present levels, which means the number of Alzheimer's sufferers will be between 13 and 18 million Americans. Among those 85 or older, almost 40 percent are likely to be affected. It is a particularly excruciating disorder because of its long time frame; it usually runs a course from onset to death lasting six to 10 years, though in some cases it may go on twice as long.

Whether pressure for change within Catholicism actually develops will depend to some extent on future scientific discoveries. Some experts believe that adult stem cells will ultimately prove to be the most productive avenue of research, in which case the ethical problem will resolve itself. As chapter six explains, there are also proposals for alternative methods of generating stem cells, such as "altered nuclear transfer," which some leading Catholic bishops and ethicists believe would be morally acceptable. At a minimum, the demographic realities of the twenty-first century will provide a powerful stimulus to embrace such an alternative.

3. A DEMOGRAPHIC DIVIDEND FOR CATHOLICISM?

Anyone even marginally active in the Catholic Church has probably attended an event recently when someone looked out at the crowd and rued: "Look at all the gray heads!" This is universally understood to be a bad thing, whereas a room full of young people would normally be interpreted as a triumph. Such reactions pivot on the commonsense assumption that youth equals growth, while old age means decline.

Yet given the "through the looking glass" demographic situation in which the global North today finds itself, in many ways the exact opposite is the case. People over 65 are far and away the most rapidly growing segment of the population in the North, well ahead of any group of immigrants. Given that the elderly are disproportionately likely to take religion seriously and to practice their faith, the "graying" of the population—far from being something to lament—actually represents a potential "boom cycle" for the Catholic Church, if it has the imagination to grasp the moment.

The material that follows pertains mostly to the United States, but the picture is much the same in other aging zones of the Catholic world.

Sociological data shows that the 65-and-older group is the most religious segment of the American population, in terms of both attitudes and practice. A recent Pew study concluded that just 27 percent of U.S. adults 18 to 34 describe themselves as "religious," as opposed to 47 percent of those 65 and older. (That difference is a barometer of religious intensity, since more young adults than seniors choose the "somewhat religious" option.) A 2006 Baylor University survey found that 18.6 percent of those 18 to 30 said they have "no religious affiliation," while the number drops to just 5.4 percent among those aged 65 and up. A *U.S. News and World Report*/PBS Religion and Ethics Newsweekly survey in 2002 concluded that 60 percent of those 65 and older attend religious services at least once a week, compared to just 34 percent of those aged 25 to 34.

Crossing the 65-plus boundary does not magically make someone religious. Sociologists refer to "lifetime stability theory" to mean that one's basic worldview generally does not undergo radical variations with age. The current crop of elderly is more likely to be religious in part because that's how they were raised; it remains to be seen how generations without a similar formation will react. Nevertheless, evidence also suggests that someone who is at least marginally open to religion at 35 is likely to be more so at 65. Sociologist Fr. Andrew Greeley says that an uptick in both prayer and attending religious services begins in the early thirties and builds as people age.

By 2030, 6.8 million additional Catholics in the United States will be entering the stage of life at which they are most likely to pray, to go to church, to reflect on religious subjects, and to be open to a deeper religious commitment. Improvements in general health mean the elderly can remain active members of the church for much longer periods of time. Three in four persons aged 65 to 74 in the United States, and two in three of those over 75, say their health is "good to excellent." They also have the means to contribute financially to the church; the advertising firm Martino and Binzer, which specializes in "mature marketing," estimates that Americans over 55 possess $1.5 trillion in discretionary spending.

The question is, will the Church take advantage of this potential bonanza by reaching out to the elderly population?

On the positive side of the ledger, the vision to do so is largely in place. Pope John Paul II published a moving "Letter to the Elderly" in 1999, which was the United Nations Year of the Elderly. The pope's own highly visible frailty in his later years stirred Catholic consciousness. The U.S. bishops published their own pastoral document in 1999, "The Blessings of Age," which states: "How the community relates to its older members—recognizing their presence, encouraging their contributions, responding to their needs, and providing appropriate opportunities for spiritual growth—is a sign of the community's spiritual health and maturity."

There are all sorts of moral and spiritual reasons why reluctance to embrace the elderly is unfortunate. Setting that aside for the moment, however, it's also self-defeating. To put this in crassly commercial terms, the 65-plus population represents the most promising "growth market" for the Church's "product," and in a boom cycle, only a dysfunctional company would fail to adjust its sales and customer service to ride the wave.

All this suggests the need for a broad "gray-friendly" consciousness in the church. To offer just one practical example, seminaries ought to be encouraging future homilists to slow down in their delivery, since elderly parishioners often struggle to hear when someone is speaking in rapid-fire fashion. Parishes should be ensuring that structures are accessible to the disabled and offering transportation programs for senior citizens. Even schedules may need to change. Parishes that cater to younger adults often start faith formation sessions or Bible study groups at seven P.M. or later, on the theory that by this hour, participants will have returned home from work, taken care of their kids, had dinner, and be ready for something else. Senior citizens often might be more comfortable with events that begin in the early afternoon. All of this should be worked out in local settings by talking to the elderly themselves.

None of this means that Catholicism ought to abandon the young. But the basic point is that far from clucking sadly when we see gray heads in the aisles, hearts ought to gladden. If someone were to dream up a program of outreach to marginal Catholics that drew 6.8 million back into active practice of the faith within a quarter century, it would be hailed as one of the great evangelical success stories of all time. Today, demographics are to some extent doing the job all by themselves.

4. GROWING SUPPORT FOR THE CHURCH'S EDUCATION AND YOUTH FORMATION

In an era of dwindling numbers of children, the perceived "value" of each individual child grows, and the protection and nurturing of children becomes a topic of immense social concern. Organizations that offer programs to nurture children, helping to mold them into morally sensitive people and productive members of society, will enjoy growing public support. In an environment in which the absolute number of children has never been so low, it becomes critical that, as American political lingo puts it, "no child be left behind."

The sexual abuse scandals that came to light in the first few years of the twenty-first century have taken a great deal of luster off the Catholic Church's reputation in this regard. Nevertheless, Catholic schools still enjoy high public esteem. Data confirm their success, both by traditional academic measures such as test scores as well as indicators of good citizenship such as rates of volunteerism. In that light, it's imaginable that concerns over church–state relations that have sometimes blocked public funding for religious schools will seem increasingly less important in years to come, as the top priority becomes promoting any program that might help higher percentages of children turn out well. Indeed, it may not be just faith-based schools buoyed by this wave of public concern for children, but any program of youth formation, including after-school programs, summer schools, and the like.

At the same time, growing public preoccupation with children also means that the damage to the Catholic Church from the sexual abuse crisis may be deeper and longer lasting than previously understood. In this cultural milieu, any institution perceived as indifferent or malfeasant in its concern for children will have a hard time winning back the public's sympathy.

Long-Shot Consequences

1. THE YOUNGEST DAUGHTER OF THE CHURCH?

In July 2006, the official French statistical office announced a new set of population projections. France's population, it said, will grow by nine million between 2005 and 2050, when it will level off at 70 million. Assuming that Germany's population continues to decline, which is almost a mathematical certainty given its current fertility rate, France would become the most populous nation in Western Europe by mid-century. This growth is not due merely to Muslim immigration, since Germany too has a rising Muslim population. It's also due to the fact that, as noted above, France has staged something of a demographic rebound and today has one of the three highest fertility rates in Europe.

It's possible that relative demographic vitality may give the French a new sense of national vigor. If so, the question is whether this rising tide could lift French Catholicism out of its doldrums. It would be a remarkable outcome, since the Catholic Church in France has long been a poster child for moribund European religiosity. Frédéric Lenoir, editor-in-chief of *Le Monde des Religions*, recently concluded that "In its institutions, but also in its mentalities, France is no longer a Catholic country." Writing in the *National Review* in 2005, Denis Boyles said summarily that "a revival of any kind is out of the question."

Still, French Catholicism could draw strength from a broad upswing in French national consciousness. In addition, the Church could get a shot in the arm from the growth of French-speaking Catholicism in other parts of the world. As outlined in chapter one, the Democratic Republic of the Congo, where French is the principal language of public life, is destined to be one of the Catholic powerhouses of the twenty-first century. By 2050, it will be the fifth-largest Catholic country in the world, at 97 million Catholics, behind only Brazil, Mexico, the Philippines, and the United States.

By 2050, the ten largest populations of Catholics where French is a principal language will be in the following nations:

1. Democratic Republic of the Congo   97,499,000
2. France   54,600,000
3. Burundi   17,294,000
4. Madagascar   11,747,000
5. Haiti   10,527,000
6. Rwanda   8,713,000
7. Vietnam   7,932,000
8. Belgium   7,830,000
9. Cameroon   6,992,000
10. Canada (Quebec)   6,781,000

French-speaking Catholicism in the twenty-first century will be an overwhelmingly Southern phenomenon. Roughly two thirds of French-speaking Catholics in 2050 will be Africans. Given the youthful demographics of those nations, one might say that Francophone Catholicism in the twenty-first century could become "the youngest daughter of the Church."

Overall, the Catholic population of the 40 nations where French is a principal language in 2050 will be roughly 280 million, making it 18 percent of the total Catholic population worldwide. This bloc could be an important force in Catholic affairs—on the condition that it thinks of itself as a "bloc," which can hardly be taken for granted. Such an awakened Francophone wing of Catholicism, if it takes shape, could offset the pro-American drift in Vatican policy outlined above, or it could drive the Church further into advocacy for multilateralism in foreign affairs.

Before one gets carried away, however, it's worth comparing the projected numbers for Francophone Catholicism in 2050 with those for the English-speaking world. The ten largest English-speaking Catholic populations in the world at that point will be:

1. Philippines   105,466,000
2. United States   98,744,000
3. Uganda   55,858,000
4. Nigeria   47,750,000
5. India   25,483,000
6. Kenya   19,938,000
7. Tanzania   19,388,000
8. Canada   11,642,000 (not including Quebec)
9. Australia   7,823,000
10. Malawi   7,068,000

The grand total of English-speaking Catholics at that point will be 434 million Catholics, 150 million more than French speakers. English speakers will constitute roughly 27 percent of the projected global Catholic population in 2050 of 1.6 billion. The point of this is not to suggest a Catholic future in which Francophones square off against Anglophones; the whole world is not going to become Quebec. Rather, the point is that even if a revival in French-speaking Catholicism does occur, one should not exaggerate its importance.

2. MATCHMAKERS AND BABYSITTERS?

Religions have always been involved in the matchmaking business (think *Fiddler on the Roof*), but in the Internet age, the process has gone high-tech. The Web site CatholicSingles.com, for example, has been in operation since 1997, and for an annual fee of $99.95, the site promises to connect clients with more than 35,000 other Catholic singles who share their interests and, most importantly, their values and faith commitments. The service describes itself as "the premier online dating site for single Catholics in the world." There's a comparable online service called Ave Maria Singles, which at one stage was affiliated with Catholic entrepreneur Tom Monaghan's Ave Maria Foundation in Ann Arbor, Michigan, and which is now based in Front Royal, Virginia.

Exactly how many Catholic dating operations the market will bear isn't clear. But in the context of declining fertility and widespread divorce, a growing number of Catholic individuals and movements, and perhaps in isolated cases even parishes and dioceses, will take it upon themselves to try to promote successful marriages by helping singles find one another.

Though it's a more remote possibility, a new movement or religious order could take matchmaking as its charism. Others might decide to specialize in providing child care for families in which both parents work outside the home. After all, the creation of new religious orders in the nineteenth century was driven to some extent by demographics, specifically the need to educate growing numbers of young people and to care for the urban poor. In an era of "through-the-looking-glass" demographics, all sorts of unlikely scenarios, such as matchmaking brothers or babysitting nuns, suddenly seem a bit more plausible.

EXPANDING LAY ROLES

M aria Luisa Chumpitaz, a Catholic mother of nine, was a local legend in an impoverished rural community of 2,000 called Villa El Carmen, located roughly two hours north of Peru's capital city, Lima. (That's as the crow flies; depending upon weather and road conditions, it can take a lot longer than that to actually get there.) The place gives a whole new meaning to the expression "off the map." Not only is there no highway exit to mark the spot, there's no highway at all. To find it, one has to exit the main road north of Lima and then follow a narrow dirt path that's more frequently traveled by donkeys than cars.

Villa El Carmen was founded in the 1980s by indigenous Peruvians from the Andes Mountains fleeing violence between Maoist-inspired Shining Path rebels and the army. The settlement is technically illegal, which among other things means that the government doesn't provide public utilities such as electricity and water. Despite the galling poverty of the place— homes without roofs or lights, open sewage, the stench of smoke, serious malnutrition—Chumpitaz, with just two years of primary education, created and ran a women's center widely seen as a regional model for female empowerment. She taught basic literacy skills to rural Andean women, most of them from mountain sites so remote that they'd never even picked up a pencil, let alone written with one. While the women did their writing exercises, Chumpitaz (known locally as Lucha) and her volunteers fed the children, checked them for disease, and coordinated food pickups and drop-offs for the families. Lucha ran the center all the way up to her unexpected death in February 2007.

She didn't do so as a limousine liberal, a member of the Peruvian middle class who drove out from an affluent neighborhood of Lima once a week in a Range Rover. She lived in a nearby poor community called Cilcal, trekking to Villa El Carmen every morning on foot and back again at night. Her father, Teodoro, had taken the family to Cilcal during the peak of Peru's bloody twenty-year guerrilla war, in which an estimated 70,000 people were either killed or "disappeared" and hundreds of thousands of Peruvians, most of them rural poor, were displaced.

After raising nine children, Lucha felt she had to do something for other women trapped in poverty and neglect. She founded her center in 1992, calling it Wawa-Wasi, meaning "house of children" in the Quechua language. In the beginning, she said in a 2004 interview, she ran the center out of her tiny family home. She had to persuade her father to leave the house early in the morning and not to come back until later in the afternoon, so classes could be held and lunch served.

"We used the only large room in the house, but it had no roof," Lucha said. "When it rained we got wet, and when the sun beat down on us we burned."

When Lucha's father died in 2001, the twelve brothers and sisters decided that his meager property should go to Lucha and the Wawa-Wasi center. Lucha decided to sell it off, and taking the limited proceeds, along with a modest grant from a Peruvian nongovernmental organization (NGO) called Pro Peru, she built a larger facility. Today, the Wawa-Wasi center consists of three classrooms, a nursery with eight cribs of different sizes, a makeshift infirmary, and a small office where Lucha acted as administrator, teacher, counselor, and sometimes even spiritual director.

The women follow a three-level course of formation. The first focuses on basic literacy, the second introduces more complex reading and writing, and the third branches out to also include some history and geography. The goal is to give them enough basic education that they can find better jobs to support their families, and stand up for themselves when they face discrimination or have to deal with public officials. The children get health checkups and participate in various group activities. The center also sponsors a child-to-child nutrition program. (The World Bank estimates that of the 3.8 million people living in extreme poverty in Peru, 2.1 million are children.)

Lucha's spiritual inspiration came from Opus Dei, a group generally classified among the more conservative elements of the Catholic Church. Lucha said its emphasis on individual holiness was a good fit with her spirituality. She wasn't looking to get involved in politics, she said, just to put her faith to work helping a few Andean women caught in a new world they don't understand, and rescuing a few children from disease, hunger, crime, and hopelessness.

In doing so, Lucha provided one face of the lay role in the Catholic Church today.

Half a world away, in Rome, American laywoman Donna Orsuto offers another.

A professor of spirituality at the Jesuit-sponsored Pontifical Gregorian University and a consulter to the Pontifical Council for Interreligious Dialogue, Orsuto is also the driving force behind the Lay Centre, a residence and support system for laywomen and -men from around the world, including non-Catholics, who want to study at one of Rome's pontifical universities. In what is arguably the most clerical company town on earth, the center provides a toehold for laity, and, in so doing, helps to form the next generation of lay scholars, activists, and pastoral workers in global Catholicism.

Orsuto was introduced to Rome in 1978, when she was a junior at Wake Forest University on a university-sponsored trip to Europe. Smitten, she returned in 1979 to begin studies at the Gregorian University, where a good number of today's bishops and priests in the Catholic Church around the world got their start. She eventually earned a doctorate in spirituality from the Gregorian, focusing on Saint Catherine of Siena. She decided to stay in Rome as a professor, teaching at an institute for religious women called Regina Mundi as well as the Dominican-run Angelicum University. Since 1994, she has been a member of the faculty at the Gregorian.

Though she is hesitant to put herself forward as a pioneer, Orsuto acknowledges that being a laywoman at the Gregorian in the 1980s made her a bit of a curiosity. When she finished her licentiate, the stage before a doctorate, she was the only woman in a class of fifty. Today, she notes, women represent 20 percent of the Gregorian's enrollment.

The Lay Centre dates from 1986, when a French group of consecrated women called the Ladies of Bethany decided to pull out of the Foyer Unitas ecumenical center in the Piazza Navona. Orsuto and a lay Dutch friend, Rickie Van Velzen, proposed keeping the facility open by turning it into a beachhead for lay students. Over twenty years, more than 100 students from twenty countries have lived at the center. The Lay Centre recently moved into larger facilities at the Monastery of Sts. John and Paul in Rome.

"The dream was to create a sense of community, of family," Orsuto said. "I heard horror stories about people having to switch apartments right before exams, or facing problems with no one to take an interest in their lives. I wanted to start a center where people would feel at home."

Encounters with ecclesiastical bureaucracy illustrate that Rome still has to play a bit of catch-up ball. When Lay Centre resident Chris Gustafson of Green Bay, Wisconsin, registered for classes at the Angelicum University each year, a standardized form required him to list his seminary residence and his religious superior. In response to the first question, he wrote "Lay Centre." In response to the second, he put down "Donna Orsuto," making him possibly the only man in Rome under the ostensible authority of a Mother Superior.

"The forms are in Latin and they're probably a hundred years old," Gustafson laughed. "It's pretty funny, but it also illustrates how the system is taking some time to catch up to reality."

Orsuto acknowledged that Rome can be a daunting place for lay-run groups to find backing, and she said that measured against the vast ecclesiastical infrastructure in the city, the Lay Centre is a modest undertaking.

"We have to constantly explain there's no big organization behind us. We're nothing more than baptized Christians trying to offer a humble service to the Church," she said. Nothing more—and, many of the center's friends and alumni would add, nothing less.

Chumpitaz and Orsuto, and millions of Catholic women and men like them all over the world, illustrate the spirit of lay activism stirring in today's Church. No one in officialdom drew up the plans for either Wawa-Wasi or the Lay Centre, and their founders didn't ask anyone's permission. Though both programs have enjoyed the support of Church leaders, probably the greatest contribution of the clergy to their success has been staying out of the way.

At one level, calling such lay activism a "trend" can seem absurd, since it's been part of the Christian story from the beginning. The early spread of

Christianity was fueled by prominent laity such as Priscilla and Aquila, Onesiphorus, and Lydia, who sometimes traveled with Saint Paul to preach the gospel and at other times operated house churches and provided leadership to the local Christian flock. Across the generations, much of the renewal in the Church has been led by laity. Saint Francis lived most of his life as a layman and only reluctantly accepted ordination to the diaconate as a condition of leadership in the new Franciscan order. Cardinal John Henry Newman of England was once asked what he thought about the laity, to which Newman is famously alleged to have responded: "Well, we'd look pretty silly without them."

Over the centuries, however, the lay role has been something of a footnote in both official Catholic theology and popular Catholic psychology. Specialized spiritual elites—bishops, priests, monks, and so on—came to be seen as the lead actors in the Catholic drama. This clericalism seeped into the popular consciousness, so much so that it's sometimes difficult to persuade outside observers, including the media, that the Catholic Church is not defined exclusively by its clerical ranks. The Second Vatican Council in the mid-1960s aimed to balance this clericalism with stronger attention to the lay role. In the period after the council, however, "lay empowerment" sometimes came to be identified with playing a quasi-official role inside the Church: distributing communion at Mass, or running the diocesan office of youth ministry. The broader vision of the laity as evangelists simply by virtue of their baptism, transforming the secular world without any formal commission or office, was sometimes obscured.

What makes expanding lay roles a major trend in the twenty-first century is that laity are emerging as protagonists both inside and outside the Church. Internally, laypeople are occupying ministerial and administrative positions once held almost exclusively by priests. Externally, laypeople are taking it upon themselves to evangelize culture and to act on Catholic social teaching. It's this one-two punch, lay ministers inside the Church and lay activists on the outside, that constitutes the trend.

To be sure, this rising lay tide sometimes butts heads with the evangelical impulse described in chapter two, with its emphasis on defending traditional markers of Catholic identity, including the authority of the hierarchy and the uniqueness of the ordained priesthood. Those who conceive of "lay empowerment" primarily by analogy to secular democracy—voting bishops in and out, or deciding Catholic teaching by plebiscites—are likely to be disappointed. For example, if the only test of hearing the "lay voice" is yielding to the strong majorities of laity in the West who, according to opinion polls, disagree with the official teaching on birth control, then it's a test the Church of the foreseeable future is almost certain to flunk.

Nonetheless, for reasons both practical and theological, laity will play increasingly visible and consequential roles during the twenty-first century, and often in remarkably independent fashion. The growth market for lay leadership won't be reformers seeking to alter official structures and teachings, but rather activists willing to take those things for granted, at least for the time being, in order to get on with the business of saving souls and changing the world.

WHAT'S HAPPENING

Expanding lay roles at the outset of the twenty-first century are so ubiquitous as to almost escape notice, the way people in rainy climates don't generally stop to think about wet weather. Today lay missionaries are scattered to the four corners of the earth, teaching, healing, and providing witness to the gospel, just as missionary priests, brothers, and nuns once did. Post-college volunteer programs for Catholic youth are booming. Lay ministers are leading parishes, catechizing, preparing people for the sacraments, and guiding people in worship. Movements such as Focolare, Communion and Liberation, and Sant'Egidio are forming highly motivated corps of laity serving the Church and the world. At the grassroots, lay pundits, bloggers, and activists are providing new sources of leadership. In several recent episodes that have convulsed American Catholicism—from the Terry Schiavo case in 2005 to Notre Dame's invitation to President Barack Obama in 2009—the tone was set by grassroots lay activists, with the U.S. bishops largely along for the ride.

Forces Driving Expansion

Advocates for expanded lay roles often point out that the dynamism of primitive Christianity was not created by priests and bishops, but rather by lay Christian women and men who were on fire with the gospel and who carried its message into every walk of life, thereby transforming the ancient world. From that point of view, it is not broad lay activism that requires explanation or theological justification, but rather the way this lay role was progressively constricted over the centuries by the emergence of clerical structures and a specialized caste of spiritual heroes. Yet from a historical point of view, the expanding lay roles of the twentieth and twenty-first centuries are not merely a matter of returning to earlier models, even if those models provide inspiration and points of reference. The trend is also a result of the intersection of at least five historical forces, all of which seem to augur further movement in the direction of lay activism.

1. PRIEST SHORTAGES

Writers on the lay role in the Church sometimes don't like to tie its expansion to priest shortages, worrying that doing so can make it seem like a temporary expedient rather than a consequence of fundamental theological convictions. In fact, the Second Vatican Council endorsed an expanded concept of lay roles well before contemporary priest shortages in Europe and the United States began to take on their current dimensions. Yet there's no doubt that persistent shortages of clergy in various parts of the world have made such a concept more attractive. Today, a growing number of Catholic leaders believe that gaps in the Church's network of pastoral care can only be filled by laypeople stepping into roles once played by priests and religious, as well as by inventing new roles to extend the Church's pastoral reach.

Growth in what Catholicism today calls "lay ecclesial ministry," outlined below, is perhaps the clearest case in point. Various forms of lay ministry in Catholicism have developed in the last quarter-century without any formal blueprint, but rather in response to the practical reality that parishes and dioceses could not catechize their new converts, run small faith groups, plan liturgies, and administer facilities if they had to rely exclusively upon priests to do so. Especially in the global South, the expanding number of pastoral centers that are not parishes promises increasing reliance on laity to deliver routine pastoral care.

2. COMPETITION

Though Catholicism is not a for-profit concern, it is not immune to the dynamics of the marketplace. Competitive pressures were keenly felt in Europe at the dawn of the twentieth century, when Catholicism seemed to be losing ground dramatically to secular ideologies. The intellectual class had opted for Darwin, skepticism, and the Enlightenment, while workers were embracing Marxism. If Catholicism was to respond, Church leaders came to believe that it couldn't address lay culture from the outside looking in; it had to do so through laity acting in the realms of art, science, commerce, and other sectors of society. One sign of ferment came in 1938, when Pope Pius XI commissioned one of the most dynamic Italian Catholic leaders of the era, Franciscan Fr. Agostino Gemelli, founder of the Catholic University in Milan, to preside over a congress in Saint-Gall, Switzerland, of leaders of twenty-five lay Catholic groups. These nascent movements were pressing to find ways for laity to live a religiously serious, committed Christian life without thereby ceasing to be laity. Many of today's new lay movements, and a broader spirit of lay activism, grew from these impulses.

Societies in the global South today are generally characterized by robust religious pluralism. Catholicism is competing with Islam in a number of zones, and with Pentecostalism almost everywhere. The determination of Catholic leaders in Latin America, Africa, and Asia to mobilize the laity is related to the reality that the Church's competitors often do a better job of drawing upon all their followers, rather than simply a clerical caste, to evangelize and to build new communities. This dynamic is especially clear in Latin America, where the Catholic bishops of the region have become steadily more committed to expanding lay roles in the face of ongoing defections from Catholicism to various Protestant groups, especially dynamic Pentecostal movements.

3. NEW THEOLOGICAL UNDERSTANDINGS

Pope Pius XI famously defined the lay apostolate as "their share in the apostolate of the hierarchy," which meant the lay role was derivative from, and dependent upon, that of the bishops. Bishops led, laity followed. The model was the powerful Catholic Action movement in Italy. According to this vision, what it meant to be an active lay Catholic was to join a group under the sponsorship of the hierarchy, and to carry out the tasks the hierarchy assigned. Pressure to turn this model around crested at Vatican II. The council stressed that each Catholic, by virtue of baptism and confirmation, is authorized to "do" apostolate. As the document *Apostolicam Actuositatem* phrased it, laypeople "ought to take upon themselves as their distinctive task this renewal of the temporal order." In contrast to Pius XI, the council fathers said: "The lay apostolate is a share in the Church's mission of salvation." Another feature of the lay contribution stressed by the document is its external orientation, meaning concern for the world beyond the boundaries of the visible, institutional Church. More than forty years after the Second Vatican Council, this vision seems gradually to be putting down roots in Catholic consciousness.

4. SEXUAL ABUSE AND FINANCIAL SCANDALS

Though the roots of the scandals that have recently marred the life of the Church in various parts of the world are complex, most Catholics seem convinced that one element has been a model of clerical leadership insufficiently accountable to the local community, and, as a result, lacking adequate safeguards for good governance. Too often, critics say, bishops and priests made financial and personnel decisions on their own, without mechanisms for ensuring that those decisions served the broader pastoral good. While evangelical Catholicism means that the Church will defend its hierarchical structures, as a practical matter there's growing awareness of the need for collaboration and shared responsibility to complement the ultimate authority of the bishops. The creation of lay review boards to advise bishops on matters related to the sexual abuse crisis is one example. In the global South, sexual abuse crises have not had the same devastating impact, but the Church's outspoken criticism of corruption and a lack of transparence in public and corporate life is similarly driving a self-examination of its own practices.

5. "PENTECOSTALIZATION" OF CATHOLICISM

Chapter ten lays out the growth in global Pentecostalism, and the various ways in which the Catholic Church is being "Pentecostalized," in terms of both the expansion of the Catholic Charismatic movement as well as informal grassroots absorption of Pentecostal spirituality and modes of Church life. One defining feature of Pentecostalism is the way it empowers laity, primarily through its egalitarian understanding of the gifts of the Holy Spirit. Prophecy, visions, dreams, healing, and speaking in tongues are not the exclusive prerogative of a clerical elite, but rather gifts bestowed upon all believers that can erupt spontaneously, without respect to formal credentials or pastoral plans. As a result, Pentecostalism bulldozes through hierarchical modes of ecclesiastical organization, relying on informal lay evangelization for its remarkable growth. The growing sector of what one might call Pentecostal Catholics means that an increasing number of laity see themselves as commissioned to act as teachers, evangelists, and activists on the basis of charismatic inspiration rather than formal ecclesiastical authorization. Even where Catholics do not formally see themselves as "Charismatic," or practice any of the spiritual gifts associated with the Charismatic movement, the Pentecostal model nevertheless can shape the Catholic imagination.

The Movements

Perhaps the most visible indicator of expanding lay roles is that there are more groups in the Church today whose explicit purpose is to encourage lay activism than at any other point in Catholic history. These forces are conventionally called the "new movements." To date, the Vatican has granted canonical status to more than 120 of these new lay movements, virtually all of them founded within the last 100 years. During that time, they've spawned a bewildering variety of projects, missions, and institutions, to say nothing of controversy. At their best, they encourage laity to see themselves as missionaries in their own walks of life, transforming the secular world from the inside out.

It's easier to document the number of movements than it is to establish exactly how many Catholics belong to them, or are influenced by them. Some movements don't have "members" in the classic sense, and others have a small core of formal members but a wider network of supporters and collaborators. By most estimates, the total number of Catholics connected to a movement is relatively small, but their visibility and official favor means the movements play a disproportionate role in setting the lay tone. Brief sketches of three movements will offer a flavor of the range of their activity and outlooks.

1. L'ARCHE

Jean Vanier, a Canadian layman and founder of the L'Arche movement, carries the rare burden of being a public figure widely flagged as a saint in his own lifetime. Born in Geneva, Switzerland, on September 10, 1928, Vanier is the son of the nineteenth governor general of Canada, George Philias Vanier, and his wife, Pauline Archer Vanier. Sainthood causes for both have been launched in Canada. His father was the Canadian ambassador to France at the end of the Second World War, and while in France the young Vanier saw ex-inmates arriving from Buchenwald, Bergen-Belsen, and Dachau. He later described "their white and blue uniforms . . . They were skeletons. That vision has remained with me—what human beings can do to other human beings, how we can hurt and kill each other."

Studying in France, Vanier befriended a chaplain for mentally handicapped men living at Le Val Fleuri, a large institution about an hour by train from Paris. Vanier later moved to the area, where he bought a small, dilapidated house that he called l'Arche, "the Ark"—a reference to Noah's Ark. Vanier welcomed two mentally handicapped men, Raphael and Philippe, into his home on August 4, 1964, marking the birth of L'Arche.

L'Arche describes itself as a series of friendships, pairing one person who has a disability with another person who does not. The idea is not merely to deliver social service, but to build relationships. A guiding principle is that "everyone is of unique and sacred value" with a "right to friendship, to communion and to a spiritual life." Vanier says that the aim of L'Arche is not so much to change the world, "but to create little places . . . where love is possible."

Vanier's movement came to international attention in the mid-1980s when Fr. Henri Nouwen, a Catholic priest whose spiritual self-help books have sold in the millions, settled in a L'Arche community in Ontario, Canada. Nouwen had suffered a nervous collapse from the pressures of worldly success, and his friend Vanier suggested L'Arche as a place he might find relief. L'Arche has since grown to some 104 communities in more than thirty countries on five continents. Vanier is no longer its director, but he still lives in a L'Arche community in France.

L'Arche has spun off two related groups. Vanier founded the Faith and Sharing movement in 1968, which brings people with developmental disabilities and others together once a month for gospel readings and prayer. In 1971, he and Marie Hélène Mathieu founded Faith and Light, which holds regular get-togethers for people with disabilities along with their parents and friends. Vanier and Mathieu founded Faith and Light after taking a group of severely disabled persons on a pilgrimage to Lourdes, where they were shocked at the hostile response. Townspeople and pilgrims actually suggested that people this badly disabled should not be taken out in public, despite the fact that Lourdes is a sanctuary for the sick.

"L'Arche is an experience born from suffering," Vanier said. "The terrible suffering of parents, of people with handicaps . . . the aim of being Christian is to reveal the compassionate face of Christ."

2. FOCOLARE

Founded in Italy in 1943 by laywoman Chiara Lubich, Focolare claims to reach 182 countries, touching 4.5 million people. Its core idea is universal brotherhood, which prompts the *focolarini*, as members are known, to be especially involved in ecumenism and interreligious dialogue.

Lubich's father lost his job under Italy's Fascist regime because he was a Socialist, and as a result the Lubichs lived for years in poverty. Lubich, who died in 2008, launched Focolare (an Italian word that means "hearth") after aerial bombings of northern Italy, including her hometown of Trento, by the Allies in 1942 and 1943. Like Vanier, Lubich said she was shattered by the reality of war, and filled with determination to promote unity within the human family. She and her friends, who formed the early core of Focolare, declared that should they be killed, they wished to have only one inscription on their tomb: "We have believed in love."

As Focolare is structured today, it has three levels of affiliation. Consecrated members take vows of celibacy, live in Focolare communities, and turn over their earnings to the community. Married members turn over what they can afford. Affiliates have a looser connection. All told, there are eighteen Focolare-related groups and associations. While Focolare is unambiguously rooted in Catholic tradition, it also welcomes members from other backgrounds, including Protestants, Anglicans, Orthodox, Jews, Muslims, Hindus, Buddhists, and Sikhs, as well as people with no particular religion. The Focolare constitution requires that the president be a woman, one of the few mixed bodies of women and men in the Church to have such a stipulation.

In the United States, one example of the Focolare commitment to unity is its standing dialogue with the American Muslim Society led by Imam W. D. Mohammed, widely considered to be the moderate alternative to the Nation of Islam. Launched in the mid-1990s, the dialogue has become a model for Christian–Muslim relations in other parts of the world.

David Shaheed, an American Muslim from Indianapolis, described the reception he got when he attended a Focolare event at their facility in Castel Gandolfo, the pope's summer residence. Shaheed said that when he and fellow Muslims were on their way to Italy, some were worried about how they were going to perform their five daily prayers. When they arrived, however, the *focolarini* had already set up a prayer room and organized the schedule so they could break for prayer seamlessly.

"They weren't trying to convert us," Shaheed said. "They were trying to help us become better Muslims."

Focolare also sponsors a network of some 750 business firms around the world called the "Economy of Communion," in which profits are pooled to fund development projects and charitable activities. Pope Benedict XVI cited the "Economy of Communion" as a promising third way between classic for-profit enterprises and nonprofit organizations in his 2009 social encyclical, *Caritas in Veritate.*

3. THE COMMUNITY OF SANT'EGIDIO

Launched in 1968 by Italian Church historian Andrea Riccardi, then a high school student in Rome, Sant'Egidio (Saint Giles in English) takes its name from an old Carmelite convent in the Trastevere district of the Eternal City where early members gathered for worship. Inspired by Vatican II and the leftist student energies of the time, members began living and working among the poor along the city's periphery. They founded "popular schools" for disadvantaged children.

For its work on international conflict resolution, Sant'Egidio is today nicknamed "the UN of Trastevere." A breakthrough success came on October 4, 1992, when they brokered a peace accord in Mozambique, ending a civil war that had left more than one million people dead. The community proudly says the Mozambique deal was "the first intergovernmental agreement ever negotiated by a nongovernmental body."

Sant'Egidio is also active on human rights issues, especially its campaign to abolish the death penalty worldwide. In 2001 the community delivered a petition with 2.7 million signatures to the United Nations supporting abolition of capital punishment. The community also enjoys a reputation for liturgical and spiritual depth. Evening vespers at the Church of Santa Maria in Trastevere attract overflow crowds, usually composed of a wide cross-section of visitors and locals, including a striking number of young adults.

Africa is a special point of emphasis. In March 2002, Sant'Egidio launched the DREAM project in Mozambique to combat HIV/AIDS. Through a combination of volunteers and donations, and relying on low-cost generic medications, some 95 percent of the over 4,000 AIDS patients under the program's care (including 1,700 on retroviral therapy) are still alive with a good quality of life. Some 97 percent of children born from HIV-positive mothers in the DREAM program do not have the disease. Perhaps most impressively, DREAM has had 95 percent compliance from its patients with the prescribed regime of treatment. This is a rate as good as or better than in Europe or the United States, and it belies that prejudice that it would be useless to give Africans complicated medical treatments because they couldn't or wouldn't follow instructions.

In 1986, when John Paul II called leaders of the world's religions to

Assisi to pray for peace, Sant'Egidio welcomed the initiative despite criticism from some quarters that it risked relativism. Every year since, they have sponsored an interreligious gathering to keep "the spirit of Assisi" alive. Members of Sant'Egidio have been leaders in ecumenical and interreligious dialogue, sometimes operating a sort of "back-channel" ecumenism alongside the Church's official dialogues and relationships.

Guerilla Evangelists

The movements are interesting not just in themselves, but as a barometer of a broader shift toward laity seeing themselves as the subjects of evangelization, not just its objects. For a case in point, consider forty-seven-year-old Peter Dobbins, founder of the Storm Theatre company in Manhattan, just off the Great White Way. Dobbins, a committed lay Catholic who has no connection to any formal movement, expresses his ambition this way: "The purpose of this theater is to lead people to God."

Since 1997, the theater has staged a series of well-reviewed productions that play to secular audiences. Some, such as *Murder in the Cathedral* and *The Power and the Glory,* have explicitly religious themes, but more often they're secular works with a spiritual and moral undertone. Dobbins said he wanted to try to do for the contemporary theater what G. K. Chesterton had done for early-twentieth-century English letters.

The Storm Theatre, founded in 1997, takes its name from a line in Shakespeare's *Titus Andronicus*: "Now is a time to storm; why art thou still?" In 2007, I asked Dobbins how he reconciles his Catholic missionary zeal with the essentially areligious, socially liberal milieu of the theater.

"Can it be a hostile environment sometimes? Sure," he said. "I'm all for a plurality of ideas. Everybody talks about that, but they don't seem to really want it. The entertainment industry actually seems terrified of it."

Dobbins said the Storm Theatre is about injecting the faith into the cultural bloodstream.

"As a guy who rejoined the church in his twenties, I feel strongly that it's not enough to say Mass on Sundays, if those thoughts and ideas are not represented in the culture," he said. "The reality is that we are going to act pretty much the way our culture teaches us to act. It's going to take lots and lots of people doing stuff like this, just so you're not being crushed by an opposite way of thinking, without any alternative.

"These ideas are eternal. They're the truth," he said. "They need to compete with the other ideas on all the other blocks around here. Not only do I think these ideas are just as good, I think they're better."

Lay Ministry

If organized movements and guerrilla evangelists such as Dobbins point to an aroused Catholic laity, so too does dramatic growth in lay ecclesial ministry, meaning laity who perform ministries such as leading parishes, preaching, teaching the faith, consoling the sick, or guiding people in worship. A study by the New York–based National Pastoral Life Center in the United States showed that the percentage of American parishes employing lay ministers at least twenty hours per week went from 54 percent in 1990 to 66 percent in 2005—in other words, from a bare majority to two thirds.

The late Monsignor Philip J. Murnion, who conducted the first studies on lay ecclesial ministry, called it "a virtual revolution in parish ministry."

1. THE UNITED STATES

In its 2005 document *Co-Workers in the Vineyard of the Lord*, the United States Conference of Catholic Bishops defined lay ecclesial ministry in terms of these characteristics:

- Authorization by the hierarchy to serve publicly in the local church;
- Leadership in a particular area of ministry;
- Close mutual collaboration with the pastoral ministry of bishops, priests, and deacons;
- Preparation and formation appropriate to the level of responsibilities that are assigned to them.

The bishops said that the sacramental basis for this ministry is baptism and confirmation, not the sacrament of holy orders.

All told, there are an estimated 31,000 "lay ecclesial ministers" working in Catholic parishes in the United States today. At first the growth of lay ministry was concentrated in wealthy suburban parishes that could afford large staffs, but today it's a fact of life in every geographical locale, particularly in the inner city, in urban business districts, and in rural settings and small towns.

As of 1990, there were just 22,000 lay ministers in the country, according to Fr. Eugene Lauer of the National Pastoral Life Center, which means that

American Catholicism generated an additional 9,000 professional lay ecclesial ministers in a decade and a half. During roughly the same period, the number of Catholic priests in the country, diocesan and religious, went down by almost 6,000, from 49,054 to 43,304. That contrast provides the clearest possible indication of which way the winds are blowing in Catholic pastoral life.

To roll the clock back even farther, Lauer estimates that fewer than one percent of ministerial positions in the Catholic Church were held by laity before the Second Vatican Council. The jobs lay ecclesial ministers are doing today either didn't exist forty years ago, or they were held almost exclusively by priests and nuns.

There are somewhere between 500 to 600 parishes in the United States that are without a resident priest and are administered by a layperson. (Titles for these positions vary; some call it "parish life coordinator," others prefer "parish life collaborator" or "parish life director.") While canon law requires that every parish have a priest assigned as pastor, even if he doesn't live there, that's often a bit of a legal fiction. In cases where the pastor is nonresident and the bishop has appointed a "parish life coordinator," that person is almost always the one who hires and fires, signs checks, and otherwise makes sure the parish trains run on time.

David DeLambo, who authored the 2005 National Pastoral Life Center study, put the trend this way: "We are developing a pool of seasoned lay ministers with a commitment to parish ministry and a history of serving the Church."

The bishops mentioned several categories of lay ministers not included in the formal counts. Laypersons who minister in the name of the Church in hospitals and health care systems, on college and university campuses, and in prisons, airports, and seaports are examples. The National Association of Pastoral Musicians had a membership of 8,500, and the National Catholic Education Association counted 5,466 lay principals of elementary and secondary schools.

The imbalance between lay ministers and priests is destined to grow under even the most wildly optimistic projections about a possible recovery in priestly vocations. There are currently more than 20,000 people in the United States in programs of formation to become lay ecclesial ministers, roughly six times the number of graduate-level seminarians preparing to become priests. Further, high median ages for priests in the United States and elsewhere across the global North suggest that the number of priests in active service in the next several decades will steadily decline, further accelerating the trend toward lay ministry.

2. THE GLOBAL PICTURE

What the United States invented with regard to "lay ecclesial ministry" is the vocabulary, not the phenomenon itself. Though hard numbers are difficult to come by in other parts of the world, growth in lay ministry, meaning the employment of laypeople to perform ministries in the internal life of the Catholic Church, is a clear sign of the times.

One global pioneer is German-speaking Catholicism, which has been able to develop a vast ecclesiastical bureaucracy thanks to the *Kirchensteuer*, or "church tax," collected by the German government. Although revenue is declining with the overall Catholic population, income in recent years has amounted to roughly $5 billion annually. Combined with other forms of public support for Church social service agencies, this income allows German Catholicism to operate a vast network of schools, hospitals, clinics, social welfare agencies, day care centers, and charitable organizations. The Catholic Church in Germany is said to be the second-largest employer in the country after Volkswagen.

Like the United States, the Catholic Church in Germany features a rapidly growing number of laypeople in traditionally clerical ministerial roles, such as running faith-formation programs, coordinating parish outreach ministries, or handling any number of specialized pastoral efforts. Because the Catholic Church in Italy also receives generous payouts from a complicated tax system known as the *otto per mille*, it too has developed a large contingent of lay employees, with a subset who perform ministerial tasks.

Outside of Europe and the United States, it's difficult to ascertain the extent to which lay ecclesial ministry has arrived. In their 2003 analysis of trends, *Global Catholicism*, Bryan T. Froehle and Mary L. Gautier basically threw up their hands, pointing to the "sheer impossibility of accounting for the dramatically growing presence in the Church ministry of laypeople who do not belong to religious communities." They called the situation "fluid and developing."

In its annual set of statistics on the global Church, the Vatican includes two line items that to some extent bear on the question of lay ministry: "catechists" and "lay missionaries." They're terms that drive analysts crazy, because there is no uniform, agreed-upon definition of either one. As a result, total figures for these categories don't mean a great deal, since it's hard to know what's being described. Those responsible for submitting the data can make whole groups of people appear or disappear depending upon how they're classified, and whether they want the numbers to go up or down.

As a rough indicator of trends over time, however, the categories are interesting. The total "workforce for the Church's apostolate," to use the official Vatican term for clergy and laity involved in Church ministries, totaled 1.6 million when John Paul II was elected in 1978. When he died in 2005 it was 4.3 million, with roughly 90 percent of that figure being laity. Catechists alone accounted for two thirds of the total. That's sixteen times more than 1978, when the official Vatican numbers said there were just 173,000 catechists in the entire world. In similar fashion, the Church didn't even have a category for "lay missionary" when John Paul II was elected, but today the official count has reached 144,000.

While these numbers have to be taken with caution, they seem to suggest that the number of laypeople occupying ministerial positions in Roman Catholicism has surpassed the number of ordained clergy by a considerable order of magnitude, and the gap is widening.

In a more recent study, Froehle points to one other trend that will likely contribute to the growth of lay ministry in world Catholicism. In the global South, Froehle observes, the proportion of Catholic pastoral centers that are not parishes, and therefore are usually not led by a resident priest, is far higher than in the United States and Europe. Most of the institutional growth in the global South in the twentieth century, he observes, came with the erection of dioceses, not parishes, owing to chronic shortages of priests. This implies that for many Catholics in the South, their primary point of contact for routine pastoral services will be a center led by a layperson rather than a priest. Froehle calls this "one of the biggest under-reported shifts occurring in the Church today," especially since theological reflection in the Church tends to follow pastoral practice.

Women in Ministry

For a Church long perceived to be a bastion of male privilege, it's interesting that these new lay professional roles are held disproportionately by women. As of 2005, roughly 80 percent of the 31,000 lay ecclesial ministers in the United States were women. *Co-Workers in the Vineyard of the Lord* provides this breakdown: laywomen, 64 percent; religious women, 16 percent;

and laymen, 20 percent. While DeLambo notes that the percentage of lay ministers who are men grew from 15 percent in 1900 to 20 percent in 2005, the overall pattern seems to be that the bulk of lay ministers will be women.

Drawing on U.S. Census Bureau data, lay ecclesial ministry thus takes its place among the following job categories in the United States that are disproportionately occupied by women:

- Secretaries/administrative assistants, 97 percent women
- Registered nurses, 92 percent
- Elementary school teachers, 91 percent
- Hairdressers, 90 percent
- Travel agents, 83 percent
- Lay ecclesial ministers, 80 percent
- Waiters/waitresses, 77 percent
- Cashiers, 77 percent

Women are not represented to the same extent in other job categories in the Catholic Church, but their numbers are generally rising. In diocesan-level administration, 48.4 percent of all positions today are held by women. At the most senior levels in dioceses, 26.8 percent of executive positions are held by women. Arguably, however, that figure should be adjusted, since by definition the diocesan "CEO" in the Catholic system (the bishop), as well as the Vicar General of the diocese, are positions restricted to men. For that reason, women probably hold a slightly higher percentage of the senior positions that are actually open to them, perhaps as much as 30 percent.

Perceptions of patriarchal bias aside, the Catholic Church actually does better in this regard than many other institutions. A 2005 study of Fortune 500 companies found that women hold only 16.4 percent of corporate officer positions and only 6.4 percent of the top earner positions. Similarly, a 2007 study by the American Bar Association found that just 16 percent of the members of the top law firms' governing committees are women, and only 5 percent of managing partners are female. According to a 2004 report from the Department of Defense, women held just 12.7 percent of positions at the grade of major or above.

In light of this comparative data, the truly interesting question may not be why there are so few women in top administrative positions in the Catholic

Church, but why there are so many. Though this is little more than a hunch, perhaps the drubbing the Church has taken in the court of secular public opinion for its ban on women's ordination has induced bishops to promote women into leadership roles, in hopes of counteracting impressions that the Church is "antiwoman."

In the Vatican, women tend to be more conspicuous by their absence. As of 2007, there was no agency in the Vatican headed by a woman, not even among those agencies that in principle can be led by laity, such as the Vatican Press Office or the Personnel Office of the Holy See. In the congregations, tribunals, and councils, which are the main decision-making offices of the Vatican, the number-one and -two positions are held exclusively by cardinals, archbishops, and bishops. There was only one woman who held a number-three position in a congregation, and she shared it with a priest. The Vatican's diplomatic corps also remains all male and all clerical.

On the other hand, there are signs of movement here too. No woman at all worked in the Roman Curia until 1952, when Pius XII created the Permanent Committee for International Congresses of the Lay Apostolate and appointed Australian laywoman Rosemary Goldie as its executive secretary. Things changed significantly over the following half-century. According to a 2005 report from the Catholic News Service, by the end of John Paul's pontificate women made up 21 percent of Vatican personnel, even if they rarely broke through to the most senior levels.

Under John Paul II, two barriers for women in the Vatican where shattered. In 2004, he appointed Salesian Sr. Enrica Rosanna to the position of undersecretary in the Congregation for Institutes of Consecrated Life and Societies of Apostolic Life, the first time a woman had ever been named to a superior-level position in the Vatican. Also in 2004, John Paul tapped Harvard law professor Mary Ann Glendon as the president of the Pontifical Academy for Social Sciences, the first woman to head a pontifical academy. None of this augurs a sociological revolution, but it is important symbolism and an indication of things to come.

The internal culture of the Vatican seems to be evolving.

"I've definitely seen a change," said Filomena D'Antoni, who worked at the Congregation for Eastern Churches for twenty-five years, in 2005. "When I came here, there were not only fewer women but they were also more closely monitored, in terms of behavior, dress, and mentality. Today it's much more open and women are more accepted."

What these developments suggest is that while there will be no change on the question of the ordination of women to the priesthood in the twenty-first century, women will continue to move into other ministerial roles in the Church, often at rates that surpass those of comparable institutions in the secular world. In the trenches, the sociological reality is likely to be that the bulk of pastoral care offered by Catholic parishes, hospitals, schools, and other institutions will be delivered by women. Aside from the priesthood and the episcopacy, ministry in the Catholic Church will progressively become "women's work."

Lay Roles in Church Governance

The 1983 *Code of Canon Law*, in canon 212, offers this statement about the lay voice in the Church: "In accord with the knowledge, competence and pre-eminence which they possess, the Christian faithful have the right and even at times a duty to manifest to the sacred pastors their opinion on matters which pertain to the good of the Church."

Reflecting post–Vatican II developments, the *Code* recognized two formal instruments through which laity can accomplish this. It required every diocese and parish to have a finance council, overseeing how assets are allocated and tracked. It also permitted, but did not require, pastoral councils in dioceses and parishes, so that bishops and parish priests could consult laity in crafting pastoral strategies. In each case, these bodies are consultative, and the authority to make decisions rests with the bishop or the parish priest.

In the United States, a survey of American parishes in 2000 found that more than nine in ten had a parish council. Various Church documents have identified a threefold role for these councils, at both the diocesan and parish level:

- To investigate the pastoral reality
- To reflect on that reality
- To recommend conclusions to the bishop or pastor

The *Code* also allows for a diocesan synod, in which priests, men and women religious, and laypeople can advise the bishops and the other leaders of the diocese on matters of special importance. Because of their size and complexity, synods are extraordinary events rather than standing bodies. As with pastoral councils, it's up to the bishop to decide whether to hold one, and what to do with its recommendations.

Usually these synods only make news if they call for changes in controversial Church teachings, as an archdiocesan synod did in Montreal in 1998, supporting the ordination of women and married men and greater openness for divorced and civilly remarried Catholics. In the main, however, synods don't take up such hot-button matters, which can't be solved on a diocesan level. They're usually more concerned with bread-and-butter issues of pastoral effectiveness; a 2003 synod in Los Angeles, for example, called for a corps of trained lay evangelists to reach out to the city's swelling immigrant population.

In the United States, another body that allows laity to contribute to governance is the review board, created in the wake of the sexual abuse crisis. Under the terms of procedures adopted by the U.S. bishops, each diocese is to have a review board with at least five lay members not employed by the diocese. These boards examine specific allegations of sexual abuse and advise bishops on the appropriate response. There's also a national review board, whose members are appointed to three-year terms. Its role is to oversee implementation of sexual abuse rules and to advise the bishops on policy.

These bodies sometimes draw mixed reviews. Some see them as well-meaning but a waste of time, reminiscent of Oscar Wilde's quip about the problem with socialism—"It takes up too many evenings." Critics say they're a sham, because ultimate power still rests with the clergy. Others say that when the bishop or pastor has the right spirit, these bodies work well.

Realists argue that whatever their flaws, these bodies, all of which have arisen in the last half-century, are the best hope of realizing the style of governance John Paul II described in a meeting with bishops from New Jersey and Pennsylvania in 2002: "Within a sound ecclesiology of communion, a commitment to creating better structures of participation, consultation and shared responsibility should not be misunderstood as a concession to a secular 'democratic' model of governance, but as an intrinsic requirement of the exercise of episcopal authority and a necessary means of strengthening that authority."

WHAT IT MEANS

Systems theorists have developed all sorts of models for explaining organizational change. Some say it's evolutionary, driven largely by alterations in the external environment. Others say it's teleological, meaning that organizations change on purpose to achieve some desired end. Still others prefer political explanations, seeing change in terms of the interaction of various interest groups within the organization; as its fortunes wax and wane, the organization moves in one direction or another. Some even adopt life-cycle models, seeing organizations as mimicking some of the stages of human development. Most people acknowledge that it's a mix of all of the above.

Further, different types of organizations change in different ways. Those with clear chains of command, few mechanisms for participatory governance, and powerful incentives for conformity can often change more quickly, if not always for the better. While those characteristics describe the stereotypical image of Catholicism, they don't always capture the reality. One can make a good case that Catholicism also contains elements of what systems theorists playfully call "organized anarchy," meaning a loosely organized system that contains multiple power and authority structures. Think of the interplay of the Vatican, national bishops' conferences, individual bishops in their dioceses, religious orders, lay movements, charismatic Catholic intellectuals and activists, and so on. Organized anarchies tend to be uncertain, unpredictable, and nonlinear. Changes are likely to be scattered throughout the system in different ways and to a different extent, depending upon local circumstances and opinion.

All these forces are at work inside the Catholic Church with regard to lay roles, which makes it difficult to anticipate how the picture will develop in the twenty-first century. Changes are unlikely to occur in uniform fashion.

Near-Certain Consequences

1. CONFLICTS OVER CONTROL

It's a perverse law of ecclesiastical life that the more successful a Catholic initiative becomes, the more the hierarchy frets about its independence. One of the prime reasons that Pope Pius XII encouraged the growth of the Catholic Action movement in postwar Italy, for example, was to ensure that the engagement of Catholics in public life—which had flowered under the grassroots leadership of Italian Catholic luminaries such as Fr. Luigi Sturzo, who founded the Italian Popular Party in 1919—pulled in the same direction and took shape under his direction. The key objective of Pius's era was to keep the Communists at bay, and he wanted to ensure that lay activism was not infected by socialism.

For a good contemporary parallel, one might consider the proliferation of Catholic media outlets in the late twentieth and early twenty-first centuries, and recent efforts by Church officials to exercise a greater degree of control over their content. While the institutional Church has occasionally attempted to enter the market of global communications itself, the track record is mixed. By and large, it has been independent Catholic initiatives that have had the best luck. EWTN in the United States, Salt and Light Television in Canada, the Rome Reports news agency in Italy, Radio Maryja in Poland—though with quite different outlooks, styles, audiences, and methods—all illustrate the point.

Yet precisely because of their success, these new media have also engendered concern. The fear is that they may be perceived as speaking in the name of the Catholic Church, especially given that they often reach a much larger audience than whatever the bishops themselves have to say. EWTN is a classic case in point, since more American Catholics could probably identify the network's founder, Mother Angelica, than their local bishop or the president of the United States Conference of Catholic Bishops. It's also been a sore point in Poland with Radio Maryja, which has one of the largest broadcast audiences in the country. Radio Maryja is generally supportive of the political right, and it has occasionally been accused of xenophobia and anti-Semitism. The Polish bishops have repeatedly attempted to rein in Radio Maryja, so far with limited results.

An October 2006 conference of Catholic television networks in Madrid, Spain, offered a sign of things to come. A new video news agency was announced, called H2O—named, organizers say, for water as the symbol of life. The impetus to create H2O came from Monsignor Enrique Planas y Como of the Vatican's Pontifical Council for Social Communications. Plans call for H2O to be available through the Internet and on cell phones, as well as through conventional Catholic television networks. Rather than creating a new network, the idea is to generate content that can be supplied to existing outlets. The project was entrusted to the Web-based Zenit News Agency, launched in 1998 with ties to Regnum Christi, the lay branch of the Legionaries of Christ.

At one level, the Vatican is concerned that wealthy Catholic networks in North America and Europe can afford to generate their own content, or to pay for high-quality content from others, while outlets in Latin America, Africa, and Asia often cannot. The idea is to create a level playing field. Parallel to this objective, however, according to observers involved with the discussions, is a desire to exercise greater influence over the content of Catholic media. This becomes a frustration, sources said, when Catholic TV outlets downplay aspects of the Church's message. Some Vatican officials, for example, feel EWTN did not give adequate attention to the Vatican's criticism of the Iraq war in 2003 for fear of alienating conservative American Catholics. In other cases, Vatican sources said, there's concern that some Catholic media outlets, especially in the global North, are run by personnel who may not be fully supportive of Church teaching on issues such as sexual morality or papal authority.

How this specific initiative will develop is anyone's guess. The broader point it illustrates is that as lay activism comes alive, especially in the realms of culture and public life, tensions over control and message will grow.

It bears saying, by the way, that there's nothing untoward about this. Church authorities have a legitimate role to play in ensuring that such initiatives don't foster confusion about what the Church stands for. To call the lay apostolate "independent" does not mean it has no accountability to the Church. The issue is not whether bishops have the right to take an interest in these initiatives. The question is *how* they do so, and this is sure to be the point upon which a great deal of Catholic conversation pivots.

2. FEAR OF "FEMINIZATION"

So far, most writers on lay ecclesial ministry tend to see its overwhelmingly female composition positively, as a means of restoring gender balance to a ministerial corps that has traditionally been all male. DeLambo has written that women ministers "bring sensitivity to lay concerns and to families, as well as to issues related to gender and inclusion," calling this "a gift to the Church." He also noted that women ministers emphasize the relational dimension of their work, favoring experiences such as staff prayer, socializing outside of work, work retreats, days of recollection, and faith-sharing. Male pastors tend to take a more functional view of parish tasks. DeLambo suggested that if parish ministry is going to work well, more attention needs to be paid to "workplace expectations," which in practice means the expectations of women.

Seeing lay ecclesial ministry as a means of including women, however, depends upon focusing on who's in the parish office. If one reverses the perspective and considers who's in the pews, things look quite different. From that angle, the predominantly female composition of the Church's ministerial workforce could be seen as another chapter in the *exclusion* of men.

Below the top levels, the sociological pattern in Christianity has long been a predominance of women, both among church workers and church-goers. Sociologists Rodney Stark and Alan Miller have studied the religious gender gap, concluding that women are more religious than men by virtu-ally every measure in virtually every culture. While the gender gap is smaller in highly traditional societies in which high levels of religious faith and practice are the norm for both sexes, nevertheless there's still a noticeable tendency for women to be more involved than men.

How to explain this gender gap is one of the great debates in the sociol-ogy of religion, and so far there's no consensus, but the underlying reality seems a fact of life.

In that light, some recent writers have voiced concern that Christianity actually alienates men. David Murrow's *Why Men Hate Going to Church* (2004) and Leon J. Podles's *The Church Impotent: The Feminization of Chris-tianity* (1999) illustrate the point. Murrow is a Presbyterian and Podles a Catholic, but both have noticed something similar about their respective de-nominations.

As Podles put it succinctly, "Women go to church, men go to football games."

Podles believes that Western Christianity has been feminizing itself for the better part of a thousand years, beginning with medieval imagery about the Church as the "bride of Christ," which he associates with Saint Bernard of Clairvaux and exhortations to "fall in love" with Jesus. While that kind of imagery has a powerful impact on women, Podles wrote, it's off-putting for men. Podles argued that Christian men have sublimated their religious in-stincts into sports, soldiering, fraternal organizations, and even fascism. When they do engage in religious activity, he wrote, it's more likely to be in a more masculine para-church organization such as the Knights of Colum-bus (note the martial imagery) or Promise Keepers. Even reviewers who didn't buy Podles's historical arguments generally conceded that he was on to something in terms of Christian sociology.

On a less theoretical note, Murrow, a media and advertising specialist, said he looked around after attending weekly church services for almost thirty years, and drew what to him seemed an obvious conclusion: "It's not too hard to discern the target audience of the modern church," he wrote. "It's a middle-aged to elderly woman."

This was never anyone's intention, Murrow said, but it's the inevitable result of the fact that these women have two things every church needs: time and money. In that light, he said, it's no surprise that "church culture has subtly evolved to meet women's needs." Murrow agreed with Podles that "contemporary churches are heavily tilted toward feminine themes in the preaching, the music and the sentiments expressed in worship."

"If our definition of a 'good Christian' is someone who's nurturing, tender, gentle, receptive and guilt-driven, it's going to be a lot easier to find women who will sign up," Murrow wrote.

Whether this diagnosis is correct, and, if so, what to do about it, is not something that can be settled here. It seems a safe bet, however, that the rapid shift in parochial leadership toward women will exacerbate alarm about the feminization of the Church. Put in its most basic form, the concern will be this: if the tone in most parishes is being set by female ministers, what will that do to the comfort level of men, since women are already over-represented? Also in the background is worry in some quarters that the overwhelmingly female composition of lay ecclesial ministry is a stalking horse for the ordination of women to the priesthood.

One might expect Catholic bishops and pastors in the future to practice a form of affirmative action, seeking to hire more men. That may indeed be the case, though to some extent they're trapped between a rock and a hard place, because they also don't want to encourage young Catholic men to see lay ecclesial ministry as an alternative to the priesthood.

One bit of data in this regard: if 20 percent of the lay ecclesial ministers in the United States are men, that works out to about 6,200 male ministers. Between 1900 and 2005, the number of priests in the United States dropped by roughly the same amount. While more study would be needed to establish a connection, it seems reasonable that at least some of those Catholic men wanted to serve the Church full-time, but didn't want the obligation of priestly celibacy, and lay ecclesial ministry provided another option. (Some men in that situation also opt for the diaconate, though it's not quite the same thing because most deacons don't draw a full-time paycheck from the Church.)

For that reason, bishops and priests will likely be cautious about targeting men as lay ministers, which probably means nonsacramental parish ministry in Catholicism will remain a predominantly female enterprise. Pastorally, that may mean a growing sensitivity to the possibility that the "feel" of Church life will exacerbate the tendency for men to opt out.

3. PROTECTING THE PRIESTHOOD

For all the reasons outlined in chapter two, defending the distinctiveness of the ordained priesthood is a major preoccupation for evangelical Catholicism. Church authorities will therefore take special pains to circumscribe lay ecclesial ministry. In their document on the subject, the American bishops issued a warning along these lines: "The application of 'ministry' to the laity is not something to be confused with ordained ministry nor in any way construed to compromise the specific nature of ordained ministry."

This agenda of protecting the priesthood is likely to take at least two forms with respect to ministry by Catholic laity: term limits, and carefully circumscribing "commissioning ceremonies."

According to traditional Catholic theology, the sacrament of holy orders produces an ontological change in the new priest, configuring him to the priesthood of Christ and allowing him to stand *in persona Christi* while celebrating the sacraments. Lay ministry produces no such ontological change. The lay minister is authorized to perform some special responsibility for the Church, but that doesn't change the essence of who he or she is. Lay ministers may experience their work as a vocation, and official Church materials often encourage them to see it this way. Nevertheless, from a theological point of view, lay ministry is a function, not a matter of personal identity, which implies it's not necessarily for life.

One way that Church authorities may choose to underline this point is by creating term limits for lay ministers, meaning appointments for a fixed period of time. These appointments could always be renewed, but the formality of reappointment could in itself serve to remind people that the status of a lay minister in the Church is different from that of a priest. It could also have the corollary benefit of making it easier for pastors and bishops to assemble their own teams rather than being stuck indefinitely with personnel inherited from a previous regime, a point that no doubt will make the idea of term limits attractive to the clergy.

In *Co-Workers in the Vineyard of the Lord*, the American bishops floated such an approach: "Bishops might consider prescribing terms of service for the exercise of certain responsibilities in the Church," they wrote. "Specifying a term of service (which of course can be renewed) also provides flexibility for a newly installed bishop or newly appointed pastor to make key personnel assignments after a period of transition."

With regard to commissioning ceremonies, many parishes and dioceses stage such events for lay ecclesial ministers, especially parish administrators who function in the absence of a resident priest. Doing so reflects the deep Catholic instinct to ritualize important aspects of the Church's faith and practice. As things develop, however, Church authorities are likely to be wary, above all to ensure that people don't get the impression that the ceremony itself imparts some new status on the lay minister. The thrust will be to communicate symbolically that a commissioning ceremony is closer to a graduation than to a sacrament.

Again, the U.S. bishops sounded a note of caution along these lines: "It should be clear that the person appointed is not a substitute for the priest who directs the pastoral care of the parish, nor should the impression be given that it is the rite itself which confers the appointment," they wrote. As a result, some parishes and dioceses may choose to suppress commission ceremonies, and others will allow them but do everything possible to make clear that what's happening is *not* a sacrament.

4. MORE SACRAMENTAL MODEL OF THE PRIESTHOOD

Ask priests what they enjoy about the priesthood, and most will mention the pastoral dimensions of their work—hearing confessions, saying Mass, giving homilies, working with couples about to get married, comforting the sick, and so on. Yet the institutional dimension of their responsibilities means that they spend a disproportionate amount of their time balancing budgets, managing personnel, and worrying about the physical plant. Many of these tasks require competencies that their seminary training never provided.

As a greater share of the burden for supervising administration, personnel, and finance shifts to laity, one result should be to free priests to focus more on their core sacramental responsibilities. As a matter of principle, clergy retain the last word, but in practice laypeople are becoming de facto decision makers. This shift requires a bit of "letting go" on the part of priests and bishops, but where it works, it allows pastors to be pastors. In this sense, one could make the argument that far from threatening the identity of the ordained priesthood, the rise of lay ministry and lay activism in the broader community actually defends that identity by allowing clergy to reallocate time and resources to those tasks that only ordained ministers can perform.

One result of expanding lay roles should therefore be a more sacramental model of the priesthood, rather than seeing the priest as the ecclesiastical equivalent of a CEO or a senior manager. This model will evolve in different ways and at a different pace depending upon local personalities and circumstances, but it's the logical result of the trajectories traced in this chapter—one that many priests will welcome.

Probable Consequences

1. BATTLES OVER BUREAUCRACY

There's an antibureaucratic humor afoot in global Catholicism today, which is one part practical, one part ideological. The practical dimension is that many dioceses and parishes, especially in the North, are struggling with declining resources and, as a consequence, facing the need to "downsize." Pinching pennies, however, is not the only motive. There's also a theological and political rationale, a basic sense that the Church should not mimic the organizational patterns of the secular world, and that doing so risks substituting secular standards of success for the criteria of the gospel. As part of this picture, there's a long-standing concern in some quarters that professional ecclesiastical apparatchiks tend to hijack the structures of the Church to serve their own agenda.

Germany, with the most extensive ecclesiastical bureaucracy anywhere in the world, has long struggled with precisely this issue, which may help explain Pope Benedict XVI's own dubious outlook. The powerful Central Committee of German Catholics, an association of German laity with a large number of professional Church employees, has often served as a thorn in the side of the German bishops and Rome. In the late 1990s, for example, the Vatican insisted that the German bishops close a series of abortion-counseling centers, on the grounds that some women who received assistance from these centers used a certificate they issued in order to have an abortion. After much back-and-forth wrangling, the bishops eventually complied. The Central Committee of German Catholics, however, defied the edict, creating an association called Donum Vitae to keep many of the centers open.

Such stands were bound to produce blowback. In 2006, Archbishop Gerhard Ludwig Müller of the diocese of Regensburg, in Bavaria, announced that he was turning off the financial faucet for the Central Committee. Under Germany's Church tax system, the Central Committee receives a significant share of tax collections; in 2005, the total amounted to almost $2.7 billion. But that money passes through the local bishops first, and Müller decided to demonstrate his disenchantment with the Central Committee by employing the power of the purse. While he was at it, Müller also suppressed a "Diocesan Council of Lay People" and thirty-three other organizations.

Müller's move built on a long history of tensions. Back in 2002, Cardinal Joachim Meisner of Cologne blasted his country's lay-dominated "structures, commissions, statutes and secretariats," which he said run the risk of "obfuscating the faith."

"They serve as the basis for the diffusion of endless debates," Meisner said. "These are alarming developments, before which we bishops cannot close our eyes. . . . To deny these facts would be to flee from reality." Meisner said instances in which lay professionals in the Church had defied the teaching or the discipline of the Church amounted to "more than sporadic cases."

This practical and political backlash against bureaucracy is in some ways a defining feature of the identity-driven Catholicism of the twenty-first century. Yet at the very same moment, the Catholic Church in the United States and in many other parts of the world is creating a large new professional class of paid lay ministers, expanding the potential for precisely the sort of "structures, commissions, statutes and secretariats" against which Meisner railed.

The stereotype of lay professionals in the Church is that they tend to skew to the left, and at least in the global North there's probably some truth to that. Lay ministers with specialized theological training tend to reflect the values and outlook of the theological guild, which on the whole is considerably more liberal than the hierarchy. This may be less true in the early part of the twenty-first century, as evangelical bishops will generally hire evangelical Catholic laity. Yet lay ministers are not exempt from the principles of human sociology, which means there's at least one contentious issue in the Church over which they are likely to line up against many bishops, regardless of their overall theological orientation: the distribution of power. In general, lay professionals favor participatory models of authority, in part because in practice it means participation by them. Bishops generally emphasize the hierarchical model, because they're the hierarchy. Of course, there are many exceptions on both sides of this generalization, but it nevertheless points to something real.

To illustrate that this is not an issue just in the United States and Europe, it's worth noting that the Brazilian National Council of Catholic Laity, a group disproportionately composed of lay professionals in the Church, proposed in 1996 transforming itself into an ecclesiastical "conference" parallel to the bishops' conference. Cecilia Bernardete Franco, who at the time served as the body's president, said that "turning into a conference would give us much more political power, especially within the Church." The Vatican took the matter seriously enough that Pope John Paul II raised it in an address to a group of Brazilian bishops in October 2002, saying: "To claim to create an autonomous organism that would be representative of the laity without referring to the hierarchical communion with the Bishops constitutes an ecclesiological error with serious and obvious implications." The pope added, "I am sure you will not delay in guiding the laity away from such initiatives." To date, it hasn't happened.

2. DEMOCRATIZATION OF CATHOLIC CONVERSATION

Once upon a time, it seemed crystal clear who speaks for the Church. At the universal level, it was the pope; locally, it was the bishop. For more than 500 years, however, this clerical monopoly has been steadily undercut. The invention of the printing press began the process, and, later, the disestablishment of institutional Christianity throughout the West meant that clergy became simple citizens in the eyes of a broad swath of the population. Content, rather than credentials, came to be most decisive in terms of who commands public attention. In the first half of the twentieth century, the great points of reference in English-speaking Catholicism included lay writers and apologists such as G. K. Chesterton, Christopher Dawson, and Ronald Knox, none of whom had a formal ecclesiastical commission, but all of whom possessed the moxie and literary talent to engage a wide readership.

Today's new burst of lay activism is accelerating this process, because it means that a growing number of laity, representing a wide variety of theological and political perspectives, are effectively competing with the bishops as the public face and voice of the Catholic Church. This can generate a bit of a paradox, because in some cases the most prominent examples are laity who enter the public arena in defense of the hierarchy. In the United States, William Donohue of the Catholic League for Religious and Civil Rights, or former Boston mayor and ambassador to the Holy See Raymond Flynn, are good examples. Ironically, their high media profile often means that these defenders of the bishops are more consequential than the bishops themselves in shaping public debate.

The growth of alternative media also renders it easier for independent lay activists and writers to assemble a following. One good example is Rocco Palmo, a young Catholic writer whose blog, "Whispers in the Loggia," is widely read, especially in the States. Without any official ecclesiastical standing, Palmo is arguably more influential than most statements from the United States Conference of Catholic Bishops in determining what many Catholics talk about and think about.

A fascinating corollary of all this is a creeping democratization among the bishops themselves: more and more, it's not the bishop with the largest diocese who looms largest, but the bishop who spends the most time on *Nightline*. In the United States, Archbishop Charles Chaput of Denver offers a good example. The Rocky Mountains are hardly a traditional center of Catholic culture, and Chaput has never been elected to a formal leadership position in the U.S. bishops' conference. Yet Chaput has developed one of the highest profiles of any bishop in the country. He's a best-selling author, a popular speaker, and a staple of TV talk shows. In that sense, Chaput is a quintessential twenty-first-century bishop, relying more on personal charisma and evangelical gumption than on the trappings of his office to gain a hearing.

Some observers worry that public impressions of what Catholicism teaches, or where the Church stands, are being skewed by today's riot of competing voices. This has been a perennial concern in the United States during recent presidential elections, when the bishops' conference has struggled to maintain an official position of neutrality while some individual prelates, to say nothing of lay activists, have insisted that the only proper Catholic position is in favor of one candidate or another. For good or ill, however, the toothpaste is not going back into the tube; if officialdom wants to project a different image of the Church, it will have to do so through effective communications strategies rather than through edicts.

Possible Consequences

1. AN EVANGELICAL EDGE

For reasons rehearsed above, one important question about lay ministry is whether it courts confusion about the distinctiveness of the ordained priesthood. In terms of determining the future prospects of the Catholic Church in many parts of the world, however, that's unlikely to be the question that truly matters. The real question is, will people (Catholics and non-Catholics alike) come to accept Catholic laity as legitimate agents of spiritual care in their own right, not as a sort of "junior varsity" beneath ordained priests?

The question takes on urgency because of the nature of competition in the religious marketplace in the twenty-first century. In many regions, Catholicism finds itself losing ground to competitors, especially to Pentecostals. One frequently cited reason is that Pentecostal churches are present in the shantytowns and barrios of rapidly expanding cities of the global South, while Catholicism is not. By "not present," what people generally mean is that there's no priest. Obviously, there are lots of Catholics in these areas, but they're not seen as representing the Church, and often they don't see themselves that way. Pentecostals, with no strong concept of the clerical role, are able to draw on rank-and-file believers to make their own presence much more visible.

From a sociological point of view, the core "products" of religion include doctrine, prayer and devotion, worship, supernatural experience, and personal morality. Aside from the sacraments, there's no reason why lay Catholic ministers can't deliver these spiritual goods just as well as Pentecostals, indigenous shamans, or anyone else. One reason they often don't is because no one has encouraged them to do so, but another factor is that even when they try, many people won't feel satisfied with the exchange unless there's a priest involved. To put the point simply, many people won't feel that the Catholic Church really cares about them until they see a priest.

Catholicism in the future, however, may evolve to a point where in many areas, a parish priest is seen a bit like bishops are today, meaning as an authority figure everyone acknowledges but no one expects to have around every day. In some regions, this is already reality. In that context, the question is whether laity will become more accepted as the routine pastoral presence of the Church. Will a visit by a Catholic lay minister to someone's hospital room, or to someone's home, become more analogous to a visit by the local Pentecostal pastor, rather than being seen as a poor substitute for a priest? To the extent this shift in consciousness occurs, it should provide Catholicism with an enormous evangelical edge, dramatically expanding popular awareness of its presence. Despite cautions regarding the identity of the priesthood, this prospect is likely to drive lay ministry forward, especially in those zones where the competition facing the Church is the most intense.

2. PARISH STRIKES

The Catholic Church has a long history of support for organized labor. In a 1986 pastoral letter of the American bishops titled "Economic Justice for All," they made no bones about it: "The Church fully supports the right of workers to form unions or other associations to secure their rights to fair wages and working conditions," the bishops wrote. "This is a specific application of the more general right to associate." Yet the Church has an equally long, if somewhat less edifying, history of unevenly applying this principle to its own workforce. The result is that lay employees of the Church often do not have the same rights and protections as people who draw their salaries from public agencies or private firms.

Two examples make the point.

In the Diocese of Brownsville in Texas in 2003, four lay ministers at Holy Spirit Church in McAllen were fired when a new pastor took over. The problem began in 2000, when Bishop Raymundo Peña terminated a pension plan for diocesan employees and substituted a new, contribution-defined system. Longtime pastoral associate Ann Cass charged that the new arrangement would deprive veteran Church employees of a third or more of their benefits. In response, employees at four parishes in Brownsville and their pastors joined the United Farm Workers union. The agreement, believed to be the first unionization of parish workers in the country, provided a union pension plan and a mandatory grievance procedure.

When a new pastor arrived at Holy Spirit, Cass and three other employees were dismissed. Reaction was heated, and eventually Peña appointed another pastor who rehired Cass and the others. The bishop then created a three-member canonical tribunal to review the situation, and in November 2005 it ruled the union contract invalid on the grounds that pastors lack the canonical authority to enter into such an agreement.

Cass said that as a Church employee, she found the situation unsettling.

"You're really vulnerable in this work," Cass said. "A pastor makes a decision one day, and you're out on your butt."

Unsurprisingly, similar tensions have worked their way through the German church. In the 1990s, German courts ruled that Church employees do not have the same right to organize and to strike that other German workers have, on the grounds that relations with the Church are determined by a concordat, or an agreement with the state, which recognizes no such rights. The courts also ruled that the Church has the right to impose adherence to Church teaching as a condition of employment, such as a ban on divorce and civil remarriage without an annulment from a Church tribunal. Those rulings were directly addressed to the 450,000 employees who work for the Catholic charitable organization Caritas, which is the country's largest provider of charitable services, but in principle they apply to all Church personnel.

As the number of lay ecclesial ministers and other paid lay employees of the Catholic Church continues to expand, this sort of tension between what might be termed management and labor in the Church will probably fester.

This is likely to be a point with special relevance for the United States, for two reasons. First, the sexual abuse crisis has made courts more aggressive about stepping into the internal affairs of religious bodies. Second, if immigration debates continue to heat up in American politics, the bishops are likely to take strong stands in favor of the rights of migrant workers to organize. In such a context, public opinion could make it more difficult for bishops and pastors to resist extending the same rights to their own workers—who, in some cases, may be the very same immigrants.

It's not out of the realm of possibility that Catholicism could witness the phenomenon of "parish strikes" in the twenty-first century; Sunday Mass goers, or parents who drop off their kids for religious education, may from time to time have to decide whether to cross a picket line.

3. A LESS PURPLE ECCLESIOLOGY

Some time ago, a producer from the BBC called me in Rome to ask for help with a documentary they were producing on women in the Church. Could I recommend, she wondered, someone from the Church with whom they might speak? I replied that they were in luck, because the Pontifical Academy of Social Scientists was meeting in Rome that week, which meant that Mary Ann Glendon was in town. As the first woman to head a pontifical academy, as well as someone who has represented the Holy See in various international conferences, I suggested that she would likely have some interesting perspective.

"I must not have made myself clear," the producer responded. "I meant someone from the Church."

What she actually meant, of course, was someone in a Roman collar, meaning a priest or bishop. Ironically, outsiders to Catholicism often have a far more "purple" ecclesiology than Catholics themselves, seeing the Church almost exclusively in terms of the activity of its clergy. Among other things, this results in a distorted perception of Catholic activity and priorities, given that a vast range of activity never registers in the public mind as "Catholic" because it's not performed by a priest.

Perceptions always lag behind reality, but as lay ministers and lay activists in the secular sphere become steadily more visible features of twenty-first-century Catholicism, a broader sense of what "the Church" actually means may gradually take hold. If so, at least some elements within the broader society may develop a deeper sense of the complexity of Catholicism, offsetting stereotypes of all sorts. For example, it may become more difficult to accuse Catholicism of being "antiwoman" in an era in which a growing cross-section of the public comes to realize that most of the Church's ministerial corps is actually composed of women.

Long-Shot Consequences

1. LAY CARDINALS

In the Renaissance period, popes would sometimes appoint members of their extended families as cardinals, even if they weren't priests, in order to make them trusted aides. This office of "cardinal nephew" evolved into the forerunner of the modern secretary of state, understood to be the pope's prime minister in the governance of the Church. From time to time, some voices in the Church have proposed that the custom of lay cardinals be revived as a way of opening authoritative positions to laity. During the Synod for Africa in 1994, Bishop Ernesto Kombo of the Diocese of Owando in Congo even proposed naming women as lay cardinals.

That idea seems unlikely to go anywhere in the near future, since evangelical Catholicism would be hostile to anything that seems to open the door to ordination of women to the priesthood. Given that custom requires the "lay cardinal" to first be ordained a deacon, this would in effect mean the ordination of women to the diaconate. While some Catholic theologians have argued for such a move, it's improbable that the idea will get off the ground soon.

It's more thinkable that a pope might decide to appoint a prominent Catholic layman as a cardinal, perhaps in an honorary capacity—in the same fashion that elderly clergy already past the age of eighty, and therefore no longer eligible to vote for the pope, are sometimes named cardinals. One can imagine that Jean Vanier or Andrea Riccardi, for example, might be considered for such an honor. Though such a move could be seen as creating greater opportunities for laypeople, it could also be interpreted in exactly the opposite fashion if Vanier or someone like him were required to be ordained a deacon before becoming a cardinal.

2. A FEMALE BOSS IN THE VATICAN

A related question is whether a woman might be named to head a decision-making office of the Vatican, such as the Congregation for Religious or the Council for Laity. Such a proposal also runs into theological quicksand. Some theologians and ecclesiologists contend that a layperson cannot hold such a position, because the congregations, tribunals, and at least some of the councils of the Roman Curia exercise delegated authority from the pope, which implies an organic connection with the sacrament of holy orders. A working group at the 1999 European Synod had proposed that a woman be named to head an agency of the Curia, but the idea did not survive in the propositions presented to the pope at the close of the synod, suggesting that at least some of the bishops were opposed and others may have regarded it as too hot to handle.

Regardless of what position one takes on this theological dispute, there's no reason in principle that a woman could not be named to head an agency such as the Vatican Press Office, a position held under Pope John Paul II by Spanish layman Joaquin Navarro-Valls. A woman could run Vatican Radio, the Vatican Observatory, or even one of the pontifical councils that does not exercise the "power of jurisdiction," such as the Council for Culture, the Council for Social Communications, or the Council for Interreligious Dialogue. Given the apparent eagerness of Church officials to promote women into senior positions, perhaps in response to criticism of the ban on women priests, it's entirely possible that the twenty-first century will see a Vatican agency led by a Catholic woman.

3. A HOLIER WORLD?

Ultimately, the purpose of promoting lay activism is not to remedy ecclesiastical imbalances or to reshape public perceptions of the Church, but rather to extend the Church's mission of sanctifying the world. Though there are extraordinary stories of success, it's tough to argue that a century of expanding lay roles in Catholicism has fundamentally transformed the human situation. Is there any reason to believe that the twenty-first century might become holier because of a rising tide of lay energy?

It's a long shot, but here's one example of potential impact.

Lay Catholic evangelists could provide a badly needed spiritual antidote to the social toxins unleashed by runaway urbanization. For the first time in human history, more than half the planet today lives in cities, and by 2050 two thirds of the world's population, some six billion people, will be urban dwellers. In rural cultures, the harshest effects of poverty are usually offset by families and extended networks of social support, which are tough to replicate in urban environments. High rates of unemployment and under-employment, along with the squalor of many urban zones and the spread of crime and drugs, too often generate a "perfect storm" of despair and dys-function.

Under any scenario, Catholicism will be unable to deploy a sufficient number of priests to provide the hands-on, retail-level pastoral care that might buffer these trajectories. If it's going to happen, it will be Catholic lay ministers and lay activists who accomplish it. Lay evangelists are also likely to determine whether a growing share of these urban populations embrace another religious option, or find a home in Catholicism. Urban areas, especially in the global South, thus shape up as the primary stage upon which the drama of lay Catholic activism in the twenty-first century will unfold.

Whether Catholic laity will be able to leaven urbanization in any measurable, significant way is impossible to say. What this observation points to, however, is the question of criteria for success. It's easy for Catholicism to compliment itself for expanding lay roles by counting the number of offices and tasks entrusted to laity, or the number of laypeople who occupy them, or the number of lay movements dotting the ecclesial landscape. Ultimately, however, that's not the evangelical bottom line. The question should be, is any of this actually making the world holier? Bearing that question in mind ought to provide an important bit of perspective as Catholicism ponders the ongoing expansion of lay roles in the twenty-first century.

THE BIOTECH REVOLUTION

In 2004, Dr. Irving Weissman, director of the prestigious Stanford Institute for Stem Cell Biology and Regenerative Medicine, did something a bit out of the ordinary, even by the occasionally bizarre standards of modern genetic science. He injected brain cells from aborted human fetuses into the developing brains of healthy fetal mice, where the cells grew into normal human neurons. Those neurons then intermingled with the naturally emerging brain cells of the mouse, eventually representing approximately one percent of the total tissue mass in the fully formed mouse's brain. To put that story in slightly more condensed fashion, Weissman gave a tiny sliver of a human brain to a mouse.

Ever since news of the protocol leaked from the scientific world into the popular press, debate over the ethics of Weissman's "Stuart Little experiment" has provided a classic illustration of the unprecedented moral and spiritual quandaries being generated by today's biotech revolution.

This was not, it should be stressed, an *Island of Dr. Moreau* farce of a madcap scientist creating genetic mutants. Weissman offered three reasons for the research, which involved allowing the mice to develop into adults and then dissecting their brains. First, he said, it offers a unique opportunity to study how human brain cells work. Second, it allows scientists to test genetic therapies to combat illnesses such as Parkinson's disease, Alzheimer's, Lou Gehrig's disease, stroke, multiple sclerosis, and spinal cord injuries. Third, it allows investigators to study brain cancers. The hope is to isolate cancer stem cells, and then to test various interventions to slow them down or stop them altogether.

Weissman's mouse is an example of an emerging new tool in genetic research, which is by now common enough that there's a scientific term for it: a "chimera," meaning an organism that carries more than one set of genetic material. The image is a reference to the legendary creature of Greek mythology that was part lion, part goat, and part serpent. Today, it refers to any organism that carries more than one set of genes.

After his first trial was complete, Weissman upped the ante. Instead of injecting only enough human cells to account for one percent of the mouse brain, he proposed injecting a sufficient quantity of cells that the mouse's brain would be composed almost exclusively of human tissue, so that genetic therapies could be tested on something more closely resembling a real human brain. In short, he wanted to breed mice with miniature human brains. In the debate that ensued, images of tiny rodent para-humans having a chat with Weissman over a cup of morning tea leapt to the popular mind, though experts issued assurances that such a scenario was out of the question.

The Stanford ethics committee to which Weissman submitted the proposal gave him a cautious green light in February 2005. The head of the panel, law and genetics professor Henry Greely, said that although the experiment might sound "creepy," there is no serious risk of Weissman transferring what he called "humanness" to the mice.

"It's not going to get up and say, 'Hi, I'm Mickey,'" Greely said. "Our brains are far more complicated."

Yet in the same breath, Greely said that his committee had also instructed Weissman to stop if his mice began to show "human-like behaviors," such as "improved memory or problem-solving." Such counsel suggests that Greely and his colleagues were perhaps not so certain after all that a speck of humanity won't make its way across the species line.

Others were less circumspect in contemplating nightmare scenarios. Technology critic Jeremy Rifkin said that Weissman's proposed experiment, and others like it, "stretch the limits of human tinkering with nature to the realm of the pathological." What would happen, Rifkin asked, if one of these mice scampers out of the lab, and all of a sudden mutant human brain cells are let loose in the wild? This sort of research, he argued, is fast becoming "a macabre journey into a Brave New World in which nature can be ruthlessly manipulated and re-engineered to suit the momentary needs and whims and caprices of just one species, the Homo Sapiens."

For his part, Weissman said the moral burden of proof should be on the opponents of the research, given that it may be critical to treating some of the most excruciating disorders known to medicine.

"Are you willing to accept the moral responsibility," he asked, "for the lives lost and the damage done because you didn't like some human cells in a mouse brain?"

Pause now and consider the following questions: From the point of view of Roman Catholic anthropology, moral theology, and social doctrine, who's right? Given that the brain is the primary locus of human personality, does the possession of a miniature human brain by a mouse—even if it isn't playing chess or writing essays on *A Critique of Pure Reason*—somehow change its moral status? Is it now something less than human but something more than animal, meaning that a new set of rights and responsibilities comes into play?

If you're having trouble answering, don't feel alone. In early 2007, I asked the same questions of Richard Doerflinger, deputy director of pro-life activities for the United States Conference of Catholic Bishops—in other words, the guy who gets paid to think about these things on behalf of the Catholic bishops in the United States. Doerflinger said that he found Weissman's first experiment, involving less than one percent of human brain cells, "probably okay," but that the second would be a step too far—and, he candidly acknowledged, it's difficult to know precisely where to fix the ethical boundary in between.

"It's easier to see night and day than to distinguish exactly when it becomes dusk," he said. "I'm not sure where the line is."

Welcome to the surreal, and ever-shifting, ethical frontiers of today's biotech revolution.

WHAT'S HAPPENING

"Biotechnology" refers to the scientific understanding of the mechanics of human, animal, and plant biology, as well as the capacity to manipulate that biology through technical means. Biotechnology covers a lot of ground, from the development of insect- or drought-resistant varieties of corn by technically adding certain genetic traits, to combining sperm and egg cells in a laboratory in order to help a woman get pregnant, or to producing artificial genetic mutants such as Weissman's mice. New biotech possibilities represent a major trend for Catholicism in the twenty-first century for five reasons:

- The issues they raise are mind-bendingly new. Though Catholics remain badly divided over matters such as abortion and homosexuality, they're comfortable with the basic contours of those debates, since they've been around for two millennia. Issues such as cloning and chimeras haven't even been around two decades.

- Precisely because the issues are so new, in some cases the Church does not yet have official positions, or the positions it does have are sketchy and in need of development. It's a period of flux in Catholic teaching, in which many important matters remain unresolved. That always invites ferment in the Church, as various parties argue for one or another outcome.

- Even if the Church were not inclined to make the biotech revolution a priority, the surrounding culture won't let it off the hook. Few matters are as anguished, and as politically explosive as the questions of when human life begins and ends, and to what extent human life ought to be manipulated at its most basic levels. The twenty-first century will witness endless upheaval over these points, and the Church, as a microcosm of society, will inevitably reflect those tensions.

- Biotechnology is big business. According to industry analyst Ernst & Young, worldwide revenues in the biotech sector approached the magic $100 billion mark in 2008, and earnings seem poised for further growth despite the global economic downturn. With that kind of money on the line, social and political pressure for rapid adoption of biotech innovations will be enormous.

- Much of the secular opposition to biotechnology comes from the political and cultural left, meaning that the generally cautious position of the Catholic Church has the potential to revise the Church's political profile and to open the door to new alliances.

Each biotech debate has its own contours, but underneath them all runs a basic ideological fault line between those who fear where the biotech revolution is headed, and those who revel in it. Former U.S. senator Larry Pressler said in 2000, "We're embarking on a hundred-year war about this issue."

Among the secular critics are Dr. Leon Kass, former chairman of the President's Council on Bioethics under President George W. Bush; technology writer Jeremy Rifkin; and political scientist and essayist Francis Fukuyama, who has warned that developments in biotechnology are ushering in a "post-human" future. Here's an example of the rhetoric biotech debate inspires, this time from British Catholic historian and essayist Paul Johnson in 1999: "In the twentieth century, we failed to stifle at birth the totalitarian concepts which created Nazism and Communism, though we knew all along that both were morally evil, because decent men and women did not speak out at the time. Are we going to make the same mistake with this new infant monster [biotechnology] in our midst, still puny as yet, but liable, all too soon, to grow gigantic and overwhelm us?"

On the other side lies a powerful constellation of scientists, research facilities, and corporations, all arrayed in support of virtually unbridled development of biotechnology. Weissman himself has compared his critics to Trofim Lysenko, a Soviet pseudoscientist who convinced Stalin in the 1930s that Darwin had been wrong and Lamarck right, devastating Russia's budding expertise in genetics and causing crops to fail for a generation. The result was mass famine. Today's anti-biotech ideologues, Weissman argues, may have a similarly catastrophic impact on scientific understanding.

That stance is shared by many ordinary people who long for new cures to diseases, or for the ability to replace damaged organs easily and virtually painlessly, or for the capacity to pass on the best possible genetic mix to one's children. American science journalist Ronald Bailey wrote a manifesto in 2005 for this group called *Liberation Biology*, styling it consciously on the liberation theology movement that grew up in the Catholic Church in Latin America in the 1960s and 1970s. Just as liberation theology strove for the emancipation of human beings from poverty and injustice, Bailey says the point of biotechnology is to create a world in which people live longer, stay healthier, feel better, and produce less harmful effects on the world around them.

In all these struggles, the Roman Catholic Church is both a protagonist and a battleground. The Church reflects within herself the opposing forces at work in the broader culture. On one side are groups such as the National

Catholic Bioethics Center in the United States, or the Linacre Centre in England, which usually line up on the side of biotech critics such as Kass and Fukuyama; on the other is a sector of theological and pastoral opinion in the Church that finds these positions rigid, pessimistic, and inhumane. James F. Drane, for example, in his 2003 book *More Humane Medicine: A Liberal Catholic Bioethics*, accused conservatives of distorting Catholic teaching to buttress "extremist" views.

To be sure, long-standing bioethical battles over matters such as abortion or homosexuality are not simply going to dissolve in the twenty-first century. If anything, the wave of evangelical Catholicism cresting through the Church, combined with increasingly secular attitudes toward sexual morality in the West, point to a chronic sort of "irresistible force versus immovable object" conflict. Alongside those traditional fault lines, however, a new cluster of conundra is arising, occupying a growing share of the Church's time and energy. The following section sketches seven poles of twenty-first-century biotech debate.

In-Vitro Fertilization (IVF)

In-vitro fertilization involves creating an embryo in a petri dish rather than through normal sexual intercourse, by extracting ova (eggs) from a woman and then combining them with sperm obtained from a man (usually through masturbation, although there are other ways of doing it). Those embryos grow for a few days in the lab and then are implanted in the woman. Pregnancy results about 20 percent of the time. In-vitro fertilization can either be homologous, which means that the man and woman use their own genetic materials, or heterologous, in which case the eggs come from another woman, the sperm from another man, or both. Embryos can also be implanted in a "surrogate" mother, a woman other than the biological mother.

The Catholic Church opposes IVF, but in some ways the debate is already over. Since the world's first "test-tube baby," Louise Brown, was born in 1978, more than three million babies worldwide have been born using in-vitro techniques. Today, 2.5 percent of all live births in the United Kingdom occur with IVF, and approximately 27,000 procedures are performed each year in the United States. The total spent on IVF procedures in the United States annually is estimated at around $4 billion.

Reasons given for official Catholic opposition to IVF include:

- IVF separates the act of love-making from procreation, rupturing something meant to be unified.

- Heterologous IVF damages the family by separating the biological and emotional aspects of parenthood.

- Because some embryos created in IVF are generally either discarded or frozen, the process involves destruction of human life.

- Sperm is generally obtained from masturbation.

- "Excess" embryos are often eliminated early in pregnancy by an injection of potassium chloride, a procedure known as fetal reduction, which the Church regards as abortion.

Some reform-minded Catholic theologians, however, have reached a more positive conclusion about IVF, especially its homologous form. Usually they make two basic arguments. First, they say that an embryo cannot be regarded as a person until it's past the point where twinning is possible. They point to wastage: scientists say that the natural rate of loss for embryos in the earliest stages after conception is 60 to 80 percent. How could God bring into being so many persons, this argument runs, only to let them perish when their lives have hardly begun? Second, while IVF separates intercourse and procreation, it does so for the purpose of procreation, not contraception. They argue that separation between intercourse and procreation is a "pre-moral" evil, meaning an evil in the abstract, which can be justified for a proportionate reason—in this case, to conceive a child.

Catholicism has always encouraged married couples to welcome children, and partly for that reason it's left the door slightly ajar to other forms of reproductive technology, such as Gamete Intra-Fallopian Transfer (GIFT). In GIFT, egg cells are retrieved from the woman in the same fashion as in IVF, while sperm is collected either by surgically inserting a needle into a testicle or by using a perforated condom during intercourse (to avoid contraception). Using ultrasound technology, the sperm and ova are inserted into the fallopian tubes, in the hope that natural fertilization will follow intercourse. Similar procedures known as Tubal Ovum Transfer (TOT) and Lower Tubal Ovum Transfer (LTOT) involve retrieval of one or more egg cells from the fallopian tubes and their reinsertion in the uterus.

Not all theologians buy it. Dominicans Benedict Ashley and Kevin O'Rourke have written: "The technology involved seems to replace the conjugal act as the sufficient cause of the uniting of the sperm and ovum, rather than simply to assist it."

Another debated question related to IVF is "embryo adoption." The debate boils down to this: Perhaps all those frozen embryos currently stored in fertility clinics should never have been created in the first place, but nevertheless they exist. Wouldn't it be better for someone to bring them to term, in effect to "adopt" them, rather than simply destroying them?

A major 2008 document on bioethics from the Vatican's Congregation for the Doctrine of the Faith, titled *Dignitas Personae,* did not address the debate over GIFT, but it appeared to offer a negative view of embryo adoption. The document says embryo adoption "presents various problems not dissimilar to those mentioned above"—a reference to a section of the text rejecting the use of frozen embryos as an infertility treatment. In the end, *Dignitas Personae* concludes, "the thousands of abandoned embryos represent a situation of injustice which in fact cannot be resolved." While this is not a definitive verdict, most experts read the document as a strong "yellow light," probably driven by anxiety that approving embryo adoption would encourage the creation of more embryos through IVF procedures.

Human Cloning

The cloning debate erupted in 1997, when Scottish scientist Ian Wilmut introduced Dolly, a sheep who was the world's first successfully cloned mammal. What followed was a brief period of frenzy about the prospect of cloning a human being, fueled by some of the kookiest characters ever to pass themselves off as scientists.

First came Dr. Richard Seed (a euphonious name if ever there was one), an out-of-work physicist who had once tried to capture the world's fish-meal market. Seed announced that he would clone anyone for one million dollars. Next was Italian fertility doctor Severino Antinori, whose prior claim to fame was helping a sixty-two-year-old woman become pregnant. He announced plans to launch a human cloning operation on a boat in international waters. In 2002, a bizarre cult called the Raelians, who believe that aliens had used genetic engineering to create human life on earth, claimed to have produced a female clone named, aptly enough, Eve. So far as we know, the only thing these people ever cloned was newspaper headlines.

Yet the debate over cloning continues on the opinion pages of newspapers, in graduate seminars on bioethics, and on the floors of parliaments around the world, seemingly taking for granted that if the technology to clone a human being is not yet fully functional today, it eventually will be.

Shortly after Dolly's birth in 1997, the Pontifical Academy for Life issued a document titled "Reflections on Cloning," which rejected cloning a human being on the basis of two considerations:

- Each human being has the right to be born as a result of a natural sexual union between a married man and woman; a human being should be born *in* and *through* marriage.

- Human dignity requires that a person never be treated as a means to an end. Cloning implies the capacity to generate human beings for the satisfaction of other motivations—curiosity, or ego, or even exploitation as a source of "spare parts" or labor.

Ten years later, *Dignitas Personae* reiterated the Church's opposition to all forms of cloning, reserving its sharpest language for the reproductive variety.

"This would impose on the resulting individual a predetermined genetic identity, subjecting him . . . to a form of biological slavery, from which it would be difficult to free himself," the document asserted. "The fact that someone would arrogate to himself the right to determine arbitrarily the genetic characteristics of another person represents a grave offense to the dignity of that person as well as to the fundamental equality of all people."

In the United States, the President's Council on Bioethics under President George W. Bush likewise identified five "categories of concern" about the prospect of reproductive cloning:

- Clones may experience an identity crisis, both because they will be genetically identical to a human being who has already lived, and because expectations for their lives may be shadowed by comparisons to the "original."

- Cloned children might come to be considered products of a manufacturing process, which could contribute to commercialization and industrialization of human procreation.

- Cloning might fuel a new eugenics, either by avoiding the genetic defects that may arise when reproduction is left to chance, or by preserving and perpetuating outstanding genetic traits.

- Cloning could confound the natural boundaries between generations. Fathers could become "twin brothers" to their "sons"; mothers could give birth to their genetic twins; and grandparents would also be the "genetic parents" of their grandchildren.
- Even if practiced on a small scale, cloning could set a precedent for future interventions into the human genetic endowment, or novel forms of control by one generation over the next.

On the other hand, the basic argument in favor of human cloning is that infertility is a medical disability, and cloning offers an additional option for infertile individuals or couples. Worldwide, the U.S.-based Assisted Conception Taskforce estimates that 90 million couples experience difficulty in conceiving a child. Advocates note that considerable debate surrounded IVF at the beginning, but by now it's become routine. With time, they say, cloning could become just as unsensational.

Pro-biotech forces dismiss worries about a potential "identity crisis" by observing that there already are human beings who share the same genes— they're called twins. Experience, they suggest, does not indicate that having the same genetic pattern as someone else makes you a robot. As Bailey has written, "Genes code proteins, not memories or souls." He also argues that clones would have greater scope for independent development than twins born the normal way, since they would grow up at a different time and in different circumstances. Bailey also rejects worries that cloned children might be more exploited. Plenty of neglected and abused children, he notes, are the product of old-fashioned sexual intercourse. In any event, he argues, since cloning will require considerable financial and emotional investment, the children who result will "be among the lucky ones, very much wanted and treasured by their families."

Embryonic Stem Cell Research

On November 6, 1998, the U.S.-based Geron Corporation announced that scientists had isolated embryonic stem cells from "leftover" embryos at fertility clinics for the first time, destroying the embryos in the process. Embryonic stem cells had long been considered the holy grail of cellular biology, because they are capable of growing into any of the 220 or so types of cells found in the human body. Many researchers believe that embryonic stem cells hold the key to cures for neurological disorders such as Alzheimer's and Parkinson's, or to restoring function to victims of spinal cord disease such as Christopher Reeve. Some envision a future of made-to-order genetic medicine, in which embryonic stem cells can be directed to replace virtually any damaged tissue in a patient's body, or even whole organs.

Excitement generated by the Geron announcement was virtually boundless.

"It is not too unrealistic to say that this research has the potential to revolutionize the practice of medicine and improve the quality and length of life," said the then-director of the National Institutes of Health, Harold Varmus, at a congressional hearing.

Moral criticism was equally swift, and equally categorical. On November 10, four days after the Geron announcement, Bishop Elio Sgreccia, vice president of the Vatican's Pontifical Academy for Life, told reporters that the procedure was morally illegitimate because it involved the destruction of embryos. As a result, Sgreccia said, embryonic stem cell research is tantamount to abortion and must be opposed with the same force.

The reactions from Varmus and Sgreccia have largely defined the fault lines of debate over embryonic stem cells ever since.

Some observers believe that science itself may leapfrog beyond the debate over embryonic stem cells, since many of the most promising breakthroughs today are coming from adult, rather than embryonic, cells. Adult stem cells can be found in umbilical cords, the placenta, amniotic fluid, adult tissues and organs such as bone marrow, fat from liposuction, regions of the nose, and even from cadavers up to twenty hours after death. The Catholic Church officially supports research involving adult stem cells. Scientists are also exploring the possibilities of "induced pluripotent stem cells," a means of reprogramming adult skin cells into the equivalent of embryonic stem cells.

Two other possibilities for morally acceptable alternatives have been floated.

One comes from Dr. Donald Landry and Dr. Howard Zucker of Columbia University, who suggest identifying a moment at which embryos are "dead." Landry suggests that death can be flagged by "the irreversible arrest of cell division," meaning a point at which the embryo stops expanding. Critics, however, have raised two objections. One is that the absence of division may not be an infallible indicator of death. The other is that such a procedure may simply encourage the creation of embryos for the sake of waiting for them to die.

A second alternative comes from William Hurlbut of Stanford University, who proposes a method called "altered nuclear transfer," or ANT. The idea is to create cellular systems that resemble embryos, but that lack some of the defining elements of human life. Certain tumors, for example, contain stem cells that can produce full body parts and organs. Hurlbut's proposal is to create such an entity on purpose, "turning off" its genes essential for development into a human being.

Hurlbut's idea has powerful Catholic backing. Signatories to a statement endorsing it include prominent Catholic ethicists such as William May and Germain Grisez, as well as Archbishop John Myers of Newark. Cardinal William Levada was positively inclined while he was still the Archbishop of San Francisco. Yet there are also strong Catholic critics, such as David Schindler, editor of the American version of *Communio*. Schindler argues that altered nuclear transfer shares the same philosophical premises as embryonic stem cell research, specifically a mechanistic metaphysics that treats organisms as machines. Others reject the claim that Hurlbut's cellular mass is not an embryo.

As with embryo adoption, *Dignitas Personae* takes a cautious stance on ANT, though one that stops short of outright condemnation. "These proposals have been met with questions of both a scientific and an ethical nature regarding above all the ontological status of the 'product' obtained in this way," the document says. Until those doubts have been clarified, the document refers to a caution from Pope John Paul II's 1995 encyclical on bioethics, *Evangelium vitae*: "What is at stake is so important that, from the standpoint of moral obligation, the mere probability that a human person is involved would suffice to justify an absolutely clear prohibition of any intervention aimed at killing a human embryo."

End-of-Life Issues

Perhaps the two best-known "martyrs" of the new biotech age are Terri Schiavo of the United States, who died in 2005, and Eluana Englaro of Italy, who died in 2008. Both were young women who had entered a persistent vegetative state, and who had been kept alive for years through artificial nutrition and hydration. Both became the center of anguished controversies, driven by a new medical capability to keep people alive even in severely diminished states.

Pro-lifers regard the withdrawal of food and water from such patients as an assault on their human dignity, in effect a way of killing someone whose life has become inconvenient. Those who take a more permissive line warn against making an idol out of continued biological existence, especially in cases where all hope of recovery seems lost. Both sides appeal to Catholic tradition—usually pitting the Church's teaching on the sanctity of life against its time-honored distinction between "ordinary" and "extraordinary" means of care (with "ordinary" means understood to be obligatory, but not "extraordinary").

The drift of official Church teaching today is clearly in favor of the more restrictive position. In March 2004, Pope John Paul II addressed a conference organized by the Pontifical Academy for Life, where he said that the provision of food and water for patients in a persistent vegetative state is always an "ordinary" means and therefore obligatory. On September 14, 2007, the Vatican's Congregation for the Doctrine of the Faith ruled that artificial nutrition and hydration for patients in a persistent vegetative state is a basic requirement of human dignity. Withdrawal of food and water from patients who are otherwise stable, the Vatican held, would be euthanasia.

Yet in the trenches, there's a wider range of Catholic opinion. Franciscan Brother Daniel Sulmasy, a doctor of internal medicine who also has a Ph.D. in philosophy, was consulted several years ago about a case of a young woman who had suffered from an eating disorder beginning at around ten or eleven years old. At twenty-one, she lapsed into a persistent vegetative state. Her parents moved the young woman into a nursing home, where she remained for four years. She repeatedly contracted pneumonia from prolonged use of a feeding tube, causing her to move back and forth between the hospital and the nursing home. The parents reached out to Sulmasy for advice as to whether they were obliged to keep their daughter in this condition indefinitely.

"I don't think they were motivated in any way to end her life prematurely because she was a burden to them or to others. I don't think they thought that she lacked dignity as a person," Sulmasy said in a 2007 interview. "They felt that she was cut off from them, living in a kind of limbo. They felt she was in a state in which she was not yet in communion with her maker, but not in union with them in a real way either."

In the end, Sulmasy said the parents opted to withdraw nutrition and hydration, and the young woman died at the age of twenty-five.

For every such case, however, there are counterexamples. Richard Doerflinger, the top pro-life official for the U.S. bishops, has personal experience to confirm that seemingly hopeless situations don't always play out that way. Thirty years ago, Doerflinger's older brother, Eugene, was involved in a car crash and lapsed into what doctors described as a vegetative state. Doctors advised the family that he would never recover. Because of that expectation, Doerflinger said, they didn't bother resetting his dislocated left shoulder or providing physical therapy to prevent his muscles from atrophying.

After roughly four months, Doerflinger said, his brother began to seem more alert, and eventually he staged a recovery, though not without some problems of short-term memory. Today, Doerflinger said, the two brothers play chess once a week. Doerflinger said his brother has been confined to a wheelchair and his mobility is restricted, in part because his doctors simply gave up too soon.

"Even in this extreme state of helplessness, we should not just assume that the patient is trying to die and is unable to do so," Doerflinger said. "We need to draw a line against abandoning these patients just because they cannot take care of their basic needs."

Ethicist Gerard Magill of Duquesne University warned that if restrictions on withdrawing nutrition and hydration are pushed too far, some people may choose to avoid Catholic hospitals and nursing homes altogether, worried that decisions will be taken out of their hands. They may fear that advance directives and living wills, for example, will not be respected.

Doerflinger, on the other hand, said that the Church's strong defense of human dignity could work in precisely the opposite direction.

"Some people want assurance that no matter how debilitated they get, they will not be dismissed," he said. Doerflinger said Catholic hospitals might carve out a "niche market" as "the only place to go if people want to be treated with respect simply as human beings."

Eugenics/Genetic Engineering

In 2002, a thirty-year-old genetics counselor in the United States was diagnosed with early-onset Alzheimer's disease, which meant that by the time she reaches forty, much of her mental capacity probably will have been wiped out. To make matters worse, she and her husband were trying to have children at the time she received the diagnosis. Given that a predisposition to Alzheimer's is genetically transmitted, this couple faced the agonizing question of whether it was irresponsible to bring a child into the world who faced a realistic prospect of losing its mind before he or she reached middle age.

The couple turned to the Reproductive Genetics Institute in Chicago for a technique known as Preimplantation Genetic Diagnosis. Using IVF procedures, embryos were created artificially and then tested to see if they carried the gene for Alzheimer's. Technicians implanted only embryos that were free of the defective gene. The result was the birth of a healthy girl.

At first blush, this might seem a biotech success story. To date, practitioners claim that this kind of preimplantation diagnosis has resulted in the birth of 1,500 children worldwide who are free of genetic disorders such as cystic fibrosis, Tay-Sachs, sickle-cell disease, hemophilia, muscular dystrophy, and Down's syndrome. Yet aside from objections over the destruction of embryos, this capacity to determine which genetic traits children will possess or lack—usually called "genetic engineering"—has raised alarm on other grounds, mostly in terms of where it might lead. Among the most frequent objections:

- **Human Freedom:** If we can screen for disease, what about personality traits, such as a disposition to irritability or laziness? Can we decide how tall we want our kids to be, what color eyes they have, or how smart they are? Anti-biotech activist Bill McKibben warns: "Down that path lies the death of the idea that people are in some way their own human beings, and not pre-programmed semi-robots." Biotech proponents see such arguments as malarkey, contending that a child whose genetic makeup is selected on purpose is no more constrained than one whose genetic profile comes together randomly. To believe otherwise, these advocates argue, is to embrace "genetic determinism," which would eradicate free will for everybody, because we all carry a genetic code.

- **Savior Babies:** A second front of controversy concerns the creation of children to provide genetic materials to save someone else's life, so-called "savior babies." In the late 1990s, American parents Jack and Lisa Nash watched their six-year-old daughter Molly suffer from a fatal genetic disease called Fanconi anemia. Jack and Lisa used pre-implantation diagnosis to sort from among thirty artificially created embryos, finding five that were a genetic match. Adam Nash was born in August 2000, and his umbilical cord and blood stem cells were used to repair Molly's marrow. Both children are now healthy. While most people celebrate Molly's recovery, the case raises unavoidable questions. What happened to informed consent? Adam was never asked if he wanted to donate his blood cells. Moreover, who's to say that such births will be limited to cases of dire medical emergencies? Do we want a world in which children become tools, designed to accomplish some specific objective?

- **Genetics Haves and Have-Nots:** Critics say that because pre-implantation diagnosis is expensive, only the privileged will be able to afford it. As a result, for the first time inequality will become written in our DNA. In extreme form, such disparities could create a new basis for conflict. George Annas, Lori Andrews, and Rosario Isasi raised this prospect in 2002: "The new species, or 'post-human,' will likely view the old 'normal' humans as inferior, even savages, and fit for slavery and slaughter," they wrote. Given this potential, the authors wrote, genetic enhancement amounts to a sort of "weapon of mass destruction," and scientists who promote it are "bioterrorists."

- **Natural Balance:** Critics point to nations such as India and China, where widespread use of cheap ultrasound technology has led parents to abort female children, perceived as less desirable than males, at an alarming rate. If use of pre-implantation screening becomes widespread, critics wonder, what other sorts of disequilibria might be created?

Catholic moral teaching seems to be striving for a middle position. In principle, it approves genetic intervention to foster human well-being. (In practice, the Church opposes current methods of genetic intervention because they rely on IVF techniques, but if the technology changes, so would the moral analysis.) In a 1983 address to the World Medical Association, Pope John Paul II said: "A strictly therapeutic intervention whose explicit objective is the healing of various maladies . . . will, in principle, be considered desirable . . . Such an intervention would fall within the logic of the Christian moral tradition." At the same time, the pope warned against "adventuresome endeavors aimed at promoting I know not what kind of superman," and said explicitly that "manipulations that tend to modify genetic inheritance and to create groups of different men at the risk of causing new cases of marginalization in society" would be unacceptable.

Genetically Modified Organisms (GMOs)

Hunger remains a persistent fact of life for hundreds of millions of people, mostly in the developing world. Data from the United Nations World Food Program indicate that 852 million people across the world were hungry in 2004, and that hunger and malnutrition claim 10 million lives every year, including six million children under the age of five.

Genetically modified crops, or GMOs, are often touted as a potential solution to world hunger, offering vastly improved yields. GMOs are held to offer other benefits as well. For example, a genetically engineered form of rice, known as "golden rice," could, according to its proponents, help prevent blindness in a half-million to three million poor children every year. Fans of genetically modified crops also argue that they're environment-friendly, pointing to a study by the U.S. Department of Agriculture that found that American farmers using biotech crop varieties reduced pesticide volume by 46 million pounds.

One might suspect that such promise would impel advocates for the world's poor to clamor for biotechnology. In fact, precisely the opposite is generally the case. The strongest critics of GMOs tend to be nongovernmental organizations, activist groups, and religious leaders, who suspect that GMOs amount to a boondoggle that delivers profits for rich agribusiness firms in the global North, while potentially jeopardizing food safety, human health, biodiversity, and environmental well-being everywhere else. Governments in the developing world have sometimes refused humanitarian aid from the West if it comes in the form of GMO food. Secular anti-GMO activists in Europe have evoked images of "Frankenfoods," meaning mutant crops with unpredictable implications for human health and the broader ecosystem.

The case against GMOs usually revolves around four arguments:

- Patent rights on GMO seeds, and the fertilizers needed to treat GMO crops, will make poor farmers more dependent upon rich agribusiness conglomerates, and will disrupt traditional farming practices;

- GMO germ lines may "stray," corrupting other forms of plant and animal life and causing unpredictable harm in the ecosystem;

- GMO food may have negative consequences for human health;

- GMO crops amount to a "false promise," when the only real way to al-
  leviate hunger is to address its underlying causes—poverty, unequal
  land distribution, lack of access to markets, and the consumer lifestyle
  in the West.

Many Catholic voices in the global South are among the strongest critics
of biotech crops. In 2002, the Catholic bishops of South Africa declared, "It
is morally irresponsible to produce and market genetically modified food."
In 2003, fourteen Brazilian bishops put out a declaration in which they condemned the cultivation and consumption of GMOs, citing three risks: 1)
health consequences, including increased allergies, resistance to antibiotics,
and an increase in toxic substances; 2) environmental consequences, including erosion of biodiversity; and 3) damage to the sovereignty of Brazil,
"as a result of the loss of control of seeds and living things through patents
that become the exclusive property of multinational groups interested only
in commercial ends." In 2004, an international coalition of Catholic NGOs
published a joint statement that concluded: "GMO crops do not address
the root causes of hunger, including lack of access to land, water, energy,
affordable credit, local markets and infrastructures."

To date, the Vatican has seemed more receptive to the pro-GMO argument.

In a 1983 address to the World Medical Association, John Paul II referred
positively to "beneficent applications in the domains of animal and vegetable biology that favor food production." In a 2001 document (published
in 2004), the Pontifical Academy for the Sciences concluded: "Rapid growth
in world population requires the development of new technologies to feed
people adequately . . . The genetic modification of food plants can help
meet this challenge." The academy sponsored a "study week" on GMOs in
May 2009, organized by German scientist Ingo Potrykus, the inventor of
"golden rice," which ended with a strong endorsement of genetically modified crops.

Such Vatican comments have alarmed anti-GMO forces. Famed French
anti-GMO activist José Bové charged in 2003 that any Vatican endorsement
of biotech crops would be "scandalous."

"I believe that Saint Francis, if he were living today, would have something to say about this stance of the Roman shepherds," he told the Italian
press.

Holy Cross Br. David Andrews, former executive director of the National Catholic Rural Life Conference in the United States, charged in a September 20, 2004, statement that "the Pontifical Academy of Sciences has allowed itself to be subordinated to the United States government's insistent advocacy of biotechnology and of the companies which market it."

Chimeras

Weissman's mouse is an example of a "chimera," meaning an organism that carries both human and animal genes. Such creatures may seem like science fiction, but in less spectacular form they're already common. Cows today are injected with human stem cells to produce a human protein in their milk, which is extracted and used to cure hemophilia; pigs have been injected with human blood cells to study how the AIDS virus appeared; mice have been injected with human prostate cancer cells to study treatments; and sheep have been injected with human blood cells to stimulate the production of clotting factors, which are later synthesized and used to treat heart attacks and strokes.

Those instances may seem benign, but it's fear of a slippery slope toward confusion between human and animal species that causes fits. That's the terrain of Michael Crichton's 2006 thriller *Next*, about a researcher at the National Institutes of Health who mixes human and chimpanzee DNA, and then tries to pass off the resulting child as fully human. (Perhaps inevitably, wags label it a "humanzee.") The riddles that would surround such a creature—what rights it might enjoy, whether it could be exploited for manual labor or have its organs forcibly harvested, and, for the religiously inclined, whether it would possess a soul—give most ethicists and theologians a migraine.

Such doubts notwithstanding, experts say the technology is largely in place to make it happen—and human history, they ruefully observe, is not exactly replete with examples of technologies that, once developed, out of a sense of restraint were never used.

Debate over chimeras has become a political football. In 2005, Republican U.S. senator Sam Brownback introduced a "Human Chimera Prohibition Act," which would have banned the creation of animals with genes from the human brain, or animals with any human genes if they could reproduce. Among other things, Brownback also contended that chimeras could exacerbate the transmission of diseases across species boundaries. The bill has not come up for a vote, but it drew support from the United States Conference of Catholic Bishops. U.S. president George W. Bush called for a ban on human–animal hybrids in his 2006 State of the Union address. In England, meanwhile, regulatory authorities have issued a cautious green light to chimeras, a decision denounced by one Vatican official as a "monstrous act against human dignity."

In fact, Redemptorist Fr. Brian Johnstone, a moral theologian at the Catholic University of America, says that the church does not have any official teaching directly on chimeras, because the issue is simply too new. Church documents on transplants, however, have carved out a clear principle: transferring genetic material across species lines is okay, as long as the identity of the individual, and its offspring, is maintained. As far back as 1956, Pope Pius II approved of transplanting animal corneas into humans, "if it were biologically possible and advisable," in an address to the Italian Association of Cornea Donors and the Italian Union for the Blind. Anything that blurs the distinction between human beings and the rest of creation, on the other hand, goes too far.

Interestingly, religious leaders concerned about human dignity are not the only forces raising questions about chimeras. Animal rights groups generally approach the issue from the other end, objecting to the exploitation of animals for human use, while environmentalists worry about the genetic manipulation of nature.

Part of what's driving today's fascination with chimeras is the connection with stem cell research. The "holy grail" of stem cell research is to be able to shape these primitive cells into healthy hearts, kidneys, and livers, in order to replace defective human organs. Those organs, however, have to be grown and tested somewhere, and that means using animals. But that raises the specter of a monkey growing up with a human heart, or a pig with human eyes—prospects that some people find disturbing.

"You're creating beings without knowing what your ethical obligations to them are," warned Richard Doerflinger of the U.S. bishops' conference.

Doerflinger said that beyond the science involved, something deeper is at stake in the chimera debate.

"Some would like to render the sanctity of human life technologically obsolete by demonstrating that species membership is fungible," he said. "If so, then the idea of natural law based on a fixed human nature is over. You'd have to come up with some other basis for rights, like sentience." Doerflinger called that prospect a "real threat, a real motivation on the part of some," and hence "something worth worrying about."

A Necessary Reminder: Global Justice in Health Care

Amid the glitter of these high-tech scenarios, it's worth pausing to recall that for most of the world, the bioethical questions that truly matter are of a much more mundane character. In developing nations, the burning public health issues are the maladies of poverty, such as tuberculosis, malaria, cholera, and HIV/AIDS. In that light, some critics contend that pouring limited health care time and treasure into the pursuit of chimeric mice and savior babies may actually make things worse for the world's poor, diverting resources away from efforts toward adequate food, water, sewage disposal, and other more basic needs.

According to World Health Organization figures, developing nations account for 95 percent of global AIDS cases and 98 percent of active tuberculosis infections. Ninety percent of malaria deaths occur in sub-Saharan Africa alone. Together, these three diseases kill six million people every year. In addition, public health experts have identified a bundle of thirteen other neglected diseases that disproportionately strike the global South, such as hookworm, leprosy, African sleeping sickness, and trachoma. They cause an additional half million deaths each year. These illnesses, experts say, respond well to intervention, but there are few market incentives in profit-driven systems of health care to make treatments available to those who suffer.

Poverty and disease also become a self-perpetuating cycle, because it's not just poverty that causes disease; high levels of disease also worsen poverty. Malaria, for example, is estimated to decrease gross domestic product growth by up to 1.3 percent in developing nations with the highest case loads. The social and economic costs of AIDS are even more astronomic.

The biotech revolution likely means that an even lower percentage of resources, in terms of both research and treatment, will be directed to combating the diseases that affect predominantly poor populations in Africa, Asia, and Latin America. An increasing share of medical research today is happening under the aegis of for-profit pharmaceutical companies, in pursuit of the next big biotech breakthrough. Michael Kremer, an expert in development economics, estimates that roughly half of all global R&D in health care in recent years has been carried out by private industries, with only about 5 percent of this total directed at diseases specific to poor countries.

As one measure of these inequities, a WHO report observes that "The Americas, with 10 percent of the global burden of disease, have 37 percent of the world's health workers spending more than 50 percent of the world's health financing. Africa has 24 percent of the burden, but only 3 percent of health workers commanding less than 1 percent of expenditures." All this is aggravated by the fact that health care systems across much of the developing world are subject to political manipulation, are dilapidated, and in many cases are dysfunctional.

Such inequities are not confined to the developing world. In the United States, current estimates are that 47 million people are uninsured, with eight of ten being members of working families. The United States is the only wealthy industrialized nation that does not ensure basic access to all citizens.

Official Catholic teaching unambiguously condemns failures to provide health care to all. In his 1963 encyclical *Pacem in Terris*, Pope John XXIII identified health care as one of the basic rights that flow from the dignity of the human person. In his 1979 address to the United Nations, Pope John Paul II also included "sufficient health care" among the human rights endorsed by the Catholic Church. In 1993, the U.S. bishops declared, "Every person has a right to health care. This right flows from the sanctity of human life and the dignity that belongs to all human persons, who are made in the image of God."

As the twenty-first century develops, a special challenge for Catholic ethicists, bishops, pastors, and activists will be to avoid becoming so intoxicated with new biotechnology that the Church overlooks the more basic, and decidedly low-tech, threats to health and human welfare that endure in many parts of the world.

WHAT IT MEANS

The rise of these new biotech quandaries will certainly not displace debates over perennial hot-button issues in sexual morality, such as homosexuality and abortion. When U.S. president Barack Obama met Pope Benedict XVI in July 2009, abortion and other "life issues" were at the top of the agenda, and in the wake of that meeting, activists on all sides scrambled to ponder what Obama's pledge to work to bring down the actual number of abortions might mean in practice. Nonetheless, as the biotech revolution continues to create new scientific possibilities, both the content and the coalitions in the broader cultural debate are likely to undergo dramatic evolution. The extent to which the Catholic Church is able to offer a compelling response to the new questions being spawned by biotechnology will go a long way towards determining its relevance in the century to come.

Near-Certain Consequences

1. BIOETHICS AS A GROWTH INDUSTRY

The most direct result of the biotech revolution for Catholicism is an explosion of interest in moral theology, particularly as it relates to genetic science. Redemptorist Fr. Brian Johnstone, currently on the faculty of the Catholic University of America and a former professor at Rome's Alphonsian Academy, said in a 2007 interview that genetics is easily the most popular area of research interest for his graduate students in moral theology these days. In 2001, the American Society for Bioethics conducted a survey of graduate programs in the field, finding that at least 42 new programs had been launched between 1990 and 2000, representing a growth rate of 182 percent. More than a third of those new programs came at institutions affiliated with the Catholic Church.

The past quarter-century has witnessed dramatic growth in Catholic institutes focused on bioethics. In 1981, the John Paul II Institute for Studies on Marriage and the Family was established in Rome. Under the leadership of then-Fr. Angelo Scola, now the Cardinal of Venice, it quickly became an important point of reference in Catholic debate. The American branch of the institute was established in 1988, and it also has affiliates in Benin, Brazil, Spain, Mexico, India, and Australia. Georgetown University created a Center for Clinical Bioethics, aimed directly at health care practitioners, in 1991. In 2002, the Legionaries of Christ–affiliated campus in Rome, Regina Apostolorum, launched a new School of Bioethics, offering bachelor's, master's, and Ph.D. degrees. Within a year of operation, it had more than 300 students from dozens of countries, both clergy and lay. St. Joseph's University in Philadelphia established an Institute of Catholic Bioethics in 2006, to serve the Catholic academic community as well as pastoral and health care workers in Philadelphia.

While much of this growth has been concentrated in developed nations, interest is also likely to grow with time in Asia, Latin America, and Africa. Southern voices will want to ensure that the agenda for Catholic conversation is not being set entirely in the North. The Bio-Medical Ethics Centre, founded in Mumbai, India, in 1981 and affiliated with the International Federation of Catholic Medical Associations, offers one example.

In the Philippines, the University of San Tomás hosts the South-East Asian Center for Bioethics.

Biotechnology seems destined to be a "growth industry" in Catholic theology. More dissertations will be written on the subject, more journals will be devoted to it, and we can expect an avalanche of books and monographs. At the popular level, biotechnology will be a central concern for Catholic journalism, apologetics, and faith formation. If one wanted to make a career these days as a Catholic writer and speaker, the two most promising specialties would probably be Islam and biotech.

2. A BOOM IN CHRISTIAN ANTHROPOLOGY

Another growth industry at both the popular level and within academia will be Christian anthropology, meaning the attempt to give a Christian answer to the basic philosophical question of what it means to be human. The biotech revolution is driving new interest in the subject for two reasons.

First, today's science blurs the boundaries between species by transferring genetic material across species lines, resulting in creatures maddeningly difficult to classify. As noted above, that's what makes the brain research of Dr. Irving Weissman controversial. Such research calls into question religious claims about a special ontological and moral status for members of the human species, since it's increasingly difficult to establish exactly who's in and who's out of the species in this category-bending age. For some thinkers who reject religious premises, the logical conclusion of making species membership fungible is that attempts to impart a special moral status to human beings are simply blind tribal prejudice, what Australian ethicist Peter Singer calls "speciesism."

Second, developments in biotechnology also give scientists the capacity to program human beings in ways that raise philosophical questions about matters such as free will and the nature of rational thought. There's already a vigorous debate in the West about whether there is such a thing as objective truth, and if so, whether the human mind is capable of grasping it. Genetic science suggests that the human mind is physically wired to think in certain ways, raising questions about how free our thought and will actually are. In a future in which offspring may be consciously designed to make certain choices and to reach certain conclusions, these question marks will multiply.

In response to these forces, Catholics of all stripes will plumb the tradition to develop new ways of explaining, and defending, human distinctiveness and human freedom. Pope John Paul II's signature issue was precisely Christian anthropology—reading the human person in the light of Jesus Christ. John Paul drew upon the European tradition of philosophical personalism to develop his anthropology, in some ways "cross-breeding" it with the classic philosophical categories of Saint Thomas Aquinas. His insights into anthropology may well be the area of John Paul's magisterium that leaves the most lasting legacy in the century to come.

3. RISE OF THE THEOLOGIAN-BIOLOGIST

During the second half of the twentieth century, the hot ticket in Catholic theology was somebody who also had a background in the social sciences, especially political science and sociology. Much of the theological conversation of the era pivoted on social questions, such as the liberation theology movement in Latin America. The question of how traditional Catholic theology should draw on social theories such as Marxism, or upon sociological data such as values surveys, was much in vogue.

In the twenty-first century, the new theological oracle is likely to be the person who has a background in science, especially the fields of genetics and molecular biology. A growing number of theologians feel ill-equipped to engage bioethical issues because they're not adequately versed in the underlying science, so those theologians who can hold their own in scientific conversation will come to play a disproportionately important role in shaping the contours of Catholic theological debate.

Fr. Tad Pacholczyk of the National Catholic Bioethics Center offers a classic case in point. In addition to his degrees in theology, he also holds a Ph.D. in neuroscience from Yale University, where he focused on cloning genes for neurotransmitter transporters in the brain. He has worked as a molecular biologist at Massachusetts General Hospital and the Harvard Medical School. Given those credentials, whatever Pacholczyk says on bioethical questions carries extra weight for many Catholics. His support of Hurlbut's proposal for altered nuclear transfer, for example, is decisive for some people, because Pacholczyk is presumed to know the scientific difference between an embryo and another kind of cellular mass.

Dominican Fr. Nicanor Pier Giorgio Austriaco, a native of the Philippines who currently teaches at Providence College in Rhode Island, is another example. Austriaco has a Ph.D. in biology from the Massachusetts Institute of Technology, and he spent a year as a fellow of the International Human Frontier Science Program at the Ludwig Institute for Cancer Research at University

College of London. He also holds a licentiate in moral theology from the Dominican House of Studies in Washington. At Providence, he's a professor of both biology and theology.

Jesuit Fr. Kevin T. FitzGerald, also a distinguished member of this emerging class of theologian-biologists, holds a chair in Catholic Health Care Ethics at Georgetown University and serves as a professor in the Department of Oncology at the Georgetown University Medical Center. He earned doctorates in molecular genetics and in bioethics from Georgetown, with his area of scientific specialization being the characterization and functional analysis of cancer genes. Another American, Fr. Peter Leonard, a member of the Oblates of St. Francis de Sales, has a similar profile. He holds a Ph.D. in cell and molecular biology from the Catholic University of America as well as a master of divinity degree from DeSales School of Theology. He teaches courses in cell biology, molecular biology, immunology, and medical ethics in the Department of Natural Science at DeSales University in Pennsylvania.

In Argentina, Dominican Fr. Domingo Basso is a biologist and professor of bioethics at the Catholic University of Buenos Aires. In 2001, when the U.S.-based biotech firm Advanced Cell Technology announced the successful cloning of a human being, Basso was among the first to denounce it as a farce—a conclusion based on his scientific training. Basso plays an important role in bioethics debates in his country, since Argentina has one of the most developed biotechnology industries in the world, especially in the field of animal engineering. The head of the scientific committee of Advanced Cell Technology at the time of the 2001 announcement, Dr. Jose Cibelli, was originally an Argentinean veterinarian.

Among other things, it's likely that Catholic seminaries of the future will beef up their offerings in bioethics, and some will even hire scientists on a full- or part-time basis to bring future priests up to speed about the biotech revolution. Those priests who have specialized scientific expertise will be in increasing demand.

In the Catholic hierarchy as well, bishops with a background in biology and chemistry—admittedly, not very many—will play steadily more important roles in global Catholic debate. In Canada, Archbishop Bertrand Blanchet of Rimouski is a biologist who serves on the bishops' Commission on Social Affairs. In Argentina, Cardinal Jorge Mario Bergoglio trained as a chemist before entering the priesthood, so like Basso, he's well positioned to engage questions of scientific ethics.

One rising star to watch in the episcopal firmament is Auxiliary Bishop Anthony Fisher of Sydney, Australia, who, like Austriaco and Basso, is a Dominican. Though strictly speaking Fisher is not a scientist, he holds a doctorate from Oxford in bioethics, where his thesis was on "Justice in the Allocation of Healthcare." From 2000 to 2003 he was the director of the Australian branch of the John Paul II Institute for Marriage and Family in Melbourne, and he's still a professor of bioethics and moral theology there. Fisher publishes and speaks widely on bioethical matters, and he is usually regarded as one of the most incisive minds on biotech questions in the Catholic hierarchy. As the twenty-first century moves forward, Fisher will be a steadily more important voice in the global Church.

4. A REVIVAL OF NATURAL LAW

Whenever Church officials in the West enter a bioethics debate these days, someone will inevitably object that they're attempting to impose a particular religious teaching upon a pluralistic culture. Confessional positions, these critics insist, cannot serve as the basis for consensus in the secular sphere. According to this way of thinking, Church teaching on abortion, stem cell research, or cloning is disqualified as a basis for public policy because it's sectarian in nature. That's a deeply frustrating reaction for Church officials, who say it puts things exactly backward. Abortion and human cloning are not wrong because the Church says so, they insist—rather, the Church says so because they're wrong.

These officials say that the Church's moral teachings are not a set of arbitrary rules for joining the Catholic club, like wearing a fez or using a secret handshake. They're based on universal truths rooted in human nature, Catholic thinkers argue, which in principle anyone can recognize. This mode of reasoning is known as a "natural law" argument. It assumes that right and wrong, truth and falsehood, are real qualities that exist in nature, and that human beings can discover using their conscience. So when Catholicism says "x is wrong," the ultimate validity of that claim rests not on the authority of the Church, but the fact that x really *is* wrong.

Church officials also worry that many Catholics accept the idea that Catholic teachings are basically the result of a legislative act, a position known as "positivism." In that sense, officials worry, too many people have come to see moral rules as closer to the speed limit than to gravity—something human beings invent, instead of something given in nature. Church leaders often say that the spread of positivism is one reason that dissent from official teaching became so widespread in the second half of the twentieth century. If Catholic doctrine is based on nothing more than Church authority, then there's no reason it couldn't be revised if those who hold authority can be persuaded (or pressured) to change their minds. As the twenty-first century moves forward, Church officials will therefore seek to promote a revival in the natural-law tradition of moral reasoning.

In November 2004, for example, then-cardinal Joseph Ratzinger wrote to Fr. John C. Maviiri, rector of the Catholic University of East Africa in Nairobi, Kenya, urging that the university take up the subject of "natural and moral truths." Ratzinger pointed to what he called "the contemporary difficulty in finding a common denominator among the moral principles held by all people, which are based on the constitution of the human person and which function as the fundamental criteria for laws affecting the rights and duties of all." In response, the university convened an international symposium on natural law in February 2007, drawing Catholic theologians and intellectuals from across Africa.

Across a wide range of matters, and especially in the arena of biotech debates, the "natural law" drumbeat from the Catholic Church is only going to get louder.

Probable Consequences

1. AN AGE OF CATHOLIC ALTERNATIVES

Under the impress of evangelical Catholicism, it's highly improbable that the Church will reconsider its opposition to in vitro fertilization or to embryonic stem cell research. At the same time, many Catholic leaders will be sensitive to impressions that the Church is antiscience, or that it lacks compassion for people suffering from debilitating genetic illness. Given that both the grassroots and the leadership class of Catholicism in the global North will skew disproportionately "gray," the disorders of old age will be an especially direct pastoral concern. Demographic trends will also create rising concern within Catholicism related to fertility, given its traditional pro-family ethic.

For these reasons, the Catholic Church could become more open in the twenty-first century to proposed alternatives to IVF and embryonic stem cell research that could provide some of the benefits but skirt the ethical objections.

For example, alternative techniques to help infertile couples, such as Gamete Intra-Fallopian Transfer, Tubal Ovum Transfer, and Lower Tubal Ovum Transfer, are likely to be defended in theory and proposed in practice by a growing cross-section of bishops, pastors, theologians, and Catholic medical personnel. The theological debate may remain open, because some elements of evangelical Catholicism will see these techniques as weakening the intrinsic link between sexual intercourse and reproduction. On the ground, however, many leaders in the Church will accept these techniques as a "Catholic form of IVF," much as natural family planning has been embraced as "Catholic birth control."

In the abstract, the Church would actually be far more inclined to approve an ethically permissible form of IVF than it was a natural form of birth control, since the limitation of births, even by morally legitimate means, cuts against centuries of pro-natalist Catholic teaching and practice. Enhancing the prospect of fertility, on the other hand, serves an end that Catholicism has always embraced, which is procreation and child-rearing.

In similar fashion, Hurlbut's proposal for altered nuclear transfer is likely to attract continued interest, the Vatican caution in 2008's *Dignitas Personae* notwithstanding. Catholic scientists and bioethicists will also be among the most enthusiastic backers of research with adult stem cells and induced pluripotent stem cells. If these methods dislodge embryonic stem cells, the Catholic Church could, ironically, be left standing as perhaps the most pro-stem cell religious institution in the world.

2. HOSPICES AND PALLIATIVE CARE

Catholicism has a deep commitment to care for the terminally ill, which the Church of the twenty-first century will want to both build upon and publicize. Doing so will be seen as important not merely as a pastoral response to human suffering, but also as a way of resisting social pressure for euthanasia. Anti-euthanasia activists in the Church believe that the more people realize they have alternatives, the less attractive euthanasia will become.

The Pontifical Council for Health published a study in 2004 that found the Catholic Church operates hospices and palliative care programs in 121 nations on five continents. Slightly more than 40 percent of these programs offer hospital-based palliative care, while just under 60 percent are hospices. Over half of the programs are in Europe, and they range in size from fewer than 10 patients to more than 200.

Some examples:

- The Archdiocese of Miami and Mercy Hospital sponsor a Catholic Hospice that provides end-of-life care to 200 terminally ill patients and their families. It offers pain control and symptom management. In an interfaith touch, the Catholic Hospice also sponsors the L'chaim Jewish Hospice Program's Camp Hope for suffering children.

- In South Korea, the Korean Catholic Hospice Association coordinates the services of a number of hospice programs throughout the country operated by the Catholic Church. The Catholic University in Seoul also operates a research institute on hospice and palliative care.

- The Church-affiliated group "Catholic AIDS Action" in Windhoek, Namibia, offers hospices, home-based hospice care, and programs of palliative care for terminal AIDS patients.

- The Catholic Church currently operates two hospices in Cambodia, both for AIDS patients, even though the roughly 35,000 Catholics in Cambodia represent just 0.15 percent of the population of 14 million.

The study found that many of these programs suffer from deficiencies in funding and staff, though most have trained medical professionals on site, including doctors. The report concluded: "A commitment is necessary at all levels to foster and support centers and palliative care units which, beyond any logic of exaggerated treatment, and in opposition to every temptation of euthanasia, assure overall assistance for sick people and their right to a dignified natural death."

One example of the growing Catholic commitment to both hospices and palliative care came in the United States in 1994, with the foundation of the Supportive Care Coalition: Pursuing Excellence in Palliative Care, a coalition of Catholic health care organizations and professionals to support both direct care of the chronically and terminally ill, as well as policy changes so that, as the group puts it, "patients can experience living well until death."

In 1998, Pope John Paul II visited the Rennweg Hospice in Vienna, Austria, which is operated by the Catholic charitable group Caritas, in effect putting the papal seal of approval upon the hospice movement.

"The hospice makes one understand that dying means living before death, because even the last phase of earthly life can be lived consciously and organized individually," John Paul said that day. "Far from being a 'home for the dying,' this place becomes a threshold of hope which leads beyond suffering and death."

During a February 2007 conference in Seoul, South Korea, in conjunction with the Catholic Church's "World Day of the Sick," Mexican Cardinal Javier Lozano Barragán, president of the Vatican's Pontifical Council for Health, called for an expansion in palliative care services, citing a "need to promote pastoral programs in local churches dedicated specifically to palliative care and to provide an appropriate catechesis. . . . With palliative care," he said, "medicine places itself at the service of life in the measure that, although aware that it cannot defeat a grave pathology, it dedicates its capacities to alleviating the sufferings of those who are terminally ill."

3. ADVOCACY FOR GLOBAL HEALTH CARE JUSTICE

As Northern theologians and pastors become increasingly preoccupied with the exotic frontiers of today's genetic science, their colleagues in the South are likely to press for greater attention to the rudimentary components of basic public health care services often taken for granted in the developed world. In the Catholicism of the century to come, this suggests that justice in global health care systems will occupy a greater share of the Church's pastoral and political energies, especially in the Vatican and in international Catholic organizations and movements.

A July 2006 gathering of Catholic ethicists from around the world organized by Fr. James Keenan in Padua, Italy, offers an example. Fr. Emmanuel Katongole of Uganda warned against "over-confidence" surrounding antiretroviral drugs as a solution to the HIV/AIDS crisis. Fascination with "miraculous medicines," he said, risks obscuring the basic truth that "something is sick and sickening in Africa's modern ways of living, playing and working," making it seem as if structural and cultural problems can be solved with a simple drug cocktail. In reality, Katongole said, many Africans have no access to safe water with which to take the medicine, no watches to keep them on a schedule, no place to store the drugs, and no food so that they won't vomit up medicines on an empty stomach. Until such problems are addressed, he said, Western innovations will not affect the underlying crisis.

Similar arguments come from other Southern Catholic leaders. When a cholera epidemic struck Rwanda in January 2006, local Catholic officials drew attention to the structural dimension of the crisis. Dr. Prince-Bosco Kanani, director of health and AIDS services for Caritas Rwanda, the Church's charitable agency, told reporters he believed the outbreak was directly related to poor sanitation and hygiene. The area in question was a typical Kigali neighborhood, with dirt roads and ramshackle houses hastily built during the 11 years since the 1994 genocide. There is little or no running water, Kanani said, and people have to fetch water every day from nearby wells and distribution centers set up by the local power utility. Until that situation is improved, he said, periodic outbreaks of waterborne diseases such as cholera will be a fact of life.

Such concerns are likely to set the tone for much Catholic engagement. In December 2006, Pope Benedict XVI addressed a letter to German Chancellor Angela Merkel, who at the time held the presidency of the G8. Among other things, the pope called upon the G8 to undertake ". . . a substantial investment of resources for research and for the development of medicines to treat AIDS, tuberculosis, malaria, and other tropical diseases."

4. ANTI-GMO PRESSURES ON THE VATICAN

Recent statements from the Vatican on Genetically Modified Organisms (GMOs) suggest a basically positive stance, so much so that some anti-GMO activists in the Church have accused the Vatican of being bought off by big agribusiness concerns in the North and their allies in the American government. The rise of the global South in Catholicism is likely, over time, to push the Vatican toward a more cautious and critical stance.

This tendency will intersect with the anti-GMO climate in Europe, which also has echoes inside European Catholicism. The Italian bishops' conference in May 2005, for example, urged caution on GMOs, concluding that more study is needed on "the possible effects of GMOs on man and his habitat, from biological, productive, economic and social viewpoints." The Italian bishops warned that, "We mustn't make the mistake of believing that new biotechnologies may be the answer for all the pressing problems of poverty and underdevelopment afflicting so many countries. . . . The possible irreversible nature of these processes, and the uncertainty linked to our partial knowledge of GMOs, call for a particularly cautious stance and further scientific research."

Given these forces, it may become more difficult for Vatican officials to move toward a formal, public approval of GMO technology.

5. THE THEOLOGY OF SUFFERING

Much cultural conversation over matters such as embryonic stem cell research, genetic engineering, and euthanasia is premised on the assumption that relieving suffering is an unalloyed good. As Ronald Tojack observed in the *Catholic New Times* in 2005, an aversion to suffering is the temper of the times: "A brief visit to any pharmacy shows that we in the so-called developed world live in an analgesic society," Trojack wrote. "Pain of any sort—recall the 'heartbreak of psoriasis'—is seen as unwarranted, indecent, improper, inappropriate. However, it's always remediable. The enormous energy and money we expend to produce and purchase remedies for fallen arches, dry skin, or body odor eloquently speak of our sense that any kind of pain is, as an old aspirin advertisement had it, 'unfair.'"

While traditional Catholic thought holds that relief of suffering is desirable, it does not regard ending suffering as an absolute value that trumps all others. In fact, traditional Catholic theology at the grassroots level has always held that "a little suffering is good for the soul." As the relief of suffering becomes an ever more potent argument to justify practices that Catholicism opposes, such as euthanasia and embryonic stem cell research, one can expect stronger efforts from the Church to assert a positive spiritual vision of suffering—not to call for additional pain in the world, but to persuade people that suffering is not pointless where moral absolutes cause anguish.

One recent focal point for such a spirituality of suffering came with the very public decline of the late John Paul II. Many Church officials and Catholic apologists insisted that his suffering and frailty was a valuable witness in a culture that worships youth, beauty, and wellness. Such ideas will be elaborated in twenty-first-century Catholic apologetics.

"No amount of suffering is wasted in Catholic theology," Robert Sungenis asserted in 2004 on behalf of Catholic Apologetics International. "Every ounce is pressed into service for the saving of souls." David MacDonald, a Canadian Catholic who specializes in outreach to Evangelicals, wrote in 2003: "Catholics are not afraid of the Cross. We love the Cross. Catholics feel that if they prayerfully offer up their sufferings to God, they can benefit those in the world who are suffering but who do not know Christ. . . . We don't go chasing after suffering, but if it is persistently there, we don't waste the opportunity to use it for good."

That's the sort of message that Catholicism will likely offer with greater frequency and intensity, in response to arguments that traditional moral norms be set aside in order to relieve the suffering of infertile couples, or Alzheimer's patients, or parents who want to use preimplantation diagnosis and IVF to make sure their children are free of disease.

Possible Consequences

1. REDEFINING THE CULTURE WARS

The politics of bioethics in the West has historically pitted a permissive left against a restrictive right. That was the dynamic when the front-burner issues were abortion and birth control, and it's still true with many of today's agonizing debates, such as embryonic stem cell research and end-of-life questions. The primary consequence for the Catholic Church has been to drive it into an ever tighter alliance with the political right.

The front-line bioethical debates of the future, however, may make today's ideological divisions much less clear-cut, as opposition to the brave new world of biotechnology will stem as much from the secular left as the religious right. This reality is already crystal-clear in Europe, where the use of genetically modified foods has basically been stopped in its tracks by the political left, not the right. Across the range of other looming biotech issues, something similar is afoot, which in the long run may upend the current marriage of convenience between Catholicism and the political right on the culture wars.

To be sure, there's strong opposition to the biotech revolution from the right, including the emergence of a group of influential intellectuals dubbed "bio-conservatives" who fear that fundamental lines of human dignity are being blurred. Yet the most ferocious criticism of today's biotech developments comes from figures associated with the cultural left. Jeremy Rifkin, for example, is often aligned with liberal environmental circles; he's served as a personal advisor to Romano Prodi, at the time the left-of-center prime minister of Italy. Rifkin is also the most acerbic critic of the biotech age, earning him the title, according to *Time* magazine, of "the most hated man in science." On the subject of GMOs, for example, Rifkin has said that they threaten humanity with "a form of annihilation every bit as deadly as nuclear holocaust."

Rifkin acknowledges that the old left–right taxonomy on the culture wars is giving way.

"The biotech era will bring with it a very different constellation of political visions and social forces, just as the industrial era did," Rifkin writes.

"The current debate over cloning human embryos . . . is already loosening the old alliances and categories. It's just the beginning of the new biopolitics."

On the grounds of protecting harmony with nature, leftist environmentalist Bill McKibben is deeply skeptical of most aspects of the biotech revolution. He's written that genetically engineering our children will be "the worst choice human beings ever make." Other socially conscious leftists harbor similar reservations. Marcy Darnovsky from the Center for Genetics and Society, along with Tom Athanasiou from EcoEquity, asserts that genetic engineering will "allow inequality to be inscribed into the human genome."

On most new biotech issues the Catholic Church will probably side with the opposition, on the grounds of respect for life as well as concern that the ultimate end of such technologies will be to erode human uniqueness. The political consequences of such values, which are obviously central to Catholic anthropology and morality, mean that bishops and pro-life activists may increasingly find themselves accompanied by unaccustomed allies from the secular left, who will have to learn anew to think of Catholicism as a friend as well as a foe.

In the coming biopolitics, the pro-life stance of Roman Catholicism may thus locate the church within a new trans-ideological constellation. In what might come to be regarded as one of the primary miracles of genetic science, the Church and at least some elements of the left may once again find themselves on speaking terms.

2. THE CHURCH AS MEDIATOR

Biopolitics of the twenty-first century will generate not only new alliances, but also new divisions. One growing divide runs between Western environmentalists and advocates for the world's poor, nonwhite majority. In May 2003, for example, the U.S.-based Congress for Racial Equality put out a public statement bitterly critical of Greenpeace for its opposition to GMOs.

"Well-fed eco-fanatics shriek 'Frankenfoods' and 'genetic pollution,'" the statement read. "They threaten sanctions on nations that dare to grow genetically modified crops, to feed their people or replace crops that have been wiped out by insects and blights. They plan to spend $175 million battling biotech foods over the next five years. Not one dime of this will go to the starving poor. . . . Greenpeace policies bring misery, disease and death to millions of people in developing countries, particularly in Africa."

In the future, elements of the left may divide along other lines as well: between those who accent choice and those who emphasize equity in access to genetic technologies, for example, or between those who demand virtually unlimited public funding for advanced biotechnology, and those who would rather see those resources devoted to the basic health care needs of the world's poor. The right could equally splinter between pro-business and pro-life forces, in a clash between profits and prophets. If things develop in this fashion, Western societies could find themselves facing a bizarre new kind of ideological warfare, in which, on certain issues, Greenpeace and the religious right face off against civil rights groups and the Chamber of Commerce.

Catholicism may be able to play a mediating role amid these tensions, for two reasons. First, the Church is broad enough that it includes people who come from all of these different constituencies, so it provides a natural common ground where conversations could unfold. Second, Catholicism is itself striving for a middle ground between progress and caution on biotech issues. Church leaders may be well suited to foster dialogue, since they'll feel the tug of the arguments all sides are likely to make. In that sense, Catholicism may have a chance of being seen as a "fair broker" in at least some of the feuding spawned by the new biopolitics.

3. WILL SIN BE "IN"?

Once upon a time, people found the Christian message that they're sinners to be fairly depressing. In the new biotech world, people may actually find the idea of being sinners liberating, because it implies that they still exercise control over their behavior, despite all the ways in which science tells us we're genetically conditioned. In the twenty-first century, the doctrine of sin may be "in."

Such an outcome might seem counterintuitive, because at face value genetic science may seem to imperil the whole concept of sin. If individuals are genetically conditioned to lie, cheat, steal, and kill, what does that do to the teaching that such conduct amounts to a free human choice to spurn God and the moral law? Most theologians and Church leaders, however, have been untroubled by that question, because they've been down this path before. Freudian psychology explained what Christians call "sin" in terms of repressed childhood trauma; Marxism explained it in terms of material determinism. In all of these cases, the Church responded that conditioning someone's behavior is not the same as causing it. No matter what constraints we face, there's always an element of free will. The forces that shape a given person's choice might mitigate subjective culpability, but as an objective matter, it doesn't make sinful behavior any less sinful.

While the biotech revolution is therefore unlikely to erode the idea of sin, there are at least a couple of senses in which it may provide a surprising boost. One lies with the question of original sin. As far back as Saint Augustine, many theologians have argued for an intrinsic connection between sexual procreation and the transmission of original sin. As Augustine wrote, after Adam's fall, our "soiled" and "corrupt" nature was "already present in the seed from which we were to spring." Over the centuries, critics have seen in such claims the basis for the Church's adoption of priestly celibacy and, in their eyes, its negative view of human sexuality overall. Yet some theologians believe that genetic science today is, in effect, vindicating Augustine. Anglican theologian John Polkinghorne, a particle physicist, says genetic science lends confirmation to the idea that corruption is written into our DNA. After all, what else does it mean that we have genetic predispositions to do morally reprehensible things, if not that we have an innate tendency to sin?

The other element driving a new interest in sin is the way it rebuts genetic determinism.

"The contemporary version of sin coming from genetic science is fatalistic," said Ted Peters, a professor of Systematic Theology at the Pacific Lutheran Theological Seminary in Berkeley, California. "It's all in the genes: 'Your Honor, I could not help myself; I committed this crime, but my genes made me do it.' In medieval Christian spirituality, we had biological propensities, but we also had spiritual resources with which to handle them, and with which to rise above them. If you're going to be a genetic determinist and a materialist, where are those spiritual resources?" Peters believes one of the central challenges facing Christian theology in the biotech era is convincing people that genetic propensities are not genetic destinies. He says that a renewed appreciation for traditional Christian teaching about sin, and the discipline to resist it, could just do the trick.

Long-Shot Consequences

PROGRAMMING THE "GOD GENE"?

To venture boldly into the fantastic, let's envision a future in which two things that presently seem improbable have happened: First, scientists have developed a technique of genetic intervention that does not involve the creation of embryos outside sexual intercourse between a married couple, and that does not subject the developing embryo to any health risks. Second, scientists have definitively identified a specific gene that predisposes people to religious belief and practice, and have developed a means to promote the expression of this gene without altering any other aspect of a person's genetic code.

In that world, would the Catholic Church approve an intervention designed to foster the "God gene?"

Talk about a gene associated with religion is not science fiction. In 2004, respected American geneticist Dean Hamer published a book called *The God Gene*, in which he claimed to have identified a particular gene, VMAT2, which correlates with spiritual sensitivity. People with one variant of the gene tend to be more religious, he found, people with another less so. Hamer is no quack; he has a Ph.D. from the Harvard Medical School and is chief of the Section on Gene Structure and Regulation for the National Cancer Institute. Still, the God gene is not a slam-dunk. Critics say the jury is still out on his findings. In any event, even if VMAT2 promotes heightened spiritual interest, that doesn't translate into support for any given religion or denomination. Someone with the "God gene" could join a New Age cult as easily as joining the Catholic Church.

Nonetheless, there does seem to be additional data supporting the idea of a genetic basis for religious interest. According to a 2005 story in the *New York Times*, identical twins separated at birth tend to have similar levels of religious faith and practice.

Catholicism would be deeply unlikely to support encoding the "God gene" into embryos, even under the long-shot circumstances assumed here. As noted above, John Paul II's 1983 address on genetics warned against "manipulations that tend to modify genetic inheritance and to create groups of different men." Moreover, Catholicism has always emphasized that faith must be a free response to God's grace, and some Catholics would worry about the free will of future generations that had been programmed for religion.

On the other hand, it's not utterly beyond plausibility that some Catholics might argue in favor of such an intervention, especially if the secularizing trends in Europe reviewed in chapter two spread to other parts of the world. After all, as the British bishops said in 1996, the genome is simply another part of the human body. Giving someone a healthy set of legs doesn't mean he'll become a champion runner, it simply means he has the capacity to do so if he makes a free choice in that direction. Similarly, passing along the

"God gene," one might argue, simply would ensure a capacity for religious faith, leaving it in the mind and heart of the individual to decide what to do about it.

Ironically, if a fixed "God gene" does become a datum of science, it may well be the secular world that decides to engineer for it, and for utterly pragmatic reasons. Put simply, religious people tend to be healthier, live longer, and be happier than everyone else. A recent study of 4,000 people in North Carolina, for example, found that regular churchgoers had a 46 percent lower chance of dying in a six-year period than those who stayed away. A similar American study of 126,000 churchgoers suggested that they live seven years longer on average than people who don't attend services. Some scientists believe that religious practice stimulates the brain to release dopamine, which makes people more optimistic and sociable, better equipping them to withstand illness. Some evidence suggests it also may make people more likely to have children. As the *New York Times* notes, some evolutionary biologists even argue that religious faith is an adaptive behavior that makes groups more cohesive and better able to withstand rivals.

For all these reasons, if a brave new world of genetic enhancement does take shape, it may be that even nonreligious parents decide that along with beauty, strength, and intelligence, they also want to program their children for religious faith. Governments might even promote doing so, as part of an effort to bolster public health, longevity, and fertility. In such a world, it may not really matter whether the Catholic Church approves of purposefully engineering the "God gene." Secularism might beat the Church to it.

GLOBALIZATION

Indian teenager Mansi Arya could be a poster child for the upside of globalization, though not in a sense that would probably give her much satisfaction. Her story reflects India's economic surge since 1980, which has propelled an estimated 300 million people into a thriving middle class. Like children of privilege in other parts of the world, Mansi comes across as bright, optimistic, looking forward to college and to a career—and, despite her best efforts, she's got a weight problem.

In late 2006, a reporter from the *New York Times* followed Arya on a trip to a nutritionist's office in Delhi, the national capital, where her family lives. She was grilled about how much she'd eaten since her previous visit. At school, Mansi explained, the cafeteria provides hot fried treats. When she gets home, her mother fries up Indian spiced bread known as *parathas,* or she digs into a package of *namkeen,* a deep-fried spicy snack. A few hours later she comes down for a full dinner, and before bed she has some late-night treats. Add to that a constant round of birthday parties featuring junk food and cakes, and it's no surprise that in the tenth grade alone, Mansi said she'd put on twenty-two pounds.

It's a typical example of the problems of plenty.

Mansi is not an isolated case in today's India. A 2006 study of Delhi teenagers by a doctor at the privately run Fortis Hospital found that the share of local teens who qualify as obese had jumped from 16 percent to 29 percent over the last two years alone. A similar study from the Delhi Diabetes

Research Center, this time of children aged 10 to 16, found almost one in five to be either overweight or clinically obese.

Compare Mansi to another child of contemporary India, Asma Bando, who lives three hundred miles to the north.

Asma is the youngest of six children, in a poor family in which the father is a day laborer and the mother cares for the children. Given her string of pregnancies over a short span of time, along with chronic shortages of food, the mother said in 2006 that she never had enough breast milk to feed Asma. She tries to scrape together enough money to buy a small amount of milk each morning, in order to make a pot of milky tea. The mother said she couldn't remember the last time she was able to buy meat or eggs; her family's normal diet consists of lentils, rice or whole wheat bread, and maybe a vegetable.

Along with the other poor children of Barabanki, Asma goes in the mornings to a local distribution point for a program called Integrated Child Development Services, designed to combat child hunger. There she receives a scoop of dry cereal, composed of a mix of wheat, sugar, and soy. Some parents complain that the cereal actually makes their children sick. No hot food is on offer. Asma has a badly distended belly, one of the telltale signs of malnutrition, and she frequently suffers from diarrhea and fever.

Like Mansi, Asma is not alone. The latest National Family Health Survey revealed that one in three Indian children under the age of three is clinically underweight. Overall, according to the International Food Policy Research Institute, India's score on the "global hunger index" falls between Sudan and Burkina Faso, among the nations with the highest rates of child malnutrition and child mortality and with the highest proportion of people who are calorie deficient.

Taken together, these two Indian children illustrate the maddeningly binary character of the outcomes associated with "globalization," referring to a growing planetary interconnectedness driven by technology, communications, travel, and economic integration, which has created vast opportunities for some and left others even farther behind. The problem is not that the glass is either half full or half empty, depending upon one's perspective. It's rather that there seem to be two glasses, one overflowing and the other almost bone dry.

In the last quarter-century, more people have escaped poverty more rapidly than at any previous point in human history. The remarkable economic growth of India and China since 1978, all by itself, has reduced the percentage of the world's population living in extreme poverty from 40 percent to 20 percent. On that basis, one could argue that globalization is the most effective humanitarian program ever devised. Yet at the same time, 29,000 children still die from preventable diseases every day, and 1.2 billion people still live on less than $1 a day. Half the population of the planet lives on less than $2 a day.

Some contemporary Catholic activism uses the slang of "globalization with a human face." But is the harsh truth that globalization is destined always to carry two human faces—the faces of Mansi and Asma? It's a question that will haunt the Catholic imagination in the century to come.

Here's another key question: Is it realistic to believe that Catholic leaders or movements can actually have any impact on a process that seems to be beyond anyone's control?

The case for hope can perhaps be illustrated with an unusual meeting that took place in September 1999, in Castel Gandolfo, the pope's summer residence in the hills outside Rome. The delegation that met John Paul II that day included Bono, of the rock group U2; Bob Geldof, another rock star from the Boomtown Rats who had launched Band Aid in the United Kingdom in 1984 to raise funds and awareness about starvation in Africa; Quincy Jones, a legendary American producer who organized We Are the World, the American counterpart to Band Aid; and economics professor Jeffrey Sachs, an expert on poverty and underdevelopment.

The objective was to pool forces on a cause dear to both John Paul II and these socially conscious rocks stars: debt relief for the world's most impoverished nations, as part of a Jubilee 2000 campaign. In the Old Testament, the jubilee was a special year marked by the Israelites in which debts were wiped clean. Advocates for the world's poor hoped to use the calendrical coincidence of a new millennium to stimulate debt relief on a much broader scale. In the end, the Jubilee 2000 campaign enjoyed remarkable success. In 1999, industrialized nations agreed to a sweeping debt relief plan in Cologne, Germany. The United States alone pledged $920 million in debt relief over four years. As a result, some twenty-three nations saw their debt load canceled or reduced. In 2005, that circle of nations was extended to forty.

Bono later told the story of what transpired in that September 1999 meeting with John Paul. As they spoke, Bono said, he noticed the pope staring at him. Bono became worried that his trademark powder-blue sunglasses were offensive, and so he removed them and put them in his pocket. The pope continued to stare. When the meeting broke up and Bono was introduced to John Paul to receive a rosary, the customary gift the pope gives to visitors, it registered with Bono that the pope still had his eyes on the shades.

"So I asked if he wanted them," Bono said. "He not only nodded, but he put them on and made the wickedest smile." Though it took a while, pictures of John Paul wearing the rocker's shades made the rounds, symbolizing the intriguing symbiosis between rock and religion in the debt relief campaign.

At the time of the pope's death in 2005, Bono insisted that John Paul had been instrumental in achieving the debt relief accomplished in 2000.

"He talked about the difference between rich and poor as the biggest threat to humanity. He meant it in the security sense and in the moral sense," he said. "We would never have gotten the debts of twenty-three countries completely canceled without him." Bono called the pope "a street fighter and a wily campaigner on behalf of the world's poor. . . . He had mischief in his eyes as well as godliness. If the Catholic Church is the glam rock of religion, this guy was just the most vivid of performers."

As he signed a debt relief measure into law in November 2000, then-U.S. president Bill Clinton also acknowledged the pope's impact. "When we get the pope and the pop stars all singing on the same sheet of music, our voices do carry to the heavens," Clinton said.

Following the pope's lead, Catholics at all levels were engaged on the debt relief issue. One visible international figure was Cardinal Óscar Rodríguez Maradiaga of Honduras, who led the Church's charge with the G8 and other international institutions. To those who said Church leaders were out of their depth, Rodríguez had a ready reply: "We're not Nobel Prize winners in economics, but we know humanity, and much of the time that's enough." Among the most energized forces in the Church were its religious orders, who for centuries have been heralds of a globalized world, with members and missions scattered all across the planet. Religious men and women in the Catholic Church learned to "think globally and act locally" long before there was a secular environmental movement to put the phrase on bumper stickers.

The Jubilee 2000 effort illustrates the contours of successful advocacy efforts in this globalized age. The debt relief movement originated from a sense of global interconnectedness, and it drew upon the global media to concentrate political energies. It also understood the multilevel character of a globalized world, in which, to achieve change, one has to simultaneously address international bodies (both governmental and private), national governments, local and regional authorities, transnational networks, and the grassroots. Leaders of the debt relief campaign grasped that the processes of economic globalization could not be relied upon, by themselves, to achieve equity or justice; it requires imaginative human intervention. Whatever its limitations, the Jubilee 2000 campaign suggests that Catholicism still has tremendous social capital, which, if invested wisely, can help change the world.

WHAT'S HAPPENING

Globalization has the curious distinction of being both almost impossible to define, and yet, by universal agreement, the most important reality of our time. In its literal sense, globalization refers to the transformation of local and regional realities into global ones, uniting the peoples of the world in a single global market and society. Globalization is the "mother of all megatrends," in the sense that it has become a catchall designation for the accelerating global integration of economics, politics, culture, communications, spirituality, and virtually everything else that matters. Analysts assert that globalization is the historical equal of the agricultural and industrial revolutions in terms of transforming social impact. As with any other major historical transition, there are winners and losers—those who benefit, such as software engineers in India and textile manufacturers in China, and those who are hurt, such as rural farmers in Africa facing falling food prices and having no access to global markets.

Beyond that broad definition, however, globalization obviously means different things to different people. To its most enthusiastic advocates, it means a level playing field in the global economy, heralding a new era of competition, efficiency, and innovation, as well as the spread of human rights and the rule of law to heretofore forgotten corners of the planet. For its most ferocious critics, globalization means colonialism on a vast planetary scale, imposing Western corporate interests and suppressing local cultures and values. Such strongly contrasting perceptions may help explain why, depending upon who's speaking, globalization can seem simultaneously like the cause of, and the solution to, all the world's problems.

The following seem among the key hallmarks of globalization:

- The rise of transnational organizations and movements both private (multinational corporations, NGOs) and public (international governmental organizations such as the International Criminal Court);

- The increasingly planetary dimensions of business, trade, finance, and technological and information flows;

- The lowering or elimination of political and economic barriers, such as tariffs;

- Increasing cultural homogenization, including the spread of liberal institutions such as free markets, limited government, and the rule of law;

- Expansion of personal relationships beyond the familial, local, regional, and even national levels;

- An equal and opposite reaction of strong assertion of local, tribal, ethnic, and regional identities, a phenomenon Roland Robertson has expressed with the term "glocal."

The globalization of opportunity also, of course, means the globalization of great mischief: terrorist networks and the exchange of weapons of mass destruction; global crime syndicates; climate changes with global repercussions; new diseases such as SARS and HIV/AIDS; the global arms trade; illicit commerce in natural resources, such as the phenomenon of so-called "blood diamonds"; and a host of other threats to peace, security, and health. They collectively represent what might be called the pathologies of globalization.

Catholic Teaching on Globalization

The Catholic Church has not issued a comprehensive statement on globalization. Catholicism does have a well-developed set of social teachings, however, that provide basic principles through which the Church analyzes what's happening. In the 2005 volume *Globalization and Catholic Social Thought*, American Jesuit Fr. John Coleman, a distinguished sociologist, offered a list of eight such principles, which are summarized here.

1. UNIVERSAL HUMAN RIGHTS

The touchstone of Catholic social theory is that each human person is created in the image of God, and therefore carries an inherent dignity, apart from that person's aptitudes or social standing. This insight grounds a commitment to universal human rights, which are unalterable and which governments and social systems are obliged to honor.

The Catholic Church has supported the development of international charters of human rights, as well as the global legal infrastructure to back them up. John Paul II put the point this way in 1979, for a celebration marking the fortieth anniversary of the UN Declaration on Human Rights: "Human rights are by nature universal, for their source is the equal dignity of every person. While recognizing the cultural diversity that exists in the world and the different levels of economic development, it is appropriate to reiterate forcefully that human rights concern every person. The argument of cultural specificity must not be used to mask human rights violations."

In 2004, the bishops of England and Wales made much the same point in their document *Cherishing Life*: "There is an equality and an inherent dignity shared by all human beings, and this is the basis of an objective moral order and of universal human rights."

2. THE SOCIAL NATURE OF THE HUMAN PERSON

As opposed to atomistic currents in modern philosophy and political theory, which tend to presume that human beings are isolated agents, the Catholic understanding is that human beings are by nature social, reaching their full potential only in relationship with others. This principle means that respect for families, communities, civil associations, cultures, and churches is a key value for Catholic thought. As Coleman notes, emphasis on the social nature of the human being also prompts Catholicism to embrace not just negative rights, which protect the freedoms of individuals, but also positive rights such as education and health care, which speak to the duty of social systems to create the conditions required for full human flourishing.

3. THE COMMON GOOD

In Catholic thought, the perfectly legitimate right of individuals and groups to seek their own advantage has to be balanced against the common welfare of all. Beneath the right to private property lies a primordial sense of the universal destination of goods of the earth. In his 1981 encyclical *Laborem Exercens,* John Paul laid out this principle.

"Christian tradition has never recognized the right to private property as absolute and untouchable," the pope wrote. "On the contrary, it has always understood this right within the broader context of the right common to all to use the goods of the whole of creation. The right to private property is subordinated to the right to common use, to the fact that goods are meant for everyone." In his 1987 encyclical *Sollicitudo Rei Socialis,* John Paul employed an arresting metaphor to capture the same idea: "Private property is under a social mortgage."

This principle has both a personal and a social thrust. Personally, it encourages people to charity and generosity with their wealth, recognizing that their property is a kind of trust, intended to build up the common good. Socially, the universal destination of goods supports efforts by governments and by nonstate actors to ensure a more equitable distribution of wealth, especially in cases of extreme need. In a July 8, 2001, Sunday Angelus address, John Paul II put an exclamation point on the importance of this principle. "The universal destination of the goods of the earth," he said, "is one of the cardinal points of the social doctrine of the Church."

According to the *Compendium of Social Doctrine,* this principle has to be translated into practice in differing ways, depending upon the local and cultural context. It also has to be done according to law; the universal destination of goods can't be invoked to justify a free-for-all in which people simply grab whatever they want.

4. SOLIDARITY

Contrary to some popular Catholic mythology, the term "solidarity" was alive and well long before August 14, 1980, when Lech Walesa climbed over the fence at the Lenin Shipyards in Gdansk, Poland, and founded the labor movement that became known as Solidarity. Pope Paul VI, in his 1967 encyclical *Populorum Progressio,* appealed for "a civilization founded on world solidarity." John Paul II cemented solidarity as a core principle of Catholic social teaching, calling for "integral development born of solidarity." Solidarity refers to a moral commitment to concern for the welfare of others that goes beyond what strict justice requires. It's not just about doing one's duty, but making the common good the baseline of moral analysis.

In that sense, solidarity has two levels of meaning.

The first is individual, meaning a personal sense of membership in a common human family for which all bear responsibility. Solidarity requires reform of the heart before reform of the social order. Pope Benedict XVI used the term in this sense in his 2005 encyclical *Deus Caritas Est.* Praising the growth of volunteer service among young people, the Pope said that such individual generosity creates "a school of life, which offers them a formation in solidarity and in readiness to offer others not simply material aid but their very selves."

At the social level, solidarity is also a principle for guiding relationships among states, corporations, NGOs, and other large-scale social actors. In recent papal teaching, it has been employed to urge wealthy nations to feel a sense of responsibility for poor nations, and for powerful nations to foster participation in global affairs by weaker ones. Solidarity functions as a measure of the success or failure of economic and political systems. If they promote solidarity, they work; to the degree they don't, they need to change.

5. THE OPTION FOR THE POOR

Over the last forty years, the "option for the poor" has been associated in Catholic thought with the liberation theology movement in Latin America, which put the phrase firmly in the Catholic lexicon. Yet the idea of an option for the poor, as opposed to the verbal formula, has a much deeper pedigree in Christianity. Pope Benedict XVI, in a May 13, 2007, address to the bishops of Latin America, asserted that it goes back to the very beginning: "The preferential option for the poor is implicit in the Christological faith in the God who became poor for us, so as to enrich us with his poverty," the pope said.

American Jesuit Fr. William Byron explained the option for the poor in a December 1999 essay.

"Any parent knows what preferential love means," he wrote. "The vulnerable three-year-old child gets preference over a more self-sufficient older sibling under certain circumstances. Let the toddler run out into the path of an oncoming automobile, and you'll see the older child left to fend for him- or herself on the sidewalk, as the parent of both runs out to extend preferential protection to the vulnerable child. So the modern Church is asking nothing unusual, unfamiliar, or extraordinary when it calls for preferential love of the poor and vulnerable."

6. SUBSIDIARITY

All of the above might sound like a prescription for extensive government intervention in the economy and social life. But the Catholic Church is not an advocate of "statalism," meaning the creation of heavy-handed bureaucracies. Instead, it teaches that decisions should be made at the lowest level possible to achieve the common good, with higher levels of authority stepping in only when lower levels can't get the job done. In practice, this means that nations and international bodies should respect the autonomy of mediating institutions such as churches and voluntary associations, and especially the family. The *Compendium* states that the principle of subsidiarity implies opposition to "certain forms of centralization, bureaucratization, and welfare assistance, and to the unjustified and excessive presence of the State in public mechanisms."

John Paul II offered a concrete example in his 1991 encyclical *Centesimus Annus,* talking about unemployment. The state, he wrote, should defend the weakest, regulate working conditions, and ensure a minimum level of support for the unemployed. But government should also foster the free market, so that entrepreneurs will create and operate businesses, leading to new employment and greater wealth. Government and private actors both have their roles to play, the pope argued, and neither should seek to do what the other can do more effectively.

7. CATHOLIC CONCEPTS OF JUSTICE

Coleman says that the Church generally accepts the classic way of dividing types of justice into three broad categories:

- *Commutative justice*, meaning fulfilling the terms of promises and contracts, ensuring the rule of law in relationships, whether on an individual or a social basis;
- *Distributive justice*, ensuring a basic equity in how both the burdens and the goods of a society are spread around, and also ensuring that everyone has a basically equal moral and legal standing apart from inevitable gaps in wealth, privilege, talent, and accomplishment;
- *Social justice*, which refers to creating the structural conditions in which the first two kinds of justice can be obtained, and the common good can be identified and defended. While Catholic thought does not mandate democracy, its understanding of social justice does require some mechanism in which people can participate in shaping the social conditions that affect their lives.

A truly just society, according to Catholic teaching, is one in which all three forms of justice are assured, not just as a pragmatic concession on the part of the state but as a fundamental requirement of human dignity.

8. INTEGRAL HUMANISM

Rather than driving a wedge between material and spiritual liberation, Catholicism seeks to foster both at once—insisting that one without the other is not only incomplete, but inherently unstable and fated to be a false promise. True humanism compels the Church to concern for both bread and prayer, seen as complementary and necessarily related objectives. Integral humanism also means that economic analysis has to be seen as one element of a broader concern for social life, which also includes culture, politics, the arts, and the environment. The Catholic instinct is to be concerned for the whole person, and for the entire cosmos in which the drama of each human life unfolds. In his 2009 encyclical addressing the global economic crisis, *Caritas in Veritate*, Pope Benedict XVI said the Church's greatest contribution to development is to promote "Christian humanism."

United in Principle, Divided in Practice

As long as we stay at the level of these abstract principles, it's easy to make it sound as if Catholicism has a clear approach to globalization, one that enjoys a broad consensus in the Church. In fact, however, there's a wide range of opinion about the merits of global capitalism inside the Church, just as there is in broader political debate. One can find Catholics who justify extreme laissez-faire views, as well as Catholics who seem to find a prescription in the Church's social teaching for virtually every imaginable form of government intervention. In part, that diversity reflects the theological point that the specifics of tax policy or trade agreements can never be dogmas of the faith, so Catholics inevitably will draw different conclusions. In the following, we'll survey a few representative Catholic responses to globalization, arising from different circles of Catholic thought and activism.

1. THE GENOA MANIFESTO

On July 20 to 22, 2001, leaders of the G8 nations met in Genoa, Italy, an event surrounded by pitched battles between police and antiglobalization protestors that left scores injured and one young Italian dead. Prior to the meeting, more than 3,000 members of Catholic movements, associations, and religious orders, and individual clergy and laity assembled in Genoa to prepare a "Catholic manifesto" for the G8 leaders.

Cardinal Dionigi Tettamanzi of Genoa, at the time widely touted as a frontrunner to become the next pope, was the keynote speaker. He called on the world's great powers to pursue policies in which "man does not exist for globalization," but "globalization for man."

"One African child sick with AIDS," Tettamanzi said to thunderous applause, "counts more than the entire universe."

Speakers urged an "ethic of responsibility," calling on people to embrace reasonable patterns of consumption. A video pointed out that one American or European consumes as much in food, goods, and services in a year as forty-three Rwandans. Another frequent refrain was the need for stronger international institutions capable of governing globalization.

"To you gentlemen of the G-8 we send a message," said Luigi Bobba, head of a Catholic pro-labor movement. "You will not be able to dream tranquil dreams as long as you are incapable of overcoming the gap between the birth of a new global consciousness and the absence of global institutions."

Filomeno Lopes of Guinea-Bissau called for struggle against merciless capitalism that operates on what he called an implicit theology of *extra mercatum nulla salus*—"outside the market there is no salvation."

In the end, the group in Genoa produced a document styled as a "Catholic approach to globalization." Its contents included:

- Rules for international trade that allow impoverished nations to offer goods at predictable prices and without barriers;

- An end to banking secrecy laws that conceal money laundering, especially illegal transfers of currency out of impoverished nations;

- Adoption of the Tobin Tax (a tax of 0.25 percent on the $2 trillion a day exchanged on global currency markets, designed to discourage speculation and to create funds for international development);

- Cancellation of debt accumulated up to June 1999; assurance that debt payments will be required only after health, education, and other basic needs are met; and a process of arbitration to identify "in terms of justice" the real debt levels of impoverished nations;

- Effective norms to protect labor;

- Stronger environmental safeguards, including adoption of the Kyoto Accords on global warming;

- National and international laws to guarantee a plurality of voices in the media;

- Augmented public funding for medical research, especially for producing drugs to combat diseases that afflict the poor;
- Efforts to halt the global arms trade, including full disclosure about the flow of weapons, and a halt to public support for manufacturers and distributors.

Signatories included Catholic Action, Pax Christi, the St. Vincent de Paul Society, Caritas, Sant'Egidio, a youth wing of the Focolare movement, as well as religious orders such as the Comboni Fathers, the Xaverians, the Missionaries of Africa, and the Salesians.

2. FREE-MARKET CATHOLICS

The pretense in Genoa to speak on behalf of the entire Catholic Church drew fierce criticism from other quarters, which saw the manifesto as an embrace of secular leftist radicalism with a thin veneer of Catholic vocabulary. Italian leaders of the Communion and Liberation movement, for example, derided the Genoa event as a flirtation with the no-global movement, reminiscent, they charged, of the way some progressive Catholics tried to baptize Marxist revolution in the 1960s.

Those objections built on a long tradition of more market-friendly thought in some sectors of Catholicism, which argues that the aim of Catholic social engagement should be to promote ways for more people to be included in what John Paul in his 1991 encyclical *Centesimus Annus* called the "circle of productivity and exchange." For this constituency, the globalization of free-market capitalism represents a fundamentally positive force opening up opportunities for a greater share of the world's population.

This Catholic defense of globalization has been elaborated most extensively in the United States. One exponent is the influential American Catholic writer Michael Novak, who made the case during a 2004 Vatican conference on "Confronting Globalization: Global Governance and the Politics of Development." Novak argued that fostering the spread of global capitalism represents a moral imperative: "Those living in the most forlorn parts of the world not yet included in the global system remain today the most desperately poor, ill and likely to die young," he said.

Another such voice is American Catholic writer Thomas E. Woods Jr., whose 2005 book, *The Church and the Market*, argues that much papal social teaching since the late nineteenth century has been well intentioned but "calamitous in practice," because it's been driven by a "prejudice in favor of the state and against the market." A disciple of the free-market Austrian School, Woods believes that economic life is governed by universal laws discovered through reason (a classic example is the supply and demand curve). Attempts to overturn or manipulate these economic laws through government fiat, Woods argues, usually make things worse. He asserts that on matters such as minimum-wage statutes, labor unions, and protective tariffs, official Catholic social teaching too often has embraced policies intended to help the poor, but which have had precisely the opposite effect.

Woods says there are resources in Catholic tradition for a more market-friendly approach, pointing to sixteenth-century scholastic theologians in Spain who argued that monarchs should not attempt to impose a "legal" price on goods and services different from their "natural" price, meaning the price fixed by free trade. In thinking about globalization, Woods suggests, Catholic social theorists almost need to return to this sixteenth-century point of departure and trace a very different path.

Other Catholics find some of the antiglobalization activism percolating in the Church out of place for a different reason. The greatest contribution to justice the Church can make, they say, is preaching Christ, not dabbling in economic theory. A six-page open letter from thirty conservative Catholic intellectuals in response to the "Catholic manifesto" in Genoa, for example, blasted it as an example of "subordination to ideologies and slogans of political groups and movements that have nothing to do with our faith. . . . The signatories of the manifesto are longwinded in talking about the most varied subjects, but nowhere consider it necessary to mention that Jesus Christ is man's only savior, and this proclamation is their fundamental duty."

Six Fronts in Globalization Debates

While there's strong debate about how Catholicism should engage globalization, few Catholics dispute that the Church has a moral and spiritual responsibility to address causes of human suffering such as poverty, war, disease, and social exclusion and how those evils may be affected by a new globalized world. This section surveys six topics that surface frequently in Catholic discussion.

1. THE GAP BETWEEN RICH AND POOR

The single most common criticism of globalization is that it widens the gap between the rich and the poor. In 2007, the total gross domestic product of the poorest forty-two nations on earth, based on data from the International Monetary Fund, was less than the wealth of the world's three richest people in that year: Bill Gates, Warren Buffett, and Mexican telecommunications mogul Carlos Slim Helu. (Their combined net worth, according to *Forbes*, was $157 billion.) According to a 2004 report from the United Nations-International Labor Organization World Commission on the Social Dimensions of Globalization, 59 percent of the world's population lives in countries with growing inequality, while only 5 percent live in nations with declining inequality.

With regard to income inequality, two issues have come to be the focus of much Catholic advocacy: the United Nations' Millennium Goals, and justice in international trading relationships.

The Millennium Goals were adopted during a United Nations summit in 2000. The eight goals, which were supposed to be achieved by 2015, are:

- Eradicate extreme poverty and hunger
- Achieve universal primary education
- Promote gender equality and empower women
- Reduce child mortality
- Improve maternal health
- Combat HIV/AIDS, malaria, and other diseases
- Ensure environmental sustainability
- Develop a global partnership for development

The chief policy instrument to fund these goals was a commitment on behalf of member nations to devote seven tenths of one percent of their gross national product each year for international development assistance. As of this writing, however, just a half-dozen developed countries have reached the 0.7 percent benchmark, with the United States being near the bottom of the list.

Catholic authorities have repeatedly endorsed the Millennium Goals. In summer 2006, Pope Benedict XVI said, "I express my fervent hope that the governments may find appropriate solutions to reach these great goals, in the spirit of harmony and generous solidarity. . . . I especially hope that effective concrete measures can be implemented to respond to the most urgent problems created by extreme poverty, sickness and hunger, which afflict so many populations."

During a March 2009 trip to Angola, Benedict XVI insisted that the poor "must not become one of the casualties" of the present economic crisis, and he demanded that developed nations live up to their "oft-repeated promise" under the Millennium Goals to devote 0.7 percent of their gross national product to assistance for impoverished nations. In a hard-hitting letter three weeks later to British Prime Minister Gordon Brown, in conjunction with a G-20 meeting in London, Benedict wrote that his Africa trip had allowed him to "see first-hand the reality of severe poverty and marginalization, which the [economic] crisis risks aggravating dramatically." The pope insisted that the elimination of extreme poverty by 2015, as called for by the Millennium Goals, "remains one of the most important tasks of our time."

In a 2006 address to the United Nations Economic and Social Council, Archbishop Silvio Tomasi, the Vatican's representative, warned that failure to honor the commitments expressed in the Millennium Goals "may provoke disorderly behavior and, surely, a less secure world."

Trading relationships are a second focus of Catholic discussion.

Many development experts believe that in order to level the global playing field, developed nations should eliminate barriers to their markets, while developing nations should be allowed to protect domestic industries, especially agriculture and basic utilities. In fact, however, the world seems to be moving in the opposite direction. The United Nations estimates that subsidies in wealthy nations cost developing countries $100 billion in each year, which is roughly twice the global total spent each year on development assistance.

Demands from international lending institutions for the cancellation of subsidies and tariffs in the developing world have sometimes seemingly made things worse. In Ghana, for example, the cost of water and electricity has doubled since the World Bank demanded an end to subsidies for public utilities. Since 1998, according to the development agency Action Aid, almost two thirds of the jobs in Nigeria's textile sector have been lost because of the elimination of trade barriers. One 2007 report indicates that after India cut its guaranteed price for cotton by more than 12 percent, some 1,200 cotton farmers in the northeastern state of Maharashtra committed suicide to escape mounting debts.

As with the Millennium Goals, the Vatican has endorsed efforts for reform.

"Rich countries' support for their own agricultural sector, which comprises a very small percentage of their populations, amounts to $280 billion per year. This amount is ten times greater than the total amount of aid destined annually to Africa, and is equivalent to the total income of the whole of sub-Saharan Africa," said Archbishop Celestino Migliore, the Vatican's representative to the United Nations, in a 2006 address. "More developed countries must finally honor the commitment to open their markets and to end the dumping of agricultural surpluses fuelled by subsidies. This is a moral imperative that cannot be delayed. If it is not taken seriously, grave consequences could result: uncontrolled movements of populations, irreparable environmental damage, even the spread of terrorism and armed conflict."

Catholic leaders have also complained about the practice of developed nations negotiating advantageous bilateral trading agreements. In mid-2006, bishops in South Korea opposed a proposed free trade agreement with the United States, especially in terms of its impact on the agricultural sector.

"We cannot help but see these free trade agreements as a desperate counter-measure to save the country's economy as a whole by selling more cars and mobile phones at the expense of local agriculture," said Bishop Boniface Choi Ki-san of Incheon, president of the Korean Catholic bishops' Committee for Justice and Peace. He called the agreement a prescription for "subordination to the United States."

2. GLOBAL CONFLICT AND THE ARMS TRADE

According to GlobalSecurity.org, thirty-one nations in 2007 were involved in armed conflicts. Most are civil or intrastate wars, and most victims are civilians, a distinguishing feature of modern warfare. During World War I, civilians made up fewer than 5 percent of all casualties. Today, 75 percent or more of those killed or wounded in armed conflicts are noncombatants.

To take perhaps the most devastating recent example on the global scene, in the Great Lakes region of Africa in 1997 a war began that, at one time or another, has involved the Democratic Republic of the Congo, Angola, Namibia, Zimbabwe, Uganda, Rwanda, and Burundi. The war is estimated by the United Nations to have caused 3.3 million deaths, mostly due to disease and starvation, and has created 2.5 million refugees. Conflict has been fueled by disputes over natural resources such as minerals and timber, as well as by ethnic and regional rivalries and internal political divisions. Although a fragile peace seemed to be holding as of this writing, no one excluded the possibility that fighting could break out again.

Many analysts believe such conflicts are stoked by the planetary commerce in weapons. In 1999, the Center for Defense Information concluded, "Africa has become an attractive and profitable dumping ground for nations and arm manufacturers eager to get rid of weapon stocks made superfluous by the end of the Cold War or by technological developments." In 2005, according to the World Policy Institute, the United States sold weapons to eighteen of the twenty-five countries that, at that point, were involved in active wars, in several cases to countries on both sides.

Worldwide, an estimated $1 trillion is spent on weaponry every year, making it by far the largest industry on the planet, according to the Center for Arms Control and Non-Proliferation. The United States accounts for 48 percent of these expenditures, roughly $500 billion. For one term of comparison, consider that the entire annual budget for the United Nations, including all of its agencies and subdivisions, is roughly $20 billion per year, making it approximately 2 percent of the world's military spending. For what it pays for weaponry, the United States by itself could fund twenty-four United Nations every year.

The United States is also the world's largest supplier of weapons, accounting for 36 percent of all sales in the year 2005. American weapons manufacturers and/or the United States government earned $97 million from arms sales that year. Developing nations are the primary market of foreign arms sales, accounting for two thirds of all arms transfer agreements in 2005.

While the United States and other developed nations are buying high-tech weaponry, the trade in conventional weapons in many other countries has skyrocketed, according to the International Action Network on Small Arms. There are a half-billion small arms around the world, with an estimated 300,000 to 500,000 people killed by them each year. They are also the weapon of choice for the estimated 300,000 child soldiers in the world. Subsidies hold prices down; in 2002, according to local media reports, one could buy an AK-47 in Uganda for roughly the price of a chicken.

It's not just Northern countries that are active in the arms trade. At least ninety-two nations now have the capacity to manufacture small arms or ammunition, about half in the developing world. For example, in the last decade, according to the International Action Network on Small Arms, Vietnam sold weapons to Myanmar; Lebanon, Liberia, Burkina Faso, and Niger all sold weapons to Sierra Leone; Namibia sold arms to Congo and Angola; and Burkina Faso sold guns to Benin.

Catholic leaders have been strongly critical of the global arms trade.

In his 1995 encyclical *Evangelium Vitae*, Pope John Paul II referred to "the scandalous arms trade, which spawns the many armed conflicts which stain our world with blood." Archbishop Migliore, in a 2006 speech to the United Nations, made the point equally crisply. "The illicit trade in small arms and light weapons is a threat to peace, development and security," he said. Migliore called for "a legally binding instrument to address the illicit arms trade." In his first message for the World Day of Peace, released in December 2005, Pope Benedict XVI expressed "dismay" at "the evidence of a continuing growth in military expenditure and the flourishing arms trade, while the political and juridical process established by the international community for promoting disarmament is bogged down in general indifference."

One intriguing chapter in the Church's response to the arms trade was a meeting in January 1996 that brought together fifteen American bishops, plus a Vatican representative, with executives of various American weapons manufacturers and trade associations, such as the Aerospace Industries Association, United Technologies, and Lockheed-Martin. Several of these executives were Catholics. Something similar occurred in August 2009, when Archbishop Edwin O'Brien of Baltimore, a former military archbishop and West Point chaplain, addressed the U.S. Strategic Command, calling for the abolition of nuclear weapons.

3. HUMAN TRAFFICKING

Some activists believe that human trafficking is the most pernicious human rights scourge created by the globalized era. Many have called it a twenty-first-century form of human slavery. Estimates are that some 800,000 to 2 million people are victims of trafficking each year, with 80 percent of them women, and most involved in the sex trade. Aside from sex, other motives for the illegal traffic in human beings include manual labor and the drugs trade (using people involuntarily as couriers).

Italian Consolata Sr. Eugenia Bonetti, a missionary who spent twenty-four years in Kenya, is among the leading voices in the Catholic antitrafficking effort. She says that in Europe alone, there are an estimated 50,000 to 70,000 women on the streets, mostly from Africa, Latin America, and Eastern Europe. Some 40 percent are minors, between fourteen and eighteen, and a high percentage are victims of cross-border trafficking of human beings for purposes of sexual exploitation.

"After many years of ministering to women on the streets, we no longer call them 'prostitutes' because at least ninety percent have been forced into prostitution against their will," Bonetti said. "We consider them victims of a modern slavery, much worse than the slavery of the past, because forced prostitution empties a human being of her inner self and inner life as a woman."

Pope Benedict XVI addressed the trafficking issue in a 2005 message for the World Day of Migrants and Refugees. Calling trafficking a "scourge," the pope said: "It becomes easy for the trafficker to offer his own 'services' to the victims, who often do not even vaguely suspect what awaits them. In some cases, there are women and girls who are destined to be exploited almost like slaves in their work, and not infrequently in the sex industry too."

4. CORRUPTION

Corruption poses a classic chicken-and-egg dilemma. It's tough to fight poverty without ending corruption, yet it's equally difficult to end corruption without reducing poverty. Poverty makes creating the legal and political infrastructure to tackle corruption next to impossible, yet antipoverty efforts are often meaningless as long as corruption means that resources never reach intended beneficiaries. Many analysts believe affluent nations could meet the Millennium Goals, throw open their markets, eliminate subsidies, and pay the Tobin Tax in full, but it would make little difference if the resulting transfers of wealth simply end up in the pockets of corrupt political and business elites.

By almost any measure, anticorruption efforts have to be a core element of social justice campaigns. The World Bank Institute reported in 2004 that countries that limit corruption and improve the rule of law can increase national incomes fourfold, calling it the "400 percent governance dividend."

In June 2006, the Vatican's Pontifical Council for Justice and Peace sponsored an international conference in Rome on the social costs of corruption. Cardinal Renato Martino, president of the Pontifical Council for Justice and Peace, said that his office would prepare a document on fighting corruption. Bishop Giampaolo Crepaldi, the council's secretary, said that while corruption is a problem for law enforcement and the judicial system, its roots must be tackled in the individual conscience, creating a need for formation of consciences by churches and other social institutions as well as for anticorruption instruction in schools.

Scholar Jong-sung You of the University of California-San Diego, a Korean pro-democracy activist and a former doctoral fellow at Harvard University's Inequality and Social Policy Program, issued a sobering warning at the conference about Catholic anticorruption efforts. Sociological research indicates, he said, that in countries with a sizeable Protestant population, controls against bribery are more effective and citizens are less tolerant of corruption than in countries where Catholics are the majority. While the findings are "disturbing and uncomfortable," he said, the Church can rebound. Just as the Church helped overthrow dictatorships and usher in democracy, You said, the Catholic Church can "switch to being an anticorruption force."

In an August 2007 address to Nigeria's Independent Corrupt Practices Commission, Archbishop John Onaiyekan of Abuja laid out a three-point program for fighting corruption. First, he said, religious leaders should reinforce social values that support honesty and integrity. In Nigeria, he said, that means joint efforts among Muslims and Christians, including an end to religious rivalries. Second, Onaiyekan called for reform in the police and the judiciary. "The honest police officer is made to look like a fool when he watches his colleagues smiling to the bank with ill-gotten proceeds of bribery and corruption," he said. Third, Onaiyekan proposed a "historic truth, reparation and reconciliation process," including a general amnesty to all who participate on the condition that looted resources be returned to the public. While addressed to Nigeria, this program could easily become a global template for Catholic anticorruption efforts.

At the same time, many Southern Catholic leaders argue that corruption cannot be resolved exclusively at home; it also depends on reforming Western practices. Onaiyekan made this case in a 2006 interview.

> African corruption would not be possible without the cooperation of the very people who are now complaining about it. The West could stop the corruption if it was a real concern. It's just not believable that a young man from Nigeria could transfer a half-million dollars to deposit in a bank in any European country, and the regulatory authorities in that country aren't aware of it. They must know where this money came from. They track suspect transactions all the time, so why do they make an exception for stolen money from Africa? With the War on Terror, they now track every cent coming into the country. . . . If the West stops doing business with corrupt governments, they will fall. Africans try to bring these governments down, but often they fail because the governments are sustained and upheld by foreign businesses who believe they can do better business with the corrupt leaders.

Pope Benedict XVI has repeatedly addressed the corrosive impact of corruption, perhaps nowhere so dramatically as in Cameroon at the start of his March 2009 trip to Africa. Standing next to strongman President Paul Biya, a former Catholic seminarian who presides over a regime in Cameroon once rated by Transparency International as the most corrupt on earth, the pope said, "In the face of . . . corruption or abuse of power, a Christian can never remain silent." Local media interpreted the line as a rebuke of Biya, who had plastered the streets of Yaoundé, the national capital, with billboards asserting a "perfect communion" between himself and the pope. The comment also seemed to energize the local church. In an interview with French radio the following day, Cardinal Christian Tumi publicly called for Biya, who has ruled Cameroon since 1982, not to extend his grip on power in what are widely viewed as faux elections set for 2011.

5. MIGRANTS AND REFUGEES

According to an analysis by the United Nations Department of Economic and Social Affairs, 3 percent of the world's population, or 191 million people, lived somewhere other than their native countries in 2005, an increase of 90 million from thirty years ago. One third of those migrants were moving from a developing to a developed country, one third were moving among developing nations, and another third were moving from one country to another in the developed world. In 2007, the United Nations High Commissioner for Refugees also reported 32.9 million "people of concern," a catchall category for refugees, internally displaced persons, stateless persons, asylum seekers, and others who for one reason or another have been uprooted.

An estimated 80 percent of refugees are women and children, who often carry the heaviest burden of survival for themselves and their families. Women and adolescent girls in refugee settings are vulnerable to exploitation, rape, abuse, and other forms of gender-based violence. Children and youth constitute approximately 50 percent of all refugees worldwide. They are often targets of abuse and are easy prey to military recruitment and abduction. They typically miss out on several years of education.

In November 2003, the Pontifical Council for Migrants and Refugees sponsored a global congress on refugees, which drew 300 bishops, activists, and theologians representing 100 nations. The gathering ended with an appeal calling for "an increasingly more active and welcomed presence" of migrants and refugees within the Church, supporting a "holistic" approach that emphasizes both pastoral care and advocacy for justice. Governments were asked to respect and protect the human dignity of people on the move, and especially not to use terrorism as a pretext to reduce their rights. Participants in the congress also called upon civil society to "combat racism, xenophobia and exaggerated nationalism."

One point of conflict between the Vatican and the UN has been over the question of reproductive services. In 1999, the United Nations issued a "field manual" on reproductive health for refugees, which called for the distribution of contraception and access to abortion. A Vatican statement in 2001 asserted, "We find ourselves in front of a current of thought that may be defined as both utilitarian and neo-Malthusian. . . . Pastors must be vigilant to ensure that practices proposed by the *Field Manual* and considered to be immoral do not gain a foothold." That dispute remained unresolved in 2009.

6. THE INTERNET

The Internet is both the leading symbol of the globalized world as well as one of its primary drivers. In 1995, according to the Web site Internet World Stats, there were 16 million Internet users in the world, representing 0.04 percent of the global population; as of June 2007, there were 1.13 billion users, or 17.2 percent of the world, remarkable growth in little more than a decade. According to the Worldwide Online Population Forecast, by 2011 roughly 1.8 billion people will be logging on, representing 22 percent of the global population—almost one quarter of all people on earth.

Experts point to three important trends in Internet usage today:

- The global shift from dial-up to broadband, which vastly increases the speed of the connection and the amount of data that can be easily transferred. Overall, there were 200 million broadband subscriptions in 2007, according to the UN Organization for Economic Cooperation and Development, most of them in the global North.

- The shift from personal computers as the exclusive means of consuming Internet content, toward multiple devices such as BlackBerries, iPods, and iPhones. The proliferation of such devices means that the percentage of time consumers spend unplugged is steadily shrinking. Soon, users will be online almost all the time, no matter where they are or what they're doing.

- The trend toward media specialization, with content pitched to highly specified subgroups. Material can be marketed to "Tennis-loving, twenty-something gay men in the greater Cleveland area," for example, or to "Catholic mothers of adopted Chinese children."

Experts also warn, however, of a "digital divide." In 2007, the International Telecommunications Union estimated that there were 800,000 villages in the world, representing more than a billion people, that had no access to the Internet at all. The G8 nations had roughly the same number of Internet users as in the entire rest of the world combined. Africa, according to Internet World Stats, has 14.2 percent of the world's population, but just 2.9 percent of its Internet users. Put another way, only 3.6 percent of Africans use the Internet, a thin elite atop a vast "unplugged" majority.

Gradually the rest of the world is making headway, due largely to market forces rather than state intervention. As explosive growth in PC sales has cooled off in the global North, many analysts believe the new sales frontier will be low-cost devices pitched to the world's poor. They call it the contest for "the next billion" Internet users. Several companies and research centers today are piloting PCs that sell for around $100. Many are hermetically sealed to keep out dust; they run off car batteries, solar power, or even hand cranks; and they connect through cellular networks that are already ubiquitous in the developing world. Critics sometimes argue that in a world in which hundreds of millions of people don't have safe drinking water or rudimentary educational or health services, trying to sell them cheap PCs is at best pointless, at worst obscene. Nonetheless, most experts believe that low-cost computers will follow the path blazed by cell phones, bringing basic service within reach for a steadily expanding share of the world's population.

According to the World Online Population Forecast, the most explosive growth in Internet use between 2009 and 2011 will occur in Brazil, Russia, India, and China. By 2011, Asians alone will represent 42 percent of the world's online population. Soon, the number of broadband subscriptions in China will surpass the total in the United States. Another sign of the times: after English, the next most commonly used language on the Internet is Chinese, representing 14.7 percent of all Internet users, according to the *Computer Industry Almanac*. Sites in Chinese between 2000 and 2007 grew at a rate of 414 percent, outpacing growth in sites in English almost four to one.

WHAT IT MEANS

As an institution concerned with social justice and dedicated to reading the "signs of the times," the Catholic Church at all levels is engaged in broad political and social debates about globalization, attentive both to its benefits but also to the need for creative intervention to ensure that globalization is at the service of the human person rather than the other way around. At the same time, Catholicism is itself arguably the oldest globalized institution on earth, and its internal life is inevitably affected in profound ways by the emergence of a new globally interconnected culture. The consequences of globalization for the Church, therefore, will play out during the twenty-first century in both the *ad extra* and *ad intra* realms.

Near-Certain Consequences

1. TENSIONS BETWEEN THE LOCAL AND THE UNIVERSAL

In 1985, Brazilian liberation theologian Leonardo Boff was placed under a gag order by the Vatican. Before the ban came down, Boff had already agreed to lead a small retreat deep in the Amazon rain forest, and he decided to go ahead on the grounds that no one in Rome would notice. As he told *Newsweek* in 1999, however, by the time he finished the retreat, a complaint from the Vatican had already reached his Franciscan superiors, based on a fax someone had sent to Rome from an outpost in the Amazon. That's life in a globalized world (in this case, pre-Internet), in which information from the most remote corners of the earth can circulate instantaneously. Globalization in that sense extends the reach of hierarchical systems of control, reducing the lag time between an event on the edge and a response from the center. The spread of global communications also fosters the construction of a single global culture, in which developments anywhere can quickly become the concern of everyone, everywhere.

As Pope Benedict XVI has observed, the traditional Catholic distinction between the "local" and the "universal" church in such a world is, to some extent, passé. Given global interconnectedness, no event or trend is so isolated that it can't quickly be swept up into global Catholic conversation. That social reality will engender much agonizing theological debate in the twenty-first-century Church about how to strike the right balance between centralized leadership and local inculturation—especially because the Catholic Church certainly also has its own forms of "glocalization," meaning a strong reassertion of local traditions and cultures. That push is especially strong in the global South, from the defense of Eastern spiritual concepts by the Asian bishops to the indigenous theology popularized by Catholic theologians in Brazil and elsewhere.

This source of tension in Catholic life, however, may also represent a unique opportunity.

For 2,000 years, the Church has insisted on a degree of uniformity guaranteed by papal oversight, and yet it's also allowed the faith to be shaped by local cultures. For example, African Catholics may use drums and festive tribal dance at Mass, but they still say the same Eucharistic prayers as Benedictine monks executing plainchant in Solesmes Abbey in France. As a result of this experience, Catholicism has developed a rich theological literature on how to balance unity and diversity, on how to build a single global community that nevertheless prizes local specificity. This tradition, however imperfectly it's sometimes applied, could inform much secular discussion in the globalized world. The extent to which theologians, diplomats, and other Church leaders are able to creatively offer these resources to the broader culture will be an important twenty-first-century trend to watch.

2. A MORE PRO-UN MOOD

Given its universal character, it's not surprising that the Catholic Church has been both a supporter and a participant in the development of the United Nations, which, at least in principle, is an attempt to give legal and political expression to what Catholicism calls the "unity of the human family." Archbishop Giovanni Lajolo, former "foreign minister" for the Vatican, observed in 2004 that there's "a particular bond of cooperation between the Apostolic See and the United Nations" because "the Holy See and the United Nations both have a universal vocation; no nation on earth is foreign to them."

In the 1990s, however, the romance between the Catholic Church and the United Nations often seemed more like a bitter separation. High-profile clashes over reproductive rights left a sour taste in the mouths of some Catholics, especially pro-life activists. Conservative Catholics devoted to the principle of subsidiarity have increasingly voiced doubt about why the Vatican is gung-ho about handing over chunks of national sovereignty to an international authority they see as unaccountable, and occasionally hostile, to religious values.

The June 2004 issue of *Catholic World Report*, widely read in conservative Catholic circles, offered a special dossier critiquing what it called this "strange alliance."

"The UN shows very little respect for the Catholic faith, or for the public positions taken by the Holy See on crucial matters of international policy," an opening editorial said. "Although the Vatican apparently views the UN as an ally, many important actors at the UN clearly look upon the church as an enemy."

Whichever side one takes in this debate, it's likely that the Catholic Church's growing engagement on behalf of anti-poverty measures, peace, and sustainable development will buttress its traditional pro-UN stance. Pope Benedict XVI's 2009 encyclical, *Caritas in Veritate*, illustrates that tendency, as Benedict asserted "a strongly felt need, even in the midst of a global recession, for a reform of the United Nations . . . so that the concept of the family of nations can acquire real teeth."

Four other considerations will drive this pro-UN trend.

First, the rise of Southern leadership will push Catholicism in this direction, as most Southern nations see the UN as their best opportunity to counteract a perceived hegemony of Northern interests, especially those of the United States. Second, the Vatican's Permanent Observer status at the UN gives it a unique capacity among world religions to act as a voice of conscience in global affairs. In a globalized age, this will be perceived as a valuable asset. Third, the demographic trend toward lower fertility described in chapter four makes it less likely, at least for the next half-century or so, that the United Nations will launch major new initiatives to promote birth control and abortion. This traditional source of tension between the Church and the UN may therefore not recur with the same intensity. (Lower-level conflicts over matters such as the distribution of condoms in UN-run refugee camps, however, will probably continue to simmer.) Fourth, the U.S.-led war in Iraq has contributed to a more positive view of the UN, since the position of the Vatican was close to that outlined by UN officials.

Church leaders will argue that a strong UN is a way of fostering democracy in international relations. They will also say that a truly effective UN, one in which small and medium-size states are empowered, would be less likely to be hijacked by powerful NGOs from the global North with an agenda hostile to Catholicism. In any event, the estrangement of the 1990s will likely be replaced with a greater willingness on the part of at least some Church leaders to view the UN as a partner.

3. TENSIONS WITH THE UNITED STATES

The Catholicism of the twenty-first century augurs a more critical stance from bishops, NGOs, religious orders, and other Catholic actors toward global capitalism and global militarism. Since the United States is perceived as the primary force behind both, this is likely to mean that global Catholicism and the United States will sometimes find themselves at odds.

Naturally, the picture is complicated. Collaboration between the United

States and various organs of the Church will continue on all manner of issues. For reasons outlined in chapter two, the Vatican in many ways is more inclined to look to the United States these days than to the European Union for leadership, given the much more secularized climate in Europe.

Yet in other ways, the twenty-first century may see a return to the early 1980s, when the administration of U.S. president Ronald Reagan looked upon the Catholic Church with alarm, especially in Latin America. In 1980, the Council for Inter-American Security, a conservative policy group that was to provide several key figures to the Reagan White House (such as Patrick Buchanan and Roger Fontaine), published "A New Inter-American Policy for the Eighties," popularly known as the Santa Fe document. Among other things, that document recommended countering the influence of liberation theology in Latin American Catholicism as an obstacle to "productive capitalism."

Some conspiracy theorists have seen in the document proof of an American plot to subvert the Catholic Church. Instead, what the document demonstrates is a reasonable, and largely accurate, judgment by American conservatives that currents in Latin American Catholicism in the late 1970s were hostile to free-market capitalism and to America's perceived security interests. As things turned out, the Cold War and anti-Soviet movements in Eastern Europe became the heart of relations between Rome and the White House during the Reagan years, and the antagonism feared on social justice issues was largely averted. That's not to say, however, that the differences have vanished.

While the Marxist revolutionary form of liberation theology is now a museum piece, the basic thrust of opposition to American-style "productive capitalism" in the Latin American Church is very much alive. During the May 2007 General Conference of the Bishops of Latin America and the Caribbean in Brazil, for example, Bishop Gonzalo Duarte García de Cortázar of Valparaíso, Chile, warned of "many signs of despair and even anger" in Latin America related to "the neo-liberal economic model" that "favors the rich minorities at the expense of the impoverished majorities." Bishop Alvaro Leonel Ramazzini Imeri of San Marcos, Guatemala, said that Central America is the "victim" of a form of globalization "in which the distance between rich and poor grows, the fruit of idolatry of pleasure and of money."

Cardinal Jorge Mario Bergoglio of Buenos Aires highlighted the region's "scandalous inequality, which damages both personal dignity and social justice."

"We live, apparently, in the most unequal part of the world, which has grown the most yet reduced misery the least," Bergoglio said. "The unjust distribution of goods persists, creating a situation of social sin that cries out to Heaven and limits the possibilities of a fuller life for so many of our brothers."

In his opening address for the Brazil meeting, Pope Benedict XVI himself, an old foe of liberation theology, nevertheless used strikingly critical language about capitalism, which would be difficult to imagine coming from any American political leader of either party.

"Both capitalism and Marxism promised to point out the path for the creation of just structures, and they declared that these, once established, would function by themselves; they declared that not only would they have no need of any prior individual morality, but that they would promote a communal morality," the pope said. "And this ideological promise has been proved false. The facts have clearly demonstrated it."

Benedict made much the same point in *Caritas in Veritate*. "The conviction that the economy must be autonomous, that it must be shielded from 'influences' of a moral character, has led man to abuse the economic process in a thoroughly destructive way," he wrote. The pope unabashedly talked about the desirability of "redistribution" of global wealth.

From the leadership class to the grassroots, the Catholicism of the century to come promises to be engaged on issues of economic justice and military policy that may prompt a future American administration to dust off the Santa Fe document, this time fretting not just about Latin America but about the world. Leaders on both sides will work hard to keep this tension in check, not least because the 70 million Catholics in the United States represent an important constituency, which neither American politicians nor Church leaders in other parts of the world want to alienate. Yet those diplomatic efforts will be steadily more complicated, because at the moment certain perceived permanent interests of the United States and of global Catholicism seem to be moving in different directions.

4. HORIZONTAL CATHOLICISM

In an October 2004 lecture at Loyola Marymount University, Fr. John Coleman, the Jesuit sociologist, pondered the paradox that Roman Catholicism should be the religious actor best positioned to engage the issues raised by globalization, but that aside from debt relief, its impact so far has been marginal. How to explain it? Citing a 1998 study by Margaret Keck and Kathryn Sikkink called *Activists Beyond Borders,* which concludes that successful global activism is "nonhierarchical, involves wide partnerships and remains truly flexible," Coleman floated the hypothesis that the official structures of the Catholic Church "may lack the inner organizational flexibility for rapid and networked response to global issues as they arise." As a result, Coleman suggests that "semiautonomous and more local Catholic subgroups will be the major actors in activist global networks."

Whether his diagnosis of Catholic officialdom is correct or not, Coleman is certainly on to something in highlighting the importance of what might be called "horizontal Catholicism," meaning a host of movements, associations, ad hoc networks, and religious communities, all engaged in the issues raised by globalization in a staggering variety of ways. These malleable, rapid-response forms of Catholicism will exercise a steadily more important role in framing Catholic social activism as the century unfolds.

One indicator is recent expansion in Catholic NGOs in and around the United Nations. According to a 2005 study by Kevin Ahern, when the UN first began accrediting NGOs in 1947, there were two Catholic groups: the International Union of Catholic Women's Leagues, and the Catholic International Union for Social Service. As late as 1989, fewer than thirty Catholic NGOs were recognized by the UN's Economic and Social Council. In 2005, Ahern reported, there were sixty-three, so the total had more than doubled. Three of these Catholic NGOs hold "general status," signifying the most important and influential nongovernmental bodies: Caritas Internationalis, the Congregations of St. Joseph, and Franciscans International.

In the Catholicism of the future, NGOs, international Catholic organizations, new movements, religious orders, and a variety of ad hoc networks without formal leadership or structures will sometimes influence the Church's public role more effectively than its official leadership. Two examples illustrate the point.

The Rome General Peace Accords were signed on October 4, 1992, between the government of Mozambique and the Renamo rebel movement, putting an end to a bloody civil war. The negotiators who brokered the deal were two members of the Community of Sant'Egidio, Andrea Riccardi and Matteo Zuppi, along with Archbishop Jaime Pedro Gonçalves of Beira in Mozambique and an informal representative of the Italian government. It marked the first intergovernmental agreement ever negotiated by a nongovernmental body, and it has been repeatedly cited by studies of NGOs and humanitarian bodies as a model for successful nonstate intervention. Though Sant'Egidio kept the Vatican apprised of its efforts, the community had no official warrant to act on behalf of the Catholic Church. To some extent, Riccardi has since laughingly conceded, this was by design; if the effort fell apart, the Vatican could duck the blame.

For an example of ad hoc, spontaneous Catholic "guerrilla activism," though in this case at a national level, consider the Catholic response in the United States to the Terri Schiavo case. Semicomatose and dependent upon a feeding tube for fifteen years, Schiavo died in 2005 after food and water were withdrawn. Her husband argued that she should be allowed to die with dignity, while Schiavo's family strenuously defended her right to life. Among other things, the parents argued that their daughter was a devout Roman Catholic who would not wish to violate the Church's teachings on end-of-life care. Schiavo's fate became the object of wide public debate, in which Catholic bishops played what many regard as a secondary role. In October 2002, Bishop Robert Lynch of St. Petersburg, Florida, where Schiavo resided, wrote that the Church would "refrain from passing judgment on the actions of anyone in this tragic moment." Two years later, Schiavo's brother, Bobby Schindler, wrote an open letter to Lynch. Schindler asked God "to spare us another successor of the apostles who would exhibit the same scandalous inaction and silence by which you remain complicit in my sister's murder via euthanasia."

What made "saving Terri" a passionate Catholic crusade was not official episcopal pronouncements, but rather a fast-moving grassroots network of pro-life activists and groups, which was organized and mobilized in the "blogosphere," meaning the vast universe of blogs, chat rooms, bulletin boards, and e-mail on the Internet that allowed concerned Catholics to find one another, to pool resources, and to spread the word in real time. The site Blogs for Terri lists 233 blogs that took up the fight to save Schiavo, a solid majority of which are identifiably Catholic in tone and temper. (Many have names such as "ExtremeCatholic," "Catholic Fire," "Pro Ecclesia," "Rerum Novarum," and "Totus Tuus.") The Catholic response to the Schiavo case, in other words, was a classic example of horizontal Catholicism in action, with officialdom swept along by its undertow.

Whatever reaction one has to either Sant'Egidio or to the Schiavo coalition, both illustrate the new possibilities for activism created by the technological and cultural changes associated with globalization. Horizontal

Catholicism will be a growing feature of Church life in the century to come, probably spawning both drama and division.

Probable Consequences

1. A NUNCIO TO STANDARD & POOR'S?

Catholic ethicist Bryan Hehir once provocatively asked, "Can Catholic social thought survive globalization?" What Hehir meant is that Catholic social doctrine arose in an age in which the primary actors were nation-states and mediating institutions within nation-states, especially families, civic associations, and churches. Formally speaking, Catholic social teaching has relatively little to say about intergovernmental organizations such as the World Bank or Interpol or the World Trade Organization, or the burgeoning sector of nongovernmental organizations.

This tendency to look to nation-states to solve social problems is especially questionable in light of the growing incapacity of the state in many parts of the world to deliver even the elemental goods citizens expect of their government: physical security, economic stability, and at least a minimal social safety net. Working out a more developed theology of governance, taking account of changing global realities, is therefore likely to be a top concern for Catholic thinkers in the years to come.

Popes are aware of the problem. In 2003, John Paul called for "a new constitutional organization of the human family."

"This does not mean writing the constitution of a global super-State," he wrote. "Rather, it means continuing and deepening processes already in place to meet the almost universal demand for participatory ways of exercising political authority, even international political authority, and for transparency and accountability at every level of public life."

Yet, as Coleman notes, these calls have been much better at diagnosis than cure; it's still not clear what those "participatory ways of exercising political authority, even international political authority" would actually look like, especially given the Catholic Church's emphasis on subsidiarity. Catholic teaching on this point, Coleman says, remains "much too vague and moralistic."

Starting from the premise that "governance is not the same as government," Coleman suggests greater attention to amorphous "global policy networks" that might be able to do the trick. He observes that Standard & Poor's is by no means a government, but it does a pretty good job of regulating the bond market. (As of 2009, over $4.85 trillion of international investments were linked to Standard and Poor's family of ratings services.) Similarly, the private Internet Corporation for Assigned Agencies, headquartered in Marina del Rey, California, oversees the assignment of domain names and IP addresses on the Internet. Some of these "global networks" flow from intergovernmental organizations, some are public–private partnerships, and some are entirely private.

Coleman argues that the principle of subsidiarity is too often understood in an exclusively "vertical" sense, in terms of relationships among global, national, regional, and local public authorities. He suggests that Catholic social thinking embrace a "horizontal" dimension of subsidiarity, in the form of these policy networks—which, he says, "bypass top-heavy bureaucracy and coordinate the many stake-holders into governance units."

Though Coleman does not draw the conclusion himself, one could make the argument that by concentrating much of its diplomatic energy on the United Nations and its member states, the official structures of the Church have not engaged where the real "action" is these days in terms of global governance. It's not out of the question that a pope of the twenty-first century will appoint a nuncio to Standard & Poor's! Whether that happens or not, it's certainly likely that the vast sector of horizontal governance will be a subject of steadily growing theological and political interest.

2. FINANCIAL ACCOUNTABILITY IN THE CHURCH

One spring evening during a 2007 reporting trip for this book, I found myself in the residence of a bishop in the developing world. We were relaxing over drinks, when an aide told the bishop that one of his nephews needed to see him. The nephew was shown in and handed the bishop some papers. The nephew, it turns out, was an officer of a local bank, and he had been placed in charge of finding buyers for a private local bond issue his bank had decided to support. In that light, he wanted the diocese to buy up some of the bonds.

"Is this going to be a good investment?" the bishop asked.

"Yes, uncle," the nephew responded.

With that, the bishop signed the papers and we got on with our evening—no meeting with a diocesan finance council, no consultation with outside experts, just the stroke of a pen. To be clear, this was not an act of "corruption," because the bishop made no personal gain from the transaction, and his nephew wasn't lining his pockets with the proceeds either (at least so far as I could tell). It is, nevertheless, a classic example of how the management of Church resources in many parts of the world stands utterly divorced from modern methods of accounting and oversight, obviously creating the potential for abuse.

This lack of clear guidelines about money management in the Church, it should be stressed, is by no means restricted to the global South. In 2007, the Center for the Study of Church Management at Villanova University announced results from a survey of Catholic dioceses in the United States, which found that 85 percent of respondents had experienced embezzlement of Church funds during the previous five years. Losses, according to the center, could run as high as $4 million nationally. In Tucson, Arizona, to take just one example, layman Philip Francis Martinez had been ordered in 2006 to repay $312,910 that he had stolen from collection plates at St. Francis Assisi Catholic Church in Yuma, and had been given a ninety-day jail term.

"Where there is money and where there are people, there is a potential for fraud," said Tucson Bishop Gerald F. Kicanas. "The best way to offset that is to have clear policies, enforce them, and investigate all allegations."

One could make several arguments why the Catholic Church ought to move in this direction, but particularly in the global South, the most convincing is likely to be that it will be difficult for the Church to challenge corruption in the broader culture if it does not model "good governance" in its own affairs. In fact, the future is likely to see a "push–pull" dynamic in this regard. Church leaders will want to develop models of accountability that they can propose to political and financial institutions; and as they demand accountability and transparency from those institutions, it will become increasingly difficult not to practice the same virtues themselves.

Various sexual abuse and financial scandals will also accelerate this development. The National Leadership Roundtable on Church Management launched by Catholics in the United States in 2005, focusing on human resources, finances, and management inside the Catholic Church, is one example of what's happening.

3. MNC THEOLOGY

Official Catholic teaching about business tends to assume a model of entrepreneurial enterprises within a free-market system, and, at least implicitly, presumes that much of its activity is circumscribed by a given social context, meaning a local community, a region, or a nation. The contemporary multinational corporation, or MNC, is not really addressed in a direct sense.

Yet MNCs are in many ways the dominant authors of today's economic globalization. Even by conservative standards of comparison, thirty-seven of the hundred largest economies on earth are MNCs. The economic might of these corporations gives them tremendous leverage over the policies of nation-states on matters such as patenting and intellectual property, environmental protections, and labor standards.

According to *Forbes*, the top ten corporations on earth as of April 2009, measured in terms of their market value, were:

1. General Electric
2. Royal Dutch Shell
3. Toyota Motor
4. Exxon Mobil
5. British Petroleum
6. HSBC Holdings
7. AT&T
8. Wal-Mart Stores
9. Banco Santander
10. Chevron

The combined market value of these ten MNCs in 2009, according to *Forbes*, was roughly $1.4 trillion. Together, these ten MNCs controlled assets of $6.2 trillion. The banking giant HSBC by itself controlled assets of $2.5 trillion, exceeding the GDP of all but five nations—the United States, Japan, China, Germany, and France. HSBC is in many ways a perfect emblem of the MNC age; the acronym stands for "Hong Kong and Shanghai Banking Corporation," but today it's headquartered in London with operations all over the world.

Given that these corporations have multiple affiliates, production sites, and sales outlets across the globe, it is difficult for any nation to regulate their activity. If a given country were to demand that a corporation stop making a given product, such as a light weapon, it could shift production to an overseas affiliate; if the government were to demand a hike in the minimum wage to the company's employees, it could shut down operations and open up somewhere else. It's also hard for national governments to tax

MNCs, because they can shift capital and assets, or incorporate in different locations, to provide maximum tax advantages. Meanwhile, companies often benefit from generous tax subsidies.

On the other hand, these global corporations are also enormous engines for innovation, technical progress, new employment, and improved living standards. Due to the ubiquity of Microsoft, for example, it's much easier for people all over the world to transfer text files, slide presentations, and data charts, because everyone is using the same software. The United States Justice Department, in seeking to break up the Microsoft monopoly, was in a sense engaged in a war not just with Microsoft, but with the global market.

What Catholic social theory needs, according to many experts, is an analysis of the multinational corporation attentive both to its blessings and its curses, locked into neither knee-jerk leftist critique of the MNC nor neo-conservative worship. While many pieces of that jigsaw puzzle may already be out of the box, somebody needs to put them together.

Possible Consequences

1. DYNAMIC DIPLOMACY

Philip Jenkins has written that the twenty-first century may witness a renaissance of Vatican diplomacy, given that many regions of the world that are likely to loom large in the globalized era have either Catholic majorities or significant Catholic minorities. If one looks at the deadliest conflict of the late twentieth century and the early twenty-first, which has been the war in Africa's Great Lakes region, he seems to have a point. The six nations most involved in that conflict, and the percentage of their populations that are Catholic according to the 2007 *Catholic Almanac,* are:

- Democratic Republic of the Congo (53 percent)
- Angola (57.1 percent)
- Namibia (18 percent)
- Zimbabwe (10 percent)
- Uganda (44 percent)
- Rwanda (47 percent)
- Burundi (67 percent)

Catholics are a majority or near-majority in five of the seven and form a significant minority of the other two. Given the high levels of religious faith and practice among African Catholics, it's probable that a sustained diplomatic initiative in which the pope was personally involved would be taken seriously.

For a contemporary parallel, one could look to the Vatican's role in avoiding war between Argentina and Chile in 1979 over the Beagle Islands. Just off the Southern tip of Latin America, the Beagle Islands are named after the British ship in which Charles Darwin explored the area between 1831 and 1836. At stake was not just the islands themselves, but 30,000 square miles of fishing and mineral rights. Preparations for war began in earnest in July 1977, an especially alarming development since both nations were then ruled by military dictators. Pope John Paul II sent a personal message to both presidents urging a peaceful solution. Through the intervention of Vatican diplomats, the "Act of Montevideo" was signed in January 1979, which settled the dispute without a shot being fired. Five years later, Argentina and Chile signed a treaty of peace and friendship. In a telling tribute to the pope's role, the treaty was signed at the Vatican.

While this sort of initiative has not been launched in the Great Lakes, or in other parts of the world where Catholics are among the primary protagonists (civil wars in Uganda, Nigeria, Colombia, and Peru come to mind), the chronic nature and staggering scale of these conflicts may well drive the Vatican into a more robust diplomatic role, especially as bishops and other leaders from these regions become more influential in setting Church policy.

2. DISINVESTMENT

One form a push for global solidarity could take in the century to come is an effort to use the investment portfolios and purchasing power of Catholicism in concentrated, targeted fashion to produce specific reforms in corporations or semipublic entities.

For example, since the World Bank is financed by bond issues on the private market, some churches, unions, and local governments have launched a "disinvestment" campaign, analogous to efforts in the 1980s to divest from South African companies under that country's apartheid regime. The criticism is that by insisting upon structural adjustment programs as a condition for loans, the World Bank has acted against the interests of the world's poor. As of mid-2007, the cities of San Francisco, Boulder, Oakland, and Berkeley had sold off their World Bank bonds. Several Catholic groups had already signed on to disinvestment, including: Maryknoll Fathers and Brothers, Sisters, and Lay Mission Association; the Mercy Investment Program;

the Conference of Major Superiors of Men; the Sisters of St. Francis of Philadelphia; and the Franciscan Friars of the Sacred Heart, Assumption, and St. John the Baptist Provinces. Given the sharper critique of global economic inequities that's likely to shape Catholic thinking in the twenty-first century, it's possible this campaign could catch on, involving not just religious orders and Catholic charitable agencies but whole dioceses, clusters of dioceses acting in concerted fashion—or, under a more long-shot scenario, virtually every agency in the Church under the order (or direct personal appeal) of the pope.

More broadly, the Catholicism of the future may take greater interest in the social consequences of its investments. One revealing hint came in December 2001, when Pope John Paul II invited Catholics to fast at the end of the Islamic holy month of Ramadan to express solidarity with Muslims. The pope suggested that Catholics save the money they would have spent on food that day, and give it to the poor. Cor Unum, the Vatican agency that oversees charitable endeavors, opened a special account at the Bank of Rome and put a pop-up window for donations on the Vatican Web site. The missionary journal *Missione Oggi,* however, called for a boycott because the Bank of Rome is a major player in the arms market. While the Vatican did not immediately switch banks, a Vatican official said on background that he agreed with the Xaverians. If you want to change corporate behavior, he said, "You have to hit them in the wallet." In the Catholicism to come, that sort of attitude is likely to wax, not wane.

Long-Shot Consequences

1. AVIGNON IN AFRICA

In the run-up to the U.S.-led invasion of Iraq in spring 2003, there was a brief flurry of speculation that John Paul II might go to Baghdad to act as a human shield. The theory was that the United States would not dare strike while the pope was in harm's way. For a variety of reasons, the Vatican never seriously entertained the hypothesis. Aside from obvious concerns about the pope's physical safety, the Vatican was under no illusions about the regime of Saddam Hussein and did not want to be perceived as giving it legitimacy. For another, there was no assurance that the American-led attack would not have gone ahead anyway.

In the Catholicism of the future, such ideas might become more thinkable. It's just possible that a future pope might decide to relocate temporarily to Africa, for example, as his predecessors did in the fourteenth century in Avignon, France—the difference being that the pope would not be fleeing feuds between noble families in Rome, but rather trying to train the papal spotlight on a region too long neglected.

As a thought exercise, what would be the impact of a pope announcing that he intended to live for a year in Goma, in the Democratic Republic of the Congo, the center of much of the carnage during the two large-scale wars in the Great Lakes region?

Immediately, the hordes of media that would follow the pope, and Catholics from all over Africa who would flock to him, would make a renewal of fighting there virtually impossible. (Thomas Friedman once said that no two countries with McDonald's have ever gone to war with one another. The Vatican corollary might be that no two countries with Catholic majorities or near-majorities will invade each other if the pope is in town.) His presence would also immediately spark a boom in roads, hotels, businesses, air and rail travel, and all the other bits and pieces of infrastructure that would be necessary. In the medium term, the stability the pope's presence would guarantee might allow businesses to invest, children to go to school, hospitals to operate. It could also be more difficult for elected officials, many of them Catholic, to brazenly misappropriate public resources facing the pope's watchful eye. In the long run, the pope might foster a renewal in eastern Congo that would have ripple effects throughout the continent.

Such a possibility is a long shot for a variety of reasons, not least the fact that Avignon is not exactly a chapter of Church history many in the Vatican are anxious to repeat. It represented a virtual captivity of the papacy by the French, compromising the pope's moral and political credibility for at least a century. Further, a pope is elected to be the bishop of Rome, not of Goma. How could a local bishop lead his church with the pope just across town? To add another layer of difficulty, how would the rest of the Catholic world react to the pope choosing Africa as the focus of his attention rather than their local crisis?

Still, the option for the poor implies that when choosing how to allocate scarce resources, the Church should try to do so in ways that benefit the most vulnerable. Perhaps the most precious resources a pope has—lacking a standing army, or a national economy—are his physical presence and his time. Spending both on a temporary "Avignon in Africa" could be a dramatic way to change the international calculus.

2. CYBER-SPIRITUALITY

On the Internet, as the famous saying goes, no one knows you're a dog. That gag about how anonymity provides cover for mischief certainly applies to ideas such as online confession, which are occasionally floated in various parts of the world only to be knocked down by Church officials. The Vatican has repeatedly interpreted the requirements for sacramental validity to include face-to-face contact, so that confessions cannot be heard at a distance, whether it's in a telegram or an e-mail. The Vatican also warned in 2003 that, in most cases, Web sites purporting to offer cyber-confessions are a hoax, so it's probably not a good idea to share your darkest secrets with the decidedly nonordained dog on the other end. Finally, the Vatican cautioned that even if it were really a priest involved, online forms of communication such as e-mail and chat rooms are notoriously easy for hackers to penetrate, so the seal of the confessional could not be guaranteed.

In 2005, the Catholic bishops of Peru had to put out a statement rejecting the validity of "cybernetic confessions," stating categorically that "the physical presence of the faithful and the manifestation of their sins to the priest in person" is an essential element of the sacrament, and hence "in no case can absolution given by a priest who is not in physical contact with the penitent be considered valid by the Catholic Church." In 2007, the Polish bishops issued a similar note when a thirty-seven-year-old Pole named Borys Cezar put a "virtual confessional" on his Web site, complete with a clickable confessional icon. (This being Poland, Cezar was actually facing jail time for the offense.)

For these reasons, Catholics will probably never see a flashing icon on their computer screen with a voice chirping, "You've got absolution!" On the other hand, the Internet and related communications technologies, such as instantaneous transmission of video, audio, pictures, and text in real time on portable personal devices, will allow individuals and communities to connect much more seamlessly across time zones and geographical borders as the twenty-first century unfolds. All this cannot help but have an impact on spiritual life.

This trend may prompt the emergence of "virtual parishes," the spiritual equivalent of the horizontal Catholicism discussed above, where Catholics find the things parishes have traditionally offered in virtual form—a sense of community, good preaching, inspired music, opportunities for charitable service and social justice advocacy, faith formation, Bible study, and all the other forms of ministry associated with parish life. This will likely be particularly true of young Catholics. A 2006 survey by Harris Interactive found that 36 percent of American teenagers say they have close friends whom they know only through online contact.

Such Catholics will continue to go down the block for Mass and confession, but most of their other spiritual needs could be satisfied online. That reality, if it unfolds in the sense sketched here, will take the Catholic practice of parish shopping to an entirely new level. Consider the Italian site pretionline.it, or "priests online," which can connect users with more than 800 priests of differing experiences, outlooks, and theological styles. It's like computer dating, helping soul mates find one another—only in this case not husbands and wives, but priests and parishioners.

Two features may distinguish these cyber-parishes.

First, they will probably be ideologically homogenized. Suzy and Bob who attend St. Rita's may not like the guitar Mass on Sunday nights, but if it's the only parish within easy driving distance, they're stuck. When Suzy and Bob go online, however, no such restraints apply, and they can seek out cyber-niches for like-minded Catholics. Communications expert Quentin Schultze has written that the greatest Internet boon has been for affinity groups, subcultures whose members thrive on finding each other and affirming their group identity. That tendency, already clear from the stratification of the Catholic blogosphere, may fuel tribalism in the Church, especially in the North where the bulk of Internet traffic is currently concentrated.

Second, in a way these virtual parishes will be doubly virtual. Not only will they be nonphysical, but they won't be unified in single locations in cyberspace either. Suzy and Bob won't go to just one site to make connections, hear good preaching, receive spiritual direction, and listen to inspirational music. Their approach will be much more bric-a-brac, drawing bits and pieces from a variety of sources. In that sense, every Catholic Internet user becomes a parish all to him- or herself, assembling a unique set of catechetical, homiletic, liturgical, and spiritual experiences, praying and singing and learning in self-chosen ways. To some extent, this eclecticism has always been part of the Catholic scene, but globalization and the Internet are accelerating the process so profoundly that this quantitative shift may become qualitative. Ironically, the end result of cyber-parishes could therefore be the disaggregation of the Church's sense of community—in a phrase, the glocalization of Catholicism.

On the other hand, the cyber-parish could also be the occasion for a sort of spiritual awakening in Catholicism, allowing best practices in the Church to reach a global audience in real time. Among other things, the cyber-parish may change how, and how often, people pray. Some studies suggest that spiritually minded Internet users actually pray more often—at the office, for example, during a brief break from work, or while surfing the Web for entertainment. Prayer could therefore become more frequent, more integrated into daily life, as the century progresses. The cyber-parish could actually turn out to spawn a sort of cyber-breviary—a high-tech mode of organizing one's life around prayer, giving each day spiritual depth.

———◆———

ECOLOGY

Whenever popes speak in the Vatican's Paul VI audience hall, Catholics believe they do so drawing upon the power of the Son. Now, however, they're utilizing the power of the Sun as well, after a battery of more than 1,000 solar panels was installed atop the building in 2008 in order to provide electrical current, light, and heating and cooling via solar energy. The project was a literal expression of the "ecological conversion" urged by Pope John Paul II in 2001 as essential to the heading off of what he called a looming environmental "catastrophe." The audience hall is usually called the *Aula Nervi* by Italians, because the building in which it's located was designed and built for Paul VI by the famed Italian architect Pier Luigi Nervi. Its sleek, minimalist design makes it easily the most modernist structure on Vatican grounds—perhaps an ideal spot for the Catholic Church's past to strain toward its future.

When the Vatican's chief engineer, Pier Carlo Cuscianna, announced the solar project, he explained that 4,800 concrete tiles currently sitting atop the building had to be replaced anyway. Given numerous calls from Pope John Paul II and Benedict XVI in favor of defending the environment, Cuscianna said his team felt installing photovoltaic panels was the right way to go. The solar panels came online on November 26, 2008, and the project captured the 2008 Euro Solar Prize, awarded by the European Association for Renewable Energy, a secular body.

Less than a month later, the Vatican announced that it had signed an agreement to become the first "carbon-neutral" state in Europe. Under an agreement with Planktos/KlimaFa, an international eco-restoration company, a "Vatican climate forest" was created in Hungary's Bükk National Park in order to offset the Vatican's annual carbon dioxide emissions. A section of land large enough to absorb the amount of carbon the Vatican puts out in a year was planted with new trees. Planktos/KlimaFa, by the way, also pledged to work with the Vatican to calculate the carbon dioxide emissions of individual Catholic churches around the world, and to offer ways to turn their carbon footprints green.

None of this means that the secular environmental movement is likely quite yet to award the Vatican a Good Housekeeping seal of approval. Coincidentally, just a day before the announcement of the solar panel project, an Italian appeals court tossed out a 2005 conviction against two former officials of Vatican Radio for generating excessive levels of "electrosmog." The case dates to 2001, when a government study showed that from 1988 to 1999, people living within a six-mile zone surrounding powerful Vatican Radio transmitters north of Rome had a higher-than-average rate of leukemia. Critics blamed the electromagnetic waves generated by the transmitters. In houses and offices nearby, it was common for computers and washing machines to turn themselves on and off, for broadcasts to break through telephone and intercom systems, even for the electrical systems of passing trains to shut down. Vatican Radio initially dismissed the complaints, though it eventually brought the emissions down. The 2005 convictions were set aside on the grounds that existing Italian law doesn't cover electrosmog, and many observers say there's no clear scientific link between electromagnetic emissions and cancer.

Whatever the merits of the case, it perhaps illustrates that the Vatican's ecological sensitivity is still a work in progress. Nonetheless, installation of solar panels and an agreement to go carbon-neutral, coupled with increasingly strong papal statements, do suggest that an era of Green Catholicism is coming into view.

WHAT'S HAPPENING

Not so long ago, the idea of Catholic environmentalism would have struck some as a contradiction in terms. In the 1960s and 1970s, it was fashionable among pioneers of the environmental movement to fault the entire Judeo-Christian tradition for humanity's savage indifference to the earth. Professor

Lynn White Jr. of the University of California published an influential article in the journal *Science* in 1967, in which he blamed the Bible for making Westerners feel "superior to nature, contemptuous of it, willing to use it for our slightest whim." (Catholic writer Stratford Caldecott notes that White's article has become the obligatory point of departure for every discussion of Christianity and the environment; the article, he says, "is famous, and famous for being famous.") While acknowledging contrary currents in Christian history such as St. Francis of Assisi, White nonetheless ended with a sweeping indictment: "We shall continue to have a worsening ecological crisis until we reject the Christian axiom that nature has no reason for existence save to serve man."

In the space of just a quarter-century, the dynamics of the blame game have shifted dramatically. Perhaps under the rubric that the best defense is a good offense, many Church leaders today argue that Christianity is actually the solution to the ecological crisis, not its source. Christianity fosters a sense of humility and restraint, they argue, essential to curbing humanity's otherwise insatiable appetite for pillaging nature. In 2001, Pope John Paul II located the birthplace of the ecological crisis in the moment when human beings stopped regarding themselves as servants of a Creator-God, and instead set themselves up as "autonomous despots." Today, the pope said, the human person at long last seems to be "understanding that he must finally stop before the abyss."

Many analysts regard Pope Benedict XVI's own strong statements on the environment as perhaps the most intriguing dimension of his social teaching. The pontiff has had so much to say on the subject, in fact, that his statements have been collected by Catholic writer Woodene Koenig-Bricker into a small book titled *Ten Commandments for the Environment,* published in May 2009.

The environmental energy taking shape inside Catholicism seems to be registering on the broader public radar screen. For example, Sarah McFarland Taylor, a non-Catholic scholar at Northwestern University, published a book in 2007 called *Green Sisters,* documenting the "pervasiveness and significance of a greening movement" among women's religious orders. The book introduces readers to sisters who are sod-busting manicured lawns around their motherhouses to create community-supported organic gardens; building alternative housing structures and hermitages from renewable materials; adopting the green technology of composting toilets, solar panels, fluorescent lighting, and hybrid vehicles; and turning their community properties into land trusts with wildlife sanctuaries. While Taylor's book focuses on

North America, the movement it describes is decidedly global. An October 2007 piece in the magazine of the Sierra Club titled "Padre Power," documenting the efforts of Catholic clergy in Latin America to defend the land and the environment against powerful multinational corporations, also illustrates growing awareness in the secular world that something is stirring inside the Church. Author Marilyn Berlin Snell called it a "liberation ecology movement."

Ecology counts as a major trend in Catholicism not only because of this stirring inside the Church, but also because it looms as one of the most potent social and political forces of the twenty-first century. It's a classic case of a transformation in Catholicism that is partly the product of the Church's own maturing theological reflection, augmented by a powerful social current that is propelling the Church forward. That development will inevitably be uneven, and there's also a powerful Catholic backlash against an overly hasty alliance with secular environmental movements that critics see as harboring hidden agendas hostile to Catholic teaching—population control, for example, or denying any unique moral or spiritual status to human beings. Even that friction, however, contributes to making ecology a major Catholic trend, because it suggests that debates over what the right Catholic shade of green ought to look like will be a major feature of the Church's life in the years to come.

Five Key Ideas

In his 1990 message for the World Day of Peace titled "The Ecological Crisis: A Common Responsibility," John Paul II urged Christians to realize that concern for Creation is "an essential part of their faith"—in other words, not something optional, but a core aspect of what it means to be a follower of Christ. On the basis of both official statements and emerging Catholic practice, at least five key ideas have come to form the heart of Catholic environmentalism. Some are theological in nature, while others are more pragmatic and legal.

1. STEWARDSHIP

No concept looms larger in Catholic environmentalism than human beings as stewards of creation, meaning caretakers rather than masters. The vision is rooted in the Genesis creation stories, and amplified in Church teaching. In its most basic form, stewardship implies that human beings do not own the natural world, but rather it has been given into their care on behalf of its rightful owner, who is God. Commitment to the common good is part of what Catholics typically mean by stewardship.

In 2003, the United States bishops defined stewardship in terms of four points:

- Receiving the gifts of God with gratitude;
- Cultivating them responsibly;
- Sharing them lovingly in justice with others;
- Standing before the Lord in a spirit of accountability.

A steward was a common function in the ancient world, but the image doesn't always translate easily today. For a modern parallel, as odd as this may sound, one could consider an ethically minded mutual-fund manager. (Granted, these two kinds of green don't normally move in the same circles, but hear me out.) The manager decides how to invest the fund's assets, and draws a reward if all goes well, but ultimately it's not his or her money. It belongs to the investors. The manager prospers only if everyone in the fund does well. Stewardship, like managing a mutual fund, also means taking the long view, building assets not just for this quarter but over a long arc of time. With regard to the environment, this means thinking not just about the current generation but those to come.

Like other principles in Catholic social teaching, stewardship has both a personal and a social thrust. At the personal level, it means avoiding addiction to consumption and making practical choices that are within one's reach to promote the common good. At the social level, stewardship means responsible policies aimed at environmental protection at all levels.

2. OPTION FOR THE POOR

At one level, the option for the poor provides an additional reason to become engaged in environmental issues. Because of factors such as cheap building materials, low levels of general health, greater dependence on agriculture, and fewer opportunities to flee at-risk zones, the poor are especially susceptible to the results of environmental irresponsibility. According to the United Nations, between 1994 and 2003 the number of deaths reported per natural disaster in the world was seven times higher in developing countries than in affluent ones. Poor people often live on steep slopes or flood-prone riverbanks, in poorly built houses, and with limited access to savings or insurance. Roughly half the jobs on earth are in farming, fishing, and forestry, and they're disproportionately held by poor people. Loss of income in these trades caused by environmental damage falls primarily upon their backs.

At the same time, the option for the poor also injects balance in environmental debates, insisting that ecology not become a fetish that would deny technologies or economic models to developing nations that could help lift people out of poverty. For example, some Western environmentalists oppose virtually any new use of coal or gas, as well as hydroelectric dams, demanding that developing nations rely on wind and solar power. Given the present state of things, many poor countries can't afford these technologies, and in any event they may not be able to supply enough power to promote real development.

To be sure, concern over runaway burning of fossil fuels in the developing world is not idle. China offers an especially telling illustration: the air in the city of Benxi was so polluted that the entire area actually disappeared from satellite maps in the 1980s. At the same time, however, one basic obstacle to improved living standards in many poor countries is chronic failure of the power grids, suggesting that some use of fossil fuels, with appropriate safeguards, is arguably a humanitarian imperative. Kenyan economist James Shikwati has said that telling Africans not to use their coal and oil resources is tantamount to telling Africa to commit suicide. Indian environmentalist Vandana Shiva complains that international conventions such as the Kyoto Protocol are "instruments to make the Third World pay for damages caused primarily by the North," calling such policies "eco-imperialism." Another Indian, Deepak Lal, was equally blunt in 2005: "Despite their protestations to the contrary, the Greens are the enemy of the world's poor."

To take another case, limited indoor use of the pesticide DDT has been shown to dramatically decrease rates of malaria, a disease that still kills one million Africans every year, but Western environmental lobbies usually oppose it. Asian authors Nagesh Kumar and Sachin Chaturvedi, in their 2007 volume *Environmental Requirements and Market Access,* also raised alarms that environmental safety standards may further exclude the agricultural products of developing nations from Western markets. For example, the cost of upgrading sanitary conditions in the Bangladesh frozen shrimp industry to satisfy EU and U.S. requirements is estimated to be $17.6 million.

The Bangladeshis, they say, can't afford it, which could mean their shrimp will be shut out of the two biggest markets on earth. While nobody is questioning the need to protect food safety, Kumar and Chaturvedi write, environmental scares could provide another justification for protectionist trade policies.

The option for the poor means wariness about proposed solutions to environmental problems that, despite the best of intentions, end up consolidating Western privilege and consigning hundreds of millions of people to permanent poverty.

3. A RIGHT TO A SAFE AND HEALTHY NATURAL ENVIRONMENT

In a 1988 address to the European Commission and Court of Human Rights in Strasbourg, Pope John Paul II referred to "a safe and healthy natural environment" as a positive human right, on a par with positive rights to health care, education, and a decent standard of living. According to Earthjustice, a U.S.-based environmental NGO, 118 nations guaranteed a right to a safe environment as part of their constitutional law as of 2007.

Church officials have argued that if such a "right" to a safe environment is to mean anything, somebody has to enforce it when it's being violated. For that reason, official Church teaching has long favored the emergence of public authorities on a planetary scale with the power to protect the common good. The *Compendium* puts it this way: "Modern ecological problems are of a planetary dimension and can be effectively resolved only through international cooperation capable of guaranteeing greater coordination in the use of the earth's resources."

4. THE PRECAUTIONARY PRINCIPLE

The precautionary principle means that in evaluating proposed interventions in the environment, if you can't be reasonably sure that the good will outweigh the harm, the best thing is to be cautious. Some critics have charged that, if pushed too far, the precautionary principle means paralysis, since it is usually impossible to establish with scientific certainty all the potential consequences of a given use of natural resources. Others charge that it's a smokescreen for consolidating Western privilege; the late novelist Michael Crichton said it's a polite way of saying, "We got ours and we don't want you to get yours, because you'll cause too much pollution." In moderate form, however, the Catholic Church has largely endorsed the precautionary principle. The *Compendium* puts it this way: "Prudent policies, based on the precautionary principle, require that decisions be based on a comparison of the risks and benefits foreseen for the various possible alternatives, including the decision not to intervene."

Catholic leaders have also invoked the precautionary principle to support immediate action to protect the environment before scientific data is complete. In a 2007 letter to the U.S. Senate, Bishop Thomas Wenski of Orlando, chair of the bishops' Committee on International Policy, made this argument about climate change.

"The traditional virtue of prudence suggests that we do not have to know with absolute certainty everything that is happening with climate change to know that something seriously harmful is occurring," Wenski wrote. "Therefore, it is better to act now than wait until the problem gets worse and the remedies more costly. This precautionary principle leads us to act now to avoid the worst consequences of waiting."

5. LIFESTYLE CHANGES

Human problems cannot be resolved purely through legislative and political remedies, according to the Church's understanding. A change of heart is also required, which leads to changed behavior at the individual level. John Paul came at the lifestyle question in *Centesimus Annus*, describing what it would take to build a just society: "This may mean making important changes in established life-styles, in order to limit the waste of environmental and human resources, thus enabling every individual and all the peoples of the earth to have a sufficient share of these resources."

Global inequities in consumption are fairly well documented. According to the World Wildlife Fund, the typical American draws on 25 acres of land to support his or her lifestyle, while the average African gets by on 2.5 acres. Pope Benedict XVI addressed the issue of lifestyle change in a session with the clergy of the Italian diocese of Bolzano-Bressanone in August 2008:

> "It's not just a question of finding techniques that can prevent environmental harms, even if it's important to find alternative sources of energy and so on. But all this won't be enough if we ourselves don't find a new style of life, a discipline which is made up in part of renunciations: a discipline of recognition of others, to whom creation belongs just as much as those of us who can make use of it more easily; a discipline of

responsibility to the future for others and for ourselves. It's a question of responsibility before He who is our Judge, and as Judge our Redeemer, but nonetheless our Judge."

Revolutionaries, Pastors, and Skeptics

Given the size and complexity of global Catholicism, one should never expect uniform development on any front. Certainly when it comes to environmental questions, the Catholic landscape is dotted with a variety of perspectives. Crudely speaking, we can divide them into the revolutionaries, the pastors, and the skeptics.

The modern point of departure for Catholic environmental theology was a revolutionary: French Jesuit Fr. Pierre Teilhard de Chardin, who died in 1955. A paleontologist, philosopher, and theologian, Teilhard believed that evolution is humanity's participation in the redemption begun by Christ. When evolution reaches its climax in what he called the "Omega point," Teilhard said the cosmos will achieve a form of "Christogenesis." Those views got him into trouble with Church officials, concerned that Teilhard's thought flirted with pantheism. Seven years after his death, the Vatican censured Teilhard's work, and in 1981, on the hundredth anniversary of Teilhard's birth, the Vatican reaffirmed that judgment.

Many Catholics still find much to commend in Teilhard. Archbishop Celestino Migliore, for example, the Vatican's Permanent Observer to the UN, said in 2007 that whenever he goes to upstate New York he stops at Teilhard's grave in Hyde Park, reflecting in the woods about Teilhard's vision of the "Christification" of the cosmos.

Descendants of Teilhard today include eco-theologians and philosophers such as Fr. Diarmuid O'Murchu and Fr. Thomas Berry, as well as Rosemary Radford Ruether, Matthew Fox, and Brian Swimme. Though each has a distinct outlook, most share a sense that if Catholicism wants to embrace ecology, it needs a radical overhaul. In 1992, Berry said: "We should put the Bible away for twenty years while we radically rethink our religious ideas." In O'Murchu's *Quantum Theology*, he suggests that institutional religion is destined for extinction. "What we cannot escape," he wrote, "is that we as a species have outlived that phase of our evolutionary development and so, quite appropriately, thousands of people are leaving religion aside."

These personalities have a small but dedicated following, and they've helped to drive ecological questions to the forefront of the Church's consciousness, but they've also set off doctrinal alarms. Fox drew a Vatican censure in 1988 and was dismissed from the Dominican order in 1992. O'Murchu attracted critical notice from the doctrinal committee of the Spanish bishops' conference in 2006. The bishops charged that O'Murchu "speaks much of God and constantly talks of human liminal values in a 'planetary' or 'cosmic' context, but says almost nothing about Jesus Christ." While the revolutionaries play an important role as catalysts, mainstream Catholic environmentalism is likely to be less ideological and more pragmatic.

For an example of just such an approach, consider a 2000 letter from the Catholic bishops of the Pacific Northwest in the United States and Canada arguing for conservation of the Columbia River Watershed. From the outset, the bishops announce their intention to steer a middle course between "economic greed" and "ecological elitism." The core principles upon which the letter is based are stewardship, respect for nature, and the common good. They promote the idea of creation as the "book of nature," a source of revelation and theological insight alongside the Bible. In general, the bishops move quickly from sketching a few brief theological ideas into direct application to concrete environmental problems. They're apparently less interested in supplying a new theological vision than in mobilizing action.

The bishops offered ten considerations to guide future discussion:

- The common good
- Conserving the watershed as a common good
- Conserving and protecting species of wildlife
- Respecting the dignity and the traditions of indigenous peoples
- Linking economic and environmental justice
- Community resolution of economic and ecological issues
- Social and ecological responsibility in industry
- Conserving energy and promoting alternative energy sources
- Respecting ethnic and racial cultures, citizens, and communities
- Sustainable transportation and recreation

The Columbia River Watershed pastoral letter is widely considered a turning point in official Church teaching on environmental questions, and it has served as a template for similar projects in other parts of the world.

Skeptics in the Catholic fold include Antonio Gaspari and Riccardo Cascioli, who teach in the master's program in environmental science at

Rome's Regina Apostolorum sponsored by the Legionaries of Christ. Both Gaspari and Cascioli have deep Catholic credentials. Gaspari has written for Zenit News Agency and *Inside the Vatican*, while Cascioli worked for Vatican Radio. Together, they published a two-volume work called *Le Bugie dei Ambientalisti* ("The Lies of the Environmentalists") in 2004 and 2006. Its argument is that the "catastrophism" of environmentalists is exaggerated. In some cases, they argue, it serves as a smokescreen for radical philosophical notions such as those propounded by the utilitarian philosopher and animal rights activist Peter Singer, who denies the unique spiritual status of human beings. In other cases, they suggest, dire warnings of ecological catastrophe may promote the interests of environmental lobby groups, law firms, and the media, by keeping public alarm at a fever pitch and thereby ensuring both funding and massive audiences.

In the United States, a group called the Interfaith Council for Environmental Stewardship put out the "Cornwall Declaration" in 1999, following a meeting of leading Catholic and Evangelical conservative intellectuals. Catholic signatories included the late Fr. Richard John Neuhaus, Robert Royal, Fr. Robert Sirico, and Fr. J. Michael Beers. Though affirming the legitimacy of environmental awareness, the statement referred to global warming, overpopulation, and rampant species loss as "unfounded or undue concerns." More broadly, it warned of setting economic development in opposition to good stewardship, describing that as a false dichotomy that would, in their view, keep the poor in misery.

While a preponderance of Catholic thought and activism may be "greening," these voices suggest it will by no means be a smooth development.

Debating Anthropocentrism

Some theologians contend that Catholic social doctrine is overly anthropocentric, meaning that it privileges humanity to such an extent that it obscures the dignity and moral status of nature. Pressing the argument, Berry says that the world needs to move from democracy to "biocracy," and that the earth needs "a United Species, not simply a United Nations."

Catholic writer John Hart argues that even well-meaning Catholic language on the environment, such as describing Creation as a "gift" from God, promotes anthropocentrism. If it's a gift, Hart argues, that implies we can do whatever we want with it. Hart offers three reasons why anthropocentric approaches to environmentalism don't work:

- It's "trickle-down ecology," and like "trickle-down economics," the problem is that very little trickles down.
- It fails to make clear that nature has an intrinsic value in itself.
- It's an appeal to pride, implying that human needs should always come first.

Dominican Sr. Miriam Therese MacGillis, founder of the eco-sensitive Creation Farm in Blairstown, New Jersey, says that traditional Catholic social doctrine puts "the human in the beginning, middle and end of our concerns." She argues for a "new cosmology," in which the human being is seen as part of creation rather than master of it. MacGillis says that while the stewardship model is an improvement, "It hasn't made the shift from a human material culture walking on a dead, material planet." Sr. Elizabeth Johnson identifies two approaches among Catholic environmentalists: the "stewardship model," which envisions the earth in service of human beings; and the "kinship model," which sees humans in service to the earth.

In some ways, this is largely a Northern debate. Hart notes that most environmental writing in the global South is not so concerned with anthropocentrism. Its point of departure is not so much defense of nature in itself, but rather the more equitable use of natural resources to help the poor.

Official Catholic teaching treats the spiritual and moral primacy of human welfare as a sine qua non of social theory. Pope John Paul II, in his message for the World Day of Peace in 1999, argued that what critics describe as anthropocentrism is not opposed to deeper environmental sensitivity.

"Placing human well-being at the center of concern for the environment is actually the surest way of safeguarding creation," the pope wrote. "This in fact stimulates the responsibility of the individual with regard to natural resources and their judicious use."

When the Pontifical Council for Justice and Peace sponsored a conference on climate change in April 2007, its president, Cardinal Renato Martino, seemed to rule out any reconsideration of the primacy of human beings. The human person has an "unarguable superiority" over creation, Martino said, and, by virtue of possessing an immortal soul, cannot be put on the same level as other living beings.

Given the clear tension between the rising environmental sensitivity in the church and its evangelical impulse to defend traditional doctrinal formulae, it seems a safe bet that the debate over anthropocentrism will continue.

Three Environmental Causes

Surveying statements on ecology from both popes John Paul II and Benedict XVI, as well as from Vatican officials, national conferences of bishops, religious orders, and Church-affiliated NGOs in various parts of the world, three environmental issues appear to be the focus of particular Catholic attention.

1. GLOBAL WARMING AND CLIMATE CHANGE

Though it seems a bad pun to call global warming "hot," the issue of climate change today undeniably enjoys a remarkable vogue. A majority of scientists—the U.S. bishops call it "a broad consensus" in their document *Faithful Stewards*—appear convinced of what's known as "anthropogenic warming," meaning that increases in the global temperature are largely attributable to human activity, especially the release of carbon dioxide by cars and trucks, industrial and electrical plants, and businesses and homes. To take just one example, scientists at the National Institute of Natural Resources in Peru report that Quelccaya, the largest tropical ice cap on the planet, located in the Andes mountains, has melted at a rate ten times faster over the last fifteen years than it did in the fifteen years before that, a change they attribute to man-made global warming. As the glacier melts, these scientists warn, it will stop releasing water during the area's dry season, causing rivers to dry up.

The primary forum in which scientists have elaborated these findings is the Intergovernmental Panel on Climate Change, created in 1988 by the World Meteorological Organization and the United Nations Environmental Programme. To date, the IPCC has delivered three reports: 1996, 2001, and 2007.

The IPCC's 2007 report found that since the beginning of the twentieth century, global temperatures have risen roughly 1.1 degrees Fahrenheit. If humans continue to burn fossil fuels at the current rate, the report found, temperatures could rise between 3.2 and 7 degrees by 2100. The IPCC links these increases to the release of greenhouse gases. The panel concluded, "There is new and stronger evidence that most of the warming observed over the last 50 years is attributable to human activities."

Among the consequences of an increase in global temperature exceeding 4 percent, according to the IPCC:

- Sea levels would climb between 7 and 23 inches because of Arctic and Antarctic ice melt. This could pose serious risks to low-lying coastal areas in densely populated regions of the developing world.

- The frequency and intensity of storms will increase.

- Greater droughts and floods will exacerbate problems with food production and distribution, worsening the problem of hunger.

- Because the number of extremely hot days will increase, heat stress may cause additional health problems, especially for the elderly, children, and those who are already ill.

- The rise in temperature could also lead to "mass extinctions" among climate-sensitive species such as polar bears.

In a separate document, the IPCC concluded that these effects can be largely avoided by limiting increases in the global temperature to a range of between 2 and 2.8 degrees. The technology exists to do so, the scientists said, pointing to increased energy efficiency, wider use of renewable energy, changes in land use and farming practices, and wider use of nuclear energy. The cost would be modest, according to the report. The most aggressive emissions-reduction scenario, the report claims, would slow economic growth by an average of 0.12 percent a year between now and 2030, or by roughly 3 percent over the entire period.

Both the scientific conclusions and the policy recommendations of the IPCC have been vigorously contested by a minority of scientists. While few dispute that the global temperature has risen slightly, they differ in how to explain it. First, some note that the IPCC findings are less spectacular than alarmist future projections make them sound. The 2007 report slightly lowered the estimate about the rise in global temperature from the 2001 document, suggesting that the findings are still in flux.

Second, such scientists say, data about temperature increases do not necessarily support a causal link to greenhouse gases. American scientist Craig Idso, who directs the Center for the Study of Carbon Dioxide and Global Change based in Arizona, claims that the highest temperatures recorded in the last 100 years were between 1930 and 1940, before the era of massive carbon emissions. (Idso spoke at a 2007 Vatican conference on climate change.) Other scientists critical of the IPCC consensus say a good deal of the rise in global temperature may be related to land use, and specifically to the greater heat output associated with urbanization, rather than to broad climate change. For example, records of average annual temperatures in New York City from 1822 to 2000 show a rise of 5 degrees Fahrenheit, yet over the same span, West Point, New York, shows no increase at all, and Albany actually recorded a drop of half a degree. New York City and Albany are just 140 miles apart, facing identical levels of atmospheric carbon dioxide, yet one got colder and the other much hotter—leading some to conclude that it's the fact that New York City grew to a city of 8 million while Albany remained much smaller, and not changes in the earth's climate, that explains the difference. Similar comparisons can be made to other large and medium-size urban areas in various parts of the world.

Without purporting to settle this debate, most Catholic leaders seem to take scientific warnings about climate change seriously. A 2007 educational document of the U.S. bishops, *Faithful Stewards,* is based in large measure upon the IPCC findings from 1996 and 2001. Catholic bishops in many parts of the world have urged their governments to ratify the Kyoto Protocol, intended to combat global warming. (As an observer rather than a member state, the Holy See is not a signatory of the Kyoto Protocol, but a Vatican official in 2005 said that the social doctrine of the Church supports many of the particulars of the treaty.)

In an April 2007 lecture to the Catholic Conference of Ohio, Migliore seemed inclined to give the skeptics a day in court. "We do hear respectable scientists and research laboratories come to different conclusions on the same phenomena. Their reports need to be read with a well-informed and critical mind," he said. Yet in the same breath, Migliore added, "There is no doubt that the latest assessments have established a strong link between human activity and climate change."

Migliore laid out a "Catholic vision for common action" on climate change that pivots on four basic points:

- Creation of a "more clear and determined environmental governing structure to implement the changes at all levels."
- "Serious public investment in clean technology," not just limited to automobiles but also involving "air and sea transport technologies."
- Strengthening links between environmental and humanitarian activities, since the poor will be the primary victims of environmental harm, especially in terms of an increased incidence of natural disasters.

- Ensuring that poor nations are not left farther behind, including "mechanisms for technological transfer and innovation intended to help the poorest communities to contain and overcome environmental degradation."

In various forms, a wide variety of bishops' conferences, religious orders, and lay groups in the Catholic Church around the world have called for similar measures, making climate change the object of a rapidly swelling wave of Catholic activism.

2. WATER SCARCITY

Though water constitutes more than 75 percent of the earth's surface, less than one percent is readily usable by human beings, and a variety of forces suggest that serious water shortages could loom on the near-term horizon. The Central Intelligence Agency has estimated that by 2015, nearly half the world's population, meaning more than three billion people, will live in countries that are "water-stressed." That's a term meaning these countries will have less than 1,700 cubic meters of water per capita, considered the threshold for extreme scarcity. In addition to northern China, the bulk of these countries are located in Africa, the Middle East, and South Asia, regions already subject to political instability. Shortages are being brought on, most experts say, by population pressures, overintensive agriculture, and erratic patterns of rainfall, evaporation, and flooding, some of which may be linked to global climate change.

In the developing world, the CIA report concluded, more than 80 percent of water usage goes into agriculture, but 60 percent of that water is lost to evaporation or leaky canals, or is contaminated by fertilizer and pesticide residues. Many developing nations will be unable to maintain current levels of irrigated agriculture, barring dramatic (and improbable) improvements in efficiency. Roughly 1,000 tons of water are needed to produce one ton of grain, resulting in overpumping of groundwater in many of the world's grain-producing regions. A 2007 Associated Press report indicated that the water table in grain-producing areas of China is falling at a rate of about five feet per year because of overpumping, leading to desperate measures in some places. Authorities in Gansu province, for example, recently ordered all farmers to vacate their properties over the next three and a half years. The government plans to replace twenty agricultural villages with newly planted grass, in a final effort to halt the seemingly inexorable advance of the Tengger and Badain Jaran deserts. Similar trends are unfolding else-where; water tables throughout India, for example, are declining by three to ten feet a year.

In the short term, there's not much optimism about turning things around. The CIA predicts that "measures taken to increase water availability and to ease acute water shortages will not be sufficient to substantially change the outlook for water shortages." Those measures include more effi-cient use of water, expanding desalinization, developing GMOs that grow on less water, and importing water.

Efforts to raise water prices in order to limit consumption are politically tricky, because in most developing nations people depend upon access to in-expensive water. As part of broader efforts to restructure national economies, lending agencies such as the World Bank have sometimes insisted upon pri-vatizing water supplies, one consequence of which is generally more realistic (i.e., higher) prices. Increasing cost, however, may trigger a spike in disease as the most impoverished populations turn to unsafe water. In 2005, for ex-ample, Elizabeth Eilor, a director of the African Women's Economic Policy Network in Uganda, told reporters that as a result of water privatization in her country, Uganda had "lots of people suffering from water-borne dis-eases like cholera and typhoid, even in some urban areas around Kampala." Privatization schemes have also led to political upheaval, including riots, in Bolivia, Ghana, and Uruguay. That blowback, however, does not seem to have arrested the trend. Today, three companies—Vivendi Water and Suez Environment, both of France, and Thames Water of England—control the water supply in at least fifty-six nations, with a combined population of over 300 million people.

All this makes water an increasingly precious resource on the global mar-ket. As *Newsweek* put it in July 2007, "The wars of the future may be fought not only over politics or oil, but water, too." *Newsweek* also noted that the av-erage amount of water used daily by one person living in Ethiopia, Somalia, Eritrea, Djibouti, Gambia, Mali, Mozambique, Tanzania, or Uganda equals that used by someone in a developed country brushing his or her teeth with the tap running.

The CIA also floated the prospect of water wars. Its report notes that more than thirty nations receive over a third of their water from outside their national borders, making the possibility of interstate conflict realistic. In fact, shortages of water may be far more destabilizing than shortages of oil, because while oil shortages cause long lines at the gas pump and put a brake on global commerce as the cost of transportation goes up, water shortages cause people to die. Not only do people die directly of thirst, they also die of hunger as crops fail when there's not sufficient water for irrigation. The CIA anticipated that water shortages would be especially destabilizing in the Middle East. Turkey operates dams that control significant water flows in Syria and Iraq, while Egypt controls waterways that provide much of the water in Ethiopia and Sudan.

In some parts of the world, fighting has already broken out over water. In July 2006, for example, in Sri Lanka, the Liberation Tigers of Tamil Eelam shut down the Maavilaru dam's sluice gate, which cut off water supplies for 60,000 people in government-controlled areas. This provoked the Sri Lankan military to commence an aerial bombardment of Tiger positions as well as a ground offensive to gain control of the reservoir's control point. More than 500 people were killed. That bloodshed over water is likely a sign of things to come.

The Vatican's *Compendium* uses strong language on water, saying that access to safe water is "a universal and inalienable human right."

"By its very nature, water cannot be treated as just another commodity among many, and it must be used rationally and in solidarity with others," the *Compendium* states. "The distribution of water is traditionally among the responsibilities that fall to public agencies, since water is considered a public good. If water distribution is entrusted to the private sector it should still be considered a public good. The right to water, as all human rights, finds its basis in human dignity and not in any kind of merely quantitative assessment that considers water as a merely economic good."

That was not a one-off Vatican statement. In a message to Brazilian bishops in March 2004, Pope John Paul II declared that water is a "gift of God" and a "right of all." In the same year, Bishop Marcelo Sanchez Sorondo, chancellor of the Vatican's Pontifical Academy of Social Sciences, called the trend toward water privatization "one of the biggest threats to equitable water rights."

Those principles have been translated into grassroots organizing by Catholic leaders in various parts of the world. Some examples:

- In the Philippines in 2007, a coalition of religious orders and Catholic NGOs noted that a government report predicts as much as 25 percent of the population of Manila could lack access to safe water in the near future. As a result, the group announced plans to "screen" political candidates for their positions on environmental issues.

- Also in the Philippines, a "businessmen's conference" issued a water conservation program in the name of the country's Catholic bishops, including a proposed ban on sand and gravel extraction to stop water losses due to quarrying, and granting land tenure to occupants of watersheds to give them a stake in preserving the water supply. The alternative, the group warned, is spreading "hydrological poverty."

- In the United States, the National Catholic Rural Life Conference has put together programs to foster a "water ethic," stating, "We watch with alarm as the privatization of water resources becomes the 'rational solution' to the public matter of water management and distribution."

- In 2006, the National Council of Churches in Brazil, together with the Catholic Conference of Bishops in Brazil, affirmed a "human right to water" in a joint statement, and expressed support for community-based alternatives to water privatization.

- In 2004, South African Catholic activist Richard Mokolo led a campaign to defend public access to water, declaring, "Privatization of water is a sin and a crime against humanity."

- A Brazilian bishop from Bahia state, Bishop Luiz Flavio Cappio, staged an eleven-day hunger strike in 2005 over the government's plans to change the course of the São Francisco river to support an irrigation project designed to bring water to arid lands in Brazil's northeast. He called the government's stance "authoritarian," saying it had not consulted the locals, and warned that it would create water shortages in the area.

3. DEFORESTATION/THE AMAZON

American historian Murray Morgan, in his book *The Last Wilderness,* described the loss of old-growth forest in Washington State's Olympic Peninsula due to commercially driven deforestation this way: "It was strangely like war. They attacked the forest as if it were an enemy to be pushed back from the beachheads, driven to the hills, broken into patches, and wiped out. Many operators thought they were not only making lumber but liberating the land from the trees."

That martial imagery captures something about the relentlessness of global deforestation due to logging and the need to clear land for agribusiness. Authors Derrick Jensen and George Draffan, in 2003's *The Global*

Assault on Forests, wrote that, "Two and a half acres of forest are cut every second, the equivalent of two football fields. That's 214,000 acres per day, an area larger than New York City." All told, Jensen and Draffan conclude that unless significant measures are taken on a worldwide basis, especially in the Amazon basin, by 2030 only 10 percent of the forests that once covered the planet will remain, with another 10 percent in a degraded condition. Along with the forests, they say, an incalculable number of species will also have been lost. Several countries in the developing world, including the Philippines, Thailand, and India, have declared deforestation a national emergency.

Aside from aesthetic objections to the decimation of natural habitats, critics say deforestation causes environmental harm in a variety of ways. For one thing, forests are a primary means for cleaning the atmosphere of carbon dioxide. Fewer trees mean more carbon in the atmosphere. Further, when these trees are cut down they're often burned, so that deforestation is itself a serious source of greenhouse gases. The loss of trees also reduces the amount of water in the soil and groundwater, as well as the moisture in the atmosphere, thereby raising the chances of both drought and fire. Half the moisture above a forest is released by its trees, so when an area covered by rain forest is cleared, it loses half its rain.

Because forests are a great source of biodiversity, their eradication always means species loss. Experts believe that given what's happening today, millions of species within the Amazon will be wiped out before they're even identified. Forests are also a source for new medical discoveries, such as Taxol, a drug used in the treatment of cancer which was extracted from the bark of a Pacific yew tree. Laying waste to large stretches of forest means eliminating the possibility of exploiting whatever medical potential lies within.

The Amazon offers the leading case in point. Generating 20 percent of the earth's oxygen and home to between 15 and 20 percent of its life forms, the Amazon covers 2.7 million square miles in nine countries: Brazil, Guyana, Suriname, Venezuela, Colombia, Ecuador, Peru, Paraguay, and Bolivia. It represents 30 percent of the world's tropical rain forest. The Amazon basin today is losing 7,500 square miles of rain forest each year, the equivalent of six soccer fields every minute. At this point, approximately 18 percent of the Amazon has been wiped away. In mid-2007, satellite imagery detected 76,000 separate fires burning within the Amazon basin. Some scientists believe that when roughly 30 to 40 percent of the forest has been cleared, a "tipping point" will be reached and the forest will start to die out on its own, regardless of what human beings decide to do.

The window for saving the Amazon, experts say, is closing fast. While the pace of deforestation has recently slowed, some scientists worry that a sufficient number of trees have already been felled to reduce the forest's capacity to remain green year-round, increasing the risk of devastating fires. A computer model designed by the Hadley Centre in England shows the Amazon beginning to turn into a savanna by 2050, completing the transformation somewhere around 2080. The woodlands of a savanna are often seen as a transitional stage between a forest and a desert. While a computer model is a hypothetical projection rather than empirical proof of anything, it nevertheless offers a warning about possible outcomes.

In the last three decades, most of the cleared land in the Amazon has been turned into grazing pastures for cattle belonging to large-scale ranching operations. More recently, the Brazilian government has increased tax and other incentives in order to stimulate agribusiness enterprises in the Amazon region, especially soybean cultivation.

Deforestation is often a human rights issue as well as a matter of environmental concern. Violent conflicts pitting landowners against peasants, as well as members of Brazil's indigenous groups, are a regular feature of life in the Amazon. Activists say that's not the only case in point. While Brazil officially abolished slavery in 1888, the government acknowledges that at least 25,000 people in the Amazon today work under "conditions analogous to slavery," clearing land and working for cattle ranches, soy farms, and other labor-intensive industries. Some groups say the true figure could be ten times that amount. In 2005, more than 4,000 people working under slave-like conditions were freed after SWAT-style teams from the Brazilian police raided 183 farms.

Catholicism has long been on the front lines of these struggles. The Church even has its own martyr of the Amazon, in the person of Sr. Dorothy Stang, a seventy-three-year-old American missionary who was killed in the rural Amazon town of Esperanza in 2005. Stang had spent thirty-nine years in Brazil, striving to protect the Amazon rain forest and to defend the rights of poor farmers. She was legendary for her perspicacity, sometimes camping out overnight in the offices of local politicians and police officials until they agreed to enforce environmental and land-use laws. Her work made her a target among the ranchers; at one point, a $50,000 bounty was put on her head.

In February 2005, Stang was approached by two gunmen working for a local rancher. They asked if she had a weapon, whereupon she pulled out her Bible from a plastic bag, saying it was the only weapon she carried. As she read from the Beatitudes ("Blessed are the peacemakers, for they shall be called children of God,") one of the men shot her six times. Shortly after Benedict XVI returned to Rome from his trip to Brazil in May of that year, a local rancher was convicted of having ordered the murder, marking the first time one of the architects of such a killing had been held accountable. At the time of Stang's death, according to local reports, more than 800 Brazilians had been killed in the Amazon region, with only nine convictions.

While in Brazil, Pope Benedict XVI came to the Amazon's defense: "The devastation of the environment in the Amazon Basin and the threats against the human dignity of peoples living within that region call for greater commitment in the different areas of activity than society tends to recognize," he said, speaking in a session with Brazilian youth. That built upon comments the pope made in 2006, when he said that the beauty and grandeur of the Amazon basin's rivers and forests "speak of God and his magnificent work for the benefit of humanity" and represent "an open book whose pages reveal the mystery of life."

Protecting the Amazon has become a national crusade for the Catholic Church in Brazil. "The Church is not against development, but it opposes development that deprives populations of their future. We have to nurture respect for nature," said Archbishop Orani João Tempesta of Belem, speaking on behalf of the Brazilian National Bishops' Council in February 2007.

"Soy planting is causing the same devastating effect as did the spread of big commercial ranching in the 1960s and 1980s," said Archbishop Odilo Scherer of São Paulo. He called on the government to strictly control the expansion of farmland, "so that measures are no longer taken after the problem is already there, after the forest is felled and burned."

WHAT IT MEANS

Given that environmentalism is a relatively new arrival on the Catholic scene, it's difficult to project where it might lead. Based on trends in official statements, political interventions, and pastoral practice, both from the hierarchy and from the grassroots, it seems clear that ecological concerns will occupy an increasing pride of place in the Church. The nature of this Catholic engagement over the next century, however, will depend on new scientific findings that are impossible to predict, and also on the extent to which political and social actors are able to prevent some of the more drastic effects of environmental damage. It's also difficult to anticipate whether environmental concerns such as climate change will retain the same political and social momentum they enjoy today, or whether, to some degree, current fears will prove to have been exaggerated. For these reasons, this section should be considered little more than a tentative peek at what might be down the road in the twenty-first century.

Near-Certain Consequences

1. GREEN DESIGN

When parishes, dioceses, and Catholic institutions find themselves facing the need to build or remodel their physical plant in the twenty-first century, there will be a strong tendency to "go green." One example is St. Joan of Arc Parish in Minneapolis, Minnesota, which recently renovated its parish center. The parish formed an "eco-spirituality committee" in 1997, with the stated purpose to "raise awareness and change behavior in all relations with the earth, its creatures and each other." When a decision was made in 2000 to remodel the parish center, this group worked with the parish's space use committee to pursue eco-friendly design. As a result, the new parish center reused or recycled 80 percent of the materials from the old structure. Builders used wood products from sustainable forests, cork flooring from oak tree bark, office chairs made from recycled milk jugs, rubber stairways made from recycled tires, and windowsills made from soybeans, junk mail, and recycled newspapers.

Parish officials say that the resulting center exceeds energy efficiency codes by 50 percent, taking advantage of natural light, energy-efficient windows, and a state-of-the-art heating and cooling system with energy ventilation to capture outgoing heat and a high-efficiency condensing unit and fan, as well as occupancy sensors to automatically turn lights off when they're not in use. The land surrounding the center has been landscaped with expanded green space, native and drought-resistant plants that require less water, vegetation to encourage wildlife, strategic shading to reduce energy consumption, and salvaged trees. While it's probably a bit of a stretch to imagine the Throne of Peter one day being constructed from recycled milk jugs, nevertheless St. Joan of Arc blazed a trail that a growing number of Catholic groups will be walking as the push for ecological sustainability gathers momentum.

For another example, consider St. Gabriel of the Sorrowful Virgin Parish in the north end of Toronto. In 2006, the parish completed a $10.5 million renovation of the church, making it, according to the Passionist fathers who staff the parish, the "greenest church in Canada." St. Gabriel's was the first church in Canada to earn silver certification under the country's Leadership in Energy and Environment Design program, which requires a 40 percent reduction in energy consumption over a standard modern church built to code. Canada has adopted programs to encourage churches to go green, such as offering $1 rebates for every 278 kilowatt hours of energy savings that show up in its energy audit. If a church can scrape together $15,000 to $20,000 to replace their boilers with a new, 80-percent-efficient modern one, estimates are they'll make back the investment in eighteen months.

On one level, all this is smart money management. The architect for the makeover said that St. Gabriel's should make back what it spent in reduced energy bills and other savings. Parishioners at St. Gabriel's insist, however, the primary motive for the project was less fiduciary than theological. The ecological commitment of St. Gabriel's is literally written in its walls. Instead of stained-glass windows inside the church, a heat-saving clear thermal glass window looks out onto a garden—connecting the congregation, its designers say, with a small sliver of God's creation.

"We did this to make a statement that needs to be made today," said Fr. Paul Cusak, the pastor of St. Gabriel's. As a member of the Passionist order, he said the redesign at St. Gabriel's had been especially influenced by Fr. Thomas Berry, who is also a Passionist. "We're in a pivotal moment in our fifteen-billion-year history," Cusak said.

2. COMEBACK FOR NATURAL THEOLOGY

Although many Christian thinkers throughout the centuries argued that truths about God can be inferred from creation, it was Saint Thomas Aquinas who laid the conceptual basis for what came to be known as "natural theology." Alongside the truths of revelation contained in sacred scripture and in the teaching of the Church, Aquinas said, there is a compatible body of truths about God that can be found in the created world. Aquinas supported his argument by appeal to ancient philosophers such as Aristotle, as well as Romans 1:20: "Ever since the creation of the world, his invisible attributes of eternal power and divinity have been able to be understood and perceived in what he has made." The First Vatican Council in 1870 enshrined natural theology as a fixed element of Catholic teaching. In its *Dogmatic Constitution on the Catholic Faith,* Vatican I held that, "God can certainly be known from created things by the natural light of human reason."

In the twentieth century, natural theology to some extent went out of fashion, first among Protestants who felt it glossed over the corrupting effect of sin upon human reason, and later among Catholics who worried that it promoted a "parallel" mode of theological argument that minimized Church teaching and tradition. Among other Catholic theologians, the recovery of scripture and the mood of ecumenical détente spawned by the Second Vatican Council (1962–65) also led them away from natural theology, toward a more biblically oriented approach.

Catholic environmentalism is likely to generate a comeback of natural theology. Among the arguments environmentalists often make is that God reveals himself through creation, and official Church teaching seems to be encouraging such a development.

"Faced with the glory of the Trinity in creation, we must contemplate, sing, and rediscover awe," said Pope John Paul II in his General Audience of January 26, 2000. "Nature becomes a Gospel that speaks to us of God.... This capacity for contemplation and knowledge, this discovery of a transcendent presence in creation, must also lead us to rediscover our fraternity with the earth, to which we have been linked since creation. This very goal was foreshadowed by the Old Testament in the Hebrew Jubilee, when the earth rested and man gathered what the land spontaneously offered. If nature is not violated and humiliated, it returns to being the sister of humanity."

The bishops of the Pacific Northwest made the same argument in their pastoral letter on the Columbia River watershed.

"The watershed, seen through eyes alive with faith, can be a revelation of God's presence, an occasion of grace and blessing," they wrote. "There are many signs of the presence of God in this book of nature, signs that complement the understandings of God revealed in the pages of the Bible, both the Hebrew and Christian Scriptures."

Pope Benedict XVI has explicitly called for a revival of what he termed the "theology of creation," in his remarks to the clergy of Bolzano-Bressanone in August 2008:

"In recent decades the doctrine of Creation had almost disappeared from theology, it was almost imperceptible. We are now aware of the damage that this has caused. The Redeemer is the Creator and if we do

not proclaim God in his full grandeur—as Creator and as Redeemer—
we also diminish the value of the Redemption. . . . If we recognize this it
will obviously follow that the Redemption, being Christian, and simply
Christian faith, also means responsibility always and everywhere with
regard to creation."

Pope Benedict also sees in the modern environmental movement a
promising route for recovery of the natural law tradition, which is an application of natural theology in the moral realm. In July 2007, the pope said
that environmentalism presumes that there are laws written into creation,
and that "obedience to the voice of the earth is more important for our future happiness than the voices of the moment, the desires of the moment."
What today's rising ecological awareness presumes, in other words, is that
there are limits inscribed in nature which humanity trespasses at its own
peril. Without any reference to religion, Benedict seems to believe, the secular world today is arriving at its own version of natural law theory. That realization, Benedict argued, could lead people to become more open to laws
of human nature as well, providing an objective basis for both personal and
social morality. To put the pope's point simplistically, if the world is willing
to limit its carbon output on the basis of the laws of nature, then maybe it
will become more willing to accept limits in other spheres of life as well.

One might call this a distinctively papal shade of green.

3. "BOTH/AND" ECO-THEOLOGY

Part of what makes Catholicism both fascinating, and at times maddeningly inconsistent, is its genetic predisposition to seek "both/and" solutions
to problems. When faced with a choice between seemingly opposed alternatives, the Catholic instinct is generally not to choose one or the other, but to
figure out a way to have its cake and eat it too. The same instinct seems
likely to be at work in the years ahead with regard to debates over environmental theology.

At one level, any move to minimize the unique theological status of humanity is a nonstarter. Given the various ways that the biotech revolution
calls human distinctiveness into question, surveyed in chapter six, defense of
humanity's privileged moral status is likely to be a cherished point for much
Catholic opinion. Evangelical Catholicism likewise cuts against a reevaluation of traditional teaching about the relationship between humanity and
other forms of life. Anything that smacks, for example, of the argument of

Australian ethicist Peter Singer, who treats "speciesism" as a prejudice comparable to racism and classism, will be immediately rejected. The challenge for Catholic environmental theology, therefore, is to find a "both/and solution," meaning a way to present the cosmos as a creature in its own right, with its own moral and spiritual character, without calling into question the privileged status enjoyed by humanity.

In some ways, the situation could be compared to liberation theology in the 1970s and 1980s. Alongside the traditionally personal understanding of redemption that had dominated Catholic theology, liberation theology proposed adding a social dimension. That project generated fears that it would replace pious devotions, charity, personal prayer, and other elements of the spiritual life with political action. The liberation theologians had to demonstrate that it could be both/and, meaning that the Church could foster both a vigorous personal spirituality alongside a serious commitment to social change—indeed, that the two could reinforce one another. Today, environmental theology is walking the same path, proposing yet another new dimension of redemption, this one cosmic, and it too will have to navigate concerns about dislodging previous elements of Church teaching and practice.

4. ENVIRONMENTAL MINISTRY

Various interdenominational and nondenominational groups are already pitching guidelines and resource kits for environmental ministries with titles such as, "Care of the Earth: An Environmental Resource Guide for Church Leaders" and "Greening of the Parish—Making the Congregation a Model for Environmental Justice." The latter offers advice for raising awareness in the parish, including:

- Purchase 100 percent recycled or tree-free stationery, and use it for everything.
- Improve lighting in your office.
- Include plants in your office décor.
- Put bird feeders outside your office window and keep them filled.
- Set up your own recycling center for office paper and trash.
- Whenever possible, hold meetings and appointments out-of-doors.
- Subscribe to at least one journal or newsletter on ecology and sustainable living.
- Ride your bicycle, walk, or take public transportation as often as possible.

- Reduce consumption of inks.
- Reduce your water consumption. (Complete with this tip: "Put a brick or full water bottle in the tank to reduce water use with each flush.")

A better example of "thinking globally and acting locally" than putting a brick in the parish toilet is, indeed, difficult to imagine.

Though it's a bit dated now, Jesuit Fr. Albert Fritsch and Angela Iadavaia-Cox coauthored a similar model for environmental ministry at the parish level from a specifically Catholic perspective in 1992, titled *Eco-Church, An Action Manual.* It includes a detailed process for creating what the authors regard as "an ecologically minded congregation," complete with audits, worship and retreat ideas, recommended lifestyle changes, and ideas for action.

As the trend described in chapter five toward lay ecclesial ministry expands, especially in the more affluent churches of the global North, "environment ministers" responsible both for changing lifestyles within a parish or diocese and for coordinating advocacy efforts could become a normal part of the paid parish staff. In some cases, this function may be merged with existing "peace and justice" or "social advocacy" personnel. In other cases, especially in the global South, these will be roles filled largely by volunteers, most on a part-time basis. But whoever does the work, Catholic pastoral life at all levels in the twenty-first century is likely to see "environmental ministry" more and more as a routine, and expected, element of the Church's ministerial corps.

Probable Consequences

1. FASTING

Chapter two made the argument that the tradition of the Friday abstention from meat, as well as an extended fast prior to the Eucharist, may make a comeback in the twenty-first century under the impress of evangelical Catholicism. The growing ecological consciousness within Catholicism is likely to lend momentum to that development, because it is perhaps the form of simplifying lifestyle and limiting consumption with the deepest roots in Catholic spiritual practice. As pressure grows on Catholics to reexamine their lifestyles from the point of view of sustainability and equity in consumption, fasting and abstention will seem an increasingly attractive form of spiritually motivated self-discipline.

The discipline of abstaining from meat on Fridays may also gain momentum from data which suggest a number of negative environmental outcomes associated with meat production. For example, the UN Food and Agriculture Organization makes the fairly stunning claim that "livestock production is responsible for more climate change gasses than all the motor vehicles in the world." In total, according to FAO, it is responsible for 18 percent of all human-induced greenhouse gas emissions. It is also, they say, a major source of land and water degradation.

The same agency says that a meat-based diet requires seven times more land than a plant-based diet, suggesting that diets based to a greater degree on crops rather than animals would be more sustainable. One of the major causes of deforestation in the Amazon, for example, is the need to clear pasture lands to allow cattle to graze in order to meet the demand for beef in the North. To add one other dimension to the picture, raising livestock for slaughter also adds to the difficulty of growing enough crops to feed the hungry, since those animals have to be fed too, and they are often quite inefficient in their consumption. Cattle, according to a 1995 report of the Canadian government, excrete 40 kilograms of manure for every kilogram of edible beef obtained from them.

For some Catholics, these considerations may lead to a growing trend toward vegetarianism. There's warrant for it in Catholic spirituality; chapters 36 and 39 of the Rule of St. Benedict, for example, stipulate a vegetarian diet. While the practice today varies from community to community, some orders such as the Trappists observe a fairly strict vegetarian diet. (The medieval belief was that eating the meat of red-blooded animals inflames the passions, contrary to the monastic aim of *apathia*, meaning control over one's emotions.) More commonly, however, Catholics whose environmental sensitivity leads them to at least limit consumption will likely see in the Friday abstention the most logical way of doing so. Ironically, evangelical Catholics and eco-Catholics may find themselves cheek-by-jowl in the lunch line on Fridays for fish sticks, once the staple Catholic dish everywhere—though their reasons for doing so, and the spiritual benefit they obtain from it, may be worlds apart.

In the U.S. bishops' document on the environment, *Faithful Stewards,* Monsignor Charles Murphy makes the case for a renewed practice of fasting: "There also should be a certain asceticism to include a rediscovery of the benefits of fasting," Murphy wrote. "Fasting is part of the Gospel. It helps us to focus on the nourishment that can only come from God. It encourages good health and enhances our enjoyment of the good things of life, freeing us from a certain deadness in spirit. A re-emphasis on fasting may not only put us in touch again with a gospel ideal but also increase our ecological awareness as we sparingly use scarce earthly resources. Fasting in the modern world can have a strong social justice meaning."

2. A CONFLUENCE WITH SECULAR POLITICS

The political role of Catholicism in the twenty-first century in the ideologically driven debates of the North is likely to be, as the saying from *Alice in Wonderland* goes, "curiouser and curiouser." The tendency to tighten up on issues of human life and reproduction, as outlined in chapters two and six, will make Catholicism seem ever more "far-right" in some circles of opinion. Yet the growing advocacy in the Church regarding issues such as economic justice, warfare and the arms trade, health care, and the new "biopolitics" of genetic engineering will all simultaneously drive Catholicism into perceived alliances with the political left. The steadily more outspoken stance from many Church leaders, though not all, on environmental questions could be another piece of that puzzle, making Catholicism seem more left-of-center and thereby making it a greater target for conservative critics.

On the other hand, it may be that as the early twenty-first century unfolds, the environment "mutates" into an issue that's less ideologically defined, especially if public attitudes continue to move in a steadily more green direction. To take the United States as a case in point, according to a May 2007 *Washington Post/Time*/ABC/Stanford University poll, 82 percent of Americans believe in global warming, and 94 percent say they're willing to make changes in their lifestyles to make the environment better. In an April 2007 CBS News/*New York Times* poll, 90 percent of Democrats, 80 percent of independents, and 60 percent of Republicans said immediate action is required to stop global warming. Those are eye-popping numbers, and if they hold up, political candidates of all formations are likely to gravitate toward more environment-friendly positions. Before long, the environment could no longer be analogous to abortion or gay marriage, meaning something over which people are divided, and could instead be more like Social Security, a program that enjoys a vast bipartisan consensus.

If so, it wouldn't necessarily be just Catholic activism driving secular politics toward greater environmental awareness, but in a mutually reinforcing way, politics could also end up prodding the Church forward.

If so, budding ecological sensitivity within Catholicism may soon encounter a political climate that encourages its rapid development. It's one thing to work on issues with no meaningful possibility of doing anything about them, but when a strong political wave crests in society, it stimulates inchoate movements within social subgroups to go "mass market." That was the case with Catholic antinuclear activism in the early 1980s, for example, which was energized by the nuclear freeze movement, and which influenced, among other things, the 1983 pastoral letter of the U.S. bishops, *The Challenge of Peace.*

Walt Grazer, a former staffer for the American bishops on environmental issues, said he finds a special zeal for the environment among younger Catholics, and not just among the usual liberal activist suspects. In part, Grazer said, this activism is being driven by the changing political climate. This trend is, if anything, far stronger in Europe, where support for climate change accords such as the Kyoto Protocol already enjoys a more or less universal consensus and has been lifted out of the normal thrust and parry of political debate.

Change in Catholicism never operates in a vacuum. Even in an era when the Church is attempting to reinforce its distinctiveness by "building a fence around the law," as argued in chapter two, it cannot remain isolated from developments in the culture. Catholics will bring into the Church many of the attitudes and values that percolate in other circles of their lives. If environmentalism moves in the direction of becoming akin to "Mom, apple pie, and baseball," this secular tendency will provide a powerful boost to the rising green tide within the Church.

Possible Consequences

1. CRUSADE FOR THE AMAZON?

While the trends outlined in this chapter point to a greater ecological awareness, it's not clear whether the Church will be a follower or a leader, and to what extent it can, or will, mobilize its resources to make a difference. One interesting thought exercise is to ask whether there's a potential Poland out there, a place where the stars could align as they did with the Solidarity movement in the 1980s, galvanizing worldwide Catholic energy and activism—in this case, for the cause of environmental protection.

If so, it's probably the Amazon.

The nine countries in Latin America that share the Amazon all have overwhelming Catholic majorities. There's a sense in which this is historically Catholic land, dotted with churches and shrines and Marian grottoes, home to one of the largest concentrations of Catholic missionaries anywhere on earth. (This is without denying the importance of indigenous traditions, or the growing Pentecostal presence.) Brazil, which forms the front line in the struggle to save the Amazon, is the single largest Catholic country on the planet, with 149 million baptized Catholics, and is destined to remain the largest Catholic country throughout the twenty-first century. One could make the argument that if Roman Catholicism can't make a stand here, there's not much hope anywhere else.

Such a suggestion may seem far-fetched, given that it's a terribly complicated picture. For one thing, while the cattle ranchers, loggers, and *sorjeiros*, or soy growers, may seem like the villains of the piece, it's not as simple as telling them all to take a hike. Were they to disappear, hundreds of thousands of Brazilians would be out of work, deeper in poverty, and more abandoned than ever. The situation doesn't have the binary moral clarity of the struggle against communist dictatorships. For another, to date no charismatic leader has yet arisen to put a "face" on the Amazon within global Catholic opinion.

Yet these difficulties may not be insuperable.

The complexity of the situation is undeniable. The goal has to be to convert the opposition, not just to conquer it, and that's always a far trickier proposition. In the end, however, this may be another enticement for the global Church to get involved. It means the Amazon offers an ideal case to flesh out the oft-stated goal of official Catholic ecology, which is to balance conservation against development, to defend the environment and to defend the poor at the same time.

On the question of leadership, the jury is admittedly out. Would it take the election of a Brazilian pope to catapult the Amazon to the top of the Church's "to-do" list? It certainly wouldn't hurt. Short of that, the scenario sketched here seems to call for a senior Catholic leader to invest him- or herself deeply in the cause, traveling repeatedly to the Amazon, standing toe-to-toe with the giants of politics and industry, crying to Heaven for justice, and adroitly marshaling the forces of the Church on the side of the reformers. At the moment, it's difficult to know who that might be.

On the other hand, maybe a single charismatic personality isn't the only possibility. Perhaps the Amazon could become the incubator for the emergence of "horizontal Catholicism" on a global scale, meaning a lay-driven grassroots mobilization, linking Catholic activists, movements, religious orders, NGOs, and other players into a fluid but powerful policy network. The nature of a globalized economy means everyone is involved in the fate of the Amazon, whether they presently realize it or not. Aside from the obvious fact that decimation of the source of 20 percent of the world's oxygen carries planetary implications, there's also the nature of global commerce. To take just one example, soy cultivation has recently replaced cattle and logging as the largest single factor in deforestation in the Amazon, as thousands of acres are being cleared for use by large multinational agribusiness firms. The largest single player is the U.S.-based Cargill Corporation, which has built its own port in the Brazilian city of Santarém, where workers load soy from the fields of the Amazon onto freighters bound for Europe. Cargill's largest single client in Europe is Kentucky Fried Chicken. As Alex Shoumatoff has noted in an article published in *Vanity Fair,* anyone who has a bucket of chicken in Liverpool or Brussels is, therefore, "eating the Amazon."

To be sure, there are multiple points at which an effort to bring global Catholic resources to bear could come unglued. For one thing, Western Catholic leaders could continue their preoccupation with the struggle against the "secularism" in Europe, consigning the Amazon to a permanent spot on the global Catholic back burner. Or, Brazilian Catholic thinkers might pursue their current fascination with "Indian theology," essentially a repackaged form of liberation theology, this time with indigenous persons as the oppressed class in a Marxist analysis rather than simply "the poor." If so, it would likely mean that much of the energy of Brazilian Catholicism would be consumed in internal doctrinal struggles and in fighting off unwanted attention from Rome.

Given the pace of deforestation, the opportunity for a concerted Catholic effort is rapidly slipping away. Were it to succeed, however, it could have a powerful effect on the Church everywhere, generating much more energetic environmental engagement.

2. A SENSE OF THE SACRED IN WATER DISPUTES

If water truly is the new oil, then working to prevent, or to mediate, conflicts over water supplies will likely be a major peace-making challenge of the twenty-first century. There may be a sense in which the Catholic Church has an advantage over other international actors as a potential broker in some of these conflicts.

For one thing, few of the potential flash points over water shape up as a Catholic country against a non-Catholic state, or even Christian versus non-Christian. In the Middle East, it's likely to be a matter of one Muslim nation contesting the water policies of another, such as Turkey versus Syria and/or Iraq. In Africa, the most acute shortages are likely to hit areas where one Muslim state abuts another, such as Egypt versus Sudan; or where two Christian states are in conflict, such as disputes over the Chobe River between Namibia and Botswana. In Asia, the most likely sources of conflict will involve states with Hindu, Buddhist, and Muslim majorities; Pakistan, Bangladesh, and Nepal are currently involved in water disputes with India. There's also great potential for tension in Central Asia, where Kyrgyzstan and Tajikistan by themselves control 90 percent of the region's water supply.

In such cases, were conflict to erupt, it would not be immediately obvious that the Church would harbor a confessional bias for one side or the other. Such perceptions have sometimes hampered Catholic diplomacy in the past. For example, efforts to bring peace to the Balkans were largely crippled by Serbian suspicions that the Vatican favored the overwhelmingly Catholic Croatians, fears that were not assuaged when the Holy See was among the first to recognize Croatia and Slovenia after they withdrew from the old Yugoslavian federation.

But why would the Church stick its nose into these conflicts in the first place?

The Catholic Church has never asserted a basic human right to petroleum or uranium, so when states deny these resources to their neighbors, it's not necessarily something with an obvious Catholic "angle." Access to water, on the other hand, is considered by the Catholic Church to be a right and a core element of basic human dignity, so the Vatican and other Catholic actors are likely to take a much more direct interest in these conflicts for reasons of both principle and humanitarian concern.

The Vatican might be able to inject an element into water disputes that no other Western actor could hope to accomplish: a sense of the sacred. All the major religious traditions whose followers might be the parties to these conflicts incorporate water in their spiritual rites, and their sacred texts are full of imagery about water. India and Bangladesh have long feuded over the Ganges River, for example, which is regarded as holy water within Hindu tradition. In Islam, purification through ablution is an obligatory component of the prayer ritual. Some strains of Buddhism practice a ritual in which lustral water is blessed by monks and then either consumed or sprinkled on one's head in order to bring blessings. Though one cannot make this statement with anthropological certainty, it's difficult to imagine a religious tradition on earth that doesn't assign some sacred attributes to water. Given that common reverence, the Vatican might be able to foster dialogue among its interfaith partners in water-stressed regions, trying to broker a cross-cultural agreement that the holiness of water should place it off-limits as a motive for conflict, or as an instrument of political brinksmanship.

3. A PONTIFICAL COUNCIL FOR ECOLOGY

As noted in chapter five, the prevailing wind in Catholicism these days is against new bureaucracies in the Church, a bias that is one part financial and one part theological (the latter being that the Church should not mimic the organizational patterns of secular bureaucracies). Yet that mood won't hold out forever, and at some point, the Church may return to its traditional pattern of erecting offices to denote its most important concerns. If so, the twenty-first century might see the creation of a "Pontifical Council for Ecology" in the Vatican, equal in stature to the Pontifical Council for the Laity or the Pontifical Council for Culture.

Aside from the general allergy to bureaucracy, there would probably be another objection to such a move. As noted throughout this chapter, the official Catholic approach to the environment insists upon linking ecology with social justice, and especially with the welfare of the poor. One could argue, therefore, that taking the environment out of the Pontifical Council for Justice and Peace (which is the office that presently tracks environmental issues) would undercut that message, both symbolically and institutionally.

Yet experience suggests that in real life, treating a topic as a subset of some broader theme cannot help but say to the world that you're not really interested in it. When Benedict XVI effectively amalgamated the Pontifical Council for Interreligious Dialogue with the Pontifical Council for Culture in February 2006, most people took it as a signal that interreligious relations were not a top priority for Benedict, his assurances to the contrary notwithstanding. Likewise, when he named a new president for the council in the summer of 2007, many people proclaimed that interreligious dialogue was "back." Symbols matter. If Catholicism does come to see ecology as a concern on a level with ecumenism, interfaith relations, and antipoverty efforts, inevitably pressures will build for that commitment to be reflected in Church structures.

In addition, the creation of a pontifical council for ecology would provide a point of reference for the burgeoning field of environmental ministry in Catholicism. The odds are good that the Vatican will want someone paying attention to all of this. In fact, a pontifical council could be the logical end result of the creation of offices for environmental ministry at other levels of the Church. Done right, the council could serve as a powerful resource for those ministries. Such a council would create a permanent advocate for ecological issues within the "bloodstream" of the Church, signifying to many eco-Catholics that their agenda has arrived.

Long-Shot Consequences

1. ECO-SANCTUARY?

Some eco-activists have argued for recognition of "environmental refugees," meaning people who flee their homes because of climate change. One especially poignant example is Tuvalu, a nation composed of a series of nine low-lying coral atolls in the Pacific, which some believe may vanish because of rising sea levels. With a population of 11,600, Tuvalu is considered the second-smallest state in the world after the Vatican, and many of its residents have already fled to Australia and New Zealand. Tuvalu's people may be the most poignant example to date of the new class of "eco-refugees," but they're hardly alone. In 2004, the Natural Resources and Environment Institute in Cairo pegged the number at several million, a figure that includes people dislodged by deforestation, nuclear and industrial disasters, and natural disasters thought by scientists to be linked to global warming.

Because "environmental refugee" is not a status recognized in international law, these people generally have no right to request asylum or protection, and hence are at risk for being deported or resettled. Environmental activists believe that industrialized nations bear a special moral responsibility to accommodate these eco-refugees, since the environmental conditions from which they're fleeing were disproportionately shaped by policies and lifestyle choices in the global North. On the other hand, advocates for traditional refugees sometimes resist extending the status to such a potentially mammoth pool of people, fearing that it might undercut the legal rights presently afforded to refugees fleeing political persecution.

However the legal and political questions are sorted out, churches in affluent nations, including the Catholic Church, will likely take an interest in these eco-refugees. One possible response is a revival of the Catholic tradition of offering sanctuary, essentially defying authorities to arrest people while they're on church grounds. Such a movement, if it happens, would be more likely to spread in wildcat fashion than in any centrally organized mode.

(To predict growing interest in a new class of eco-refugees is not, by the way, to suggest that the underlying forces believed to be generating these refugees are necessarily well documented. In the case of Tuvalu, for example, there is ongoing scientific debate about whether sea levels are truly rising and whether the atolls are actually in danger. Many activists, however, will take the view that it would be irresponsible to wait for scientific certainty before acting to protect vulnerable populations.)

2. URBAN PARISH FARMS

According to a 2005 UN report called *World Urbanization Prospects*, by mid-century, at least two thirds of the world's population, some six billion people, will be living in cities. Migration toward the cities has been moving at three times the rate of global population growth. Runaway urbanization poses environmental risks on many fronts. For one thing, cities now account for 60 percent of all water allocated for domestic human use, which puts enormous pressure on governments to allocate water away from agriculture, depleting watersheds and worsening soil erosion. In China, farming communities are being cut off from water supplies so that Beijing's domestic, industrial, and tourist demands can be met. Another difficulty is the treatment and disposal of human and industrial waste. Every year the number and concentration of toxins leaching into soils and rivers from improperly buried and managed urban landfills soars. Urban pollutants are another source of concern. Nitrogen, sulfur oxides, ozone, carbon compounds, and other particulates are pumped out by urban areas in ever-increasing amounts. In many cities automobile traffic is the single greatest source of pollution, such as in São Paulo, where over 8,000 tons of pollutants are poured into the air on a daily basis. As cities grow, more land is cleared, contributing to deforestation, ecosystem depletion, and species loss.

While classic forms of environmentalism generally look to local, regional, and national governments to offset these risks, the reality of the developing world is often that governments have little effective control, and some governments are so riddled with corruption and inefficiency that what influence they do have is wasted or misdirected. Most analysts believe that if the environmental and social hazards of urban sprawl are to be addressed, it may not be realistic to expect that response to come from formal structures of governance. Instead, they point to informal networked initiatives at the community level as the best hope of doing something constructive.

One such community-based response is the practice of urban agriculture, utilizing small plots of land, balconies, walls, rooftops, public roadside land, and river banks to grow fruits, vegetables, and other crops. The produce it generates can be used to support a single family or a small community, or it can be sold in urban markets. Urban agriculture not only increases the total food supply, but it also means that the produce reaching urban consumers is often more fresh, promoting general health. In terms of protecting the environment, urban agriculture is often an example of sustainable development in action. Using urban waste as fertilizer, for example, helps to solve sewage disposal problems and reduces the need for potentially toxic chemical inputs. Producing food within the city also reduces the need to clear land in nearby rural areas, protecting forests and promoting biodiversity. One 2002 study in Australia found that for every one acre of land in a city devoted to agriculture, five acres of marginal rural land or rain forest were saved. Further, vegetation inside cities acts to remove carbon from the atmosphere, potentially contributing to reducing the harmful effects of carbon-based emissions.

According to the Food and Agriculture Organization, the major brake on the spread of urban agriculture is land security. Looming over many urban farmers is the constant threat of losing access to their plot and being forced to stop production, because in many cases they don't hold legal title to the land. Pressures for commercial development often end up taking potentially arable land out of agricultural use. In many urban areas, FAO says, the inability to access land in the city is the major reason people give for not farming.

Perhaps this is where the Catholic Church could enter the picture.

The Church is often among the largest private landowners in many urban areas, operating an extensive network of parishes, schools, colleges, hospitals, hospices, social service centers, youth centers, and other facilities. In theory, every one of those buildings represents a roof and a set of walls that could be made available to grow something. In addition, many of these facilities have large grounds. Again in theory, if each Catholic parish, school, and hospital in urban areas were to set aside one tenth of its grounds for urban agriculture, working with the local community to decide how that land could be best used, it could make an enormous difference in both hunger eradication and environmental protection—bringing together the two elements of official Catholic ecology, defending the earth and defending the poor. To take the possibilities one step further, in some urban areas in the global North, the Church has a large number of underutilized buildings such as seminaries and houses for religious orders, built to accommodate populations well in excess of those presently occupying the structures. Some portion of those buildings and grounds could also be converted to low-intensity urban farming.

Will this happen on a broad scale? Maybe. If it does, it probably won't be the result of any edict from Rome. Public mythology to the contrary, neither the Vatican nor the local bishops "own" most of the properties mentioned above, such as schools, hospitals, and colleges. These facilities belong to religious orders, or to independent Catholic associations, and by now many are governed by lay boards of directors. Opening the Church's property to small-scale, sustainable urban farming would have to happen place-by-place.

One way to start, however, might be for the Pope to invite low-income people in the Rome area, perhaps including recent migrants and refugees, to make use of a small plot of land in the Vatican gardens. The Vatican also owns at least 700 buildings in the Rome area, which theoretically could be put to similar use. Giving recent immigrants access to the rooftops of these buildings could also have the side benefit of promoting their social integration, quite literally "opening doors" to them. Such symbolism could have a significant impact.

3. A SPIRITUALITY OF SIMPLICITY

Perhaps the biggest long-shot in the realm of environmental concern would be that large numbers of people in affluent nations will fundamentally change their own lives, especially their patterns of consumption and waste, in order to promote global sustainability. At least at the conceptual level, doing so enjoys strong official Catholic support. In November 2006, for example, Pope Benedict XVI called on modern women and men to "adopt a style of life and consumption compatible with safeguarding creation." To date, however, it's difficult to see much by way of results from these exhortations.

Personal consumption is a classic example of a zone of human affairs into which the long arm of the law generally cannot reach. If the West is to inoculate itself against what critics call "affluenza," meaning the addiction to consumption, what's required is a change of heart, something notoriously difficult to produce by legislative fiat. Religious leaders arguably have a decisive role to play, since they can appeal to conscience and accountability before God, rather than simply to pragmatism. Catholicism is the largest single religious denomination in the affluent West and the Church may need to shoulder the largest share of this load.

To date, the Church's response has largely taken the form of moral argument. In the future, pressure may grow for something more imaginative by way of personal example. Consider the impact, for example, if every bishop and priest in the world were to announce that he's walking or cycling to work, eating fewer processed foods and less meat, recycling whatever he can, checking books out of the library rather than buying them new, and limiting his annual consumer spending. The ripple effect of such simple gestures throughout the Catholic world could arguably be enormous.

In doing so, however, the Church faces a couple of question marks.

First, it's not immediately obvious that lowered consumption in affluent nations would actually benefit the world's poor. Developing nations seek greater access to Western markets precisely because those markets are so immense. According to the Worldwatch Institute, the United States accounts for 30 percent of global consumer spending, despite having just 4.6 percent of the population. Those numbers are facts, but how one interprets them is a different matter. Is it a tremendous inequity? Or does it mean that the United States is potentially the leading engine for economic growth in the developing world, if it allows products from developing countries to stand a better chance of satisfying its voracious demand? There's a broad consensus among antipoverty experts in favor of growing developing economies, thereby creating employment and lifting people out of poverty. If so, the best strategy may not always be to persuade the West to spend less, for spending less would close doors to opportunity more effectively than any tariff or subsidy. The trick is moving toward a responsible form of voluntary simplicity, ensuring that resulting shifts in trade and investment don't make things worse in the name of making them better.

Second, it's important to ensure that "voluntary simplicity" doesn't become a kind of grim, moralizing abstemiousness, which in some ways is the opposite of "simplicity of heart." As Chesterton put it in his book *Heretics,* "There's more simplicity in the man who eats caviar on impulse than in the man who eats Grape-Nuts on principle." The goods of the earth are meant to be enjoyed, and Christian life is supposed to be about a rhythm between the feast and the fast. In fostering a lifestyle of simplicity, Catholicism needs to take care that it is also promoting an ethic of joy. Otherwise its variant of the "simplicity movement" won't last, and probably wouldn't deserve to.

MULTIPOLARISM

Growing up in Taiwan in the early 1980s, Te-Sheng Cheng would sit in a darkened bedroom and listen to *American Top 40* with Casey Kasem on his AM radio, straining to understand the English commentary in between the week's top pop songs. English was obligatory in Taiwan's public schools, and this was one way to practice. Cheng and his wife, who is also Taiwanese, eventually ended up in Rothschild, Wisconsin, a small community of 4,900, where they own and operate the Kobe Teppanyaki Steak House. When they arrived, it was suggested to Cheng that he might want to take a nickname, so in Wisconsin he became "Tommy" Cheng.

One understands the instinct. As of the 2002 census there were 120 Asian Americans in Rothschild, so Chinese names don't exactly roll off most tongues—though that appears set to change. Beginning in 2007–2008, the county school system decided to drop French and to offer Mandarin Chinese as one of its core foreign languages. Cheng now plans to get out of the restaurant business and to teach Chinese to Wisconsin kids in kindergarten through the twelfth grade instead.

"It's exciting that this small farming town will accept foreign culture," Cheng told a reporter in May 2007. "As immigrants, we want to do what we can do to help."

Rothschild's interest in Chinese is hardly an isolated case. In 2007 alone, school districts in Detroit; Fort Worth; Tulsa; New Haven; Carmel, California;

and Lancaster, Pennsylvania, all added courses in Mandarin Chinese. Fort Worth is also adding Hindi, the dominant language in India. Most of these districts dropped existing romance languages, usually French. Today, there are roughly 50,000 students in American schools studying Mandarin. While that doesn't hold a candle to the 200 million Chinese students studying English (it's a required course), it's a significant jump from the 5,000 who were taking Chinese just seven years ago, according to the American Council for the Teaching of Foreign Languages.

Over and over, school officials offer variations on the same theme in explaining the switch.

"I think educators have come to the realization that Americans need to engage with China for diplomatic reasons and certainly economic reasons," said Jessica Stowell, director of the Oklahoma Institute for Teaching East Asia at the University of Oklahoma-Tulsa. "Twenty-two percent of the world's population speaks Mandarin Chinese as a first language. When we understand the language, we can understand the culture. And when we can understand culture, we have a level playing field."

It's not just the United States that's catching on.

In Peru, which has an active Chinese immigrant community and a growing economy driven in part by Pacific Rim trade, business people are leaping at the chance to study Chinese. Lima's Catholic University plans to offer a course for business executives costing $2,200 a year, a hefty sum by local standards. The course will deal not only with Chinese grammar and vocabulary, but also with the trappings of Chinese culture and history, from Confucian philosophy to the importance of tea. The University of Buenos Aires in Argentina started a Chinese-language department in 2004. Bogota's National University in Colombia offers classes in Chinese on Saturdays for business executives, in addition to its normal classes for undergraduates.

This Mandarin surge is a clear sign of the times. It reflects a transformation in the drama of global power relationships, with a series of former bit players or character actors stepping into starring roles. The show is mutating from a monologue dominated by the United States into something more like the movie *Syriana,* with multiple actors and several complicated storylines unfolding at once.

WHAT'S HAPPENING

"Multipolarism" refers to a political, military, economic, and strategic arrangement in which it's not just one great power that shapes history (as in the Roman or British empires), nor tension between two such powers (as in the Cold War), but the interaction of multiple points of influence. The most frequently cited candidates to become the new poles of this multipolar system are Brazil, Russia, India, and China, famously dubbed the BRIC nations in 2003 by the investment firm Goldman Sachs. The firm's analysis predicted that by 2040, the combined economies of the BRIC countries would be greater than those of the United States and Europe together, a forecast that still holds despite the global economic meltdown that began in 2008. By mid-century, these four nations should also represent almost 40 percent of the world's population.

Before going too far down this road, however, it's worth doing a reality check.

Economic guru Nicholas Vardy observes that the early twentieth century had its own list of "BRIC nations," meaning four emerging states seemingly destined to replace Great Britain as global superpowers: Argentina, Russia, Austria-Hungary, and the United States. These were the fastest growing economies in the world, and they seemed headed for steady expansion. Vardy says people bought up Russian railroad stock in the early twentieth century for the same reason they're buying Chinese Internet stocks today—because they felt the market simply *had* to get bigger. In the end, only the United States and Russia emerged as global titans, and, as things turned out, even Russia's claim to superpower status rang a bit hollow.

In the same way, it's far from clear that all the BRIC nations are destined to be the dynamos of the twenty-first century, or that other candidates might not pop up to take their place: the EU, Japan, Mexico, Turkey, South Africa, and Nigeria are all sometimes rumored for the part, to say nothing of the Iranian-led "Shi'a crescent" stretching from the Mediterranean to Central Asia. (Some wags have coined an acronym for these overlooked options, CEMENT, for "Countries in Emerging Markets Excluded by New Terminology.")

While the BRIC nations have done spectacularly well in the last decade and a half, they remain economic midgets compared to the United States. The U.S. economy grows by the equivalent of the entire Indian economy roughly once every eighteen months. Only one in fifty Indian households has a credit card, and only one family in six has a refrigerator. Likewise,

China's raw GDP of $11 trillion looks great until it's divided across its vast population. On that basis, China ranks as one of the poorest nations on the planet; it doesn't even crack the top 100 in terms of per-capita income. In terms of military might, the United States is so far ahead of the rest of the world that it makes comparisons seem almost silly.

One should therefore be careful about forecasts of a "Chinese century" or a "resurgent Russia." If China's economy overheats and slides into recession, it could turn inward for a decade or more, withdrawing from broad global questions. India could become embroiled in a bloody war with Pakistan. Russia's oil-based economy may implode as the world shifts to alternative energy sources, slinking back into being, in that famous Cold War aphorism, "Upper Volta with nukes." In any conceivable scenario for the twenty-first century, barring an asteroid strike wiping away half of North America, the United States will remain the richest and most influential actor on the global stage.

The key point to make, however, is that multipolarity is not like pregnancy: the world *can* be just a little bit multipolar. It's not a question of whether the twenty-first century will or won't see the rise of a multipolar system, but how much and how fast. Present trajectories tell us that, however the actual distribution of power shakes out, non-Western nations such as India and China seem poised to wield more of it.

What does this mean for the Catholic Church? One way to begin thinking about it is this: For the first time since Christianity became the state religion of the Roman Empire in 380, Catholicism seems destined to find itself in a world not clearly dominated by a state, or a group of states, shaped by the Christian tradition. Of course, the Church has seen great non-Christian powers come and go, from the Sassanids to the Ming dynasty, from the Mongols to the Ottomans. Those empires, however, were largely external to the mental world Catholicism inhabited. In the twenty-first century the mental world of the Catholic Church is fully global, and it's a globe in which non-Christian cultures will exercise a growing share of influence.

This section offers a brief overview of the economic, political, and ecclesiastical situation in the four BRIC nations: Brazil, Russia, India, and China. The point is not necessarily to predict that these nations will be the great new powers of the twenty-first century, though they are all important actors. Rather, laying out the basic interests and tensions that characterize each country, both from a secular and a Catholic point of view, will at least suggest something of the complexity and diversity awaiting the Church in an increasingly multipolar world.

China

1. THE ECONOMY

Given its vast human capital and natural resources, China was always destined to be an economic titan. The surprise is not that it's becoming one in the twenty-first century, but that it took this long to happen. In the 1980s, Deng Xiaoping unleashed China's potential with his program of "socialism with Chinese characteristics," which in practice means free markets without democracy. Deng was fond of a folk proverb from his home province of Sichuan: "Black cat, white cat, all that matters is that it catches mice." In other words, ideology is less important than results.

Deng's reforms—export-oriented markets, privatization, deregulation of financial markets, currency adjustments, allowing direct foreign investment, shrinking subsidies, lowering protectionist tariffs, and introducing more flexible labor laws—are generally held up as exhibit A in the case for globalization. In 1990, the World Bank reported that 375 million people in China were living on less than $1 a day. By 2001, that number had fallen to 212 million, and if current trends hold, by 2015 it will be 16 million. China now has a middle class of more than 200 million people, 80 million of whom are quite well off. It's conventional wisdom that more people have been lifted out of poverty in China over the last quarter-century than at any other point in human history in a similar span of time.

China's economy grew at an average annual rate of 9.4 percent over the last twenty-five years, and in 2008 it had a GDP of 4.4 trillion, making it the third-largest economy in the world after the United States and the Euro zone. Foreign companies have poured more than $600 billion into China since 1978, according to Robyn Meredith in her 2007 book *The Elephant and the Dragon,* far eclipsing what the United States spent rebuilding postwar Europe in the Marshall Plan. China exported more in a single day in 2007 than it did in all of 1978. China still faces enormous challenges, such as environmental degradation, political unrest, and corruption, but to date none of that has been sufficient to derail the Chinese locomotive.

2. POLITICS AND FOREIGN POLICY

Westerners have long taken it on faith that countries can't have free markets without free societies. A primary argument for admitting China to the World Trade Organization in 2001 was that economic liberalization would inexorably produce a more open society. Critics, however, say that this theory is contradicted by facts. Two decades after the Tiananmen uprising in 1989, strict one-party control of the country's political life has been firmly reasserted. The NGO Reporters without Borders, for example, considers China to be one of the least free countries in the world for the press. Meanwhile, the economy chugs merrily along, maintaining 9 percent growth in 2008 despite the global crisis.

This combination of political centralization and economic liberalization has led some observers to talk about a "Beijing consensus," in contrast with America's global evangelization on behalf of democracy. Some analysts believe the rise of quasi-authoritarian leftist regimes in Venezuela and Bolivia, or Iran's near-theocracy, draw strength from this "Beijing consensus." Whether China will be able to sustain its authoritarian politics over the long haul remains to be seen, but in the early part of the twenty-first century, China's rise to power casts doubt upon the inevitable march of democracy and human rights across the globe.

China's principal regional aspiration seems to be to make the China Sea and the Taiwan Strait its own Caribbean, excluding others from military influence and economic advantage. Some Chinese maps already claim most of the China Sea, which is the primary route for oil supplies to reach East Asian nations, as part of China's territorial waters. That ambition has fueled a tough line toward Taiwan and the semiautonomous territory of Hong Kong, as well as skepticism about American efforts to exert influence over North Korea.

Outside Asia, China is aggressively developing relations with Russia, Western Europe, Africa, and Latin America, relying on its economic might to expand its political influence. The total value of trade between China and Latin America, for example, rose from just over $10 billion in 2000 to $50 billion in 2006. Chinese companies are investing in farmland and energy installations in Brazil, and Beijing has signed a free-trade agreement with Chile and has announced investments in gas and oil fields in Ecuador, Argentina, and Bolivia. China has also cemented a $5 billion oil deal with President Hugo Chávez of Venezuela, who is seeking to diversify exports to other countries beyond the United States. Chinese diplomats often argue that their foreign policy is less ideologically driven and more respectful of a nation's autonomy than that of the United States, since China does not impose political demands as a condition of trade, such as human rights reforms. Critics, however, say that China's willingness to do business with pretty much anybody is, in effect, a choice to support even corrupt or authoritarian regimes.

There's a growing and influential Chinese diaspora of roughly 31 million in Pacific Rim nations such as Thailand, Indonesia, Malaysia, Vietnam, and Singapore, which reinforces the Chinese interest in regional affairs. In the early twentieth century, Thailand's King Rama VI called these Chinese minorities the "Jews of the East," because they were disproportionately represented in the business class and sometimes were the object of hostility. If China continues to flex its regional muscles, these communities could feel new backlash. The Chinese in diaspora are disproportionately Christian, leading Philip Jenkins to imagine an ironic future in which officially atheistic China comes to be seen as the great protector of Christianity in Asia.

3. THE CATHOLIC CHURCH IN CHINA

If there were any lingering question about whether there's a spiritual boom in China today, it now has a two-word answer: Yu Dan. A forty-two-year-old female talk show host and pop culture icon, Yu Dan is the author of *Notes on Reading the Analects*—a sort of Confucian *Chicken Soup for the Soul*—which sold somewhere between 3 and 4 million copies in 2007, making it one of the biggest best-sellers in China since Mao's *Little Red Book*. Dan's success illustrates that China has become, according to writer Zha Jianying, the "largest soul market" in the world. With a population of 1.3 billion, China is trying to fill an ideological void left by the collapse of Communism as anything more than a system of political control, and by the dislocations of astonishing but uneven levels of economic growth.

Post-modern Confucianism is not the only spiritual option riding this wave. In northwestern China, an estimated 20 to 30 million Muslims are also in the grip of a revival. According to a 2006 report in the *Asia Times,* new Muslim schools are opening with a strong accent on Islamic orthodoxy, while young Chinese Muslims are studying across the Middle East and bringing new missionary energies home. China's post–Deng Xiaoping economic opening has expanded opportunities for Muslim nations, especially Saudi Arabia, to fund Islamic enterprises. The *Boston Globe* found in the same year that a growing number of Chinese Muslim women are wearing veils, and attendance at local mosques is mushrooming.

Perhaps the most remarkable burst of religious energy is in China's burgeoning Pentecostal Christian population. At the time of the Communist takeover in 1949, there were roughly 900,000 Protestants in the country. Today, the Center for the Study of Global Christianity, which issues the much-consulted *World Christian Database,* says there are 111 million Christians in

China, roughly 90 percent Protestant and most Pentecostal. That would make China the third-largest Christian country on earth, following only the United States and Brazil. The Center projects that by 2050, there will be 218 million Christians in China, 16 percent of the population, enough to make China the world's second-largest Christian nation. According to the Center, there are 10,000 conversions every day.

Religious data is notoriously imprecise in this officially atheistic state, and not everyone accepts these eye-popping estimates. In the 2006 update of his book *Jesus in Beijing,* former *Time* Beijing bureau chief David Aikman puts the number of Protestants at 70 million. Richard Madsen, a former Maryknoll missionary and author of *China's Catholics,* puts the number still lower, at 40 million. That's in line with the *CIA World Factbook.* Even those conservative estimates, however, would mean that Protestantism in China experienced roughly 4,300 percent growth over the last half-century, most of it since the Cultural Revolution in the late 1960s and 1970s. Notably, Protestantism took off after the expulsion of foreign missionaries, so virtually all of this expansion has been home-grown.

Curiously, this booming "soul market" seems largely to have bypassed the Catholic Church. In 1949, there were 3.3 million Catholics, while the most common estimate today is 12 million. Between 1949 and 2005, China's population increased by a factor of four, which means that Catholic growth has done little more than keep pace. A half-century ago, Chinese Protestantism was three and a half times smaller than Catholicism; today, it is at least three and a half times larger.

Given the harsh persecution of Chinese Catholics, the fact that the faith survived at all is in some ways a miracle. The heroism of Chinese clergy and laity is without a doubt one of the most inspirational chapters in church history, and their trials continue. When Pope Benedict XVI published a letter to Catholics in China in 2007, the government-controlled Patriotic Association, the regulatory body for Church affairs, banned its publication and some priests who had distributed it were arrested. Those moves came despite the letter's conciliatory tone toward the government, and despite the fact that its primary effect inside China was to encourage many underground bishops, priests, and laity to cooperate with the above-ground church recognized by the government. In addition, in early 2009 several bishops recognized by the government were forced to attend "political sessions" sponsored by the Communist Party, and at least three underground bishops had vanished in police custody.

Yet Catholicism is hardly alone in facing such persecution. Protestants, Buddhists, Taoists, Muslims, the Falungong, and others have similar stories of martyrdom to tell. One Protestant pastor told Aikman, "Chinese prison is my seminary. Police handcuffs and the electric nightstick are our equipment. That is God's special training for the Gospel."

Despite similar experiences, Catholicism has not experienced the same recent surge. China-watchers generally offer four explanations as to why not.

Lack of Ecclesial Infrastructure

According to a 2005 analysis by Maryknoll Sr. Betty Ann Maheu, there are 6,000 Catholic churches in China but 3,000 priests, which would mean that roughly half the Catholic churches in the country lack a resident priest. Overall, the priest-to-Catholic ratio in China is one to 4,000, better than Latin America (one to 7,000) or the Caribbean (more than one to 8,300) but considerably worse than in Europe (one to 1,100) or the United States (one to 1,300). Maheu said the shortage is likely to deepen. There was a vocations boom in the early 1980s, she said, but today numbers are dropping, as expanding economic opportunities make recruitment and retention more difficult. Madsen said that even in Shanghai, normally held up as the most dynamic urban Catholic community in the country, most seminarians come from rural Catholic villages whose populations are in decline.

China has 110 dioceses and 114 active bishops, which in theory means that most dioceses should have a bishop. At least a dozen bishops, however, are in jail, under house arrest, or subjected to severe surveillance. Because of doubts over the legitimacy of bishops who have registered with the government, their leadership is often contested. Given chronic tensions between China and the Vatican, dioceses sometimes remain vacant for extended periods. Some of the youngest bishops in the world today are in China, many appointed in their early thirties, in part out of fear that the opportunity to name another one might not roll around again soon.

Sociological Profile

Historically, Catholicism in China was almost entirely a rural phenomenon. Madsen says that despite runaway urbanization, 70 to 75 percent of Catholics are probably still concentrated in largely homogenous Catholic villages, especially in Hebei and Shanxi provinces in the northeastern area around Beijing. Even the urban footprint of Catholicism, he said, is largely composed of villagers who have relocated to the city, and experience suggests it's sometimes difficult for them to maintain the faith in this new environment.

The tenacity of these Catholic villagers is the stuff of legend. *China's Catholics* tells the story of a village in Shanxi Province where a family-planning team arrived in 1985 to try to distribute contraception in accord with the state's "one-child" policy. Villagers surrounded their car, and when the team retreated to their living quarters, the villagers hurled rocks through the windows. Eventually the team had to be rescued by the police, and they fled the area.

Yet the rural character of the Church also means that it is handicapped in terms of missionary expansion, since preserving Catholic communities is often a higher priority than making new converts. Catholics are under-represented in urban areas, which are creating the most vibrant "growth markets" for new spiritual movements.

The insularity of some rural communities, Madsen says, also means that many reforms triggered by the Second Vatican Council (1962–65) never really arrived. Even in cosmopolitan Shanghai, the first Chinese-language Mass wasn't celebrated until 1989. (Ironically, this is one point upon which Chinese Communists and Catholic traditionalists agree. Both prefer Mass in Latin, in the case of the Communists because it means that most people won't understand it.)

Internal Division

The Chinese church remains lacerated over the question of cooperation with the Communist regime. Some Catholics accept state oversight, even if most of them do so not out of enthusiasm for the Communist project of a "self-governed, self-funded, self-propagated" church, but because it seems the best survival strategy. Other Catholics reject this option out of unwavering loyalty to the pope, frequently regarding these "open church" Catholics as compromised. In their most extreme form, the divisions can turn violent. In 1992, an "open" priest in Henan was murdered by a disgruntled seminarian who claimed he had been denied ordination because of his ties to the unofficial church. The priest died at Mass after drinking from what was literally a poisoned chalice.

Recent years have seen significant efforts to heal this breach. Conventional estimates are that as many as 90 percent of bishops ordained without the authority of the pope now have asked for, and received, Vatican recognition. Yet the bitterness is hardly a museum piece.

Pope Benedict XVI released a "Letter to Chinese Catholics" in May 2007, which called for unity and pledged that Catholicism is not an enemy of the state, but also insisted that the Church cannot accept interference in its internal life. Benedict revoked faculties given in 1978 for "underground" bishops to appoint successors and to ordain priests without contact with Rome. Fierce debates broke out over how to interpret the letter. One testy exchange was between Belgian missionary Fr. Jeroom Heyndrickx, a frequent Vatican advisor on China, and Cardinal Joseph Zen of Hong Kong, an outspoken critic of the Communist regime. In early July, Heyndrickx published a commentary on the pope's letter, suggesting it meant that unregistered bishops should come out into the open. Zen published a tough response, charging that Heyndrickx has lost the "vast consensus and positive regard" he had once enjoyed among Chinese Catholics by becoming unacceptably close to the government-controlled Catholic Patriotic Association.

Missionary Strategy

Much Catholic conversation about evangelization in China is usually phrased in the subjunctive: "If China were to open up on religious freedom . . ." or "If the Holy See and China were to establish diplomatic relations . . ." The implicit assumption is that structural change is required before Catholicism can move into an expansion phase. Pentecostal talk about mission, on the other hand, is phrased in the simple present. Most Pentecostals would welcome being arrested less frequently, but they are not waiting for legal or political reform before carrying out aggressive evangelization programs.

The most audacious even dream of carrying the gospel beyond the borders of China, along the old "silk road" into the Muslim world, in a campaign known as "Back to Jerusalem." As Aikman explains in *Jesus in Beijing,* some Chinese Evangelicals and Pentecostals believe that the movement of the gospel for the last 2,000 years has been westward: from Jerusalem to Antioch, from Antioch to Europe, from Europe to America, and from America to China. Now, they believe, it's their turn to complete the loop by carrying the gospel to Muslim lands, eventually arriving in Jerusalem. Most experts regard that prospect as deeply improbable; Madsen said he doubts more than a handful of Protestants in China take the "Back to Jerusalem" vision seriously. Aikman is more sanguine, reporting that as of 2005 two underground Protestant seminaries in China were training believers for work in Islamic nations. In any event, it's revealing as an indication of missionary ferment.

One exception to this general Catholic hesitancy has been Bishop Jin Luxian of Shanghai, in his early nineties and in failing health as of this writing. He's long been a controversial figure because of his willingness to cooperate with the government, but he enjoys the respect of many senior Catholic leaders internationally. The subject of a flattering profile in a 2007 issue of the *Atlantic*, Luxian does not mince words about his missionary aspirations.

"The old church appealed to three million Catholics," he said. "I want to appeal to a hundred million Catholics."

India

1. THE ECONOMY

India was dominated by a Soviet-style planned economy for most of its post-colonial history since 1947. Beginning in the early 1990s, however, the country embarked on a course of reform, and as of 2007 it was experiencing a 9 percent annual rate of economic growth. India is now a world leader in information and communications technology, light engineering, biotechnology, and pharmaceuticals. It's also the Microsoft of outsourcing, controlling 85 percent of market share in an industry growing 40 percent every year. India has become self-sufficient in food, a remarkable accomplishment for a country with the world's largest population and a history of chronic hunger. One way of putting the point is this: A generation ago, American mothers told their children to finish their vegetables because there were starving kids in India. Today they're more likely to tell their kids to finish their homework, because smart kids in India will take their spots in college.

There are, to be sure, multiple points at which things could still go into tilt. Infrastructure in India is dreadful. Roads are perennially congested, and many rural villages, where 60 percent of the population lives, are cut off from the rest of the country. Airports and seaports are overtaxed. The power grid reaches only about 50 percent of the country, and there's a growing threat of water shortages. Most basically, India's economic miracle has left an enormous share of its people behind. An estimated 300 million live in extreme poverty, meaning less than $1 a day. India also faces potential instability from a Muslim minority of roughly 150 million people, making it the third-largest Muslim nation on earth. The permanent underclass of "untouchables," or Dalits, is estimated at somewhere between 150 million and 250 million people, and they are still subject to appalling discrimination and violence.

2. POLITICS AND FOREIGN POLICY

Indians generally look upon their economic success as an augury of rising political importance. Writing in *Foreign Affairs* in 2006, noted Indian journalist C. Raja Mohan described his country as "the first large, economically powerful, culturally vibrant, multiethnic, multireligious democracy outside the West," predicting that India "will play a key role in the great political struggles of the next decade."

The first aim of Indian foreign policy is to establish the Indian Ocean region as the country's zone of influence. Indian leaders have moved, albeit unevenly, to improve relations with Pakistan, apparently realizing that a war would harm the economy and drain resources away from broader foreign policy goals. India's second aim, according to analysts, is to counter China. To that end, India seems to be pursuing a double-edged policy of constructive engagement and competition. Indian–Chinese trade has risen from less than $200 million in the early 1990s to $20 billion in 2005, and by 2015 China will have surpassed both the EU and the United States as India's largest trading partner. At the same time, India has campaigned to be admitted to the UN Security Council, not content to allow China to be the de facto spokesperson for Asia.

Indian–U.S. ties hit a low point in 1998 when India successfully tested a nuclear weapon, leading to talk of a regional arms race. Just ten years later, many analysts rate India as one of former president George W. Bush's few foreign policy breakthroughs, finding common ground on Islamic radicalism and growing Chinese power. India backed the U.S.-led invasion of Afghanistan and nearly sent troops to Iraq. It echoed American opposition to both the International Criminal Court and the Kyoto Protocol, and India voted with the United States in the International Atomic Energy Agency in favor of sanctions against Iran's nuclear program. According to the most recent Global Values Survey, the percentage of Indians with a positive view of the United States went from 51 percent in 2002 to 71 percent in 2005. In return, Washington has embraced a doctrine of "Indian exceptionalism," basically meaning that it dropped objections to India's nuclear weapons. In 2005, the United States and India signed a nuclear pact, formally declaring the 1998 dispute resolved.

Yet India's tradition in foreign policy is to be nonaligned, and there are signs of hedging its bets. For example, India has strengthened ties with Russia. Its largest single foreign investment is a $1 billion stake in the Sakhalin 1 oil and gas development project in Siberia. In 2006, India received Russia's then-president Vladimir Putin as a guest of honor on Republic Day, January 26, considered the highest compliment that the country can bestow upon a visiting dignitary.

3. THE CATHOLIC CHURCH IN INDIA

Though Catholics represent only 1.6 percent of the population, India is so big that this works out to a sizeable Catholic community of 17.6 million. The Church is divided into three rites: Syro-Malabar, Syro-Malankara, and the Latin Rite. The Syro-Malabar rite has an estimated four million adherents, the Syro-Malankara about 500,000, and the rest belong to the Latin Rite. Local tradition credits the apostle Thomas with the introduction of Christianity, and believers who trace their ancestry to him are known as "Thomas Christians." Missionary efforts in the south, centered on Kerala and Goa, followed the Portuguese conquest of Goa in 1510.

In many ways, Indian Catholicism is thriving. The Church is growing at a rate ahead of overall population growth, and by 2050 there could be almost 30 million Catholics. Outside its traditional base in the south, Catholicism is also expanding in the northeast. In the state of Arunachal Pradesh on the eastern border with China, where Catholicism arrived barely twenty-five years ago, there are today 180,000 Catholics out of a total population of 800,000. Catholicism enjoys wide respect for its network of schools, hospitals, and social service centers. When Mother Teresa died in 1997, the Indian government afforded her a state funeral, only the second private citizen after Mohandas K. Gandhi (known as Mahatma) to receive the honor. Her casket was borne by the same military carriage that had carried Gandhi's remains in 1948.

Yet as the twenty-first century dawns, Indian Catholicism also faces three major headaches.

First, India has acquired a reputation for some of the most adventurous theology in Catholicism today, especially in "religious pluralism." Thinkers such as Michael Amaladoss, Felix Wilfred, Raimon Panikkar, Aloysius Pieris, and Jacques Dupuis, all of whom are either Indian or influenced by India, have been controversial because of the various ways in which they try to give positive theological value to non-Christian religions. That's a logical development given India's religious diversity, but it has raised alarms in quarters of the Church identified with evangelical Catholicism. Catholic leaders will want to encourage theological exploration that can open up dialogue, but without transgressing doctrinal limits.

Second, a noteworthy point about Catholic demography in India is the disproportionate share of Dalits, or untouchables. Estimates are that somewhere between 60 and 75 percent of Indian Catholics are Dalits, who often see Christianity as a means of protesting the caste system and of affiliating with a social network to buffer its effects. Beginning in the 1970s, the Catholic Church took up the Dalit cause in Indian society, yet the Church itself has a mixed record. Archbishop Marampudi Joji of Hyderabad, the first Dalit archbishop, said in a 2005 interview that "discrimination against Dalits has no official sanction in the Church, but it is very much practiced." Joji told a story about a meeting between Catholic leaders and the former prime minister Indira Gandhi in the 1970s. When the bishops complained about the treatment of Dalits, according to Joji, Gandhi shot back: "First do justice to the Dalits within your Church, and then come back to me and make your representation on their behalf. I shall do my best for you then." Yet as of 2000, just six of the 156 Catholic bishops in India were Dalits, and out of 12,500 Catholic priests, only about 600 were Dalits. Sensitivity to caste distinctions in the Church still runs strong. When Joji was appointed to an archdiocese where Dalits are not a majority, outgoing Archbishop Samineni Arulappa of Hyderabad complained, "Rome is being taken for a ride. Rome does not know the ground realities."

Third is the rise of aggressive Hindu nationalism. Radical Hindu movements often claim that Christians engage in duplicitous missionary practices in an effort to "Christianize" India. Though by most accounts the Hindu nationalists represent a tiny fraction of the population, they have the capacity to create tremendous grief. Organized radical groups today sometimes move into Christian villages, preaching a gospel of *Hindutva*, or Hindu nationalism, and urge people to take part in "reconversion" ceremonies. These groups also routinely stage counter-festivals during Christmas celebrations. Fear of a Christian takeover is pervasive; in 2001, when Italian-born Sonia Gandhi ran in national elections, one national newspaper carried the headline, SONIA—VULNERABLE TO VATICAN BLACKMAIL! Sometimes these tensions turn violent. In 2006, for example, Archbishop Bernard Moras of Bangalore and two priests were attacked by a mob in Jalahalli, ten miles south of Bangalore. The three clerics had gone to inspect the damage after St. Thomas Church and St. Claret School in Jalahalli had been sacked by Hindu nationalists. Members of Catholic religious orders are also exposed. In April 1995, nationalists cracked the skulls of two nuns in a convent on the outskirts of New Delhi; another mob broke into a residence of the Franciscan Sisters of Mary Angels and beat the five sisters, along with their maid, using iron rods.

Russia

1. THE ECONOMY

Not long ago, the twilight of Russia was taken for granted. The failure of post-1991 shock therapy had left the economy a shambles, with roughly the same output as the state of Texas. The only business sector experiencing growth was organized crime. When asked about economic opportunities in Russia in 2005, one of Warren Buffett's top financial advisors testily responded, "We don't invest in plutocracies." As outlined in chapter four, Russia's abysmally low fertility rate means it could shed as much as a quarter of its population between now and 2050, dropping from 146 million to 110 million—a drop that would threaten further disruption as the country struggles to fund pensions and health care for a rapidly aging population.

Yet despite all this, Russia is once again taking a seat at the great power table. Why? In large measure, because Russia sits atop one third of the world's gas supplies. To be sure, the global economic crisis that began in late 2008 has hit Russia especially hard. In the summer of 2008, when oil was trading at more than $140 a barrel, Russia seemed awash in new wealth; one year later, when prices had dropped to roughly $40 a barrel, much of that new affluence had been wiped out. Unemployment stood at around 7.5 percent, industrial output was contracting, and per-capita earnings were in freefall. Some of the impact of the crisis, however, was buffered by the fact that under former president and current prime minister Vladimir Putin, Russia managed to squirrel away $60 billion of oil profits into a rainy-day fund. Moreover, despite wide fluctuations in the global price of oil, Russia's vast deposits mean that it will be a major player in global economic affairs for the foreseeable future.

2. POLITICS AND FOREIGN POLICY

Russia is sometimes viewed as an autocracy, largely because of the strong presidential system developed under Putin, known as "managed democracy." One sign of managed democracy in action came in 2008, when Putin, barred from another term as president, propelled his protégé Dmitry Medvedev into the presidency while retaining a hold on power by becoming prime minister. Yet for precisely this reason, Russia is arguably the most politically stable of the BRIC countries. Putin centralized control by changing the system of tax collections, ensuring that revenues flow to the central government rather than to the regions. Moreover, Putin has also virtually guaranteed that a strong-hand mode of rule will continue by stacking the upper echelons of the Russian government with current or former members of the country's intelligence community. According to a December 2006 study by Russia's Academy of Sciences, officials with an intelligence background now hold 80 percent of senior government posts.

On the global stage, Russia's policy elites feel trapped in a strategic vise between a rising China on one side, and NATO, the European Union, and the United States on the other. In effect, Russia is caught between the Old West and the New East. In a February 2008 essay, foreign policy analyst Robert Kagan observed that the basic difference between Europe and Russia today is that for Europe, the nightmare to be avoided remains the aggressive nationalism of the 1930s; for Russia, it's the national collapse of the 1990s. Thus for Europe, the key foreign policy aim is overcoming the nation-state and military power; for Russia, it's restoring them. Kagan described this as a collision between twenty-first- and nineteenth-century views of the world.

Over time, Russia will likely become more willing to assert key perceived long-term interests: maintaining preeminence in the Caspian Sea area and Central Asia, since these are the main transit points for its oil and gas exports; opposition to U.S.-led plans for a global nuclear defense system, which could render irrelevant the only strategic advantage Russia inherited from the Soviet era; and opposition to further EU expansion in the East. If Ukraine were to be seriously considered for membership, many experts regard that as a red-line issue that could provoke a major crisis. On the other hand, EU–Russian trade more than tripled between 1999 and 2005, and Russia is now the European Union's third-largest trading partner after the United States and China. According to the Oxford Institute of Energy Studies, the European Union is now dependent upon Russia for as much as 60 percent of its energy supplies. This provides Moscow with a powerful incentive to maintain European stability. Russia and the United States also share strategic interests in combating Islamic radicalism and in countering China's rising influence.

As the twenty-first century unfolds, what one can likely expect to see in terms of Russia's relationship with the rest of the world is an alternating cycle of chills and thaws.

3. THE CATHOLIC CHURCH IN RUSSIA

Getting a fix on how many Russian Catholics there are is tricky, since counts are subject to manipulation on all sides. The official Vatican tally says

809,000. Local Catholic leaders say that projections based on the size of traditionally Catholic ethnic groups (mostly Poles, Lithuanians, and Germans) indicate there should be around 1.5 million Catholics. Whatever the number, levels of practice may not be terribly high. When a team of Catholics in 2002 called up all 270 priests in Russia to ask how many people usually come to Sunday Mass, the total was 200,000. If there are 1.5 million Catholics, this means 13 percent of them go to Mass.

Sociologist of religion Nikolai Mitrokhin, who directs the Institute of the Study of Religion in the CIS and Baltic Countries, believes the real number of faithful Catholics in Russia may be substantially lower.

"If you want to talk about really practicing Catholics, meaning going to church at least once a week, it could be as low as twenty thousand or thirty thousand," Mitrokhin said in a 2004 interview in Moscow. "You couldn't find a single Catholic parish in Russia that draws more than five hundred people on a regular basis."

One issue above all towers over the present and future of Russian Catholicism: relations with the Russian Orthodox Church. For a variety of historical and theological reasons, the Vatican's ecumenical policy assigns priority to the Orthodox, and in Russia this means the local Catholic Church's prime directive is to build bridges with its Orthodox neighbors. Some Russian Catholics believe their church is in danger of being sacrificed on the altar of ecumenical progress.

For one thing, Catholicism in Russia is under virtually a no-growth policy. Under Vatican instructions, if a Russian shows up at a Catholic parish and asks to join, the first response is supposed to be: "Why don't you go back to the Orthodox Church?" In any other country, a small Catholic community would trumpet conversions and baptisms; here, Catholic officials do everything possible to play them down. There is no overt evangelization, and church leaders are hesitant to engage in public policy questions for fear of usurping Orthodox prerogatives. Even pastoral activity such as feeding the poor, teaching languages, and running orphanages can be problematic. The result is that, despite centuries of tradition on Russian soil, the Catholic Church is all but invisible to most Russians.

Compounding Catholic frustration is the dramatic growth of Pentecostals, Baptists, and Jehovah's Witnesses, who expanded at a clip of 20 to 25 percent a year during the 1990s. Today, Mitrokhin believes there are at least one million practicing Protestants in Russia, and he calls their growth "the most important religious trend" in the country. Despite that,

Catholicism in Russia for the near future seems likely to continue to move in the shadows, meeting the pastoral needs of its small flock but playing a subaltern role to the Orthodox in national cultural and spiritual debates.

Brazil

1. THE ECONOMY

"Brazil is the country of the future," Charles de Gaulle once said, "and always will be." Until the mid-1990s, that was the international diagnosis: Brazil had great potential, along with a tragic aptitude for never realizing it. Certainly the potential is obvious. Physically, Brazil is enormous; one could fit Texas twelve times into its landmass. It also has the second largest population in the Western hemisphere after the United States, with 190 million people. With the Amazon basin, Brazil is wealthy in natural resources. Yet for a variety of reasons—including sharp swings from left to right in domestic politics, corruption, and basic failures in poverty relief, health care, and education—Brazil never seemed to get its act together. The old pattern was a brief growth spurt, followed by backsliding into recession and political crisis.

Until the mid-1990s, there was little reason to think the twenty-first century would be much different. From 1986 to 1996, Brazil's annual rate of inflation ran around 180 percent. Yet beginning in the mid-1990s, Brazil turned a corner. It tamed inflation (in 2008, despite the impact of the global economic crisis, inflation was just 4.4 percent) and slashed its external debt, and the country now runs both a trade and a fiscal surplus. Brazil's economy grew by 5.1 percent in 2008, according to the *CIA World Factbook,* giving Brazil the eighth-largest economy in the world. From an investment point of view, Brazil enjoys several advantages. It's a robust democracy with no serious territorial disputes, and it's the only BRIC country without a nuclear bomb. On virtually all major indices of freedom and transparency, Brazil scores better than its BRIC counterparts. One of the reasons Brazil has a lower rate of GDP growth than China, India, and Russia is that it was wealthier and more urbanized to begin with.

None of this is to suggest that Brazil has entered a golden age. According to the United Nations Human Development Report, Brazil has one of the widest gaps between rich and poor in the world. Those disparities generate alcohol and drug addiction, crime, corruption, and violence. The northeastern city of Recife has a murder rate twice that of the most violent cities in the United States. Despite that, most analysts believe that Brazil is set for a decade or more of sustained growth, moving past traditional European powers such as Italy and France in terms of GDP.

2. POLITICS AND FOREIGN POLICY

Brazil has the most idealistic foreign policy of the BRIC nations, seeing itself as the leader of the developing world. Particularly under charismatic President Luiz Inácio Lula da Silva, it's strongly pro-UN and pro-multilateral. In no other BRIC nation are trading interests so clearly subservient to political goals. Instead of focusing on the United States and the EU, Brazil has instead invested heavily in "South–South trade," meaning exchange with Africa, Asia, and the Middle East, as well as with other Latin America nations. Over the last twenty years, Brazil's share of the U.S. market has actually dropped from 2.2 percent to 1.4 percent.

Brazil has organized summits for Latin American and Arab leaders, trying to promote greater integration in terms of both trade and political concerns. U.S. representatives were excluded. Brazil has also been a driving force in assembling the G20, a bloc of developing nations organized to make sure the voices of the developing world were heard by the G8. Brazil's Southern emphasis has irritated even some of its own diplomats. In 2007, Roberto Abdenur, former Brazilian ambassador to the United States, complained that Brazilian foreign policy is excessively "anticapitalistic, antiglobalization, anti-American."

Brazil has pushed for a permanent seat on the United Nations Security Council, which Brazilian leaders argue is an extension of the country's "developing world" foreign policy. It's not obvious to some other developing countries, however, why the voice of the developing world should belong to Brazil. Argentina has opposed Brazil's candidacy, seeing it as a means of extending Brazilian dominance in the region.

3. THE CATHOLIC CHURCH IN BRAZIL

Brazil is the largest Catholic country on earth, at least in baptismal totals. According to the Vatican, Catholics are 85 percent of the population, which would translate into 153 million people. The national census, however, indicates that only 67 percent of Brazilians identify themselves as Catholic, which would mean a total of 122 million, a gap of 31 million people—equivalent to the entire Catholic population of both India and China.

In the period following the Second Vatican Council (1962–65), Brazil was one of the most creative and controversial forces in world Catholicism, forming the laboratory in which liberation theology took shape. Many of that movement's great thinkers, such as Leonardo Boff and Frei Betto, and its most stalwart episcopal defenders, such as bishops Hélder Câmara and Pedro Casaldáliga, as well as cardinals Paulo Arns and Leo Lorscheider, are Brazilians. More recently, Brazil has been a pioneer in environmental activism, as well as in protection of indigenous cultures. Another distinguishing feature of Brazilian Catholicism are the "ecclesial base communities," meaning small groups of Catholics who meet for Bible study and faith formation, as well as various forms of social and political advocacy. Brazilian Catholic leaders say there are somewhere between 60,000 to 80,000 such communities.

Like the rest of Latin America, Brazil has seen remarkable growth among Protestant groups, usually Pentecostals. Today 15.4 percent of Brazilians identify themselves as "Protestant," with at least two thirds being Pentecostal. One response has been the growth of the Catholic charismatic movement. A 2006 study by the Pew Forum on Religion and Public Life found that 57 percent of Brazilian Catholics call themselves "charismatic," the second-highest percentage in Latin America after Guatemala.

Despite the fact that Pentecostalism tends to get the headlines, one expert on Brazil's religious situation says the more important, albeit less discussed, phenomenon is the striking rise in the percentage of Brazilians with no religious faith at all. Fr. José Oscar Beozzo, who directs the Center for Evangelizing Services and Popular Education in São Paulo, said in 2007 that between 1980 and 2000, the percentage of the Brazilian population that identifies itself as Protestant, with most of that number being Pentecostal, rose from 12 to 17 percent. Over the same period, Beozzo said, the percentage who say they have no religious affiliation went from 0.7 percent to 7.3 percent, a tenfold increase.

"This is the infinitely more important movement in the Brazilian religious situation," Beozzo said.

Beozzo attributes this trend to the intersection of two factors. First is Brazil's economic development over the last thirty years, which has created new affluence at the top of the economic ladder but left millions of people behind. Second is rapid urbanization, creating new urban peripheries where the traditional social networks of family, community, and church have broken down.

A shortage of priests in Brazil has created holes in the Church's network of pastoral care. While the priest-to-person ratio in the United States is 1 to

1,229, in Brazil it's 1 to 8,604. Though there are upticks in vocations in some countries, there's no foreseeable future in which there will be a sufficient number of priests to staff all the parishes in Brazil, to say nothing of comforting the sick, teaching the young, and conducting the other ministries of the church. For many Brazilian Catholic leaders, the answer is obvious: lay empowerment. Given, however, that liberation theology also promoted lay empowerment in a way that critics saw as forming a kind of "Church from below" in opposition to the hierarchy, some remain wary.

Beozzo said Brazilian Catholicism's future is nevertheless as an increasingly lay-led Church. "That's not by choice," he said. "It's simply the Church we've got."

WHAT IT MEANS

Population and economic output alone mean that these four countries will be important players in the twenty-first century, whether they live up to their full potential or not. How Catholicism responds to their emergence, including whether the Church takes advantage of the new possibilities a multipolar world creates, will be fascinating to watch.

Near-Certain Consequences

1. BOON FOR INTERRELIGIOUS DIALOGUE

By 2050, world population is projected to be 9 billion, with India and China accounting for one third of that total by themselves. China and India will have two of the world's four largest economies, both are nuclear states, and both have strong regional ambitions. The most salient fact for Catholicism is that both are overwhelmingly non-Christian. Given that both China and India are emerging as major world powers, Catholicism will feel the need to expand its understanding of their religious traditions. While the rise of Islam means the Church's chief interreligious priority in the immediate future will be Catholic–Muslim relations, over the long term, Catholic–Hindu, Catholic–Buddhist, and Catholic–Taoist dialogue may become equally important. Catholicism will try to produce more priests and theologians who speak the languages of these cultures, who have studied their sacred texts and practices, and who know how they think. Theologians such as American Jesuit Fr. Francis X. Clooney will command steadily larger audiences.

While teaching in Kathmandu, Clooney developed a fascination with Hinduism, and he ended up earning a doctorate in Hindu studies at the University of Chicago.

As important as such experts are, Church leaders will also want to ensure that dialogue does not become the province of experts who are not always representative of the mainstream of their own traditions. Leaders will strive to promote interreligious studies across the spectrum of Catholic opinion.

In part, this trend is likely to mean that pioneers in Catholic dialogue with Asia, such as Matteo Ricci in seventeenth-century China and Robert de Nobili in sixteenth-century India (both Jesuits), will become the focus of new rounds of academic study. Like Ricci, de Nobili tried to blend the Christian gospel with deep respect for Hindu traditions, adopting the lifestyle of a Hindu *sanyasi,* following a vegetarian diet, learning and writing in Sanskrit and Tamil, and engaging Hindu scholars in philosophical and religious dialogues. Catholic institutions will create new "Matteo Ricci chairs" and "Robert de Nobili fellowships."

For a variety of reasons, Hinduism may become a special magnet for Catholic attention. While the bulk of Hindus are Indian, there are also substantial Hindu communities in Nepal, Bangladesh, Sri Lanka, Pakistan, Indonesia, Malaysia, Mauritius, Fiji, Suriname, Guyana, and Trinidad and Tobago, usually associated with an Indian diaspora in those nations. As Indian migrants move around the world, Hinduism is becoming a steadily more global religion. Because Hindu nationalism is an important force in Indian politics, one can expect the Indian government to draw upon its growing resources and prestige to foster a Hindu revival as an expression of Indian national identity. If Hindu nationalism were to become further radicalized, the Bush policy of quietly approving India's admission to the nuclear club could look like a significant miscalculation. Catholic leaders will want to try to engage Hindu leaders, promoting moderate voices.

Some Asian Catholic leaders believe they have something to teach the rest of the Church about how to manage interreligious relationships.

"The West may not always have felt it was imperative, but for us it's a question of survival," said Cardinal Oswald Gracias of Mumbai, India, in a 2006 interview. "The West has got to start learning from Asia about how to deal with a multicultural, multireligious situation. We've been involved in this dialogue for a long time, and we've learned from some of our mistakes. You can't be insular, and at the same time you can't compromise on principles. The key question is, how do we live together for everyone's good?"

2. BOON FOR ECUMENISM

Ecumenism should draw strength from the rise of the BRIC nations, in different ways depending upon local context. In China and India, the fact of being a tiny minority promotes a feeling of kinship among Christians, especially because the majority tradition in both nations often fails to distinguish among Christians based upon denominational allegiances. To the typical Indian Hindu, for example, a Christian is a Christian. The surrounding culture is not only non-Christian, but at times it can actually be anti-Christian. In China, pressure comes from the government, which scrutinizes Protestant Christianity just as it does Catholicism. In India, the threat comes from Hindu nationalist media, movements, and politicians, as well as discriminatory application of "anti-conversion" laws. In both cases, Christians often feel an "ecumenism of the gulag."

Russia may produce ecumenical momentum of another sort. In general, trends do not augur well for Catholic–Orthodox dialogue: evangelical Catholicism is dubious about ecumenism generally, and its key figures are often frustrated with what they see as Orthodox intransigence and double standards. Pentecostalism, not Orthodoxy, will be the primary Christian "other" for much of the Catholic Church of the twenty-first century; and the demographic implosion of Eastern Europe means the Orthodox population will shrink and age rapidly. In that context, Catholicism will be tempted to reallocate time and resources away from its relationship with Orthodoxy. Only two forces seem to cut in the opposite direction. One is perennial—the ecclesiological conviction that because the break with Orthodoxy is the primordial schism, ecumenism should start here. The other is political: in a world in which Russia is steadily more important because of its oil and gas reserves, and in which its foreign policy is in flux, the Catholic Church will see its ties to the Russian Orthodox as its best opportunity to understand what's happening in Russia, and in some measure, to influence it.

Brazil will push forward the Catholic interest in Pentecostalism, given that it's the largest Catholic country on earth and one of the places where the erosion to the Pentecostals has been most dramatic. The sometimes antagonistic stance of some Pentecostals will also elicit a more feisty response on the Catholic side, emphasizing apologetics and missionary work. But Pentecostals also are likely to be among Catholicism's natural allies in Brazil's version of the culture wars, and that will promote a warming of relations.

3. A CHURCH OF THE POOR

The issues that frame the Catholic agenda in any era are often those that the culture presents. Benedict XVI has battled a "dictatorship of relativism" in part because he believes that's the dominant cultural reality in the West. In a Church that takes its cues to a greater degree from the BRIC countries, however, relativism is unlikely to loom as large. Levels of religious faith and practice remain high in India and Brazil, and there's a growing spiritual interest in China. According to the Pew Global Attitudes Project, 77 percent of Brazilians and 92 percent of Indians say that religion is a "very important" force in their lives. There are also stirrings of a revival in Russian Orthodoxy, despite Russia's dwindling overall population numbers.

The dominant issue likely to be lifted by the rise of the BRIC countries is not relativism, but poverty and social exclusion. All told, the number of people in extreme poverty in China and India is over 500 million, according to the World Bank, more than one and one-half times the size of the present population of the United States. In Brazil, some 35 million people are below the $1/day threshold, according to the same World Bank figures, and the country has one of the widest gaps between rich and poor on the planet. An estimated 35 million Russians live in poverty—"estimated" because the Russian government in 2005 stopped collecting statistical data on poverty. As the BRIC nations emerge as global powers, their capacity to manage social unrest related to poverty and exclusion at home will take on increasingly planetary implications.

In both India and China, the Catholic community itself tends to be disproportionately poor. In India, a substantial majority of Catholics belong to the "untouchable" Dalit class. In China, Catholics are concentrated in rural areas often left behind by the affluence of China's gleaming new cities. Despite representing tiny statistical fractions of the total population in India and China, the combined Catholic population of those two nations in 2050, even assuming no net gains due to conversions, would be 42 million—roughly the size of the Catholic population of France today.

4. NATURAL LAW AND HUMAN RIGHTS

Chapter six argued that the biotech revolution will promote a revival of the natural law tradition in Catholicism, because Catholic activists will seek to avoid the impression that their interventions are based on nothing more than sectarian positions. Chapter eight predicted a boon for natural theology from ecological consciousness, which revives interest in seeing the universe as the "Book of Creation." Global multipolarity will provide the third leg of the stool, because arguments about sexual ethics, religious freedom, or social justice that are rooted in specifically Christian concepts or categories will fall on deaf ears in a world increasingly led by non-Christian powers.

In practice, this implies that alongside biblical language about the human person as "created in the image of God," or the example of Jesus' outreach to the poor and the sick, the Catholicism of the future will also increasingly draw upon the vocabulary of human rights. Despite criticism from some quarters that talk of "human rights" is a Western way of putting things, it seems the best hope for fostering cross-cultural consensus about moral issues and the requirements of justice. In order for the concept of human rights to have teeth, the rights have to be rooted in a common human nature that makes them universal, inalienable, and eternal. It's reasonable to anticipate that human rights and natural law will not only be the subject of a rising number of Catholic dissertations and seminars, but will also occupy the place of honor in much interreligious and ecumenical conversation.

Probable Consequences

1. REEVALUATION OF TEACHING ON DEMOCRACY

In principle, Catholicism is neutral among the various forms of government. The Church has made its way under empires, monarchies (both absolute and constitutional), feudal systems, and totalitarian regimes. No system of government is good or bad in itself, or so the traditional Catholic theory runs; it's a question of whether the instruments of power are exercised for the common good. Think of this as the Catholic equivalent of Deng Xiaoping's dictum about it not making any difference what color cat it is, as long as it catches mice.

Since the launch of Catholic social theory in its modern form in 1890, however, the Church has moved steadily closer to asserting that democracy not only is consistent with the common good but is the best way to organize social life. That seems to be the position of the *Compendium of the Social Doctrine of the Church* in paragraph 395: "The subject of political authority is the people considered in its entirety as those who have sovereignty," that section reads. "Although this right is operative in every state and in every kind of political regime, a democratic form of government, due to its procedures for verification, allows and guarantees its fullest application."

That assertion probably seemed unremarkable to the consulters who edited it, most of whom live in Europe and the United States. One wonders, however, what a Catholic living in China might have made of it, or for that matter one of the handful of Catholics living in Putin's Russia, with its "managed democracy." In those cultures, putting the Catholic Church on the side of democratic government could sound dangerously like allying the Church with the ideological positions of the West.

The rise of nondemocratic regimes, or at least limited democracies, to global superpower status may once again make democracy a matter of ideological division, as it was during the Cold War. Given its special interest in China, Catholicism will be careful to avoid the impression that there is something inherent in Catholic faith incompatible with the "Beijing consensus." In their hearts, most Church officials may hope that true democracy arrives in China, but as a formal matter Catholicism will be careful not to be seen as an advocate of exporting democracy.

Pope Benedict XVI moved in this direction in his 2007 letter to Chinese Catholics, quoting the Second Vatican Council to the effect that the Church "is not identified with any political community, nor is she tied to any political system." That language at Vatican II was crafted against the backdrop of the Cold War. (The first session of the council opened on October 11, 1962; the Cuban Missile Crisis began just three days later, on October 14.) In that context, the bishops didn't want to appear to be taking sides in the great ideological struggle of the day, and a similar logic may influence the Church's social teaching in the twenty-first century.

2. MISSIONARY PUSH IN CHINA

Both John Paul II and Benedict XVI have expressed hopes for a "great harvest" of faith in Asia. Above all, those hopes are pegged on China, given the obvious spiritual revival described above. Catholicism will feel pressure to concentrate its missionary resources in China, lest it be left behind in the scramble for new adherents. Gains made by Pentecostal Christianity in China from the period of the Cultural Revolution forward lend urgency to this sensation. The Pentecostals are not the only competitors. Aside from Islam, Richard Madsen foresees a rise of repackaged Buddhist and Taoist movements with what he calls a "Confucian overlay." Such movements are today flowering in Taiwan, he says, and have nascent parallels in mainland China.

How things shake out religiously in China may be of tremendous strategic importance, even for people who don't feel any particular spiritual stake in the result. If Christianity ends up at around 20 percent of the population, for example, China could become an exponentially larger version of South Korea (where Christians are between 25 and 50 percent of the population, depending upon which count one accepts)—a more democratic, rule-oriented, basically pro-Western society. On the other hand, if dynamic Muslim movements create an Islamic enclave in the western half of the country, with financial and ideological ties to fundamentalist Wahhabi forms of Islam in Saudi Arabia, at least that part of China could become a wealthier and more influential Afghanistan. If growing religious pluralism in China becomes fractious, it could result in a well-armed and wealthy superpower being destabilized by internal conflict, posing risks to global peace and security. Imagine a much larger version of the Christian–Muslim conflict in Nigeria.

Catholicism could potentially offer a positive ingredient in China's new spiritual stew. The Church could realize significant numbers of new members. Perhaps just as importantly, Madsen believes, a dynamic and growing Catholicism could be an important force in building a healthy civil society in China. For that to happen, the four liabilities outlined above would somehow have to be addressed. At present, it's difficult to envision. Sr. Betty Ann Maheu, the Maryknoll sister cited above, said in 2005, "Short of a series of miracles, the journey of Catholicism in China will continue to be uphill in the foreseeable and even distant future."

One key to Pentecostalism's expansion, however, is that Pentecostals live in constant expectation of just such a series of miracles. Perhaps rather than waiting for the "one step forward, two steps back" ballet between Rome and Beijing to reach conclusion, Chinese Catholics will steal a page from the Pentecostal playbook and embrace a vision of "the future is now." At the very least, it would be fascinating to watch them try.

3. PRESSURE FOR INCULTURATION

In their own ways, each of the BRIC nations will propel the question of cultural adaptation onto twenty-first-century Catholicism's radar screen. In both India and China, the quest for an authentically inculturated faith is a natural result of the fact that Christianity arrived in Asia as a Western import, but in order to flower, it has to respond to the yearnings and expectations of cultures shaped by non-Western religious traditions. That implies a delicate theological balance between preserving the essentials of the faith, while expressing them in new ways.

One example came in October 2005, when a conference of priests and bishops at the Pune Papal Seminary in India recommended a sweeping program of "Indianization" of the Church, including performing the Hindu ritual of *aarti* (a ritual that involves lighting candles and singing) during Mass, studying Sanskrit and the Vedas, experiencing ashram life, and participating in a *satsang* (a form of meditation and spiritual study under the guidance of a master). In part, these practices were justified as a response to criticism that Christianity is hostile to Hindu traditions: "It would definitely put a check on the so-called fundamentalists who keep blaming us for conversions," said Fr. Lionell Mascarenhas.

Cardinal Gracias of Mumbai said that the rise of India and China inevitably will lend new urgency to this sort of effort to express the faith in new ways.

"The Holy Spirit guides us in a particular direction at a particular time, and today we're being led towards inculturation," he said. "In Asian societies, religion is seen as a necessary part of the culture. I believe the West has got to learn to respond to the signs of the times. Change and adaptation is necessary, and maybe the churches of the South, especially in Asia, can offer an example. Today, we try to be open to the Spirit with self-confidence, believing that inculturation is not going to take the church to the ruins."

In Brazil, there is no great religious "other" against whose traditions the question of inculturation might be measured. One of the deepest currents in modern Brazilian politics and social activism, however, is concern for the country's indigenous populations, concentrated in and around the Amazon basin. There are roughly 750,000 indigenous persons in Brazil, divided into more than 400 ethnic groups that speak more than 180 languages. They're all that remains of a population estimated to have been 10 million at the time the Portuguese arrived. At that time, ethnographers believe there were more than 2,000 ethnic groups in Brazil.

For many Brazilian Catholics, preserving the traditions and cultures of these indigenous persons is a moral obligation. A high percentage of these indigenous are Catholic, and many today are exploring ways that their ancestral religious traditions can be integrated into contemporary Catholic faith and practice. They're supported in that project by a broad swath of opinion among Brazilian theologians, clergy, and the hierarchy.

With regard to Russia, the question of inculturation takes on a more ecumenical hue. By common consensus, the main obstacle to unity between

Orthodox and Catholics is the papacy, specifically how much autonomy the Orthodox would have to surrender were they to place themselves under the jurisdiction of the pope. In its own way, this too is a matter of inculturation: can Catholicism make room for semiautonomous local churches, which follow their own liturgical and doctrinal customs and largely regulate their own inner life, and yet are in substantive communion with the pope and the universal Catholic Church? Catholicism has already accommodated twenty-one Eastern-rite churches, which enjoy a significant degree of autonomy—though to what extent that's respected in practice is a matter of debate. Perceptions of the importance of Russia, and therefore the desirability of moving toward greater ecumenical ties with the Russian Orthodox, will also drive Catholicism to consider new ways in which local traditions can find space within the one Church.

Possible Consequences

1. LOCAL SELECTION OF BISHOPS

Though it's impossible to predict when or if the Vatican and Beijing will establish formal diplomatic relations, a key element of any deal would likely be a role for the Chinese government in vetting the appointment of bishops. Such an arrangement is already in place in Vietnam, where the custom is for the Vatican to submit three names and for the government to pick one. When the controversial Bishop Michael Fu Tieshan of Beijing died in April 2007, Cardinal Jean Baptiste Pham Minh of Ho Chi Minh City proposed a "Vietnam model" for the selection of a successor. The bishops of China, Pham suggested, should forward a set of candidates to the Vatican, which would put together a set of acceptable options and submit it to the Chinese government. The government would make its selection, and then the pope would formally appoint the bishop. (The eventual selection of Joseph Li Shan more or less corresponded to this procedure, though without a formal act of appointment by Benedict XVI.)

If the Vatican grants such a concession to China, it might inadvertently promote a broader reexamination of how bishops are selected in the Catholic Church, which is already the object of wide theological and political debate. As late as the middle 1800s, direct papal appointment of diocesan bishops outside central Italy was rare. Beginning with the fall of the Papal States in 1870, however, the power to appoint bishops was progressively centralized in the papacy. In the second half of the twentieth century, arguments arose from some quarters that this way of doing business doesn't take sufficient account of the needs of the local church.

In the late 1990s, for example, retired Archbishop John Quinn of San Francisco wrote a book titled *The Reform of the Papacy*, in which he claimed that "testimony from all over the world points to a widespread dissatisfaction with the present procedure for the appointment of bishops." Quinn argued that the lack of effective participation from laity, clergy, and even other bishops neglects the teaching of Vatican II about the local church. It also results, he said, in the selection of bishops solely on the basis of doctrinal orthodoxy.

One can imagine the following argument taking shape if the Vatican were to strike such a bargain with China: If the Chinese Communists, who are officially committed to a dogma of atheism, can be allowed a say in who becomes a bishop on their soil, why can't the faithful Catholics of the local Church be afforded the same privilege?

Given the momentum of the Catholic identity impulse, it's difficult to see any movement in that direction soon, but the twenty-first century is young. Some Catholics may argue that China and Vietnam represent peculiar local situations with limited importance for the rest of the Church. That contention, however, is at least arguably undercut by the fact that the Catholic population of those two countries in 2050 should be around 25 million, which will be roughly equivalent to the projected Catholic population for England and Wales, Australia, and Canada (excluding Quebec) put together—in other words, a sizeable chunk of the Catholic pie.

2. MULTIPOLAR DIPLOMACY

Multipolarism will force the Vatican to rethink the "Great Power" theory and to forge a more bric-a-brac diplomatic style. One likely scenario would be for the Holy See to look to the developing world, especially Brazil, to be its natural partner on social justice questions; to the United States on religious freedom, anti-Christian persecution, and human rights; and to Muslim states as its best allies in the culture wars. As outlined in chapter three, such a partnership with Muslim states took shape in the mid-1990s at UN conferences in Cairo and Beijing in opposition to a press for international recognition of rights to abortion and contraception.

On matters such as justice in trading relationships, arms control, environmental protection, and multilateralism, Brazil and the Vatican are often closer to one another than either is to the United States. As the century unfolds, it seems plausible that the Vatican will naturally be drawn into Brazil's orbit on these issues and in turn will look for opportunities to promote Brazilian leaders and interests. One way of doing that, for example, would be to support Brazil's candidacy to become a permanent member of the UN Security Council.

This scenario does not necessarily imply coarsening relations between Rome and Washington. In a multipolar world it might actually become easier for the Vatican to overtly back American initiatives and to support American policies. At present, Vatican diplomats are often reluctant to do so too openly, for fear of becoming indentified with the "lone superpower" and thus alienating other states. If the United States no longer exercises global leadership all by itself, then partnerships between the Catholic Church and American embassies in various parts of the world, or joint diplomatic initiatives, would arguably become less problematic.

In this light, Benedict XVI's "Brazil policy" in the first four years of his papacy begins to look less like the former doctrinal czar healing old wounds, and more like a forward-looking player thinking a couple of moves ahead on the chessboard. In October 2006, Benedict called Cardinal Claudio Hummes, the popular Franciscan archbishop of São Paulo, to Rome as the prefect of the Congregation for the Clergy. There hadn't been a Brazilian in a senior Vatican job since Cardinal Lucas Moreira Neves died in 2000. By putting Hummes at his side, Benedict signaled that Brazil matters. The same logic may have been at work, at least in part, in the pope's decision to choose Brazil as the site of the 2007 meeting of the General Conference of the Bishops of Latin America and the Caribbean, and to canonize a Brazilian while he was there.

To finish the job, Benedict will need to appoint more Brazilian cardinals. As of this writing, Brazil had just eight cardinals, and only four of them were under the age of eighty and hence eligible to vote for the next pope. By way of contrast, the United States had seventeen cardinals, and thirteen were still "electors." In Catholicism, red hats matter, and the pope will probably want to fit more of them on some Brazilian heads. In similar fashion, if Catholics in Brazil who care about justice, peace, and inclusion want to see their country and their Church become better partners, they might be well advised to steer clear of avant-garde theological and political movements that would inevitably drive a wedge between Brazil and Rome.

3. THE FABC CENTURY?

Catholicism has three great regional groupings of bishops in the global South: the Episcopal Conference of Latin America and the Caribbean (CELAM), the Symposium of Episcopal Conferences of Africa and Madagascar (SECAM), and the Federation of Asian Bishops' Conferences (FABC). CELAM is the only one that predates the Second Vatican Council, having been founded in Rio de Janeiro in 1955. SECAM was launched in Kampala, Uganda, in 1969, and the FABC emerged from a meeting of the Asian bishops in Manila in 1970.

For most of the second half of the twentieth century, CELAM was the body that by and large provided the voice of the global South in the Catholic Church. The twenty-first century arguably ought to belong to SECAM, given the explosive growth of Catholicism in Africa. To date, however, the more interesting, and controversial, movements seem to be stirring in the FABC. Given that the most important new poles of a multipolar world will be Asian, it's possible that the baton may pass to the Asian bishops.

The countries of the FABC encompass just over 110 million Catholics, which means that all of Asia has fewer Catholics (at least in terms of baptismal counts) than Brazil. Even this picture is a bit distorted; if one takes the Philippines, with 68 million Catholics, and India, with 17 million, out of the equation, the resulting total is 25 million—roughly equivalent to the Catholic population of Germany. Yet size doesn't always matter, because despite their relatively small numbers, the Asian bishops have managed to galvanize much conversation in the global Church by pioneering what they call the "Triple Dialogue":

- Dialogue with the great cultures of Asia, leading to a deeper inculturation of Christian faith;
- Dialogue with the great religions of Asia, leading to mutual understanding and concrete cooperation where possible;
- Dialogue with the poor, leading to efforts at what the bishops call "integral liberation."

Since the Second Vatican Council, the FABC has worked out a positive theological reading of religious diversity, downplaying anything that might be seen as intolerant or exclusivist. That's often presented as an especially important point in the context of some regions of Asia, above all India, where suspicions of Christian proselytism are a frequent flash point for conflict. The press for inculturation, meaning a creative synthesis of the Christian gospel with Asian culture, is a paramount concern.

While few would dispute the point in theory, where the rubber meets the road is how to apply it in practice. To take just one example of how things can get sticky, the Asian bishops gathered in Rome in 1998 for the Synod for Asia. Its theme was chosen by the Vatican: "Jesus Christ the Savior, and His Mission of Love and Service in Asia." At the time, some Asians complained the Vatican was insensitive to how exclusive-sounding language comes across in the context of Asia's religious diversity. When the FABC organized its own plenary meeting in 2000, the bishops decided to revisit some of the conversations from the synod. This time they picked their own theme: "A Mission of Love and Service."

To put that editorial choice into a sound bite, the Asian bishops deleted Jesus. To be fair, their purpose was not to compromise church teaching, but to choose a phraseology that would not be seen as provocative in Asia. Nonetheless, in an era in which defending traditional doctrine on Christ is an evangelical watchword, it's probably not surprising that such moves raise blood pressure levels in Rome. Yet as both India and China become more prominent both on the global scene and within the Church, it's possible that some of this resistance may fade.

Long-Shot Consequences

1. A PRO-DALIT CRUSADE IN INDIA

For those who despair of social change, it's worth recalling that a three-year period from 1991 to 1994 saw the largely peaceful collapse of two of the most deeply entrenched regimes in recent history: Communism in Eastern Europe, and apartheid in South Africa. In both cases, nonviolent protests within those systems, sustained by international support outside, brought about change that few had initially considered plausible.

Surveying the scene in the early twenty-first century, is there another place in the world where a nonviolent humanitarian protest movement, perhaps with Catholic leadership, might be able to end a similarly egregious form of injustice? If so, it may well be in India, where savage inequalities continue to face the Dalit class.

The Indian caste system recognizes four groups: the Brahmins, traditionally priests and intellectuals; the Kshatriyas, soldiers and administrators; Vaisyas, the artisan and commercial class; and the Sudras, farmers and the peasant class. Beneath these four groups is another category, the so-called "untouchables," who are regarded as outside the community. Many Hindus believe that one is born into a given caste based on sins in a past life. While India formally abolished its caste system in 1950, virtually everyone concedes that caste distinctions still undergird deep inequities in employment, education, health care, housing, and treatment by police and the judiciary.

A variety of ethnic and social groups make up the excluded category, whose members are generally referred to as Dalits, a term meaning "broken person." Estimates of the size of the Dalit class in India vary from 160 million to 250 million.

Examples of daily anti-Dalit discrimination, according to human rights monitors, include:

- Dalits are expected to bow to members of the upper castes, drink from separate wells, and clean latrines and other public sanitation facilities as a matter of obligation.

- In many dominant-caste families, after a Dalit servant has cleaned the rooms, pots, and pans, a family member will sprinkle "holy water" to purify all that has been touched by the Dalit.

- In rural areas, Dalits are often not allowed to cycle or walk through the dominant-caste area of the village.

- Dalits are usually not allowed to sit at bus stops. They have to stand back until dominant-caste people have entered the buses. Dalits are also not allowed to sit on the bus seats, even if they are vacant.

- If a Dalit's shadow falls on a member of one of the upper classes, they may consider themselves polluted and perform a ritual of purification.

- Dalits are not allowed to enter some Hindu temples, for fear of ritual pollution. Dalits have been chased out, abused, and beaten.

Prime Minister Manmohan Singh in 2007 explicitly compared the caste system to apartheid in South Africa, calling it "not just prejudice, but a blot on humanity."

The application of this system varies tremendously, and most Indians say the twentieth century saw significant improvements. Kocheril Raman Narayanan, a Dalit, served as the president of India from 1997 to 2002. Another Dalit, Narendra Jadhav, has served as chief economist for the Reserve

Bank of India. Many Hindu temples have opened their doors to Dalits, and some Dalits have cashed in on India's newfound prosperity, moving into the middle and upper classes. Nonetheless, sociological data also indicates that Dalits are far more likely to be born into poverty, to suffer childhood malnutrition and disease, to work in low-paying, low-prestige jobs, and to die earlier.

While there has long been a Dalit civil rights movement in India, and while the right to vote means some politicians actually court Dalit support, none of that has fundamentally altered the caste dynamics. India's higher profile in international affairs means that these structural injustices will draw greater levels of scrutiny in the twenty-first century. In addition, since the fastest-growing sector of the Indian economy is outsourcing from other countries, its dependency upon the global market provides foreign companies and governments with potentially enormous leverage on Indian policy.

If there is to be an international effort to promote reform, the Catholic Church is a good candidate to play a central role. There's even a potential Desmond Tutu waiting in the wings: Archbishop Marampudi Joji of Hyderabad, the country's first Dalit archbishop. Pro-Dalit efforts could be the global Catholic Church's next great human rights crusade. To date, there's little sign of such a movement, at least anything that might rival the anti-apartheid efforts of the 1980s and 1990s. But as the global spotlight on India grows more intense, the potential will mount.

2. AN AMERICAN POPE?

So far, there's never been a serious American candidate for the papacy. Although the election of John Paul II, a Pole, in 1978, and Benedict XVI, a German, in 2005, seems to have broken the Italian monopoly on the job, it's long been taken for granted that an American is out of the question because the Church can't have a pope from the world's lone superpower. It's the same logic that would bar an American from becoming Secretary General of the United Nations—most countries believe the United States already has too much influence, and bloggers would have a field day speculating about Vatican policy, or UN policy, being dictated by the CIA and American industrialists.

Yet as multipolarism gains ground in the twenty-first century, it's possible that this bias against an American pope may lose some of its force. The economic crisis that erupted in 2008 may already have revised the calculus, since it created a new global context in which America is no longer able unilaterally to dictate the terms of economic life to the rest of the world. In a global milieu in which China, India, Brazil, Russia, and a variety of other nations are more commonly seen as equals, it's possible that for the first time, an American could emerge as a serious contender for the papacy.

Indeed, it could happen sooner than one might expect for an institution that typically thinks in centuries. After the death of John Paul II, conventional wisdom held that the cardinals would not turn to a European, but to a candidate from the developing world. In the end, however, they decided that Benedict XVI was the right man for the job, despite the fact that he is German. The next time around, it's just possible the cardinals might decide that multipolarism has made the question of what passport a given *papabile*, or candidate to be pope, happens to hold irrelevant, and be willing to give an American a serious look.

Looking around, there seems to be just such a candidate waiting in the wings.

In February 2009, Pope Benedict XVI named Archbishop Timothy Dolan, then of Milwaukee, as the new archbishop of New York. The appointment means that Dolan, fifty-nine as of fall 2009, is almost certain to become a cardinal the next time Benedict XVI holds a consistory, and thus enter the ranks of serious contenders for the papacy.

If it weren't for the fact of being American, Dolan would probably be considered a front-runner. He's seen as a reliable theological conservative, although open and pragmatic in his judgments. He's perhaps the most media-savvy figure in the American church, and such an extrovert that his scores on a Myers-Briggs personality test would be off the charts. His stock in Rome is high, having served there as rector of the North American College, the American seminary, from 1994 to 2001. Despite a strong populist streak, Dolan is also a serious intellectual, holding a Ph.D. in church history from the Catholic University of America. He's got an aptitude for forging friendships, and thus has strong ties with fellow prelates around the world.

Of course, the trash heaps of history are littered with the carcasses of journalists who have tried to predict the next pope. Whether Dolan will emerge as a serious contender when the time comes is anyone's guess. The point, however, is that multipolarism implies a sort of Catholic irony: As America's unchallenged global dominance recedes, the prospects for an American *papabile* increase.

PENTECOSTALISM

If someone called the central casting office in a Hollywood studio and asked for a Catholic version of the magnetic Pentecostal preachers today marching across much of the world, it couldn't do much better than Oscar Osorio. An articulate Honduran layman with a wife and four children, Osorio is a leader in the Catholic Charismatic movement in Central America. He's also a star of Channel 48, the Catholic television network in Honduras, where his high-octane, Bible-based preaching opens each morning's programming. In a Catholic culture without much tradition of lay activism, Osorio is a rare bird: a full-time lay preacher with a wide regional following.

Part of Osorio's appeal is that he unabashedly speaks the same deeply personal, spiritual language that has driven the phenomenal growth of Pentecostal Christianity across the globe, especially in Latin America. Osorio, laughing, says that a growing number of Pentecostals attend his retreats, some telling him afterward: "Great preaching, brother . . . it's hard to believe you're Catholic!"

Osorio was born into a Seventh-Day Adventist family, but he says he only went to services twice in his life. His father abandoned the family when Oscar was five years old, and he was basically "unchurched" until he met his future wife in his early twenties. She was involved in the Catholic Charismatic Renewal and insisted that Osorio attend Mass with her. By this stage, Osorio was a cutthroat businessman, running a successful printing company, and well on his way to killing himself with booze. (Osorio said he had been an alcoholic since he was fourteen.)

"I didn't believe in God, and I especially didn't believe in priests or in the church," Osorio said.

Eventually, his wife demanded that he go to a Catholic Charismatic retreat. As part of the experience, everyone was supposed to make a confession.

"There were five priests, and I decided to look for the oldest one, because I thought he would be the easiest. There was one elderly priest who could barely hear, and I saw all the men lining up to go to him," Osorio recalled, laughing.

When his turn came, Osorio said he felt an inexplicable need to open his soul. For the next two hours, he said, he reviewed his entire life, and in the process he decided it was time to break with the man he had been before. The next day, Osorio made his first communion.

"I was the only one to drink from the cup," he said. "I felt something burning in me, something powerful, but it didn't hurt. It was a feeling of joy and liberation."

From that point forward, Osorio said, he felt like a changed man. During the next day at the retreat he tried to take a drink of rum, but he felt such physical revulsion that he spat it back out. When he got home, Osorio reconciled with his father, with whom he had not spoken since his father had walked out on the family. He joined a Bible study group. For the next eight years, Osorio worked hard at mastering the teachings, practices, and traditions of the Catholic Church. As part of that experience, Osorio went to Mexico for a formation program, where he had another brush with what he considers divine intervention.

"I was at an all-night vigil before the Blessed Sacrament when I heard a voice saying, 'I need you,'" Osorio said. "At first, I thought it was the priest speaking, so I said, 'What do you need?' He just told me to be quiet. Then I closed my eyes and I heard the voice again, and I told the priest what had happened."

The next morning, Osorio said, he expected the priest to explain the theological significance of the experience. Instead, he said, the priest simply told him: "Learn how to listen to God."

Over time, Osoiro concluded he was being called to become a full-time lay preacher. The only problem was that such a concept didn't exist in Honduras.

"My confessor went to the bishop to ask his permission and his advice,"

Osorio recalled. "The bishop said yes . . . but he didn't say how!" For a husband struggling to support a wife and family, this amounted to a fairly serious gap in the plan.

Eventually, a priest involved in the Charismatic movement promised that his parish would support Osorio's mission. So he began, a modern-day version of the medieval itinerant preacher: roaming from parish to parish, speaking to any audience that would have him. Osorio's message is unambiguously rooted in Catholic tradition—the sacraments, devotions, the office of the papacy, and a strong Catholic ecclesiology. Yet it's delivered with the fire and the wit of the most animated "tent revival" preacher.

Osorio quickly built a following in Honduras. He helped to form "Schools of Evangelization" in Tegucigalpa, and before long he was teaching at the archdiocesan seminary. By now, Osorio said, he has spoken to hundreds of thousands of people throughout Central and South America. His daily television program reaches some four million Honduran homes, and he says the time has come to put his life story in a book.

Honduras, once 98 percent Catholic, reflects the Pentecostal explosion that has eaten into once-homogenous Catholic populations in much of Latin America. One common estimate is that Honduras today is 35 percent Protestant, most of that Pentecostal. Some analysts believe that eventually the population could be divided fifty-fifty between Protestants, most of whom will be Pentecostals, and Catholics.

Osorio said he's actually optimistic about the future of Honduran Catholicism, claiming that perhaps as many as 30 percent of Catholics today are active in the faith—which, if true, would represent an all-time high. He said the heart of the matter is preaching the gospel.

"It's something that we laity must do," he said. "We can't sit back and wait to be led. We have to want it, to feel it, to burn to evangelize."

Osorio is one face of the Catholic response to Pentecostalism, the fastest-growing religious movement in the world.

WHAT'S HAPPENING

"Pentecostalism" refers to a movement within Christianity emphasizing direct personal experience of God through the "baptism of the Holy Spirit," which often, though not always, is believed to produce spiritual gifts such as healings, visions, and speaking in tongues. Pentecostals often regard themselves as reviving the spiritual power and enthusiastic worship of the early Christian church.

When future histories of Christianity are written, the late twentieth century will probably come to be known as the era of the "Pentecostal Explosion." From less than 6 percent in the mid-1970s, Pentecostals finished the century representing almost 20 percent of world Christianity, according to a 2006 study by the Pew Forum on Religion and Public Life called *Spirit and Power*. Combining organized Pentecostal denominations such as the Assemblies of God and the International Pentecostal Church of Christ, plus the vast galaxy of independent churches around the world with a Pentecostal flavor, such as the African Zionists, the Spiritual Baptists in the Caribbean, and the True Jesus Church in China, brings the total worldwide number of Pentecostals to around 380 million. That would make Pentecostalism the second-largest Christian "denomination" on earth, lagging behind only Roman Catholicism. There are more Pentecostals today than all the Orthodox, Anglicans, and Lutherans put together.

As remarkable as those numbers are, they underestimate the real Pentecostal footprint. Established Christian denominations have also spawned their own versions of Pentecostalism, usually called Charismatics. Combining Pentecostals and Charismatics into an amalgam scholars refer to as "Revivalist Christianity" brings the global total to a staggering 600 million, according to Cardinal Walter Kasper, president of the Pontifical Council for Promoting Christian Unity, during a 2006 ecumenical conference in South Korea. That's more than one quarter of all Christians.

The birth of Pentecostalism in North America is conventionally dated to the Azusa Street Revival in Los Angeles in 1906, meaning that L.A.'s top cultural export of the last century was not Hollywood sleaze but muscular biblical Christianity. At around the same time in the early twentieth century, other forms of Pentecostalism arose spontaneously in different parts of the world, such as massive revivals in Chile, Korea, and India. Some experts believe Pentecostalism is the main religious beneficiary of globalization, perhaps even the mode of spiritual expression best suited to a global age.

Collapsing such multifarious religious activity under one label, however, risks a false impression of unity. For example, some Pentecostals follow a "Oneness" doctrine of the Trinity, softening distinctions among the Father, Son, and Holy Spirit, while other Pentecostals defend a classic Trinitarian theology. That Pentecostals can be divided on such a core dogmatic question illustrates their diversity; there's no Vatican that has the last word. Salvadorian Pentecostal anthropologist Ronald Bueno prefers to talk about "Pentecostalisms," meaning a welter of highly differentiated and localized groups, loosely united by an emphasis upon miracles, healings, speaking in tongues, and the other gifts of the Holy Spirit.

The same diversity makes keeping track of Pentecostalism a hazardous enterprise. The authors of the Pew Forum study admit their numbers are best-guess estimates, fraught with ballpark figures (often self-reported) and debatable definitions of a "Pentecostal." Some experts peg the number of Pentecostals much lower, between 150 million to 200 million. Even allowing for these nuances, however, Pentecostalism remains the most important new arrival on the world religious scene in the last 100 years.

Luis Lugo, who directed the Pew Forum report, put its bottom line this way: "I don't think it's too far-fetched to seriously consider whether Christianity is well on its way to being Pentecostalized," he said.

At least two thirds of Pentecostals are in the developing world, and some believe Pentecostalism is emerging as the de facto Southern way of being Christian. Sociologist Paul Freston says the major global centers for Pentecostalism are in Chile, Guatemala, Nigeria, Ghana, South Africa, Korea, the Philippines, and China. The largest single Christian congregation in the world is the Yoido Full Gospel Church, a Pentecostal church founded in 1958 and located on an island within Seoul, South Korea. Every Sunday, 250,000 worshippers show up for nine services simultaneously translated into sixteen languages.

Looking around at the Pentecostal explosion, *The Economist* reported in December 2006: "The evidence can be seen everywhere in America and the developing world, in churches the size of football stadiums in Latin America, in 12,000-acre 'redemption camps' in Nigeria, and in storefront churches in the slums of Rio and Los Angeles." The most successful Pentecostal church in Guatemala, the Fraternidad Cristiana de Guatemala, recently built a $20 million facility, said by church members to be the largest building in Central America, complete with seating for over 12,000, parking for more than 3,500 cars, 48 Sunday-school classrooms, a baptism pool with space for hundreds, and a heliport. The church even has corporate sponsorship, as its entryway is called "Burger King Drive."

Yet Pentecostal growth is not confined to the South. Sociologist of religion Nikolai Mitrokhin, who directs the Moscow-based Institute of the Study of Religion in the CIS and Baltic Countries, said in 2004 that denominations generally viewed as Pentecostal in flavor, such as the Assemblies of

God, expanded at a clip of 20 to 25 percent a year in Russia during the 1990s. In 2005, Mitrokhin estimated that there are at least one million practicing Protestants in Russia, many of them Pentecostals, and he believes that Pentecostal and Evangelical Christianity could be the religious preference of a plurality of Russians by mid-century.

Pentecostalism has long been viewed as the religious choice of the poor and backward, a motley band of "hillbilly holy rollers." Today's research, however, contests that view. Sociologist Fr. Andrew Greeley says that the Pentecostals in Latin America enjoy greatest success among the "aspirational" class, meaning white-collar groups not yet among the social elites but hoping to move up. Mitrokhin says the same thing is true of Russia; the greatest expansion of Pentecostal movements, he said, has come among the country's urban entrepreneurial class.

While public fascination surrounds the spectacular number of entries into Pentecostalism, there hasn't been as much attention to what some experts say is an equally remarkable number of exits. In the late 1990s, sociologist Kurt Bowen found that in Mexico the drop-out rate for second-generation Pentecostals was as high as 48 percent. For a significant percentage of new converts, Pentecostalism may be a way station between nominal membership in a traditional church and a complete lack of religious affiliation; several Latin America nations today have growing pockets of people who say they have no religion, a historic novelty on this intensely religious continent, and sociologists report that many of these new "nones" are ex-Pentecostals. Some experts say Pentecostalism should be understood as the most visible expression of a whole series of deep religious reconfigurations associated with globalization, which is producing mounting diversity across a wide range of options, from intense Pentecostal devotion and reinvigorated Islam, to a smorgasbord of New Age and "emergent church" options, to no religion at all.

A Pentecostal Profile

As the term "Pentecostal" indicates, the motor force of the movement is the conviction that the eruption of the Holy Spirit associated with the Feast of Pentecost in the New Testament did not stop with the close of the biblical era. Adherents believe that the Holy Spirit can enter ordinary mortals and work miracles today, from speaking in tongues to healings to prophecy and visions. The Spirit also has the power to change lives, leading people out of self-destructive patterns of behavior such as crime, alcohol and drug addiction, marital infidelity, and laziness.

Pentecostalism generally has a "low church" ecclesiology, emphasizing the capacity of ordinary believers to make contact with the spiritual realm without the need for sacraments or special clerical intermediaries. It also has a powerful missionary impulse, oriented toward leading others to experience the power of the Spirit in their own lives.

The 2006 Pew report found that renewalist Christians (the umbrella term for Pentecostals and Charismatics) have the following characteristics:

- Belief in the gifts of the Holy Spirit, such as speaking in tongues, prophecy, or prayer for miraculous healing;
- A literal reading of the Bible;
- Strong belief in divine healing of illness or injury;
- Belief in the possibility of direct divine revelation;
- An emphasis on evil spirits (many Pentecostals say they have personally witnessed the devil or evil spirits being driven out of someone);
- Belief that Jesus will return to earth during their lifetimes;
- Belief in a "rapture," meaning that the faithful will be gathered up before the end of the world and transported to Heaven;
- Belief that miracles still occur as in biblical times;
- Commitment to "evangelization," meaning sharing the faith with nonbelievers;
- Emphasis on Christ as the lone path to salvation;
- A conservative moral code on issues such as homosexuality, extramarital sex, abortion, divorce, and alcohol consumption;
- Higher-than-average rates of attendance at church services.

The Pew Forum study found that most Pentecostals support a strong role for religion in public life, though in seven of the ten countries surveyed, majorities also uphold the separation of church and state. Pentecostals are more likely than other Christians to say it's important for political leaders to have strong religious beliefs. In most countries, according to the Pew data, Pentecostals are likely to sympathize with Israel, in part because of eschatological beliefs about the Second Coming occurring in Israel. Some Pentecostal churches in various parts of the world actually fly the Israeli flag to symbolize this conviction.

Relations between Catholics and Pentecostals have occasionally been frosty, in part because a few of the biggest names in the Pentecostal firmament are also among the most antiecumenical voices in global Christianity. Frances Swaggart, wife of famed Pentecostal televangelist Jimmy Swaggart, wrote a book in 2006 titled *Catholicism: A Modern Babylon,* which offered a cocktail of time-honored complaints about Catholicism such as the sale of indulgences. When asked in 2006 whether the Catholic Church was the "whore of Babylon," the best another famed Pentecostal, Jimmy Bakker, could do was, "We don't know for sure." A decade earlier, Bishop Sergio von Helde of Brazil's Universal Church of the Kingdom of God, one of the largest Pentecostal denominations in Latin America, went on TV on the Feast of Our Lady of Aparecida, the national patroness of Brazil, and kicked an icon of the Madonna, declaring, "This is no saint!" Uproar ensued, in which outraged Catholics attacked Pentecostal churches and von Helde was convicted of public disrespect for a religious symbol. While these figures are not representative of the Pentecostal mainstream, their hostility to Catholicism is a real current in some Pentecostal thought.

Yet on some key issues that formed the fault lines of the Protestant Reformation, Pentecostals are arguably closer to Catholics than to the Evangelicals. While classical Protestants stress the doctrine of *sola scriptura,* that the Bible alone is the only guide to faith, Pentecostals believe in ongoing revelation through the Spirit. Similarly, classical Protestantism believes in salvation through faith alone, while many strains of Pentecostalism believe in a faith manifested in holy living and the fruits of the spirit—in other words, both faith *and* works. Pentecostals and Catholics also tend to see grace and nature as complementary, unlike classic Reformation theology, which sees a radical discontinuity. Pentecostalism has a sensual, earthy spirituality similar to some forms of popular Catholic devotion. For these reasons, Harvey Cox has dubbed Pentecostalism "Catholicism without priests," meaning an expression of folk spirituality without the Roman juridical system or complicated scholastic theology. Despite strong tensions between Pentecostals and Catholics, these structural parallels suggest a basis for long-term dialogue. They also may help explain why so many Catholics in various parts of the world have found Pentecostalism congenial, since it's not entirely foreign to their own religious instincts.

Prosperity Gospel

Perhaps the most controversial element of the Pentecostal outlook is the so-called "prosperity gospel," meaning the belief that God will reward those with sufficient faith with both material prosperity and physical health. Some analysts distinguish between "neo-Pentecostalism," which they see as focused on the prosperity gospel, and classic Pentecostalism, oriented toward the gifts of the Spirit such as healings and tongues. Yet the Pew Forum data suggests that the prosperity gospel is actually a defining feature of all Pentecostalism; majorities of Pentecostals exceeding 90 percent in most countries hold these beliefs. The Pew report also found that Pentecostals tend to be more optimistic than other Christians about their future financial prospects.

For one example of the prosperity gospel, consider the Maximum Miracle Centre in Nairobi, Kenya. On one Sunday in April 2006, a guest preacher blamed poverty and joblessness on the devil, promising the large congregation that, "If you are sleeping on an inch-thick mattress, tell the devil '*kwaheri*,' and you will sleep on a seven-inch or ten-inch one." The term *kwaheri* roughly means, "Get lost." In Bolivia, female preacher Magneli de Guachalla at the New Pact Power of God Church told her congregation in spring 2007 about a woman who went from sleeping in a mud hut to owning a chain of stores within six months of her conversion, and an out-of-work man who now is a shoe manufacturer because "he's crazy about God."

"God will give you a house!" Guachalla shouted. "If you think I'm materialistic, I am! Everything is possible with the power of God! Disbelief is a sin!"

For Christians who embrace the option for the poor, such messages can seem troubling, implying that poverty is the result of a failure of faith rather than structural injustice. Writing in *Christianity Today* in 2007, Ted Olsen said that while it's important to listen to the voices of Christians outside the West, it's also essential to counter this "health and wealth" view. In that light, Olsen wrote, "The spiritual gift most needed in the twenty-first century is discernment."

On the other hand, Ghanian theologian Kwabena Asamoah-Gyadu believes that in the context of developing nations, the prosperity gospel fosters "an indomitable spirit in the face of life's odds." Writer Katharine Wiegele offered a similarly favorable reading in her 2004 book about the Charismatic Catholic El Shaddai movement in the Philippines, arguing that the prosperity gospel allows members to recast their poverty as something personal and temporary, as opposed to left-wing readings of poverty as structural and enduring. If it's personal, Wiegele argues, an individual can do something about it, which generates both hope and effort.

There's a sense in which the prosperity gospel sometimes acts as a self-fulfilling prophecy, since many Pentecostals regard their churches as extended networks in which members have an obligation to help one another. In the trenches in various parts of the world, Pentecostals sometimes give preference to one another in hiring, promotions, and business relationships. In Nigeria, Catholic Archbishop John Onaiyekan of Abuja says that some members of his flock complain that they don't get the same preferential treatment from other Catholics that Pentecostals give one another. (Onaiyekan says he discourages this sort of intraconfessional networking, because, in his view, it too easily veers off into corruption.)

Catholic Charismatics

Catholicism's version of the Pentecostal explosion is the Catholic Charismatic Renewal, the roots of which in North America date to a 1967 retreat at Duquesne University in Pittsburgh, when a group of Catholic professors and students say they experienced baptism in the Spirit. Like Pentecostalism, the Catholic Charismatic movement has become especially pervasive in the global South. It has also penetrated the upper reaches of the Church; the Preacher of the Papal Household, Capuchin Fr. Raniero Cantalamessa, is a Charismatic.

The World Christian Database estimates the total number of Catholic Charismatics in the world at 120 million, which would be roughly 11 percent of the total Catholic population. The Pew Forum survey found that 14 percent of Catholics in the United States, a bloc of almost 10 million people, consider themselves "Charismatic," with Hispanic Catholics nearly five times more likely to take part in charismatic activities. Samuel Rodriguez, president of the California-based National Hispanic Christian Leadership Conference, said of Hispanics in America in 2007, "There are more Catholic Pentecostals than Pentecostal Pentecostals."

Brazilian Charismatic Fr. Marcello Rossi offers one example of the highly eclectic global Charismatic scene. Rossi regularly draws crowds of more than 70,000 to Masses he celebrates four times a week in a former bottle factory on São Paulo's south side, where signs and wonders abound. In the late 1990s, his CD titled *The Lord's Aerobics* became the best-selling album of all time in the country. In the Philippines, the El Shaddai movement founded by Mike Velarde has a following estimated at eight million. At services in packed stadiums, these charismatic Catholics raise their passports to be blessed, believing this will help them obtain the visas they need to work overseas, and carry upside-down umbrellas in order to catch the material blessings they believe God will shower upon them.

Like Pentecostalism, the heart of the Charismatic Renewal is baptism in the Holy Spirit. That experience leads to a spontaneous, joyous form of worship; an emphasis upon miracles, healing, and visions; and, in many cases, speaking in tongues. Charismatics strongly believe in the spiritual world, including the influence of evil spirits, and thus engage in a kind of "spiritual combat." For this reason, Charismatics are often particularly interested in the Catholic practice of exorcism.

In 2003, international Charismatic leader Charles Whitehead listed what he regards as the gifts to Catholicism offered by the Charismatic Renewal:

- Prayer, praise, and worship, empowered by the gift of tongues.
- Our *expectant* faith: we are confident that God *is* going to act. Sadly this expectancy is often missing in the Church. Many have a creedal faith but no expectation that the Lord will ever *do* anything.
- The conviction that the Lord heals and works miracles through ordinary people.
- A sense of joy and celebration.
- A desire to be witnesses, secure in the knowledge that we are empowered for the New Evangelization.
- Bringing alive one of the theological virtues: hope.
- A prophetic voice in the Church and in the world. In our materialistic and selfish society, we desperately need to hear God's voice.
- Intercession and spiritual warfare. Through the Holy Spirit we understand that there is a spiritual battle going on and we are part of it; we recognize the presence of evil spirits as well as the Holy Spirit. We therefore have a role and a task to defend the Church against the power of the evil one, which those who are not aware of the spiritual battle cannot do.
- A concern for justice, peace, and social issues. These things are important, and we are called to bring them to greater prominence. We know we must be practical as well as spiritual.

Many Catholic leaders have supported the Charismatic movement in the Church, seeing it as a means to promote deeper faith and practice. It has a natural ecumenical dimension among Charismatics in other Christian traditions. On the other hand, critics have charged some Charismatic communities with "cult-like" attitudes in terms of submission to magnetic leaders, and alleged spiritual elitism. Others have raised doctrinal questions, arguing, for example, that an exaggerated emphasis on "baptism in the Spirit" could seem to render the sacrament of baptism insufficient or defective.

One sign of official caution came with a September 14, 2000, Vatican document entitled "Instruction on Prayers to Obtain Healing from God." The instruction stipulates that the ordinary rules for celebration of the Mass must not be set aside in order to accommodate healings and exorcisms; that extra-liturgical healing services must have the approval of the bishop; and that a Charismatic leader said to have a gift of healing must not supplant the sacraments as the basic way grace is distributed.

Catholic Losses

The hundreds of millions of new Pentecostals generated in the late twentieth century did not step out of a vacuum. Unlike global gains in Catholicism or Islam, increases in Pentecostalism cannot be explained primarily by overall population trends. Instead, Pentecostalism has drawn followers from other religious traditions. Paul Freston says that Pentecostals have made gains among Hindus in India and among Buddhists in China and other parts of Asia, as well as among Muslims in Africa. Pentecostals have also done well among followers of traditional tribal religions and shamanism in various parts of the world.

Catholicism has been hit particularly hard by the Pentecostal wave, especially in Latin America. Belgian Passionist Fr. Franz Damen, a veteran staffer for the Bolivian bishops, concluded in the 1990s that conversions from Catholicism to Protestantism in Latin America during the twentieth century actually surpassed the number of conversions incited by the Protestant Reformation in Europe in the sixteenth century. A study commissioned in the late 1990s by CELAM, the Episcopal Conference of Latin America and the Caribbean, found that 8,000 Latin Americans were deserting the Catholic Church every day. A 2005 poll by Latinobarometro, a Chile-based firm that conducts polls in seventeen Latin American countries, found that 71 percent of Latin Americans considered themselves Roman Catholic in 2004, down from 80 percent in 1995. If that trend continues at its current pace, the authors speculated, only 50 percent of Latin Americans would identify themselves as Catholics by 2025. (Whether that actually happens remains to be seen; straight-line projections over a considerable arc of time almost always turn out to be false.)

It's not just Latin America. According to the World Christian Database, Pentecostals today are 12 percent of Africa's population, some 107 million people, up from less than 5 percent of the African population in 1975. Many new Pentecostals have come from Catholicism and mainline Protestantism; in January 2007, Reverend Nyansako-ni-Niku of the All-Africa Conference of Churches, Africa's main Protestant ecumenical body, referred to Pentecostalism as a "disease." During a 2008 gathering of bishops in Rome, Cardinal Polycarp Pengo of Tanzania warned of an "exodus" of Catholics to Pentecostal movements all across Africa. In Asia, Pentecostals have become 3.5 percent of the population over just a quarter-century, meaning 135 million people, and again some of these new Pentecostals are ex-Catholics. The Catholic bishops of India carried out a national study of Pentecostalism in 1997 after a wave of Catholic conversions, including a priest who at the time was the editor of India's only Catholic news service.

Though it's more of a sound bite than serious sociology, one could put the reality this way: in the global North, dissatisfied Catholics usually become secularized; in the South, they usually become Pentecostals.

On the other hand, the news is not all bad for the Catholic Church. While Pentecostalism often eats away at the raw numbers of Catholics, sometimes it can be an index of religious ferment that, in the long run, may also benefit Catholicism. In his 2008 book *Conversion of a Continent,* Dominican Fr. Edward Cleary argues that Latin America today is in the grip of a religious upheaval, with Pentecostalism as its leading edge. Catholicism, Cleary says, is also becoming more dynamic in Latin America, generating higher levels of commitment among those who remain. Cleary believes that this Catholic awakening had its roots in lay movements that go back to the 1930s and '40s, but it's been jump-started by healthy competition from the Pentecostals. Cleary argues that despite its statistical losses, Catholicism in Latin America is actually much stronger because of the Pentecostal presence.

Some data suggests that at least in Latin America, the explosive growth of Pentecostalism has cooled. It's also worth noting that Pentecostals too struggle to hold on to their people, perhaps more than many other religious movements. In three Latin American countries where Pentecostal expansion has been the most impressive—Brazil, Guatemala, and Chile—there's a growing segment of the population that says it has no religion at all, representing 15 percent in both Guatemala and Chile and 8 percent in Brazil, according to the 2006 Pew Forum data. Those are remarkable numbers for a continent where religious nonaffiliation was essentially unheard of just a generation ago, and a disproportionate share of those without religion is thought to be made up of ex-Pentecostals.

Trying to explain these losses, Cleary concluded that the "perfectionist character" of Pentecostalism, meaning its high moral and social demands, is simply too much for some people. Pentecostal groups in Latin America tend to shed their less committed members, so that the more committed can continue unimpeded. Cleary said that the drop-outs often move into a "dark pool" of no religion at all; Fr. Andrew Greeley, who has studied the situation in Brazil, says some also gravitate to one of the many syncretistic religious movements on the Brazilian landscape. What they don't generally do is return to the Catholic Church.

Church leaders in Latin America often say the majority of Catholics who have become Pentecostals were never practicing Catholics in the first place, a conclusion Cleary echoes. The fact that some become active Christians, albeit in a different denomination, could actually be seen as a positive development.

"For many of them, what's happening is a discovery of religion for the first time," said Auxiliary Bishop Edgar Moreira da Cunha of Newark, the only Brazilian-born bishop in the United States, in a 2007 interview. He was speaking about converts in Brazil as well as Hispanic converts in the United States. "In a practical sense, this is not a 'loss' to Catholicism, because most of those people were never practicing Catholics. In a sense, this might be a good thing, because they're practicing some religion, whereas they were not doing anything before."

In other parts of the world, however, losses appear to have come from the ranks of practicing Catholics. Fr. Paul Parathazham, who coordinated the national study of Pentecostalism on behalf of the Catholic bishops of India in the late 1990s, said that converts "are by and large the well educated and devout Catholics who have been brought up in traditionally religious families."

There's anecdotal evidence that the growth of the Charismatic movement within Catholicism may have helped reduce losses to Pentecostalism. Reverend William Okoye, founder of the All Christian Fellowship, a Pentecostal community in Nigeria, and chaplain to the country's president, said in March 2007 that the "explosive growth" of Pentecostalism in his country initially came at the expense of other Christian bodies, "especially the Anglicans and the Catholics."

"Some years ago, this was an ecumenical problem," Okoye said in the office of his sprawling church in downtown Abuja in March 2007. "Now, the other churches are more accommodating. The Catholics allow the Charismatic Renewal movement. The Anglicans do the same thing, so their people can remain Catholics and Anglicans, but they act like Pentecostals."

Okoye said that in his own congregation of several thousand, he notices substantially fewer ex-Catholics than was the case ten or twenty years ago. Today's growth, he said, is more likely to come in the north of Nigeria, among people who were once nominally Muslim but who today are attracted to the dynamism and family spirit of Pentecostal Christianity.

In the traditionally Catholic Philippines as well, many experts say the defections would have been far more severe if it were not for El Shaddai, which has given Catholics attracted to Pentecostal spirituality a home within the Church.

Explaining the Growth

Ask any Pentecostal or Charismatic to explain the remarkable rise of "Renewalist Christianity," and you'll get the same answer: the Holy Spirit. Pentecostalism and the various Charismatic movements within established churches, they believe, represent the most awesome work of the Spirit in the modern age, and any attempt to explain the phenomenon in human terms will miss what's most essential about it.

Sociologists of religion naturally seek explanations in more human terms, and trying to account for the global expansion of Pentecostalism is one of the more wide-open parlor games in the field today. (This search for sociological insight does not contradict belief that conversion is a fruit of the Spirit; the Spirit, after all, may well be working through human sociology.) This section surveys fourteen popular explanations, both from academics as well as from the protagonists themselves. It's impossible to say which of these theories is correct, though most experts believe that there's probably at least some merit to all of them—and that any one of them, pushed too far, becomes an ideology rather than a useful hypothesis.

1. AMERICAN INFLUENCE

Among some members of non-Pentecostal religions, it has become a standard rhetorical trope to argue that Pentecostalism has grown because of access to vast resources from patrons in the United States. In Africa, this hypothesis is remarkably ecumenical; it surfaces both from Catholic and Anglican bishops and from Muslim imams. When asked in 2004 to explain the expansion of Pentecostalism in Uganda, the late Monsignor Joseph Obunga, at the time the secretary general of the Ugandan Episcopal Conference, offered a two-word answer: American money.

"They have got baits, the riches," said Obunga. "Most of these sects come from America, and the Americans give them money. They entice the members with free scholarships, clothing. Some people here are very poor, and if you come, they will give you something."

In their 1996 book *Exporting the American Gospel*, Steve Brouwer, Paul Gifford, and Susan D. Rose laid out this case, charging that the developing world has "a rapidly growing sector of Christianity closely related to, and heavily dependent upon, the United States." They warned of an "Americanization" of global Christianity. Gifford said that Pentecostalism in particular often amounts to a "neo-colonialism propagated by American prosperity preachers."

2. AMERICAN POLICY

A variant of the "America is to blame" theory holds that it has been a conscious policy of the United States government to promote the spread of Pentecostalism, primarily as an ideological boost for free-market capitalism.

Peruvian Catholic journalist Federico Prieto Celi made this argument during an interview in Lima in 2005. Prieto cited a remark of Theodore Roosevelt to the effect that, "I believe it will be long and difficult to absorb these countries into the sphere of the United States as long as they remain Catholic." In a similar vein, Prieto pointed to a 1969 essay by Nelson Rockefeller on American policy in Latin America, which included the observation, "The Catholic Church has stopped being a trusted ally of the United States, and on the contrary is transforming itself into a danger because it raises the consciousness of the people. It's recommended to give support to fundamentalist Christian groups and churches of the sort of Moon and the Hare Krishna."

Other Latin Americans point to the Reagan administration's "Santa Fe document," which recommended efforts to subvert the growth of liberation theology in Latin American Catholicism.

3. LACK OF PASTORAL CARE

In those countries where conversion to Pentecostalism has come primarily from Catholicism, many observers believe that something the Catholic Church has done, or failed to do, is responsible. In Latin America, the most common diagnosis is that historically the Catholic Church baptized people but often did very little else for them, leaving them spiritually adrift and thus easy prey to competitors.

In June 2007, Monsignor Carlos Quintana, the expert on Latin America for the U.S. bishops and a former official for the Latin American bishops, put the point into a sound bite: "*católico ignorante, futuro protestante*," he said, roughly meaning that "an ignorant Catholic is a future Protestant."

This view seems now to be the quasi-official explanation of the Episcopal Conference of Latin America and the Caribbean.

"The majority of Catholics on this continent no longer participate, or never have participated, in the life of our ecclesial communities," said Cardinal Claudio Hummes of Brazil, who now serves as prefect of the Congregation for Clergy in the Vatican, during the May 2007 assembly of Latin American bishops in Aparecida, Brazil. "We baptized them, but for many reasons, we never really evangelized them sufficiently."

It's not just Latin America. A 1997 study by the Catholic bishops of India concluded that one factor in why Catholics chose to join Pentecostal bodies is that they felt "anonymous and unconnected" in large Catholic parishes with little direct pastoral care.

4. THE PRIEST SHORTAGE

A more specific form of the "pastoral failure" hypothesis is that severe priest shortages in the developing world, coupled with a passive view of the lay role, have left enormous gaps in the Catholic pastoral network. In the United States, the priest-to-person ratio is one to 1,300, but the average in Latin America is one to 8,000, and in many places the situation is far worse. Fr. José Óscar Beozzo of Brazil described the practical reality: "We have only eighteen thousand priests for something like one hundred forty million Catholics," he said. "Meanwhile, the Assemblies of God have eight and a half million faithful in Brazil, and over fifty-two thousand pastors." That works out to a ratio of one minister for every 163 members of the Assemblies of God, and one priest for every 7,777 Catholics.

In Honduras, a woman who is the last remaining Catholic in a family that can trace its roots back to Columbus explained in a 2007 interview how her relatives had become Pentecostals. Several years ago, she said, her mother-in-law had cancer and was hospitalized for six months. During that time, her overtaxed parish priest managed to visit her only twice, briefly, and the Catholic hospital had no resident priest-chaplain. Meanwhile, a group of women from the local Pentecostal church spent hours every day in her room, holding her hand during chemotherapy treatments, praying for her, helping her to eat and to keep clean. They also looked in on her house and kept track of her children. At the end of that experience, the mother-in-law began attending the Pentecostal church, and the rest of her family followed.

5. THE LIBERAL CASE: THE CHURCH IS TOO HIERARCHICAL AND DISTANT

For liberal critics of Catholicism, the rise of Pentecostalism is often interpreted as a popular referendum against perceived defects of the Catholic Church. Most commonly, the critics cite clericalism, refusal to adapt unpopular teachings, and distance from the people.

"People feel alienated by a Church that condemns divorce and is not willing to listen, an authoritarian church that opposes the use of condoms, and isn't willing to adapt to the times and the real needs of people," said Elio Masferrer, a Mexican who serves as chairman of the Latin American Religious Studies Association and a researcher at Mexico's National School of Anthropology and History. Protestant Israel Batista, the general secretary of the Latin American Council of Churches, charged in 2006 that Catholicism is losing ground in the region because it has maintained "hierarchical structures that are distanced from the people."

"When you go to an Evangelical church, you are taken into the community, which is relatively free of hierarchy, whereas in the Catholic churches, the faithful are scattered and receive advice and even orders from faraway places like the Vatican, which often do not relate whatsoever to the reality of the people," Batista said.

6. THE CONSERVATIVE CASE: BLAMING LIBERATION THEOLOGY

Catholic conservatives sometimes point to the historical coincidence that defections to Pentecostalism in Latin America began at roughly the same time that Catholicism was embracing liberation theology, suggesting a causal relation between the two. By moving into politics, they argue, Catholicism left a spiritual vacuum that Pentecostal movements were able to fill. Cardinal Juan Luis Cipriani of Peru, a member of Opus Dei, made this argument in 2004.

"In Latin America you see how much people are asking for spiritual life, how hungry they are. How stupid we are when we think they are asking only for bread," he said. "Of course, we have to do social work. Of course, we must do pastoral work. But spirituality . . . that's where the sects are moving in." Cipriani said Church leaders should return to the spiritual basics: "Speak with God, forgive each other, go to confession, pray."

A related critique is that liberation theology styled itself as a populist movement, but Pentecostalism better expresses grassroots religious sensibility. In a mid-1990s study in Brazil, John Burdick found that many poor women said they felt inferior and illiterate at meetings of progressive Catholic base communities, but in Pentecostal churches they felt empowered through the gifts of the Spirit.

7. THE "ECSTASY DEFICIT"

So far, most of these explanations suggest that some outside force is responsible for the success of Pentecostalism. Many analysts say these theories fail to do justice to its inner attractiveness, which exercises a natural gravitational pull. Harvey Cox has argued that Pentecostalism offers a remedy to the "ecstasy deficit" created by forms of religiosity shaped by modern science and Enlightenment-era philosophies.

Mainline denominations, Cox said, fail to take account of the "Dionysian" dimension of the religious experience. The joyous, exuberant type of worship provided by Pentecostal denominations, Cox argues, taps into a primal religious instinct. Echoing this view, *The Economist* described typical Pentecostal worship as "part religious service, part spectacle, part rock-and-roll rave." In Pentecostal parlance, there's an aphorism about grim worship that captures this point nicely. Such Christians, the saying goes, appear to have been "baptized in pickle juice."

Once again, this isn't just a North American or Latin American phenomenon. India's Fr. Paul Parathazham said a commonly cited factor among new converts to Pentecostalism is that they never had a "God experience" within Catholicism, meaning something that got the heart pumping and put them into direct contact with the supernatural realm.

8. HEALTH

Given the injustices in global health care described under trend six, it's little surprise that fear of disease is an enormous day-to-day preoccupation of many people, especially in developing nations. In a 1997 study on

Pentecostalism in Brazil, Andrew Chestnut found that the illnesses flowing from poverty and the consequent desire for instruments of healing were a powerful factor in attracting many people, especially women, to Pentecostalism. Chestnut observes that prayer and hoped-for miracles are only part of the picture. By encouraging members to abstain from casual sex, to renounce drugs and alcohol, and to lead industrious lives, Pentecostal churches actually foster a healthier lifestyle. Pentecostal churches also mobilize social networks to support families in moments of crisis related to poor health. In effect, Chestnut concluded, Pentecostalism often does a better job than its competitors of addressing the primal human concern for health and sickness, making it little mystery why a growing number of people are drawn to it.

9. EMPOWERING WOMEN

Though it may seem counterintuitive, many observers see Pentecostalism as a vehicle for the emancipation of women, even a form of feminism in its own right. In a 2003 article in the *Latin American Research Review,* Anne Hallum of Stetson University argued that Pentecostalism empowers women to "confront the demon of *machismo*" associated with excessive drinking by men, violence against women, chronic infidelity, abdication of household duties, and a general identification with the street rather than the home.

Andrew Chestnut quoted one recent female convert making Hallum's point:

> "Look, the majority of women who attend church have problems with their husbands. For example, sometimes the husband suddenly 'arranges' another woman out there. So at church we have prayer groups and through prayer, God removes the other woman from her path. . . . A wife often has problems with her husband when he drinks too much, and they fight constantly. And so here at church we get together to pray and through prayer, God blesses the couple."

On the basis of such reports, Hallum describes Pentecostalism as "a collective survival strategy chosen by tens of millions of Latin American women," yet one that many Western feminists ignore because it doesn't reflect their expectations of what women's liberation is supposed to look like.

10. INCULTURATION

By stressing religious experience without always having to think through the doctrinal implications, Pentecostalism is able to smoothly incorporate the religiosity of different cultures, such as folk healing, ancestor worship, and shamanism. Pentecostalism has a built-in openness to inculturation that often gives it a powerful advantage over more structured forms of religion. The Brazilian Pentecostal Church of Christ's Spit, for example, draws on indigenous beliefs about the spiritual potency of a healer's spittle. David Martin's study of Pentecostalism in Korea suggests that its growth is related to its capacity to tap into archaic Korean shamanism. Martin argued in the mid-1990s that this feature of Pentecostalism appeals especially to "upper lower" levels of Korean society.

Lamin Sanneh argued in his 2003 book *Whose Religion Is Christianity?* that those forms of Christianity that have done well in the global South are generally the ones that "allow Christian engagement to produce results that have indigenous credibility rather than just foreign approval." He wrote that Islam did well in Africa in places where indigenous religions had been destroyed by colonialism, while Christianity thrived where the indigenous religions had been preserved. No branch of Christianity has shown a greater capacity to adapt elements from those indigenous traditions than Pentecostalism.

11. AN ANSWER TO URBANIZATION

Pentecostals have posted some of their most impressive gains in the peripheries of the sprawling cities in the developing world, where millions of people uprooted from rural villages and kinship structures often find themselves dislocated, isolated, and forgotten. In that context, many Pentecostal churches have been able to offer new social networks and experiences of community. As noted in chapter one, a popular saying in Brazil has it that the only two things that work in the favelas are organized crime and Pentecostal churches.

Uganda's Monsignor Obunga said that effective urban ministry has been one key to the expansion of Pentecostalism in Kampala, and at the time of his death he was promoting the formation of small communities by Catholics in neglected urban areas. Luis Lugo, who coordinated the Pew study, said that one of the keys to Pentecostal expansion has been its capacity to foster "a sense of community by reaching out to the displaced, including migrants to the city, providing a spiritual home in a world that is quickly changing."

12. PERSONAL MORALITY

Listening to the stories of people who have converted to Pentecostalism, it's striking how often personal moral reform plays a central role in their accounts. Pentecostalism, they say, helped them stop drinking or abusing drugs, stop stealing, stop gambling, stop abusing their spouses or children, stop cheating on their wives or husbands, to take their work more seriously, and in general to become more upright, sober people. Fr. Andrew Greeley said sociological data indicates that giving people a strong sense of personal morality has been an important ingredient in Pentecostal expansion.

Hispanic theologian Cecilia Loreto Mariz argues that the strict morality of Pentecostalism has a direct social payoff.

"When individuals confront serious personal crises and find it difficult to survive, they usually lack the conditions necessary to develop social consciousness or to become politically involved," she wrote in a 1996 essay that was part of the book *The Power of the Spirit*. "By giving them the means to overcome these personal difficulties, the Pentecostal churches help poor people on a microsocial level, that is, in the daily life of the individual, his family, and organizations."

13. ECONOMIC ADVANTAGE

On the subject of Pentecostalism, Peter Berger has famously quipped, "Max Weber is alive and well and living in Guatemala City." The reference is to Weber's argument that by promoting a strong work ethic, Protestantism contributed to the rise of modern capitalism. In a similar fashion, Berger believes that by teaching people they are "dynamite in the hands of God," Pentecostalism inoculates them against fatalism, making them more likely to believe that hard work can change their lives.

In the mid-1980s, anthropologist Sheldon Annis found that the single greatest factor separating those who improved economically in a small Guatemalan town from those who didn't was Pentecostalism. Overall, Catholic wealth averaged 81 percent of Pentecostal wealth, and Pentecostals were twice as likely to own a car. Pentecostal children were more likely to go to school, and Pentecostal adults were more likely to work in upwardly mobile occupations such as sewing, tourism, and transportation that could lead to microbusiness ownership.

Analysts point to several characteristics of Pentecostalism that foster good business skills. Pentecostal churches typically rely on ordinary lay people to spread the word, teaching them the rudiments of public speaking—in effect, how to make a good sales pitch. Pentecostal churches are also locally owned and operated, so laypeople learn administration, financial accounting, and personnel management.

Pentecostalism creates a "competitive economic advantage," according to Don Miller, a professor of religion for the Center for Religion and Civic Culture at the University of Southern California. When the Pentecostal church encourages men to give up gambling, booze, and womanizing, the men end up with "surplus capital" that can be invested in small-scale business enterprises and the education of their children. In turn, these families pull ahead of their neighbors and peers, creating a powerful incentive for other people to embrace the Pentecostal message.

14. COMPETITION

Barriers to market entry in Pentecostalism are notoriously low. Any Pentecostal who feels dissatisfied with the offerings at the local church is free to move on to another, even to start his or her own church in a basement or garage. As a result, Pentecostalism tends to spawn thousands of competing churches. (According to experts, this reality has sometimes contributed to an exaggerated perception of the spread of Pentecostalism, because the number of separate churches is not always a good barometer of the total number of Pentecostals. One hundred Pentecostals may be divided among twenty or more different congregations.)

As *The Economist* observes, "Pressure to perform is relentless. If you can't preach a mesmerizing service, people will go elsewhere." This inner dynamic within Pentecostalism, admirers believe, prevents it from going stale, enabling it to sustain growth. At the same time, it means that growth is inherently unstable; individual churches and denominations will rise and fall as the market shifts, but overall the Pentecostal version of the "gross domestic religious product" will grow.

One young Pentecostal preacher quoted by *The Economist* put it this way: "We have to work against the competition as well as the devil."

WHAT IT MEANS

Russian sociologist Nikolai Mitrokhin believes that if Pentecostalism didn't exist, globalization would have invented it. In a pluralistic world, he says, religious monopolies such as those enjoyed by the Orthodox churches in Eastern Europe, or Catholicism in Latin America, or Hinduism in India, cannot be sustained. Those traditions may remain the religious choice of the majority, but diversification of the religious market is irreversible.

Mitrokhin argues that Pentecostalism is "the ideal form of religion for the globalized world":

- It empowers individuals to act apart from formal structures;
- It provides a sense of community in an atomistic and urbanized culture;
- It's perfectly post-modern, so Pentecostals can assemble a personal spirituality from a smorgasbord of options without incurring doctrinal sanctions;
- Pentecostalism has no clerical caste, so newly self-confident "aspirational" laity don't have to feel subordinate to priests or experts with advanced doctrinal studies;
- Pentecostalism fosters aptitudes in participatory government, since the local church is usually run on a congregationalist basis;
- In a mobile world, Pentecostalism is highly portable.

For at least the next half-century, the most important Christian "other" for the Catholic Church will be Pentecostalism. The implications of that encounter will cut across multiple zones of the Church's life.

Near-Certain Consequences

1. ANOTHER BOON FOR APOLOGETICS

Chapter three made the argument that the rise of Islam, especially its radical elements, will promote growth in Catholic apologetics. In similar fashion, the rise of Pentecostalism will transform the nature of Catholic ecumenism, restoring "defense of the faith" as a central element of the Church's ecumenical strategy. Oscar Osorio, the Catholic Charismatic preacher in Honduras, said that intra-Christian polemics are alive and well in Central

America, where some Pentecostals don't hide their objections to Catholicism.

"They say the Catholic Church is a prostitute, that the pope is the anti-Christ," he said. "They say that we worship the pope and the Virgin Mary. We need to know how to answer these things when people hear them."

Given those pressures, the future is likely to see a growing cottage industry of Catholic apologetic tracts along the lines of "Up from Pentecostalism," written in 1995 by Kathleen M. Gavlas, a convert from the Assemblies of God. Gavlas argued that claims by Pentecostals to do away with the need for clerical intermediaries by insisting that each believer can be directly illuminated by Scripture turned out to be hollow.

"Just the opposite was true," she wrote. "We relied almost entirely on our sect's interpretation of every verse. Any lay person's 'personal interpretation' that didn't line up with the sect's was not tolerated."

Moreover, Gavlas wrote, by putting such a high premium on being "Spirit-filled," Pentecostalism does not provide adequate resources for moments of spiritual aridity or doubt. Catholicism's capacity to root faith in both sentiment and reason, she said, is ultimately a more satisfactory bulwark against tough times.

Robert Sungenis, president of Catholic Apologetics International, has likewise warned of the dangers of what he calls "fanatical Pentecostalism and their fallacious interpretations of Scripture." In his seven-part study on speaking in tongues, Sungenis argues that while the Catholic Church in principle is open to it, and that great saints such as Teresa of Avila and Anthony of Padua had such experiences, that doesn't mean that every Pentecostal claim is legitimate. In fact, he suggested, some Pentecostal practices might actually be demonic.

"It is reasonable to postulate that, if the true gift of tongues were manifested among certain people today, then either the demonic world or the psychologically unstable and egotistically motivated would seek to mimic such divine manifestations in an effort to grab the limelight and/or to deceive the followers of Christ," Sungenis wrote.

In a 2007 discussion among Catholic apologists in the Philippines, several participants expressed a desire to debunk oneness Pentecostalism. They voiced concern that the rapid rise of the Charismatic movement within Catholicism might act as a backdoor to introduce a "oneness" theology of the Trinity into Catholicism.

Such concerns are likely to loom large in the twenty-first century, as the sometimes-turbulent encounter with Pentecostalism breeds a greater willingness on the Catholic side to push back.

2. HORIZONTAL ECUMENISM

As these apologists joust with Pentecostals, other Catholics will strive to keep lines of communication open, believing that détente rather than debate is the best way to win hearts and minds.

At the international level, a formal Catholic–Pentecostal dialogue has existed since 1972. It wasn't easy getting it off the ground; in the early days, according to Pentecostal writer Walter J. Hollenweger, some Pentecostals who met with Catholics asked to have their identities protected out of fear of being ostracized in their own churches. In 1977, the World Pentecostal Conference formally discouraged its members from participating in relationships with Catholics. In the 1980s, Pentecostal scholar and pastor Jerry L. Sandidge, who did advanced studies at the Catholic University in Louvain, wrote a paper titled "A Pentecostal Perspective on Mary" to serve as a basis for discussion in one of these dialogues. For his trouble, the Assemblies of God in the United States kicked him off the payroll. (Perhaps these Pentecostal leaders had in mind the well-known quip of British sociologist Brian Wilson, who said that "churches become ecumenical only when they're in trouble.")

In classic Pentecostal fashion, the answer to official disapproval was private revelation. In the late 1960s, a British plumber named Smith Wigglesworth told a South African Pentecostal minister named David Du Plessis that God was calling Du Plessis to go to all churches, including the Catholic Church, to bring them the message of Pentecost. Du Plessis took the message seriously and became the architect on the Pentecostal side of the first wave of Catholic–Pentecostal conversation.

Things have warmed considerably over the years. In 2000, Pentecostal leaders from twenty-seven denominations took a pilgrimage to the Vatican in order to build closer ecumenical relations. Over 170 members of the Joint College of African-American Pentecostal Bishops attended Pope John Paul II's general audience at the Vatican on February 9, 2000, and worshipped in a Catholic church on February 13. The pope told the Pentecostal bishops, "I am confident that your visit will help strengthen ecumenical relations between Catholics and Pentecostals."

Monsignor Juan Usma Gómez, who since 1996 has overseen Catholic–

Pentecostal dialogue in the Vatican's Pontifical Council for Promoting Christian Unity, said in a 2006 interview, "The Church must not be afraid of the Pentecostal growth" and must not respond "with aggressiveness, even if at times some of these groups act aggressively." Gómez was speaking on the margins of a Rome conference on the Catholic–Pentecostal relationship, where several Pentecostal scholars said that Pentecostalism might be able to help Catholicism deepen its experience of the Holy Spirit.

While such formal dialogues will continue, it's an open question what impact their results will have on wider circles in either Catholicism or Pentecostalism. Given the extraordinarily diffuse nature of Pentecostalism, the model of one global body in conversation with another may not be the best way to structure this exchange.

What is likely to evolve is "horizontal ecumenism," in which individual Catholic parishes, or even Catholic lay movements, associations, or small faith communities, invite local Pentecostal congregations or groups into conversation—sometimes for formal theological exchange, sometimes for concrete cooperation on a matter of local concern, sometimes simply to get to know one another. This form of ecumenism will be sporadic, and the result of chance and individual initiative rather than central planning. If it catches on, it could transform the Pentecostal–Catholic relationship from the bottom up. As these conversations take root, they may build upon Harvey Cox's insight that in many ways, there's already a great deal of common ground between Catholics and Pentecostals.

In the global South, this horizontal ecumenism is already developing organically. As the story of Oscar Osorio demonstrates, Pentecostals are attending Catholic Charismatic retreats, nights of recollection, and prayer meetings, and vice versa. In many ways, some of these Charismatics and Pentecostals probably already think of themselves as more closely related to one another than to nonrenewalist strains in their own traditions. In other parts of the world where the Charismatic movement is not as widespread, this horizontal ecumenism may have to be a bit more intentional.

3. POLITICAL ECUMENISM

Another force that will likely drive Catholics and Pentecostals into one another's arms are the culture wars on issues such as abortion and homosexuality. A pragmatic alliance on these issues will grow in the twenty-first century, especially if the high levels of movement from Catholicism to Pentecostalism cool off, allowing interconfessional antagonism to dissipate.

Brazil offers a classic case in point, where estimates are that there are somewhere between a million and two million clandestine abortions each year. In 2007, Brazil's president, Luiz Inácio Lula da Silva, a Catholic, said that he's personally opposed to abortion, but that "the state cannot abdicate from caring for this as a public health question, because to do so would lead to the death of many young women in this country." To date Brazil has not liberalized its abortion law, but forces in the parliament are pressing to do so.

That's where the Pentecostals come into play. Of all the political and social forces in Brazil, the Pentecostals are most receptive to the Catholic Church's pro-life message. They are a considerable force in Brazil's political galaxy; as of this writing, the Pentecostal bloc in the national legislature represented about 10 percent of the total, roughly sixty members. While the Pentecostals come from different parties and hold different positions on issues such as tax policy and international relations, they are compactly in favor of conservative positions on social questions. Some Pentecostal legislators and ministers were damaged by corruption scandals in 2005 and 2006, but they still represent a potent political force.

This situation presents the Catholic Church with a dilemma. On the one hand, the Church hopes to stop its attrition toward Pentecostalism, and, if possible, to recapture some lost ground. Yet the Church does not want to alienate Pentecostals, because few other constituencies sympathetic to Catholic positions on moral issues can claim the same popular following.

"It's not just the specific question of abortion or homosexuality," one Brazilian journalist explained during the pope's 2007 trip. "It's the broader question of the 'religiousness' of Brazil. If the pope had to rely just on the Catholics, the country would be much more secularized than it already is." One irony of evangelical Catholicism, with its emphasis on hardening the battle lines in the culture wars, may be that it inadvertently ushers in a new era of Catholic–Pentecostal "good feelings."

4. PASTORAL HUSTLE

Pentecostalism may help accomplish something that generations of Catholic bishops, theologians, popes, and pastoral agents were unable to engineer: rousing Latin American Catholicism from its slumber, creating pressure for more personal pastoral care for the Catholics of the continent. A little old-fashioned competition seems to be producing a new sense of pastoral hustle. While the trend is most clear in Latin America, the same phenomenon can be found in other zones where Catholicism faces a stiff Pentecostal challenge.

At the level of formal Church policy, the 2007 General Conference of the Bishops of Latin America and the Caribbean in Brazil marked a sharp break with the past practice of blaming outside forces for the Church's losses. Instead, the Latin American bishops offered a frank admission that 500 years of Roman Catholicism as a near-monopoly in some ways put the Church to sleep, leaving it content with the formal externals of religion but often failing to impart any real sense of personal faith. Recognizing the bankruptcy of that approach, the bishops called for a "Great Continental Mission," driven by old-fashioned, door-to-door pastoral outreach, rather than sitting around in parishes and waiting for people to show up. As the bishops conceived it, this mission would be driven mostly by lay evangelists and would be directed especially at the favelas and barrios of the continent's cities. Whether it gets off the ground successfully is almost beside the point; the very idea reflects a new sense of urgency.

Below the level of official episcopal statements, there are hints that things are moving. Independent lay activists such as Osorio are also a novelty in a Church that for centuries prompted a relatively inert vision of the lay role. Various other forms of lay ministry are now common. In Central America, tens of thousands of laity called "delegates of the word" function as pastoral coordinators for small faith communities. Lay movements such as Focolare, Schönstatt, and Communion and Liberation are growing.

Osorio says Catholicism will be "stronger and better" because of the Pentecostal challenge, because those Catholics who remain will be "passionate about living and sharing their faith."

"We're not losing," Osorio insists. "We're gaining."

If Osorio is right, and a smaller but more dynamic Catholicism emerges, one might compare the result to the impact of the Protestant Reformation in the sixteenth century. Luther's uprising ended Catholicism's monopoly in Europe, but it also contributed to the fruits of the Counter-Reformation. In a similar sense, the rise of Pentecostalism may be stimulating a new burst of creative energy in Catholicism, the outlines of which are only starting to come into focus.

5. MINISTRY TO THE NONES

As noted above, Latin America has a growing share of its population that professes no religious affiliation, sometimes referred to among sociologists as "nones." The term was first coined in the North to describe swelling ranks of secularized Europeans, but some experts caution this is not the best way to understand what's happening in Latin America, where perhaps the single largest category of "nones" is composed of people who left Catholicism for Pentecostalism, and then Pentecostalism for nothing.

Fr. José Oscar Beozzo of Brazil said disaffiliation in his country is an index not of secularization, but of despair.

"I talk to these people," Beozzo said in 2007. "What they tell me is that they do not believe that religion has any meaning for them. They don't believe it has any capacity to change their lives." In that sense, Beozzo said, being a "none" is not so much a specific lack of faith in God or the Church, he said, as a collapse of faith in virtually everything.

Fr. Edward Cleary addressed the growing segment of Guatemalans without religious affiliation in 2004, saying "we know almost nothing about this category." He asked: "What is it like to be without religion in this hotly religious country? Would one feel relief to be on an island of calm away from the heat of religious passion? Do people who say they have no religion still believe in God? Are they hurting and in need of help?"

Attempting to respond to those questions, and to craft pastoral strategies appropriate to the answers, will be an important form of ministry for Catholicism in the twenty-first century. This will be driven not merely by concern for the spiritual well-being of the "nones," but also by the fear that if the phenomenon endures, at some stage a tipping point may arrive in which "none" becomes "anti," and the same ideological hostility to institutional religion characteristic of some zones of Europe may become a mass phenomenon elsewhere.

Probable Consequences

1. ANOTHER BOON FOR INCULTURATION

Chapter seven outlined a paradoxical feature of globalization: it spreads a single global culture at the same moment that it also fosters a reassertion of the local and the particular. Pentecostalism is tailor-made for this process, because it is an expanding global network that leaves tremendous scope for preserving and expressing local beliefs and traditions. This flexibility reflects its emphasis upon the Holy Spirit, which "blows where it will."

For that reason, it's possible for a Pentecostal to see native magic or healing practices as a valid work of the Spirit, which can be reexpressed and incorporated in a Christian guise, and to readily adopt local languages, music, and ritual. Allan Anderson, professor of theology at the Centre for Missiology and World Christianity at the University of Birmingham in England, argues that the "localization" of Pentecostalism is its greatest strength. Byron Klaus, president of the Assemblies of God Theological Seminary in Springfield, Missouri, calls Pentecostalism "the quintessential indigenous religion, adapting readily to a variety of cultures."

The global rise of Pentecostalism is likely to promote inculturation within Catholicism in at least two ways.

First, the size and scope of the Pentecostal movement will mean that Catholic ecumenical dialogue becomes increasingly focused on Pentecostalism. As it does, this will drive pneumatology, meaning the doctrine of the Holy Spirit, to the top of the theological agenda, just as the dialogue with the Eastern Orthodox made ecclesiology, especially the papacy, a key focus of theological concern in the 1980s and 1990s. As the focus shifts to pneumatology, Catholicism will deepen its theological reflection on the activity of the Holy Spirit outside the visible bounds of the Church.

Second, Catholicism will also be led in this direction by the Pentecostal instinct within itself, meaning the rise of Charismatic Catholicism. This form of "Catholic Pentecostalism" is itself strikingly open to adapting local spiritual practices, and as a greater share of priests and bishops in Africa, Asia, and Latin America bring this background with them into leadership roles, it will reinforce the already strong pressure within Catholicism for greater inculturation.

2. A COMEBACK FOR EXORCISM

One concrete form this rising tide of inculturation is likely to take is a renewed interest in the Catholic ritual of exorcism. Chapter one made the argument that the rise of the global South will make exorcism a more regular feature of the pastoral practice of Catholicism, and the Charismatic movement in the Church will likely be the primary vehicle through which this occurs. It will mean both wider use of the formal ritual of exorcism as provided in the liturgical books of the Church, but also a wide variety of informal and "para-liturgical" ceremonies and prayers for the casting out of evil spirits. All this builds on strong interest in spiritual combat and casting out evil spirits in the traditional religious beliefs of cultures all over the world.

For Pentecostals, the struggle with demons is not confined to the arena of formal rituals. In the Pentecostal approach to social ministry, for example, exorcism is a routine part of the picture. Alcohol and drug recovery programs run by Pentecostal churches not only provide counseling and twelve-step programs, but they also typically cast out the evil spirit of drunkenness and teach the recovering addict a range of spiritual disciplines. Such an approach to ministry will be increasingly common in Catholicism, in part because of competitive pressures.

The Catholic Church in the twenty-first century will not only battle poverty and environmental degradation, but it will also challenge the "spirits of this world." In fact, along with the Pentecostals, an increasing share of Catholics will come to see this as one and the same fight.

3. EMPOWERING CATHOLIC WOMEN

Given that Pentecostals tend to foster a strictly traditional moral code that often sees women primarily as wives and mothers, it may seem a curious candidate to be a primary agent for the empowerment of women. Yet there is an implicit egalitarianism in the Pentecostal movement that has allowed women to assume new roles in surprising ways. One of the most powerful Pentecostal pastors of the twentieth century, for example, was Aimee Semple McPherson, founder of the Foursquare Church. "Sister Aimee" was, among other unusual accomplishments for her time, the first woman to own a radio station west of the Mississippi River. From the beginning, women have acted as worship leaders and evangelists in early Pentecostalism, even if men tend to dominate senior leadership positions, and even if many Pentecostal churches formally permit only men to enter the ranks of ministers.

In *Fire from Heaven,* Harvey Cox argued that the Pentecostal emphasis on direct revelation is one key to understanding its emancipatory approach to women.

"It went a long way in answering my question about how so many women win the right to preach in a church which, at least technically, forbids it. It clearly demonstrated why Pentecostals, who take the authority of the Bible very seriously but also believe in direct revelation through visions, have opened a wider space for women than most other Christian denominations. What the Bible says is one thing, but when God speaks to you directly, that supersedes everything else."

For the reasons outlined above, Pentecostalism also tends to be experienced by ordinary women in developing nations as liberating. Pentecostal churches insist that men become better husbands and fathers—not cheating on their wives, not bullying or beating them, and accepting their fair share of the responsibility for raising children. To the extent that men actually do these things, the result is a transformation in the quality of life for Pentecostal women and a corresponding increase in their prospects.

Under the pressure of competition from the Pentecostals, Catholicism across the global South is likely to place a greater premium on empowering its own women, both in terms of Church activity and also in the social sphere.

Cardinal Julio Terrazas Sandoval of Bolivia, speaking during the 2007 assembly of the Latin American bishops in Brazil, addressed the first point.

"One of the things that Protestants do very well is to energize their women," he said. "For the Church to be able to reach out to those who are distant from her, we too must look to our women to help lead the way."

In light of evangelical Catholicism, this push to mobilize women in the twenty-first century will almost certainly not lead to their ordination as priests, but it will produce a climate in which Church leaders are attentive to promoting women into positions of leadership in ways that don't require sacramental ordination. The rise of the Charismatic impulse within Catholicism will also push in this direction, since it encourages spontaneous, noninstitutional participation that's as open to women as it is to men.

Greater attention to the microeconomic impact of Pentecostalism for women will also create pressure for Catholicism to examine its own contribution. Looking at the Pentecostals, some Catholics are likely to argue that if the Church really wants to do something about poverty and injustice, it needs to encourage lifestyle change at the micro level that can provide a "one-person-at-a-time" basis for social reform.

4. A COMEBACK FOR BASE COMMUNITIES

One of the great strengths of Pentecostalism is its capacity to form a sense of community, especially in urban environments where the old networks of social support and identity have broken down. That success creates a strong competitive pressure within Catholicism to cultivate similar social networks, which will often take the form of small Christian communities—what the Latin Americans call "base ecclesial communities," usually meaning groups of no more than fifteen to twenty people who come together for Bible study, prayer, and mutual support. In some cases, these groups may also analyze the social circumstances of the local community and opt to engage in some form of activism.

In 2004, Monsignor Obunga said that the primary pastoral response of the Ugandan Church to the spread of Pentecostalism was promotion of small faith communities. Obunga described them as a vehicle to foster "holistic evangelization."

"This is what small Christian communities are geared towards, personal well-being," Obunga said. "They promote the overall well-being of the human person, body and soul. The sects are doing well in that, because they are very intertwined. They are small groups, so they know each other. They are concerned about the overall welfare of their members. . . . We have something to learn."

In a press conference toward the end of the 2007 conference of Latin American bishops, Cardinal Hummes of Brazil offered an unqualified endorsement: "There are many ecclesiastical base communities, and they are a great accomplishment of the church in Latin America," he said. "They suffered a crisis, but they continue to make contributions . . . they must not be lost, but rather they should be strengthened." The fact that the comments came from a senior Vatican official make them significant, in effect giving "cover" for the bishops to build upon the base community model.

5. MUSIC MINISTRY

Anyone who has been to a thriving Pentecostal church understands that in many ways, the glue that holds the whole thing together is the soundtrack. As Miller of the University of Southern California put it, "The punch behind a lot of it is the music; the originality of the music, its energy, and the cultural embeddedness and appropriateness of the music. Pentecostalism is oftentimes attracting a fairly young constituency. In my opinion, it's because they are initially attracted to the music. That's the portal into this movement."

Music is perhaps the most important, and most distinctive, element of Pentecostal worship. Even former Pentecostals who have been turned off by what they see as exaggerated deference to charismatic leaders, or by what they experience as a lack of depth and intellectual rigor, often say that what they miss most is the music. In a critical March 2006 piece on Pentecostalism in *Christian Century*, Roger Olson describes this sentiment.

"Most of the formerly Full Gospel men and women I know still remember fondly the excitement and passion of the movement," Olson wrote. "Some of us listen to Pentecostal music on CDs, and occasionally raise our hands or clap to its ecstatic words and beat."

Music is an important pastoral priority within Pentecostalism. The U.S.-based Pentecostal Music Association sponsors a sort of Pentecostal version of *American Idol,* holding an annual "North America Talent Search" to identify the best rising stars among Pentecostal male soloists, female soloists, and vocal groups. In many Pentecostal churches, the pulsating sounds of the house band are the primary draw for tens of thousands of regular worshippers. Many Pentecostals call this "raise-the-roof" worship; as one put it, "We don't believe Satan should have *all* the good music."

The success of Pentecostalism in using contemporary and indigenous forms of music in praise and worship has already spawned imitation by the Catholic Charismatics, and this tendency is likely to penetrate even nonexplicitly Charismatic parishes and Catholic gatherings as the twenty-first century moves forward.

Music is one of those areas in Catholic life in which differing trends are steering the Church in different directions. Evangelical Catholicism is driving a renewed interest in musical forms traditionally associated with Catholicism, especially Gregorian chant and polyphony. A 2004 Vatican conference sponsored by the Congregation for Divine Worship, for example, issued a strong call for the recovery of the Church's traditional sacred music. The most dramatic moment came in an address by Monsignor Valentin Miserachs Grau, president of the Pontifical Institute of Sacred Music, who called the abandonment of Gregorian chant in the post–Vatican II era a "deplorable amputation."

Especially given that Pope Benedict XVI has encouraged wider celebration of the pre–Vatican II Mass, one can expect that the recovery of chant and polyphony will be a growing feature of Catholic liturgical life. At the same time, however, the Charismatic movement and the example of the Pentecostals will also push Catholicism in the opposite direction, toward music that's more modern, saucy, and upbeat. Among other things, this suggests that music ministry will be one of the primary arenas in which new tensions in the Church in the twenty-first century are worked out.

Monsignor Giuseppe Liberto, former maestro of the Sistine Chapel Choir, offers one way of trying to reconcile these forces.

"Vatican Two had two beautiful phrases," he said in a 2004 interview. "We must conserve, but we must also augment. Conservation of the antique musical repertory is a custodial duty, but this can't block the charism and the prophecy of inventing new forms."

Possible Consequences

1. THE FAULT LINE OF THE TWENTY-FIRST CENTURY

For more than forty years since the close of the Second Vatican Council, the primary fault line in Catholicism, at least in the North, has run between two camps conventionally known as "liberals" and "conservatives." While everyone knows it's more complicated than that, at a very high level of abstraction the distinction captures something real across a range of issues, such as moral teaching, papal authority, liturgical reform, and the lay role in the Church. Knowing if Catholics identify themselves as "liberals" or as "conservatives" is often a fairly good predictor of which side of the fence they'll occupy on those matters.

Under the influence of evangelical Catholicism, these debates will be increasingly dead letters in the twenty-first century, at least in terms of official policy. The most consequential fault line of the future is more likely to run instead between Pentecostal and non-Pentecostal Catholicism. "Pentecostal Catholicism" is a broader term than "Charismatic," because even Catholics who don't identify themselves as "Charismatic" may share a largely Pentecostal outlook.

It's not a distinction that corresponds with ideology, because there are conservatives and progressives on both sides. Nor is it a doctrinal argument, because for the most part the underlying ideas of both sides are orthodox.

Instead, it has to do with worship, prayer, biblical interpretation, the relationship between institutional and charismatic authority, the balance between tradition and innovation, attitudes toward the supernatural, and a host of other matters that shape the warp and woof of the Church. Will Catholic charities in the twenty-first century dispense prayers for prosperity as well as sandwiches? Will parish councils make decisions on the basis of visions as well as votes? Will pastors vie with laity baptized in the Spirit in terms of setting the parish tone? Will Catholic hospitals make exorcisms as routine as X-rays? Will the soundtrack of the Sunday Mass sound more like Soundgarden than the St. Louis Jesuits? In general, will the Church still see the fruits of the Holy Spirit primarily in terms of the formal sacraments, or will a much wider range of eruptions of the Spirit come to define pastoral practice?

The drama of the next century may hang on the extent to which Catholicism feels compelled to choose between Pentecostal and non-Pentecostal options, or whether it can craft a "both/and" solution.

2. PRO-ISRAELI PRESSURES

Chapter three illustrated how sensitivity to Jewish concerns in world Catholicism is diminishing as the World War II–era generation of European Catholic leaders passes from the scene. If there is a force that might come to occupy the same place in terms of acting as a pro-Israeli balance in Catholic reflection, it may be ecumenical dialogue with Pentecostals. As noted above, many Pentecostals believe in an end-time scenario in which believers will be gathered in Israel, the Jews will convert to Christianity, and then the Second Coming of Jesus will bring history to an end. On the basis of this conviction, the safety and security of Israel has become a major political concern for many Pentecostals.

The Pew Forum data show that in the United States, 60 percent of Pentecostals say they "sympathize with Israel" in the Israeli–Palestinian conflict, as opposed to 40 percent of other Christians. In Brazil, 37 percent of Pentecostals say they sympathize with Israel, as opposed to just 14 percent of other Christians. In the Philippines, 67 percent of Pentecostals feel this way, as compared to 54 percent of other Christians.

At the very least, Pentecostal reaction will factor in Catholic thinking on Israel to a higher degree than has previously been the case.

For the moment, it doesn't seem that pro-Israel sentiment is quite as strong among Catholic Charismatics. According to the Pew Forum data, in most countries Charismatics are less likely than Pentecostals to be pro-Israel, though they are slightly more likely than the general public to hold pro-Israel attitudes. In only three countries are Catholic Charismatics more pro-Israeli than Pentecostals: Nigeria, India, and South Korea. That may be because Pentecostals in those nations better reflect prevailing local attitudes, which tend to be strongly pro-Palestinian, whereas Catholics are more influenced by the balancing mechanisms at work in the global Catholic Church.

Long-Shot Consequences

1. WILL THE PARISH PERISH?

While Pentecostalism is localized, that doesn't mean it follows traditional geographical patterns of assembling congregations. The entrepreneurial nature of Pentecostalism means that few Pentecostals feel stuck in their neighborhood church. If they're dissatisfied, they either go somewhere else, or they start a church of their own. By its nature, Pentecostalism subverts traditional modes of ecclesiastical organization, especially those based on territorial boundaries.

At least on paper, Catholics are firmly committed to a decidedly non-Pentecostal territorial system in the form of parishes and dioceses. The logic is not simply that this is a mode of bureaucratic organization inherited from the Roman Empire. It also makes an ecclesiological statement, which is that the local community ought to be the entire Church in microcosm, the place where Catholics of differing socioeconomic status, ideological outlooks, backgrounds, and experiences check their differences at the door.

Yet in the twenty-first century, it's a fair question to ask if neighborhoods actually perform this function any longer. Across much of the world, the poor are crowded into urban barrios while the rich live in gated communities, meaning that neighborhoods often don't perform much of a mixing function. Geographical mobility also erodes the traditional notion of the parish as a stable community since people move in and out all the time. In such a world, Catholics may come to believe that the Pentecostal form of ecclesiastical organization—which assembles congregations on the basis of attraction to charismatic personalities, preferences in liturgical style, or simply the warmth of community experience—is the most logical way to structure the local Church.

In some ways, Catholicism is already moving in this direction. Catholics who belong to one of the new movements often receive most of their spiritual formation and even sacramental life within the movement. Catholic Charismatics often mimic the patterns of Pentecostal spirituality, gravitating to where the most dynamic preaching, praise, and worship can be found.

Parishes and dioceses aren't going to die off, but they may become steadily more akin to the titular sees that popes assign to bishops in the Vatican, a diocese that's still on the books but doesn't have any actual flock. It's possible that in the Catholicism of the future, most Catholics won't think of themselves as members of "St. Ann's Parish," but rather as members of the Charismatic community, movement, or small faith group that best corresponds to their spiritual inclinations. The way in which priests are assigned could change. Rather than being the "Pastor of St. Anne's Parish," Fr. Tim would become "Pastor of the Awesome Power of God Catholic Community," which might assemble at multiple locations, even bringing a patchwork collection of various parishes into its orbit.

Some of these networks might morph into Catholic churches, with their pastors (or their lay founders) becoming the de facto equivalent of bishops.

That's more or less what happened in the Philippines with the El Shaddai movement, leading to serious tensions in 2000 when then-cardinal Jaime Sin of Manila wanted President Joseph Estrada to step down, while El Shaddai's lay founder, Mike Velarde, supported Estrada. Given the size and devotion of Velarde's following, it was an open question to some observers whether Velarde or Sin actually had the greater political influence.

One structure Catholicism might draw upon in this regard is the "personal prelature," currently utilized only by Opus Dei, but which in principle is designed to allow priests and lay faithful to be attached to nonterritorial groupings rather than to physical parishes and dioceses. The twenty-first century could see an explosion of these personal prelatures, many of which would rise and fall depending upon how they fare in the Catholic spiritual marketplace. In a sense, this scenario is one specific application of the more basic question raised earlier, which is how far Catholicism will go in the direction of "Pentecostalization."

Parishes in this new world could shut down not just because Catholics have physically moved away, but because they've taken their business elsewhere. Again, that's already the case in some ways; every diocese has parishes that thrive and those that seem to be sleepwalking, and lots of Catholics go out of their way to avoid the latter. Nevertheless, the traditional Catholic emphasis on the "givenness" of a parish acts as a brake on that development. In the Catholicism of the future, it may seem a brake that has outlived its usefulness.

TRENDS THAT AREN'T

The list of ten trends in this book didn't just fall from the sky. At one point or another, I considered at least a couple dozen other trajectories in the Church as possible trends. The list mutated as I added and subtracted trends, collapsed some currents into others, and either expanded or contracted the number of items under review. At one stage I had twenty trends, at another five. Of the ten trends as they now stand, only four were on the list of fifteen I sketched when I had the original idea for the book, though elements of many of the remaining eleven have been subsumed under other headings. In a way, I developed this list the way a scientist works out a theory in the lab, forming hypotheses and testing them experimentally to see if they really explain the data, then adjusting the theory as the results roll in. I certainly don't claim that the final list carries scientific certainty, but I can at least promise that I didn't just jot down the first things that occurred to me on a cocktail napkin.

One way I experimented with the trends was by periodically publishing draft lists in my online column, "All Things Catholic," and inviting comments from readers. Thousands took me up on the offer, from every corner of the world. Another series of experiments came in the form of presentations to roughly 200 audiences in various places, and those folks weren't shy about voicing their thoughts either.

The feedback, as one might expect, has been staggeringly diverse, covering all points of the Catholic compass. One ultratraditionalist insisted that I name the illegitimacy of every pope since Pius XII as a Catholic trend, while an avant-garde advocate of women priests argued passionately that wildcat ordinations of women by rogue bishops in various parts of the world deserved to make the list. Some suggestions were even more idiosyncratic. One persistent reader, for example, has informed me repeatedly that this entire project will be a sham if I don't make reference to the work of René Girard on "mimetic desire." (I wonder if that sentence means I'm out of the woods.) Another said that I'll miss everything that matters in the twenty-first century if I don't include String Theory. One rule of thumb I developed, in light of such proposals: if I have to google a proposed trend to figure out what it means, it's probably not setting the Catholic world on fire.

In a striking number of cases, recommendations seemed to cancel one another out. One reader suggested I identify "squelching Vatican II" as a trend, for example, while another proposed "recovering the real Vatican II." "Dissent" and "conscience" commonly popped up, usually from people who either wanted to condemn the former or celebrate the latter. One reader tipped "ecumenism," and the very next e-mail in the box proposed "the death of ecumenism."

Drawn completely at random, here's a sampling of other proposed trends:

1. The priest shortage
2. "Clown Masses"
3. Fundamentalism
4. Eucharistic adoration
5. Pets replacing children
6. Homosexuals
7. Recentralization of authority in the Church
8. The permanent diaconate
9. Catholic TV
10. Feminism
11. Sexuality
12. Species loss
13. Systematic corruption in the Church
14. Mysticism
15. Intellectual dishonesty
16. John Paul II's New Evangelization
17. The Globalization of Gang Wars

18. Dissolution of the Family
19. Cyber-spirituality
20. Return to orthodoxy
21. "Hierarchicalism"
22. Confession
23. Secularization of Catholic colleges
24. Divorced and remarried Catholics
25. Gregorian Chant

Sometimes, people offering these ideas didn't quite seem to grasp the descriptive thrust of this project. In the end, they weren't so much suggesting that their favorite candidate really is a trend, but that it deserves to be. This helps explain the obvious ideological edge to some of these suggestions. (It's hard to think of "Clown Masses," for example, or "Systematic corruption," as neutral descriptive terms, even though there's probably some degree of reality behind both.) In the end, many of these suggestions were fairly easy to discard. Often, they ended up as pieces of a larger picture, or they didn't make the cut at all.

Criteria for a Trend

As I struggled with how to make these judgments, I eventually developed six criteria for what counts as a trend:

First, the trend has to be global, as opposed to something associated primarily with a given country or region. That doesn't mean it has to be happening everywhere, but rather that it's broad enough to transcend boundaries of language, ethnicity, socioeconomic profile, and regional differences.

Second, the proposed trend has to have a significant impact at the Catholic grassroots, indicating that there's really movement in the direction it indicates that goes beyond a small clique of theologians, activists, clergy, or (perhaps the worst of all possible worlds) journalists. "Significant" is a slippery word, but in the end I applied the "know it when you see it" standard.

Third, there has to be evidence that the official leadership of the Church is engaged on the issues that fall under the trend, and that it carries at least the potential to influence Catholicism in terms of its institutional resources and structures. As much as Catholics might grumble about the bishops or the Vatican, it's fantasy to believe that one can project the Catholic future without attention to their interests and priorities. If the Church is to move in the direction the trend suggests, it can't be something that officialdom would rule out on principle, or that in practice it's likely to ignore.

Fourth, the trend has to have explanatory power. That is, it has to provide a context in which a wide variety of events, issues, and developments in the life of the Church, which on their own might seem random or isolated, can be understood as expressions of a deeper impulse. For that reason, a trend shouldn't be a single issue or a cause, but rather a broad category within which disparate pieces of the Catholic puzzle can be assembled. One test for explanatory power is whether the trend explains developments not just in one area, such as liturgy or moral theology, but across several.

Fifth, the trend also has to have predictive power. That is, understanding this current should help anticipate where the Church might go on a variety of fronts, even if the details of how the trend might work itself out are open-ended and dependent on a number of contingent circumstances. A trend that's too ripped from today's headlines would fail this test. A trend shouldn't pivot on a transient episode or a closed chapter in history, but rather should be a deep current that seems likely to keep flowing.

Sixth, the trend cannot be ideologically driven. It shouldn't imply a judgment about what's happening in the Church. Rather, it should describe a current that Catholics of all theological outlooks and political persuasions should be able to recognize, even if they might draw very different conclusions about its meaning or what to do about it.

By those standards, it should be reasonably clear why the twenty-five items listed above fail one or another of those tests. The priest shortage, for example, is global, and it's certainly got the attention of both the grassroots and the hierarchy. Yet it's too specific to be a trend by itself. It's better understood as a component of several different trends, such as the expansion of lay roles in the Church and the phenomenon of Catholic losses to Pentecostalism. "Return to orthodoxy" and "hierarchicalism" represent suggestions that clearly betray a particular stance on intra-Catholic debates.

As I developed the project, there were five persistent candidates for trends that at one stage or another were on my list, and for which one can make a convincing case based on the criteria set out above. Each one is discussed at length at some point in the book, yet in the end none seemed to work as a trend in its own right. It's worthwhile to explain briefly why each didn't make the cut, because doing so illustrates something important about pondering the future of the Church in the twenty-first century.

Women

Far and away the most frequent comment I received as I developed this project is that any list of Catholic trends has to include something on women. Sorting through the feedback, it seems that people intend this assertion in one of two ways: either as an ideological statement about needed reforms in the Church, or as a practical insight regarding the evolving nature of leadership and pastoral practice.

At the ideological level, those who insist on women as a trend sometimes mean the ordination of women as priests, which they see as a remedy for long-standing patriarchal bias, or the adoption of less "masculine" religious imagery in Catholicism, such as a transition to inclusive language in prayer and worship (referring to "people" rather than "man," or talking about God as "Mother" as well as "Father"). More broadly, some refer to pressure for "feminization" of the Church, by which they mean the evolution of a Church that, as they would put it, is less hierarchical and male-dominated, more inclusive and participatory, and less absolute on doctrinal matters, especially on sexual ethics.

Such Catholics often report that they feel deep anguish over the present state of affairs. One religious sister in Michigan wrote in early 2007 with these reflections: "Many women struggle bravely to effect change within the sexist, hierarchical structures, but the cost is very high and painful. Many have silently slipped away, too disillusioned and determined not to live in a way that contradicts their dignity as images of God. . . . John, it is a very sad and painful time for many critically conscious women within the Catholic Church right now."

Without in any sense questioning the sincerity of those views, it's relatively easy to knock down "women" as a trend in this sense, because it contradicts my third criterion, meaning some indication that the Church will move in this direction officially and institutionally. There is no serious reason to believe that within the arc of time under consideration in this book, meaning the rest of the twenty-first century, the Church will ordain women, abandon its hierarchical structures in favor of something more inclusive, or significantly relax its teachings on sexual ethics. These issues will continue to be the subject of intense theological debate, and they will remain a source of personal suffering for Catholic women who feel alienated. But especially in light of evangelical Catholicism, the institutional Church of the twenty-first century is unlikely to adopt this canon of proposed reforms.

At the other end of the spectrum, some Catholics argue for the emergence of a "New Feminism" as a trend, meaning a new reading of male–female relationships informed by the anthropology of Pope John Paul II, which sees the relationship between the sexes in terms of complementarity: that their roles are equal in dignity but nonetheless different, and that men and women complete one another. Often this approach is set in opposition to classical feminism, which some critics see as promoting competition between men and women. In general, this new feminism takes Catholic teaching on sexuality, marriage, family, and the priesthood as a point of departure. American Catholic writer Helen Alvaré, for example, put the point this way in a 1997 essay: "A new feminism also remembers that it is a waste of time to rail against objective truths. Trying to be free of our bodies' reproductive abilities or of the emotional consequences of promiscuity is as futile as trying to be free of gravity." There's no question that this new feminism has become an important topic of discussion in evangelical Catholic circles, but to date it's difficult to see evidence that it has had a sufficiently significant impact on the broader cultural conversation, or within the confines of Catholic theological debate, to count as a trend in its own right.

What other people seem to mean by "women" as a trend is a bit more descriptive, such as the accelerating tendency for women to play visible leadership roles in ways short of priestly ordination, such as female chancellors of dioceses or Vatican officials. Or, they sometimes mean reliance on women as grassroots evangelists, catechists, and lay ministers. Both of these things are indeed happening, and they're described in detail in chapter five.

In terms of institutional leadership, however, the same thing is also true of lay men. This suggests the trend is really about a redefinition of the roles of clergy and laity, rather than those of men and women. For that reason, it made more sense to treat this trajectory under the aegis of "expanding lay roles."

At the grassroots, it's certainly true that Catholicism in the twenty-first century will rely upon women as its principal evangelizers and catechists. But then, so did Catholicism in the twentieth century, and the tenth, and for that matter the first. This overrepresentation of women among the most active faithful is characteristic not just of Catholicism, but of any religion you care to name. Sociologists Rodney Stark and Alan Miller have studied the "gender gap" in religion, and they conclude that women are more religious than men by virtually any measure and in virtually every culture. Catholicism has always depended upon women to transmit the faith within families and within communities. To call this a "trend" therefore would be akin to asserting that the rising of the sun is a trend. The difference today is that a growing subset of Catholic women are occupying formal ministerial roles, which the Church in the United States calls "ecclesial lay ministry." That's important, and it's described at length in chapter five, but it amounts to a formalization of a function that Catholic women have performed since the very beginning.

I'm conscious, of course, that a book about the most important currents in the Catholic Church written by a man that doesn't put women on the list courts criticism of masculine blindness. For a time, I flirted with titling my fifth trend "Women and Laity"—which, as several people pointed out, is one of the most redundant expressions coined in recent Catholic memory. In the end, I hope readers will perceive that I don't intend to take sides in debates over whether Catholicism is hostile to women, nor do I mean to gloss over the staggering contributions women make to the Church. In terms of a trend, however, the point boils down to this: If we're talking about "women" in terms of sweeping theological changes, it's not likely to happen soon; if we mean "women" in terms of leadership in the trenches, it happened a long time ago.

The Sexual Abuse Crisis

If this were a book about mega-trends in American Catholicism, the sexual abuse crisis would inarguably deserve a spot on the list. If the criteria for inclusion were exclusively moral and spiritual, the crisis once again would make the cut. The pain inflicted upon the victims and their families, all by itself, ought to command the attention of Catholics everywhere, especially of Church leaders in a position to ensure that such abuses do not recur. During his visit to the United States in April 2008, Pope Benedict XVI rightly referred to the sexual abuse of children by priests as "evil" and a "sin," candidly acknowledging that the crisis was "sometimes very badly handled" by Church leaders. The pontiff's meeting with victims of sexual abuse during that trip, and a similar session later in 2008 with victims during a trip to Australia, were important signs of pastoral sensitivity.

Nor, to be sure, is the story over. In May 2009, for example, a report by a government commission in Ireland documented decades of rapes, humiliation, and beatings of both boys and girls at Church-run reform schools, reawakening the wounds of the crisis in that once ultra-Catholic nation. In the same month, the Diocese of Bridgeport, Connecticut, in the United States was hit with an appeals court decision demanding the release of thousands of documents related to the handling of sex abuse cases. It seems safe to say that the shadow of the sexual abuse crisis will continue to fall across the Catholic Church for some time to come.

Yet from a purely descriptive point of view, it's difficult to make the argument that the crisis looms large in the day-to-day concerns of either the Catholic grassroots or the hierarchy anywhere outside the English-speaking zones of the world, meaning principally the United States, Canada, the United Kingdom, Ireland, Australia, and New Zealand. This is not to say, of course, that only English-speaking priests sexually abuse children. Similar episodes have cropped up all over, and there's no reason to believe the behavior of priests is worse in the United States, Canada, and so on, than anywhere else. Yet nowhere outside the English-speaking zone has sexual abuse by priests generated anything like the same cultural reaction. Though there are many reasons why that's the case, one important factor is the evolution of corporate liability in Anglo-Saxon civil law, which makes it easier to hold institutions accountable for wrongdoing by their personnel, as well as to use the instruments of the civil law to compel public disclosure of that wrongdoing. The capacity to generate massive financial settlements is also part of this picture.

However one explains it, the fact is that nowhere else has the sexual abuse crisis gripped the public imagination to the same degree. In December 2006, Redemptorist Fr. Don Kirchner, a missionary in the Amazon for thirty-eight years, wrote to tell me that he had just returned from the annual National Moral Theology Congress in São Paulo, which brings together priests, nuns, and laypeople from all over Brazil.

"Never once was the subject brought up," Kirchner said of the sexual abuse crisis. "It is simply not an issue in the wider church, if for no other reason than things like sexual scandals have always been around." That captures the reality I have heard time and again from Catholics in various parts of the world.

Moreover, even within the United States the crisis has not had quite the transformative impact that some predicted. Alarmists warned that a collapse of confidence in the official Church, or outrage about massive payouts, would cause severe declines in financial contributions. Instead, the Center for Applied Research in the Apostolate conducted a survey in 2006 that found "either a very minimal decline or no substantive change in parish giving at all" attributable to the sexual abuse crisis. A February 2008 survey by CARA found that more than eight in ten American Catholics described themselves as "somewhat" or "very" satisfied with the leadership of Pope Benedict XVI, and more than seven in ten were at least "somewhat" satisfied with the job performance of the American bishops. That data, it's worth noting, was collected six years after the peak period of the sexual abuse crisis in 2002, meaning that sufficient time had elapsed for at least some of the long-term impact to become visible. Whatever one makes of the ultimate lessons of the crisis, the swift implosions of Church structures and episcopal authority that seemed obvious or inevitable to some observers seven years ago have not materialized.

What this illustrates is the danger of evaluating trends on the basis of the here and now—"here" in the sense of a given location, and "now" in the sense of the present, especially if that present happens to fall in the middle of a crisis that's making front-page news. In thinking about the future of Catholicism, perspective is critical. Developments have to be seen against the backdrop of a complex global Church, and against a long enough arc of time to separate transient currents from those that produce deep and lasting change.

None of this is to minimize the gravity of the crisis, or the pain of those most affected by it. As of this writing, the Catholic Church in the United States has paid more than $2 billion in settlements related to the crisis, and five dioceses have gone into bankruptcy, both of which suggest the mammoth dimensions of what has happened. Nor is it to suggest that every issue the crisis generated has been satisfactorily resolved. Several deep questions highlighted by the crisis, such as the accountability of bishops and structures for lay participation in governance, are treated in this book. Yet from a global point of view, the sexual abuse crisis is more akin to the priest shortage than to Islam or the biotech revolution—meaning a specific development that forms part of a bigger picture, rather than a deep current that supplies the context to make sense of other developments.

Polarization

In many sectors of Catholicism these days, it can be difficult to have a rational conversation on the merits of almost anything, because discussion is immediately swept up into the Church's version of the culture wars. A classic illustration has recently been offered by debate over whether the Church might approve the use of condoms in the highly limited circumstance of a married couple in which one partner is HIV-positive and the other is not, on the grounds that in this specific situation the intent would not be to block pregnancy but rather to block disease. In the language of classical Catholic moral theology, it's a question of what's known as "double effect." If a proposed action can be foreseen to have both a good effect and a bad effect, one can do it if the action is not morally wrong on other grounds; if the intent is the good effect, not the bad; if the good effect does not result from the bad; and if there's a reasonable proportion between the good to be achieved and the harm to be done.

Catholic moral theologians are divided, as are members of the hierarchy, as to whether those standards apply to condoms for couples in which a partner is HIV-positive. It's exceedingly difficult to take up the question dispassionately, however, because forces on all sides rush to impute a broader agenda. For pro-life Catholics, this often seems like the beginning of the end for the Church's ban on birth control; for reform-minded Catholics, this could be the opening salvo in doctrinal changes across the board. As a result, discussion becomes frozen in place because we're not talking about the issue anymore, but about what it symbolizes for various constituencies.

This situation is conventionally referred to as "polarization," though that's misleading if it's taken to mean that there are only two poles that matter, labeled "liberal" and "conservative." In fact, the reality is more akin to tribalism, with a variety of groups each vying to promote their own causes and outlooks. There are social justice Catholics, liturgical traditionalists, Charismatics, reform Catholics, neoconservatives, and a variety of other factions. In principle that diversity should be a source of strength, but in practice it often amounts to a kind of voluntary ghettoization in which members of the various tribes speak their own language, follow their own heroes, and engage members of the other tribes largely as sparring partners in ideological debates. This situation is frustrating and counterproductive, to say nothing of its inconsistency with Catholic ecclesiology, but it shapes the way everything in the Church is understood, including the trends described in this book.

Yet it too fails to rise to the level of a trend, for two reasons.

First, it's not truly global. The sort of ideological splintering I've described is by and large characteristic of the global North. The tendency to form interest groups is not a feature of the Church in most parts of the South to the same degree, in large measure because Southern Catholics are not as preoccupied with internal Catholic questions. In fact, as outlined in chapter one, the rise of the South may drive a reconfiguration of existing party lines.

Second, it's not ideologically neutral. That may sound paradoxical, because the point of naming polarization (or tribalism) as a trend is to stand apart from ideological partisanship. Yet in some sectors of opinion in the Church, "polarization" is by now a loaded term. It suggests to some that one should go gingerly in defending Church teaching for fear of creating division. In reality, these Catholics argue, polarization is a manifestation of dissent. The Catholic Church stands for things, they say, and fear of stepping on toes cannot become an excuse for soft-pedaling the Church's positions. This is a view, for obvious reasons, especially associated with evangelical Catholicism. To name polarization as a trend would therefore be read by some as taking a position in intra-Church debates.

The point is that operating on the descriptive level, trying to find analytical frameworks that people won't suspect of harboring hidden agenda, requires sensitivity to language. Ironically, the very act of naming polarization as a trend could inadvertently contribute to the phenomenon it purports to describe. Instead, I deal with polarization and tribalism under the rubric of several trends, especially world Catholicism and evangelical Catholicism. I also came back to these themes in the final chapter, this time in a slightly more prescriptive key.

The Movements

The twentieth century was one of those periods of Church history in which a new form of Catholic life arose to respond to a new social or cultural challenge. The fifth and sixth centuries generated European monasticism, especially the Benedictines, as the old world of the Roman Empire collapsed. The twelfth and thirteenth centuries gave the Church the mendicant orders, such as the Franciscans and the Dominicans, in response to urbanization and the consequent need to evangelize the cities as well as the countryside. The Counter-Reformation gave birth to the Jesuits, and the period following the French Revolution saw the foundation of a wide variety of orders intended to rebuild the Church after a century of devastation.

What made the twentieth century unique is that Catholicism spawned not a new mode of religious life, but a new way of harnessing the energy and commitment of laypeople, in the form of the "new movements." To date, the

Vatican has given canonical recognition to more than 120 such groups, which encompass a wide variety of aspirations, theological outlooks, and spiritual inclinations. The better-known movements include groups such as the Focolare, the Neocatechumenate, Regnum Christi, L'Arche, and Opus Dei. (Opus Dei is technically a prelature rather than a movement, but that's a detail for another time.)

Though most of the new movements were founded in Europe, many now have a global reach, so they pass muster as a trend on that score. While some Catholics see them as predominantly conservative, closer examination reveals considerable diversity, so elevating them as a trend would not be tantamount to taking sides in Catholic debate. They're by definition a grassroots phenomenon, and they also enjoy tremendous support from the hierarchy.

Where the movements fall short, however, is in terms of explanatory power. On their own, the movements really explain only one phenomenon: the movements. It's only when they're seen in terms of a broader ferment in the lay role in the Church that they can be properly understood. In fact, there's a sense in which treating them as a trend almost undersells their importance. In isolation, the movements tell the story of their own membership, which is a relatively small piece of the larger Catholic pie, and their own activities. Seen as part of expanding lay roles in the Church, the movements can be understood as incubators and laboratories for new approaches to the lay vocation in its broadest sense, which means that they carry implications for virtually every member of the Church, whether they belong to a formal group or not.

John Paul II

When the Beatles recorded the song "Fool on the Hill" in 1967, one theory that made the rounds was that the song was an oblique reference to Pope Paul VI, who by that time was seen in some quarters as a rather sad and lonely figure ignored by the world. "Nobody ever hears him, or the sound he appears to make," seemed to some a rather apt description. While there's no particular reason to think that's actually what was in the heads of John Lennon and Paul McCartney, the fact that the idea even occurred to people is revealing in terms of public perceptions.

Had the song come out twenty years later, in 1987, it's unlikely anyone would have taken it as a reference to John Paul II. Whether people liked what John Paul had to say or not, it would have been difficult to suggest that nobody heard him. By virtually any standard one might apply, John Paul II was one of the most consequential players on the global stage in recent memory: from his role in the collapse of Communism to his vocal opposition to the U.S.-led war in Iraq, from his pioneering travels to his staunch reassertion of traditional Catholic teaching, this was a pope who mattered. As the third-longest-reigning pontiff in history, he shaped Catholicism for more than a quarter-century. Perhaps most consequentially, he took a Church that had been locked in internal debates and turned it inside out, confidently urging it to "set off into the deep," reawakening its capacity to evangelize and to engage the broader social and political causes of the day.

This "Wojtyla Revolution" is undeniably global, and it certainly has a footprint in the Church both from a "bottom up" point of view as well as "top down." It's a bit more problematic in terms of ideological neutrality, because there's wide debate in the Church about various aspects of the late pope's legacy. Even the most ferocious critics of John Paul II, however, would have a hard time arguing that he was inconsequential.

Where this proposed trend comes up short is its predictive power. Put simply, the "Wojtyla Revolution" is a better category for a chapter (or several chapters) in recent Church history than it is a tool for discerning the Catholic future. It makes too much depend upon one personality. Many impulses associated with John Paul's pontificate will continue to exercise a profound impact on the Church, especially because an entire generation of bishops, priests, and laity came of age under his leadership, but those impulses won't shape the future because John Paul II is pushing them forward. They'll do so because they correspond with deep movements of history, which need to be tagged and understood on their own. As a trend, "John Paul II" sweeps together a cluster of disparate trajectories under the heading of a single charismatic figure, which doesn't contribute very much in terms of analysis.

Moreover, such a trend runs the risk of "presentism," of presuming straight-line developments from current realities, which almost never adequately anticipates the wild cards that the future always deals. For these reasons, John Paul's legacy is better understood as a force within the trends presented in this book, providing one baseline for how Catholicism may perceive and react to the challenges these trends create.

CATHOLICISM IN THE TWENTY-FIRST CENTURY

I f past history were all there is to the game," American investment tycoon Warren Buffett once remarked, "the richest people in the world would be librarians." In typical homespun fashion, the Oracle of Omaha's point is that strategies premised on the assumption that the future will be like the past, only more so, generally turn out to be wrong. The trick is anticipating where things are moving, not where they've been. The point of this book has been to do that for global Catholicism, surveying the most important trends shaping the Catholic future. To review, the ten trends are:

1. A World Church
2. Evangelical Catholicism
3. Islam
4. The New Demography
5. Expanding Lay Roles
6. The Biotech Revolution
7. Globalization
8. Ecology
9. Multipolarism
10. Pentecostalism

It's time now to try to see the forest composed of all these trees. This final chapter synthesizes the impact of these mega-trends on the Catholic

Church, especially what they might mean for the Church's contribution to the great challenges facing the human family in the twenty-first century. The chapter is designed as a stand-alone summary of the main ideas of this book, offering a big-picture sketch of what the upside-down Church of the future will be like. For teachers, book club moderators, leaders of small faith groups, or anyone else wishing to foster a discussion about the trends I've surveyed, the present chapter would be the best chunk of material to refer to by way of an overview.

Before coming to that, however, an industrial-size caution is in order, because the presumption that these mega-trends necessarily will turn the Catholic Church upside down rests on a potentially shaky premise.

One might reasonably ask whether Buffett's law really applies to the Catholic Church. Catholicism famously thinks in centuries; the modus operandi tends to be, "Talk to us on Wednesday, and we'll get back to you in three hundred years." In the Vatican, no reaction to any proposal garners consensus more readily than, "It's not yet opportune," which translates as, "Let's do nothing." The multiple layers of authority in Catholicism, its strong emphasis on tradition, and its deliberately self-referential ethos are all designed to ensure that the Church doesn't march to the beat of a given culture or historical moment. Facile claims that the Church must move in this direction or that are almost always projections of someone's agenda rather than sober analysis. One can imagine a book on Catholic trends in the early nineteenth century, for example, spotting the collapse of European monarchies as a force that would also bring down the papacy, and look where that prediction would have ended up.

So, are claims of important changes looming on the Church's horizon almost by definition overwrought? Only time will tell in individual cases. But even in Catholicism, change can sometimes sweep away old paradigms in what may seem historically like the blink of an eye. Perhaps an example will help.

A Precedent for Paradigm Shift: Mastro Titta

Though it's a bit off the beaten track, Catholic visitors to Rome owe themselves a quick trip to the state-run Criminology Museum just across the Tiber River from the Vatican. There, in a back room on the first floor, twelve feet tall and looking to be in perfect working order, stands the papal guillotine.

A gift from Napoleon, the guillotine was used in the Papal States throughout the nineteenth century. The man who wielded it in the pope's name was Giovanni Battista Bugatti, nicknamed Mastro Titta (a Roman corruption of *maestro di giustizia*, or "master of justice"). In his time, Bugatti was a celebrity. Byron jotted a few lines about him, and Charles Dickens left a lengthy recollection in *Pictures of Italy* after watching him work one afternoon in 1845. Today, his memory lives on as legends often do, in half-remembered anecdotes and obscure ditties. Roman mothers sing their little ones to sleep with a rhyme that goes: "*Sega, sega, Mastro Titta.*" *Segare* is the Italian verb "to saw," so the mental image implied is ghoulishly accurate.

Ironically, Italy in the era of Mastro Titta actually formed the vanguard of the abolitionist movement on capital punishment. The Grand Duchy of Tuscany had become the first sovereign state to ban the death penalty in 1786. It did so under the influence of Italian essayist Cesare Beccaria, whose 1764 anti-death-penalty tract "On Crimes and Punishments" is considered a classic. So strong had Italian aversion to capital punishment become that when an anarchist named Angelo Bresci assassinated King Umberto I in 1900, Italian courts sentenced him to life in prison. It was the first time a man had killed a European king, without toppling his regime, and not been executed.

The Catholic Church was not part of this development. Its guillotine was busy up to the very last minute of the pope-king's regime. Its final use came on July 9, 1870, just two months before Italian revolutionaries captured Rome. What explains that stubbornness? For one thing, the clear witness of Church tradition. Saint Augustine defended capital punishment in *The City of God* in the fourth century: "Since the agent of authority is but a sword in the hand [of God], it is in no way contrary to the commandment 'Thou shalt not kill' for the representative of the state's authority to put criminals to death," he wrote. Aquinas followed Augustine in the thirteenth century in *Summa Contra Gentiles*. "The civil rulers execute, justly and sinlessly, pestiferous men in order to protect the state," he wrote. Nor was this tradition confined to the Middle Ages. As late as September 14, 1952, Pope Pius XII echoed its logic. "It is reserved to the public power to deprive the condemned of the benefit of life, in expiation of his fault, when already he has dispossessed himself of the right to live," the pope said. Leading abolitionists of the eighteenth and nineteenth centuries were Enlightenment-inspired critics of revealed religion, so popes defended the right to send people to death because to do otherwise seemed tantamount to abandoning belief in eternal life.

As part of this tradition, Mastro Titta experienced execution as a sacred liturgy, rich with ritual and spiritual meaning. The morning of each execution, the pope said a special prayer for the condemned in his private chapel. A priest would visit Mastro Titta to hear his confession and to administer Communion, symbolizing in the sacramental argot that the executioner was fully christened by the Church. The execution was solemnized by a special order of monks, the *Arciconfraternita della Misericordia*, or Brotherhood of Mercy. They delivered pastoral care to condemned prisoners and celebrated the rituals surrounding their deaths. Pope Innocent VIII in 1488 assigned them the aptly named Roman church of *San Giovanni Battista Decollato*—St. John Baptist Beheaded.

The brotherhood stayed with the condemned in their last twelve hours of life, praying with them, offering the sacraments, and encouraging them to ask God's forgiveness. Under papal law no execution could take place before sundown, the time of the Ave Maria, if the monks had not succeeded in eliciting a confession. Members of the brotherhood wrote prayer books and catechisms for death-row inmates, paying special attention to the requirements for a *mors bon Christiana*—"a good Christian death." The monks led the condemned through the streets in a sacred procession. Altar boys went first, ringing bells, while the monks chanted special litanies. Incense was burned as they walked. The monks donned hooded whitish-brown robes and carried a crucifix, usually wrapped with a black shawl. (Some of these robes and crucifixes are also on display in the Criminology Museum.) They would hold the crucifix toward the condemned, so that it was the last thing he saw. Historian James Megivern describes the theology underlying this liturgy of execution as "gallows pietism." The idea was that an execution was a form of expiation, a way for the condemned person to atone for evil done. Devotional literature compared the redemptive value of the blood spilled to Christ's sacrifice on the cross.

All of which makes the shift in thinking in the Catholic Church over just the last fifty years nothing short of astonishing.

When the new *Catechism of the Catholic Church* appeared in 1992, it did not ban capital punishment outright, but expressed a strong preference for "bloodless means." Such strategies, it said, "better correspond to the concrete conditions of the common good and are more in conformity to the dignity of the human person." In his 1995 encyclical *Evangelium Vitae*, Pope

John Paul II further tightened this teaching, writing that the only time executions can be justified is when they are required "to defend society," and that "as a result of steady improvements . . . in the penal system such cases are very rare, if not practically nonexistent." On the stump, John Paul used still sharper language. During a visit to St. Louis in January 1999, he said that the death penalty is "both cruel and unnecessary." Human life must not be taken "even in case of someone who has done great evil." Popes have also relentlessly interceded on behalf of death-row inmates, and the St. Louis trip occasioned John Paul's best-known success. Then-Missouri governor Mel Carnahan commuted the death sentence of Darrell Mease in response to a direct plea for mercy from John Paul II.

Church historians locate the roots of changed Catholic thinking on the death penalty in the Second Vatican Council, as well as in John XXIII's 1963 encyclical *Pacem in Terris*, both of which endorsed universal human rights and especially the right to life. Papal criticism of the death penalty became more explicit under Paul VI. When the Vatican city-state came into existence in 1929, its Fascist-era constitution included a provision for execution of anyone who tried to kill the pope. When the law was updated in 1969, Paul VI removed this provision. He also begged governments on several occasions not to carry out executions. At the grassroots, Catholic groups such as the Community of Sant'Egidio have become leaders in the global press to ban capital punishment.

Reflecting on this mutation, then-cardinal Joseph Ratzinger, now Pope Benedict XVI, said in the late 1990s that Catholicism has witnessed a "development in doctrine" on the death penalty. For a Church that thinks in centuries, however, the word "development" hardly does justice to what has happened. It is more akin to a doctrinal revolution, one that would have dumbfounded no one more than Mastro Titta.

In the end, Warren Buffett may have a point: even in the Catholic Church, libraries (or, for that matter, criminology museums) are not always the best place to seek the future.

Sociological Notes of the Church

Every time Catholics go to Mass they recite the Nicene Creed, which contains the four theological notes of the Church, meaning the four defining characteristics regarded as essential to its God-given identity: "One, Holy, Catholic, and Apostolic." Being theological in nature, these notes are believed to express the inner identity of the Church, regardless of how much observable facts may seem to contradict them. Catholicism today, for example, is anything but "one," yet Catholics believe that "one" is what the Church is supposed to be, and, in some deep ontological sense, that's what the Church always is.

This book isn't a work in theology, but in descriptive journalism. In that spirit, I'll offer four notes for Catholicism in the twenty-first century that are sociological rather than theological. They attempt to describe what the observable Catholic Church, the Church one can see, hear, touch, taste, and smell, is actually going to be like over the next 100 years. Drawing together the main lines of development expressed in the ten trends we've surveyed, I believe the Catholic Church in the twenty-first century will exhibit these four sociological notes: "Global, Uncompromising, Pentecostal, and Extroverted." Taken together, these four notes could trigger a series of upheavals in Catholic thought and life every bit as breathtaking as the shift from Mastro Titta to Pope John Paul II.

GLOBAL

Not only is multipolarism a trend in international relations, it also describes the Catholic future. The global North in the Church is not going away, and places such as Paris, Barcelona, Chicago, Los Angeles, and Toronto—to say nothing of Rome—will continue to be important centers of Catholic thought and life. Theologians and activists in the North will continue to command a disproportionate share of resources, allowing them to wield tremendous influence on Catholic conversation.

Yet Catholicism in the twenty-first century will also be led to a steadily greater degree by the global South, meaning Africa, Latin America, and Asia. This will be where many important theological and pastoral currents originate, where political energy begins to stir, and where a growing share of the Church's leadership class comes from. At some point in the twenty-first century, Catholicism may well have an African, Asian, or Latin American as pope. At the grassroots, Catholicism in this century will become steadily more non-Western, nonwhite, and nonaffluent. The Catholic South will also be arriving at the doorstep of the North to an increasing degree through immigration patterns. If demography is destiny, the Catholic future is quite clearly ever more global.

The following represent broad generalizations to which there are, inevitably, significant exceptions in various parts of the world. Nonetheless, the emergence of a "World Church," featuring a rising Southern tide, will mean a Catholic Church which is more

- **Morally Conservative:** Across much of the global South, there's a mainstream social consensus on the issues that shape the culture wars in the West, such as abortion and homosexuality, that strikes most outside observers as remarkably traditionalist. That consensus is vigorously shared by most Southern Catholics, both at the leadership level and among the rank-and-file. Combined with the strong defense of traditional Catholic identity that's part of evangelical Catholicism, this Southern consensus makes the chance of any significant revision in Catholic teaching on the hot-button issues of sexual morality virtually zero for the foreseeable future.

- **Liberal on Social Justice:** Because large majorities of Catholics in the South are poor, combating economic injustice is a towering pastoral priority. Southern bishops tend to talk about the World Bank and the IMF the way many Northern bishops talk about Planned Parenthood, as the Church's main bête noire. The political outlook of Southern Catholics is often suspicious of capitalism and free markets, dubious about the global dominance of the West and especially the United States, and strongly antiwar and pro–United Nations. Neoconservative Catholics in the West currently cheering the rise of the South because of its conservative views on the family and sexual morality may not be so content when the focus shifts to other matters.

- **Biblical:** For most Southern Catholics, the Bible rather than the *Catechism of the Catholic Church* or the *Code of Canon Law* is the touchstone of their faith. Higher criticism is restricted to a small intellectual elite; many Southern Catholics would qualify as biblical literalists by Northern standards. Preaching and catechesis are structured according to biblical narratives and images, not formal theological categories. Leaders who move opinion in the South are those able to successfully appeal to biblical teaching. Southern Catholics are also not shy about speaking the language of biblical faith in public, so there will be a more robustly evangelical tone to the way many Catholics engage social and cultural issues. (Example: Rather than saying cloning violates the dignity of the human person, one might say it "stands under God's judgment." The idea is the same, the argot is different.)

- **Concerned with Pluralism, not Secularism:** Evangelical Catholicism, the trend that dominates the policy-setting level of the Church today, is to some extent a reaction against the inroads of Western secularism. In sociological terms, however, secularism doesn't have a terribly large footprint anywhere outside the West, particularly outside Europe. In Africa especially, but also in much of Asia and Latin America, religious faith and practice remain strong. At the grassroots, the real challenge to Catholicism comes not from secularism, but from the dynamics of a remarkably competitive religious marketplace. As a result, Catholicism in the twenty-first century is likely to spend less time concerned with defending itself against secular indifference, and more time developing a new sense of entrepreneurial "hustle."

- **Young and Optimistic:** In terms of demography, the global South is considerably younger than the North. Forty-three percent of the population of sub-Saharan Africa, for example, is under fourteen years old. The Catholic Church across the South reflects those demographics, giving it a strikingly youthful "feel." The Church in the South is also young in another sense. Outside Latin America, Catholicism doesn't carry the weight of centuries of history and tradition. In most zones of the global South, Catholicism is either growing (as in Africa and parts of Asia) or contracting in terms of absolute numbers but experiencing an inner revival (as in Latin America). As a result of all this, Southern Catholicism usually strikes visitors from the North as dynamic, innovative, and ultimately hopeful.

- **Alien to Europeans and Americans:** Under Southern influence, Catholicism will be driven to provide greater scope for indigenous spiritual practices such as divination, reverence for ancestors, and folk healings, as well as more robustly inculturated forms of liturgical worship and theological expression. (Asian "negative theology" offers one example.) All this may make parts of the Church seem increasingly alien to its white minority in the developed world, especially in Europe and the United States. Southern Catholics also tend to believe that the theological agenda set in the West sometimes doesn't address their pastoral concerns. When Catholicism in the twenty-first century ponders the family, it's more likely to be talking about polygamy rather than gay marriage; when it considers popular attitudes to religion, it's far more likely to be concerned with witchcraft rather than atheism.

Seen through Western eyes, the emergence of World Catholicism augurs a Church that is ever more enmeshed in contradiction. As the social drift in the West toward permissive stands on same-sex marriage, euthanasia, and other moral questions intensifies, a Catholicism buoyed by its Southern contingent will not only oppose that drift in principle, it will become more aggressive in practice. At the same time, Catholicism under Southern influence will also mount a strong challenge to Western political and military dominance; to the West's corporate interests; to its patterns of consumption and waste, approach to immigration and the environment, and cultural traditions of individualism and nationalism; and to its role as the architect of the globalized economic order. Western theologians of both left and right, long accustomed to setting the agenda for global debate, will increasingly find that their issues occupy back-burner positions. Whose ox will be gored will depend on the issue, but it's hard to imagine many constituencies in the West, including the United States, that won't come to think of global Catholicism in some sense as the opposition, and a fairly brash opposition at that.

UNCOMPROMISING

When Cardinal Joseph Ratzinger was elected to the papacy in April 2005, a mock newspaper front page made the rounds in the Vatican, poking fun at the astonished secular reaction to the choice of a conservative's conservative. The faux banner headline proclaimed: CATHOLIC ELECTED POPE! That bit of mirth reflects a fundamental shift in psychology, at both the grassroots and the leadership level, which is today the most powerful trend in the Catholic West.

Post–Vatican II, any teaching or behavior that made Catholics seem alien was frowned upon, and a good bit of it was simply cast aside. In 1967, for example, the bishops of England and Wales eliminated the requirement of abstaining from meat on Fridays with this explanation: "Non-Catholics know and accept that we do not eat meat on Fridays, but often they do not understand why we do not, and in consequence regard us as odd." Given the temper of the times, this was clearly understood as an argument against the practice. Today, the winds are blowing the other way. A perception of Catholic singularity has become an argument *in favor* of doing things, such as wearing religious habits and saying the Mass in Latin.

What changed? In today's highly secularized Western world, observant Catholics increasingly perceive themselves to be an embattled minority. They feel misunderstood and ostracized by cultural elites hostile to the Church. In response, Catholics are behaving as embattled minorities generally do, practicing a politics of identity. They're vigorously reinforcing traditional markers of group identity as a way of protecting themselves from assimilation. This impulse is described in chapter two as a Catholic version of the Evangelical movement in Protestantism. Evangelical Catholicism is reshaping wide regions of the life of the Church, from theology to liturgy to spiritual practice, down to how it delivers education, health care, and social services.

The evangelical Catholicism of the twenty-first century will be:

- **Doctrinally Traditional:** Catholicism innovates theologically from a position of strength; under threat, it reasserts traditional teachings and generates new pastoral models to defend them. Facing the Protestant challenge in the sixteenth century, the Counter-Reformation reaffirmed Catholic doctrines and founded the Roman Inquisition, while also producing the Jesuits, the Capuchins, and other new orders. Today, the perceived threat is from what Benedict XVI has termed a Western "dictatorship of relativism," and the Church is engaged in a similar project of doctrinal retrenchment: Christ as the lone Savior, the Catholic Church as the one true church, a sharp distinction between the priesthood and laity. New lay movements and an expanded notion of the lay apostolate are among the Church's emerging pastoral instruments.

- **Politically Assertive:** The evangelical impulse means that Catholicism is becoming bolder in the public realm, engaging in overt activism and using the threat of disciplinary sanctions against Catholics in public life who hold positions contrary to Church teaching. This trajectory promises sharper church–state tensions, especially on the culture wars. In some parts of the developed world, increasingly blunt criticism of homosexuality could run up against legal protection of gay rights, ending in prosecutions of Church officials under "hate speech" statutes, and bringing legal pressures on Church institutions. On matters of sexual morality and the family, this probably means Catholicism will be perceived as "far right."

- **Deliberately Different:** One thrust of evangelical Catholicism is to emphasize those things that set Catholicism apart. At the personal level, this means a return to practices such as individual confession, Eucharistic adoration, and Marian devotion. At the institutional level, it means vigilance about the Catholicity of Church-run schools, hospitals, and charitable agencies, ensuring that their policies and procedures do not blur Church teachings. This thrust also has implications for ecumenism and interreligion relations, since it implies a Church more concerned with defending its peculiarity than in finding common ground. The Catholic growth industry in the realm of relations with other churches and religions is likely to be apologetics rather than dialogue.

- **Dynamic, yet Divided:** New energy in twenty-first-century Catholicism will be palpable, as constituencies in the Church emboldened by this politics of identity will produce all manner of new apostolic works: religious orders, magazines and TV networks, Web sites and ad hoc action networks, small faith groups, and social action projects. At the same time, the liberal wing of the Church in the West will feel increasingly despondent. Catholics not in sync with the identity movement will migrate to non-Catholic settings, such as secular universities, think tanks, and humanitarian organizations, creating an informal Church in exile and further exacerbating Catholic tribalism.

PENTECOSTAL

By any measure, the fastest growing religious movement in the world today is Pentecostalism, which, according to one recent estimate from the Pew Global Forum, now represents 20 percent of all Christians on earth, up from roughly 5 percent as recently as the middle of the twentieth century. If one combines that figure with the Charismatic Christians within existing denominations, the total Pentecostal footprint rises to 25 percent, meaning one quarter of world Christianity. Within the Catholic Church, some 11 percent of the world Catholic population today identifies itself as Charismatic, and in some Southern Catholic churches, the Charismatics are a majority. In effect, Pentecostalism is becoming the de facto Southern way of being Christian. Luis Lugo, the director of the 2006 Pew Forum study, has said that Christianity is well on its way to being "Pentecostalized." Popular devotional Catholicism in some ways has a special affinity for

Pentecostalism, given that both foster an earthy, sensual spirituality. For just that reason, Harvey Cox has defined Pentecostalism as "Catholicism without priests."

To put the point into a sound bite, one could say that the recent past of Catholicism belonged to the liberals, its present belongs to the evangelicals, and the future belongs to the Pentecostals.

While evangelical Catholicism cuts toward decidedly non-Pentecostal modes of worship and ecclesiastical organization, both trends also promote doctrinal orthodoxy, explicit evangelization, an assertive Catholic presence in public life, and strict personal morality. There will be much tension between these impulses in the twenty-first century, but in important ways they will also reinforce one another. This Pentecostal Catholicism will be:

- **Supernatural:** Angels and demons, possessions and exorcisms, and curses and hexes are an integral part of the worldview of Pentecostals, and not just the uneducated or poor. The spirit world is tangible, close, and a direct force in human affairs. The vicissitudes of both personal and social life are interpreted as the result of spiritual forces. Miracles, healings, and casting out of demons—along with the other gifts of the Holy Spirit—will become a routine part of pastoral practice. Even the Church's work for social justice will increasingly involve a supernatural dimension: Catholic activists won't just protest the G8, they'll exorcize it.

- **Prosperity-Oriented:** The liberation theology movement popularized the notion of "structural sin," which has since been ratified in papal social teaching. Pentecostalism, on the other hand, tends to see poverty and other forms of misfortune as either the result of personal sin or the effect of malevolent spiritual forces. The "prosperity gospel" emphasizes that prayer and effort can translate into material gain. While Catholicism will still protest social injustice, it will also tend toward a more Pentecostal reading of the circumstances of individual poor people, regarding material prosperity (within reason) as a legitimate blessing, and prayer for that prosperity as part of the Church's mission of liberation.

- **Entrepreneurial:** One key to Pentecostal success is that it creates a constant competition for followers. Anyone dissatisfied with the music, preaching, or fellowship at a given church can move on; given the low barriers to market entry, they can even start a church of their own. Though Catholics have no license to create parishes, the tendency to found movements, prayer groups, and small faith communities will accelerate in the twenty-first century, as Charismatic Catholics take a page from their Pentecostal counterparts. In the Catholic future, the parish system may no longer be the primary point of reference for Catholics. They may think of themselves not as members of St. Rita's Parish, but as members of the "Awesome Power of God Charismatic Crusade," always with the implied capacity to switch movements or to found one of their own.

- **Lay-Led:** Another asset of Pentecostalism is its reliance on ordinary believers rather than a clerical elite to build up congregations. Catholics will move in this direction as well, partly because competitive pressures from Pentecostalism will drive the Church in this direction, partly because the mounting priest shortage in many regions of the world makes it inevitable. Much of this lay leadership will come from women, which may help address perceptions that Catholicism consigns women to a second-class status but will also create concerns in other quarters about a creeping "feminization" of the Church.

EXTROVERTED

In traditional Catholic argot, the terms *ad intra* and *ad extra* refer to the internal life of the Church and its engagement with the world outside. For much of the post–Vatican II period, the drama in Catholicism was largely *ad intra*: Would the Church change its teaching on birth control? How far would liturgical reforms go? To what extent would power be redistributed from Rome to bishops' conferences, or from the clergy to the laity? Would women be ordained, and could priests get married? How far could theologians push the doctrinal envelope, and to what extent should the Church recognize a right to dissent?

In the Catholicism of the future, those questions will be largely a dead letter, at least in terms of the potential to shape official Church teaching and practice. Under the impress of evangelical Catholicism, the debate has been closed. As a result, the real action for the Church in the twenty-first century, where its most creative energies will be found, will be mostly in the *ad extra* realm. Historically, this is perhaps the greatest irony about evangelical Catholicism: It began life as an *ad intra* impulse, intended to shore up a strong sense of traditional Catholic identity. Yet by closing doors and constricting debate over most *ad intra* matters, evangelical Catholicism seems destined to fuel a strong burst of *ad extra* activism.

The Catholic Church of the twenty-first century will be more extroverted as a result of the intersection of four forces: Many Catholic liberals will embrace *ad extra* causes because, from their point of view, there's little to be accomplished *ad intra*. Evangelicals will hunger to take their unabashed Catholicity to the street, as an expression of the Church's missionary impulse. The theological and pastoral concerns of Southern Catholicism are predominantly *ad extra*, concentrating more on poverty and war and less on matters such as power in the Church or the fine points of doctrine. Finally a vast range of pressing new questions in the outside world, such as the biotech revolution and the rise of Islam, will demand answers from Catholicism.

Catholicism in the century to come will be defined by its theology and activism in at least five areas:

- **Islam:** Islamic radicalism today occupies the role once played by the Soviet Union during the Cold War, as the chief perceived rival of the West. Unlike the Soviet system, however, there is no prospect that Islam will simply implode, which means that the future will either be one of unrelenting conflict between Islam and the West or some new modus vivendi. Catholicism reflects within itself these tensions—deeply alarmed about religious freedom, violence, and missionary competition from Islam, but also eager for collaboration with Muslims in defending traditional moral and spiritual values against a "dictatorship of relativism" in secular culture.

- **Aging:** Given current demographic trends, Western societies will struggle to cope with rapidly aging populations, putting severe strains on pension and health care systems and potentially fraying the bonds of solidarity between generations. Catholicism will be called upon to address policy implications of these shifts, as well as to generate networks of care and social support for the mushrooming number of elderly who won't be able to rely upon caregivers in the family or neighborhood. Catholicism will also have to respond to the aging of its own congregations, which could represent a demographic boom for the Church: growing numbers of people at the stage in their lives when they're most open to religion, with the means and general health levels to make important contributions. How the Church reacts will have a great deal to say about its pastoral viability.

- **Biotechnology:** From cloning to chimeras to genetic enhancement, revolutions in biotechnology are generating new ethical questions to which the Church's traditional teaching on bioethics is at best an imperfect guide. Catholics and people of conscience will look to the Church to provide a moral compass, which means these issues will eat up an increasing portion of the Church's time and energy. The politics of biotechnology shatter the classical liberal–conservative fault lines, so these issues also create the possibility for new alliances and a reconfiguration in the perceived ideological profile of Catholicism.

- **Social Justice and the Environment:** Globalization is throwing into ever sharper relief the gap between those who've made it in today's flat world and those who haven't. It also means that conflicts that once were only local or regional quickly take on a global character. A growing environmental consciousness will elicit Catholic theological reflection and political activism. All this will be turbocharged by the rise of the global South in the Church, since these are often the most burning pastoral concerns of Southern Catholic leaders.

- **International Relations:** Global trends toward multipolarity, meaning multiple centers of power rather than dominance by the United States, will challenge the "Great Power" theory of Vatican diplomacy, creating the potential for new partnerships but also new conflict. In particular, the rise of China and India creates a new situation for modern Catholicism, meaning a world not unambiguously dominated by nations with a Christian cultural heritage. This reality will make Asia, including the great religious traditions of Asia, a top-shelf priority.

Catholicism and the Great Questions of the Twenty-First Century

If the dynamism of the Catholic future is likely to unfold *ad extra*, the central question becomes which of the era's great social, cultural, and political challenges represent areas where new Catholic energies could make a decisive difference. Surveying the world scene at the close of the first decade of the twenty-first century, four topics seem to offer compelling examples of how the Catholic Church might have something to say about whether the future is one of greater virtue or greater vice, and in each case it's an open question which way things might develop:

- **Islam:** The struggle for the soul of global Islam, especially the impact of a rising Shi'ite tide from Lebanon to Central Asia, as well as the growing force of transnational Shi'ite movements such as Hezbollah;
- **McWorld vs. Jihad:** Whether the processes of globalization will result in permanent structural conflict between a homogenous global culture and resurgent local forces, a clash that Benjamin Barber famously described as pitting "McWorld" against "jihad";
- **Human Rights:** The rise of non-Western, and sometimes nondemocratic, cultures as the new poles of a multipolar world, and whether that will imperil the construction of a universal legal architecture of respect for human rights;
- **Water Wars:** The potential for global political volatility over shortages of water, in a world in which half the population of the planet lives in areas that are "water-stressed," and more than thirty nations receive over a third of their water supply from outside their national borders, including nations already marked by chronic instability.

These are hardly the only serious challenges on the horizon, but they represent four areas in which Catholicism is a global actor with unique resources that could be harnessed to promote positive outcomes.

1. CATHOLICISM AND SHI'A ISLAM

Chapter three outlined several structural similarities between Shi'a Islam and Catholicism, such as the emphasis on clergy and saints, belief in intercessory prayer, popular feasts and devotions, the centrality of sacrificial death and atonement, and belief in tradition alongside scripture. Iranian writer Vali Nasr has argued that in terms of beliefs and spiritual practice, Shi'ism represents the "Catholic branch" of global Islam. Catholicism can claim a presence in traditionally Shi'a cultures that predates the rise of the West—for example, Maronite Catholics in Lebanon and Syria, Chaldean Catholics in Iraq, and Armenian and Chaldean Catholics in Iran. Those local churches, despite the severe pressures they face today, nevertheless produce Catholics who speak the languages and know the cultures of the Shi'a world. For all these reasons Catholicism is arguably the global actor best positioned to engage Shi'a Islam, at a moment in which the importance of Shi'ism within the Islamic world is gaining ground.

Catholics can do so in a way in which Western ambassadors and United Nations officials cannot, which is to engage Shi'ites not only on a political and humanitarian level, but from within shared spiritual and religious commitments. Both regard secularism and privatization of religion as an aberration. In this sense, evangelical Catholicism, which is driving Catholicism to mount an aggressive challenge to secularism, may also be repositioning the Church to become a more reliable interlocutor for many Muslims. There is a recent history of cooperation between Islamic nations and the Catholic Church in the form of joint opposition to creating rights to abortion under international law during United Nations conferences in the mid-1990s.

Demographics may also lend a hand to Catholic efforts to reach out to Shi'ites. Declining fertility rates are beginning to take hold across the Middle East, especially in Iran, where fertility has fallen by two thirds since 1950 and now stands below replacement level. That's likely to take some of the wind out of the sails of radicalism, because aging societies tend to be less belligerent. As children become scarcer, parents and relatives are far less likely to romanticize martyrdom. Catholicism and Shi'a Islam may also be able to find common ground in discussing spiritual responses to the social and cultural pressures created by this demographic transition.

2. GLOBALIZATION VS. GLOCALIZATION

Sociologist Peter Berger has observed that the Catholic Church is "the oldest globalized institution there is." As the lone centrally organized branch of Christianity with a truly global profile, Catholicism struggled with the tension between McWorld and jihad long before it occurred to political scientists and policy wonks to ponder its implications. The missions of Jesuits Robert de Nobili to India in the sixteenth century, for example, and Matteo Ricci to China in the seventeenth, put the balance between universal faith and local expression squarely at the center of the Church's reflection. Whether Church authorities addressed those questions adequately five hundred years ago is beside the point; the point is, can you name another global institution that has been thinking about them for five hundred years?

While some simplistic readings of Church history would have it that in

Catholicism the universal has always swamped the local, things are actually more complicated. Consider, for example, this 1659 ruling from Propaganda Fidei, the Vatican's top office for missionary work: "What could be more absurd than to transport France, Spain or Italy or some other European country to China? Do not introduce all that to them, but only the faith. It is the nature of men to love and treasure above everything else their own country and that which belongs to it. In consequence, there is no stronger cause for alienation and hate than an attack on local customs, especially when these go back to a venerable antiquity."

For every example one can cite of popes and missionaries who were not animated by the spirit, there are others who clearly were, such as the sixteenth-century Dominican missionary Bartolomé de Las Casas, who was the first bishop of Chiapas in Mexico, and whose 1552 book *A Brief Account of the Destruction of the Indies* is one of the most forceful pieces of advocacy on behalf of indigenous cultures ever written.

The theological debate within Catholicism on the proper relationship between the universal and the local continues into the present. A public exchange of essays by Cardinal Walter Kasper and then-cardinal Joseph Ratzinger in the late 1990s and early years of the twenty-first century pivoted on precisely this point and illustrates that different currents of reflection exist at the most senior levels of the Catholic Church. This tradition, still in many ways a developing one, is potentially the Church's most valuable intellectual and cultural asset in addressing the perplexing contradictions of globalization.

3. UNIVERSALITY OF HUMAN RIGHTS

For more than 200 years, both the development of the theory of human rights and its legal expression in the form of various charters, conventions, and treaties have been almost inseparably linked to the spread of democratic government. The primary forces behind the various modern statements of human rights have been democracies, most of them shaped by a Christian heritage.

In a new multipolar world, one in which an officially nondemocratic China, a democracy in India that sits in uneasy tension with the caste system, and the "managed democracy" of Russia all represent increasingly consequential points of reference, what becomes of the concept of human rights? Will the various legal agreements governing human rights come to be seen as expressions of Western culture, appropriate for the West but largely inapplicable elsewhere? Will budding resentments against globalization, and the perceived imposition of Western cultural forms, sweep the notion of human rights under the same indictment? If so, what other instruments does the world have to forge moral and political consensus around the protection of minorities and individuals? In China, for example, the current trend is toward greater economic and social freedom, but the trend is clearly understood as a pragmatic concession by the state, not as a matter of individual rights. In a world in which this "Beijing consensus" is steadily more influential, is the concept of a universal standard of human rights passé?

Catholic natural law theory and theological anthropology could make an important contribution here, starting from an analysis of the spiritual dignity of the human person rather than from political ideas derived from the Enlightenment. Recent attempts by the United States to "export democracy" have illustrated the difficulties of imposing these ideas on cultures to which they're largely alien. If there is a future for human rights under nondemocratic or partially democratic regimes, it arguably lies in the direction pointed by Catholic social theory, beginning with a strong defense of the right to life.

The Church's capacity to advance such an agenda could be strengthened if missionary efforts in China gather steam, which would allow a growing Chinese Catholic community to make these arguments from within Chinese culture and experience. For that reason, the looming missionary contest in China, which is likely to pit indigenous Chinese spirituality, Islam, Catholicism, and Pentecostal Christianity in a four-way contest, appears rife with potential global implications.

4. WATER WARS

As outlined in chapter seven, many geopolitical experts are convinced that "water is the new oil," meaning that scarcity of water supplies and political disputes over control of water resources are likely to become to the twenty-first century what conflict over oil was to the twentieth. As *Newsweek* put it in July 2007, "The wars of the future may be fought not only over politics or oil, but water, too." The difference is that the instability created by water shortages is exponentially more explosive, because when water becomes scarce, the results show up not just in the price of gas, but in human lives lost due to thirst, disease, and crop failure. As these scenarios play out, the landscape is further complicated by the fact that the water supply of an estimated 300 million people has been commercialized, and now rests in the hands of private multinational corporations such as Veolia Water and Suez that cannot necessarily be relied upon to act on behalf of the common good.

Given the enormous commercial and political stakes involved in water disputes, it's an open question whether strategies based upon humanitarian or strategic interests by themselves will be able to avert the feared water wars of the twenty-first century. Religious bodies may have the capacity to make a deeper contribution, because the sacredness of water is a common theme to virtually all of the world's great religions. In the Middle East and the Indian subcontinent, where the potential for violence related to water scarcity is greatest, Hinduism, Buddhism, Islam, Judaism, and Christianity all regard water as a symbol of life and employ water in their sacred rites. That commonality means that religious leaders may be able to bring a depth to discussions about water that would be difficult to achieve beyond the level of platitudes in other forums.

Most experts believe that problems of water scarcity cannot be resolved in a lasting fashion in isolation from broader environmental questions such as climate change and systems of sustainable development. Catholic ecology may be able to provide a badly needed bridge between efforts to protect the environment and efforts to help the poor. The dynamic of some contemporary environmental debates sometimes pits ecological preservation against economic development; official Catholic environmentalism has developed a conceptual framework for seeing these aims as complementary rather than competitive, which puts the Church in a position to be an important voice in global conversations on environmental policy.

Will It Happen?

The decisive question is not whether Catholicism will address these challenges, and many others like them, but to what extent and with what outcomes. On each front, Catholics at all levels are already engaged; and in each area, Catholic activism has not yet produced noticeably transforming results. It's not that Catholicism lacks the capacity to change history. If anyone doubts that, just ask an ex-member of the politburo in any former Communist state in Central and Eastern Europe what an aroused civil society shaped by dynamic Catholic leadership can accomplish. At the same time, such results are hardly automatic; for every example of successful Catholic activism, there are dozens that never quite caught fire. So, aside from dumb luck and divine providence, what are the variables likely to be most significant in determining the quality of Catholic answers to the questions presented above?

At least four factors seem especially relevant. (Warning: From here on in, the material veers into prescriptive territory.)

1. PRIORITIES

Driven by the momentum of evangelical Catholicism, the Church today is increasingly sensitive to questions of Catholic identity, including the importance of revitalizing traditional Catholic modes of language, practice, and thought. The architects of this effort see it as a bulwark against assimilation to secularism and relativism, what European critics call the "weak thought" of postmodernity. An inherent danger, however, is that the resulting focus on the inner life of Catholicism could become so overpowering as to constrict the Church's capacity to tackle anything else. For some, this may seem a price worth paying. The distinguished American Catholic scholar Robert Louis Wilken articulated this view with respect to American Catholicism during a 2004 conference at Boston College: "At this time in the Church's history in the United States," Wilken bluntly said, "it is less important to communicate the gospel to American culture than to rebuild the Church's distinctive culture."

That instinct reflects a core premise of evangelical Catholicism, which is that a satisfactory response to human problems cannot be given by a culture constructed *etsi Deus non daretur*, "as if God does not exist." Efforts to buttress Catholic identity are themselves, according to this way of thinking, the Church's most valuable contribution to the construction of a better world, and that implies first restoring what Wilken called "thickness and density to Catholic life." In itself, this is a legitimate enterprise, and it is doubtless true that Catholicism will have no distinctive contribution to offer the world if it is not clear about what it stands for. Yet problems of the urgency and the global scope of those described above cannot simply be put on hold for a century as the Catholic Church gets its own house in order. Charles de Gaulle once said that "to govern is to choose," and Church leaders will face some difficult choices as these trends play themselves out.

2. PROXY BATTLES

A related danger is that some Catholics may indeed take up questions such as dialogue with Shi'a Islam or human rights, but approach them largely as a pretext for scoring runs in insider Catholic baseball rather than respecting the complexity of these problems on their own terms. This sort of sleight-of-hand has become common in some circles of Catholic discussion.

One case in point is offered by the flurry of literature produced over the last decade about Pope Pius XII. Although debate over the wartime pope's record on the Holocaust is often phrased as a sticking point in Catholic–Jewish relations (and it is), the most acerbic exchanges have come among Catholics, with Jewish commentators often reduced to the role of spectators to an intra-Catholic wrestling match. While this literature is styled as history, one can't escape the impression that the real motor fuel is current events, especially competing Catholic visions of the papacy and the hierarchy. Critics of Pius XII frequently offer his alleged failures and silences to buttress the case for reform in Catholic authority structures, while his defenders sometimes hint subtly (and not so subtly) that exonerating Pius XII is tantamount to defending the papacy itself. For this reason, the eventual unsealing of remaining Vatican records from the World War II era will probably do little to end the debates over Pius XII, because what's at stake for partisans on both sides cuts far deeper than this particular pope's record.

To take another example, interfaith dialogue in some ways today is complicated by a bitter intra-Catholic theological divide between those who stress the activity of the Holy Spirit outside the visible bounds of Christianity and those who insist upon the singularity of Christ and the Church. How to interpret religious pluralism theologically, and what it implies for classic Christian doctrines about Jesus, the Holy Spirit, and the Church, has been the most agonizing subject in Catholicism for the last two decades, and it has transformed interreligious exchange into a hot potato. Because of these divisions, the Catholic Church does not have one functioning network of thinkers, linguists, pastors, and experts in inter-faith dialogue—it actually has several, often working at cross-purposes. Catholicism's best minds on Islam, for example, probably spend at least as much time arguing with one another as they do actually talking to Muslims, or helping to guide the discussion of Islam in the West in productive directions.

Such tensions cannot be dissolved with the wave of a papal magic wand, and doing so wouldn't be desirable even if it were somehow possible. The challenge is not to evaporate any given party to these debates, but to see their views for what they are—valuable but incomplete insights into difficult problems. This is not tantamount to relativism, as if all views in the Church are equally valid, but rather to recognizing that any one perspective rarely enjoys a monopoly on wisdom. As Pope Benedict XVI said during a July 2007 meeting with priests from the northern Italian dioceses of Belluno-Feltre and Treviso, the historical spirit of Catholicism is its passion for synthesis, for "both/and" solutions to seemingly binary "either/or" oppositions. As long as Catholics see themselves locked in zero-sum struggle with rival camps in the Church, however, such a spirit of synthesis is difficult to generate.

Any of the issues outlined above could easily be transformed into a proxy battle for internal Catholic struggles. Debates over the promotion of human rights on the global stage, for example, could become code language for what some might see as the need for greater protection of human rights in the Church; Catholic activism around protection of water resources could morph into a broad critique of what some consider the anthropocentrism of traditional Catholic theology. While these topics certainly merit serious discussion, the question is whether a unified, balanced Catholic approach to the trends will be a casualty of this conflict.

3. IDENTITY FEARS

Another danger for the Church in the twenty-first century is that much creative energy could be stifled, not on its merits, but rather due to suspicions of a slippery slope leading to confusion about Catholic identity. One sees this today in Latin America, for example, in continuing ambivalence about "base ecclesial communities," meaning small groups of faithful who come together for prayer, worship, and social analysis. Because some liberation theologians in the 1970s and 1980s saw the base communities as a "church from below" in opposition to the hierarchy as a "church from above," support for the base communities became an ideologically loaded concept. Some bishops and pastors are still hesitant to throw their weight behind the communities, due to a kind of muscle memory about a danger they once posed. Meanwhile, Pentecostal and Evangelical movements using similar techniques—such as the G12 model pioneered by the International Charismatic Mission in Colombia, based on each church member assembling a group of twelve other believers, which is spreading like wildfire in the region—are meeting the practical spiritual needs of Latin America's swelling urban population in a way the Catholic Church is not. Like military generals, some Latin American bishops and activists seem to be fighting the last war. In such cases, conversation is shut down or redirected because an "identity wire" has been tripped, in some cases quite accidentally.

Awareness of this danger prompts two cautions.

First, the cornerstone of any effort to respond to the challenges of the ten trends outlined in this book must be a clear, unambiguous embrace of Catholic identity—of the teachings of the Church, and of the authority of Church leaders to defend those teachings. Initiatives, movements, and campaigns in the twenty-first century will either be firmly rooted in a strong sense of Catholic identity, or they will arrive stillborn. To be as blunt as possible, if these initiatives want to go anywhere, their leaders need to be as clear about what they're *not* proposing as what they are, and to avoid anything that smacks of adversarial tactics or interest-group organizing. They will have to phrase their arguments in the language of the Church, appealing to its own traditions and concepts, rather than drawing on secular democracy or corporate management. In a Church determined to be unabashedly itself, arguments that it ought to be more like somebody else won't have much of a shelf life.

Second, Church leaders have a special responsibility to balance their legitimate concern for vigilance about Catholic identity against the urgency of fostering creative Catholic thinking and activism. Clarity does not have to mean paralysis, and discernment does not have to mean turning a deaf ear to new perspectives because of anxiety about their provenance or possible implications. There's an old bit of Vatican wisdom that's relevant here: "Not every sentence of a heretic is heresy." In other words, even if personalities or movements in the Church sometimes give bishops and other authorities heartburn, that doesn't mean they have nothing to contribute on any possible subject. When Pope Benedict XVI met with his old friend Hans Küng at Castel Gandolfo in September 2005, the two men did not discuss their long-standing differences over papal infallibility or theological dissent, but rather focused on Küng's efforts to foster a "world ethic" among global religions. The encounter hinted at a model of Church leadership rooted in a thick Catholic identity, yet unafraid to glean insights even from figures who may chafe against some particulars of that identity. Bishops and other leaders will be pressed to embrace this model in the century to come, if for no other reason than the maddening complexity of the challenges they face.

4. THE HORIZONTAL DIMENSION

American Jesuit sociologist Fr. John Coleman has observed that despite its rich intellectual and human resources, Catholicism has played a curiously "subaltern" role in most contemporary debates over globalization, with the lone exception perhaps coming with the Jubilee 2000 debt relief campaign. In trying to account for this mismatch between the Church's potential and its actual impact, Coleman cites a 1998 study of NGOs called *Activists Beyond Borders* by Margaret Keck and Kathryn Sikkink, which argued that successful global actors today are generally loosely organized policy networks without multiple layers of command. Perhaps, Coleman has suggested, Catholicism's hierarchical mode of organization lacks the flexibility needed to keep up with the intense pace at which issues mutate in a globalized world.

In fairness, Catholicism does have a wide variety of successful horizontal actors in the form of religious orders, lay movements, and a variety of grassroots coalitions. When these players join forces, they can produce striking results. One example came with debates in the United States over the fate of Terri Schiavo, the Florida woman in a persistent vegetative state who died in 2005 after life support was removed. Most of the Catholic energy in favor of keeping Schiavo alive came not from the Church's official leadership, but from a variety of pro-life groups and an ad hoc movement formed largely on the Internet. Whatever one makes of the position taken in that instance, it illustrates the capacity of an energized horizontal Catholicism to mobilize opinion and to get results. In this case, the movement didn't prevent Schiavo's death, but it did generate a national examination of conscience around end-of-life issues that is still a work in progress.

Yet Coleman has a point that this horizontal dimension of Catholic activism remains underdeveloped, at least in comparison with the Church's vertical structures. Remedying that deficit is not primarily a task for the hierarchy; indeed, in many cases their most valuable contribution may be to stay out of the way. The construction of a more forceful, articulate horizontal sector in the Church on the issues sketched above depends upon a growing share of lay Catholics, especially the vast majority who don't belong to any formal movement or group, taking it upon themselves to translate their faith into action. Authentic horizontal Catholicism cannot be willed into existence by hierarchical fiat. It has to well up from the grassroots, reflecting a popular determination to get something done.

Waiting for the Vatican or the bishops to act, or blaming them for doing it the wrong way, won't cut it. It's the ultimate in clericalism to believe that everything in the Church depends upon its clergy, or that nothing useful can be done until Rome turns over a new leaf. Such a position misreads both the theory and the practice of how change in the Church works. When everything else is stripped away, the core responsibility of the hierarchy is to ensure that when Christ returns the faith will still be found upon the earth. By definition, in many ways, this is a conservative, cautious, defensive role. To also expect the hierarchy to be the primary "change agent" in Catholicism, the chief source of its vision and new energy, is both unfair and unrealistic. To borrow a sports metaphor, it's akin to expecting your defense to score all your points. When a bishop comes along who's a visionary, one should receive it as a grace, but to expect it as the normal course of events is a prescription for heartburn.

In reality, change in Catholicism typically percolates at the grassroots and is then subject to a long period of theological and spiritual discernment at multiple levels, well before it is ever ratified and assimilated by the hierarchy. The Church did not spawn mendicant orders in the twelfth and thirteenth centuries, for example, because a pope decreed that it should be so, but because creative individuals such as Saint Dominic and Saint Francis saw an emerging need and responded to it. Similarly, the great burst of new teaching and missionary orders in the nineteenth century was the work of visionary Catholic women and men who seized the initiative, often struggling for most of their lives with recalcitrant superiors and bishops worried about where things might lead.

The plain reality is that if Catholicism is to generate the imagination required to meet the challenges of the trends we've surveyed, it is not principally a task for the hierarchy. It should be carried out in communion with the Church's leadership, of course, but it cannot depend upon them. To think otherwise is to succumb to a sort of "purple ecclesiology," in which the Church is reduced to its bishops. Yes, bishops can sometimes abuse their authority, and they can artificially stifle creative energies. Their natural caution sometimes translates into rigidity or closure. Ultimately, however, time and the tides stop for no one, and good ideas will endure whatever their initial reception by the powers that be.

The real question, therefore, is not whether the bishops are up to the challenges of the twenty-first century. The question is whether the rest of us are.

POSTSCRIPT

The Courage to Be Globally Catholic

One of American Catholicism's most influential writers, George Weigel, published a book in 2004 in the wake of the sexual abuse crisis urging believers to have "the courage to be Catholic." Weigel's analysis was that the crisis revealed a deep failure of nerve within the Church, the antidote to which, as he saw it, is a more robust embrace of the fullness of the Catholic faith. The book is a manifesto for evangelical Catholicism, reflecting the particular historical moment in which it arose. Whatever one makes of the argument, the kind of courage Weigel described was already percolating among a significant constituency in the Church—namely, Weigel and those who think like him. The change of heart to which he called people was, in that sense, selective.

The twenty-first century will call forth another type of courage, one that will challenge all Catholics, regardless of which ecclesiastical tribe they presently inhabit. What this century will demand is the courage to be *globally* Catholic, moving out of the parochialism of a given language, ethnicity, geographical region, or ideology, and embracing membership in a truly "catholic" Church.

Forging Catholic identity in a global key involves far more than dropping a few extra coins into a second collection on Missions Sunday, or feeling a sense of solidarity with Catholics suffering persecution in the Middle East or in China, though both are worthy gestures. The courage to be globally Catholic means rethinking deeply entrenched patterns of thought and behavior. It means no longer defining one's Catholicity primarily in terms of allegiance to a faction or to a fixed set of views on issues in the Church— a challenge that, like the rain, falls upon everyone, the just and the unjust alike.

This undertaking is perhaps especially urgent for Catholics in the United States. A quick story makes the point. In 2005, the BBC broadcast a documentary called *The Monastery*, a three-part series filmed at Worth Abbey in England about five young men with little or no experience of either Catholicism or monasteries, who were chosen to spend forty days living the monks' life. It was a ratings hit, and Abbot Christopher Jamison of Worth Abbey later published a book about the experience called *Finding Sanctuary*. In 2006, Abbot Christopher came to the United States for a series of lectures based on the book. I happened to be in London shortly afterward, and I spoke with him over lunch. The abbot said that as he had traveled around the United States, he had been struck by a peculiar feature of American Catholicism. Rather than simply accepting his identity as a Benedictine monk, he said, many Catholics in the United States had seemed to want to know more. Specifically, their implicit question had seemed to be,

"What kind of Catholic are you?" Was he liberal or conservative, charismatic or traditional, horizontal or vertical in his spirituality? It almost had seemed in some cases, Abbot Christopher said, as if people had wanted him to declare a party allegiance.

The abbot's experience is not isolated, and it reflects a distressing truth about Catholicism in the United States. American Catholics spent the first half of the twentieth century clawing their way out of a ghetto that had been imposed upon them by a hostile Protestant majority and the second half reconstructing ghettoes of their own ideological choice. They ended the century as badly divided as they had begun, only this time divided not from the Protestants but from one another. This situation is sometimes described as polarization, but that's misleading if taken to mean that Catholics are clustered around two poles, conventionally labeled "conservative" and "liberal." In reality, the situation is more akin to tribalism, with a whole series of camps attending their own meetings, reading their own publications, and following their own heroes, generally viewing the other tribes with a mixture of disinterest and suspicion. Liturgical traditionalists, peace and justice Catholics, charismatics, reformers, pro-lifers, and neoconservatives are a few of the tribes an ethnographer would probably identify.

Under any circumstances, this sort of Balkanization would be regrettable. Diversity is wealth, but division is impoverishment. This is one sense in which Catholicism in the West, and especially in the United States, is actually more evangelized than evangelical. Too many Catholics have been evangelized by the psychology of secular politics, seeing the Church as a terrain upon which interest-group battles are fought, rather than as the common table of the Lord around which these differences dissolve. The tenor of much Catholic conversation these days might be expressed as an ideologue's spin on the Lord's Prayer: "MY will be done."

In the twenty-first century, tribalism will be not merely unfortunate, but utterly unsustainable. Every one of the ten trends outlined in this book is fraught with the potential for deep new fractures, this time on a planetary scale. The global Catholicism of the twenty-first century will rattle neoconservative cages with its emphasis on reform of economic systems and critique of American militarism, will distress liberal Church reformers with its immobility, will unsettle liturgical traditionalists with its Pentecostal-style praise and worship, will gall some Asian theologians by the way Church authorities reassert the uniqueness of the salvation won in Christ, and will concern Catholics invested in ecumenical and interfaith work with its more robustly apologetic tone. No one will inhabit the Church of his or her personal dreams, and all Catholics will face the primal choice of whether that reality will close them down, or will open them up to new possibilities.

Global Catholicism is giving sociological expression to one of Catholicism's core theological claims about itself: that the Church is the "sacrament of the unity of the human family." That abstraction is taking on flesh and blood in the twenty-first century, and as with any deep realignment of tectonic plates, the tremors it generates are unsettling. In response, the Church will need to live far more deeply what recent popes and theologians have called the "ecclesiology of communion," because the strains on that spirit of communion will be immense. Catholicism has the opportunity to pioneer what a form of globalization that prizes both the universal and the local might look like, or it could model within itself the clash of civilizations that alarmists fear for the rest of the world. Both are eminently plausible trajectories, and which way things develop will not depend primarily upon decisions made in Rome or in bishops' offices. It will depend upon what happens in Catholic hearts, upon the capacity of more than a billion individual Catholics to embrace both the promise and the peril of this new historical moment. These trends will be a mixed bag for everyone, but they are also an invitation to adventure, to the hope that bold souls always feel at the beginning of a journey whose outcome is unknown.

Some Catholics—to be painfully honest, many Catholics, and not just professional critics or chronic grumps—will object that such talk of adventure is Pollyannaish, maybe even obscene, in the face of any number of crises in the Church. Catholics in the United States and other parts of the world scarred by sexual abuse from priests, and further traumatized by the failure of bishops to prevent it, may see talk of rebirth as a grotesque denial of what they regard as endemic corruption. Dalit Catholics in India appalled to find in the Church the same caste prejudice they fled in the broader society may feel the smoldering rage that only comes from a dream deferred. Catholics everywhere who feel betrayed by the unwillingness of their pastors or their fellow Catholics to stand up for the truth, or to act compassionately when they were in need, or for any number of other shortcomings, may wonder if the Church is capable of anything in the twenty-first century other than maintenance of the status quo. Such sickness of heart is often justified, and Catholics at all levels need to hear it, regardless of how they might assess its rights and wrongs.

Yet if one were to throw a dart randomly at a continuum of 2,000 years of Church history spread out against a wall, at whatever point that dart fell, whether it's the ninth century or the nineteenth, it would have been possible in that era too to make a convincing case for despair—and without a doubt, some Catholics did exactly that at the time. At that very moment, however, new life was also stirring that would carry the Church in new directions. The raw truth is that Catholicism is enormously complex, often enormously ambivalent, and much of the time it lifts your soul and breaks your heart in roughly equal measure. Faith in the Church has never meant believing it does everything right; it means never abandoning hope despite all the things it does wrong. Today, as always, there is a basis for hope, regardless of the content of our desires, if we have but eyes to see—and if we're willing to accept that satisfying half a desire is better than none.

An upside-down Church implies contradiction, tension, and in some cases disillusionment. Yet spiritually speaking, the turbulence that comes from being turned upside down is part of the Christian experience. In his classic work *Heretics*, G. K. Chesterton offered the example of how Christianity audaciously upended the ancient pagan reverence for the human family. The ancients venerated the time-honored structure of father, mother, and child. Christianity capsized the sequence, thereby producing the Holy Family of child, mother, and father. As Chesterton epigrammatically observed, "Many things are made holy by being turned upside down."

Fostering holiness in the upside-down Church of the twenty-first century will require special courage—the courage of humility, of patience, of perspective. Above all, it will require the courage to think beyond the interests of one's own Catholic tribe, conceiving the Catholic future not in zero-sum terms but as a bold synthesis of the best of each of the Church's constituencies. If Catholicism can generate that kind of courage on a mass scale, it could form an eleventh trend, arguably the most consequential of all.

SUGGESTIONS FOR
FURTHER READING

I've always felt that one of the best arguments for being a journalist rather than an academic is that I'm not required to use footnotes. Accordingly, when I provide statistics or some nonobvious point of fact in this book, I generally cite the source right in the text, leaving it to readers to track down the specifics if they're interested. For those who want to pursue one or more of these trends in greater depth, however, I'll provide details here on some of the main resources I drew upon in each chapter, any of which would provide excellent points of departure for further reading. Every chapter also made extensive use of reporting and analysis I've done over the years for the *National Catholic Reporter*, much of which can be found through keyword searches in the archive to my Internet column "All Things Catholic." That archive can be found here: http://nationalcatholicreporter.org/word/archives.

One important resource for statistics on world religion is the World Christian Database, maintained by the Center for the Study of Global Christianity at the Gordon-Conwell Theological Seminary. As of 2007, the annual edition is published by Brill. As with any attempt to track global population, the World Christian Database has its critics, but it remains an authoritative and widely cited source of this kind of data. Information can be found at http://www.gordonconwell.edu/ockenga/globalchristianity/. For Catholic data, I consulted two other sources: *Global Catholicism: Portrait of a World Church*, by Bryan T. Froehle and Mary L. Gautier; and the 2009 *Catholic Almanac*, published by *Our Sunday Visitor* and edited by Matthew Bunson. Both books belong in the library of anyone who wants a grasp of the global Catholic situation.

For overall population numbers, I relied upon the United Nations Population Division's invaluable Population, Environment, Resources and Development database, along with its annual publication, *World Population Prospects*. The latest update available as of this writing was the 2008 edition. This material can be consulted online at http://www.un.org/esa/population/unpop.htm. Where I found it useful, I supplemented these numbers with data from the *CIA World Factbook*, which can be found online at https://www.cia.gov/library/publications/the-world-factbook/index.html. For data about the United States, I turned to the United States Census Bureau, which also has an online service: http://www.census.gov/population/www/.

TREND ONE: A WORLD CHURCH

Berryman, Phillip. *Religion in the Megacity: Catholic and Protestant Portraits from Latin America* (Orbis Books, 1996).

Donovan, Vincent J. *Christianity Rediscovered* (Orbis Books; originally published in 1978, reprinted in 2005).

Escobar, Samuel. *Changing Tides: Latin America and World Mission Today* (Orbis Books, 2002).

Fox, Thomas. *Pentecost in Asia: A New Way of Being Church* (Orbis Books, 2002).

Gray, Richard. *Black Christians and White Missionaries* (Yale University Press, 1990).

Jenkins, Philip. *The Next Christendom: The Coming of Global Christianity* (Oxford University Press; originally published in 2004, updated in 2007).

———. *The New Faces of Christianity: Believing the Bible in the Global South* (Oxford University Press, 2006).

Kukah, Matthew Hassan. *Democracy and Civil Society in Nigeria* (Spectrum Books Limited, 2003).

Sanneh, Lamin. *Whose Religion Is Christianity? The Gospel Beyond the West* (William B. Eerdmans, 2003).

TREND TWO: EVANGELICAL CATHOLICISM

Barker, Eileen, and Margit Warburg. *New Religions and New Religiosity* (Aarhus University Press, 1998).

Benedict XVI (Joseph Ratzinger). *Jesus of Nazareth: From the Baptism in the Jordan to the Transfiguration* (Doubleday, 2007).

Berger, Peter, ed. *The Desecularization of the World: Resurgent Religion and World Politics* (William B. Eerdmans, 1999).

———. "Globalization and the Rise of Religion." Interview with American Public Media, available at http://speakingoffaith.publicradio.org/programs/globalization/transcript.shtml.

Carroll, Colleen. *The New Faithful: Why Young Adults Are Embracing Christian Orthodoxy* (Loyola Press, 2004).

Congregation for the Doctrine of the Faith. "Dominus Iesus: On the Unicity and Salvific Universality of Jesus Christ and the Church." Declaration issued August 6, 2000, and available online at http://www.vatican.va/roman_curia/congregations/cfaith/documents/rc_con_cfaith_doc_20000806_dominus-iesus_en.html.

Hoge, Dean R. "Center of Catholic Identity." Published in the *National Catholic Reporter,* September 30, 2005.

Oden, Thomas. *The Rebirth of Orthodoxy: Signs of New Life in Christianity* (HarperOne, 2002).

Stark, Rodney, and William Sims Bainbridge. *A Theory of Religion* (Rutgers University Press, 1987).

Weigel, George. *The Courage to Be Catholic: Crisis, Reform, and the Future of the Church* (Basic Books, 2004).

TREND THREE: ISLAM

Aslan, Reza. *No god but God: The Origins, Evolution, and Future of Islam* (Random House, 2006).

Bergesen, Albert. *The Sayidd Qutb Reader* (Routledge, 2007).

Dulles, Avery. *A History of Apologetics* (Igantius Press; originally published in 1971, reprinted in 1999).

Elad-Altman, Israel. "The Sunni-Shia Conversion Controversy." Published in *Current Trends in Islamist Theology*, April 6, 2007.

Gerges, Fawaz A. *Journey of the Jihadist: Inside Muslim Militancy* (Harcourt Inc., 2006).

Kreeft, Peter. *Ecumenical Jihad: Ecumenism and the Culture War* (Ignatius Press, 1996).

Madigan, Daniel. *The Qur'an's Self-Image: Writing and Authority in Islam's Scripture* (Princeton University Press, 2001).

Nasr, Vali. *The Shia Revival: How Conflicts within Islam Will Shape the Future* (W.W. Norton, 2006).

Pontifical Council for Interreligious Dialogue. *Recognize the Spiritual Bonds which Unite Us: 16 Years of Christian-Muslim Dialogue* (Vatican, 1994).

Tabler, Andrew. "Catalytic Converters." *New York Times Magazine*, April 29, 2007.

Weigel, George. *The Cube and the Cathedral: Europe, America, and Politics Without God* (Basic Books, 2006).

TREND FOUR: THE NEW DEMOGRAPHY

Gallagher, David P. *Senior Adult Ministry in the 21st Century: Step-by-Step Strategies for Reaching People over 50* (Wipf & Stock Publishers, 2006).

Johnson, Adrian. "Suddenly, the Old World Looks Younger: Europe's Population." Published in *The Economist*, June 14, 2007.

Longman, Phillip. *The Empty Cradle: How Falling Birthrates Threaten World Prosperity and What to Do about It* (Basic Books, 2004).

President's Council on Bioethics. *Taking Care: Ethical Caregiving in Our Aging Society* (U.S. Government Printing, 2005).

United Nations Population Division. *World Population Prospects: The 2006 Revision* (United Nations, 2007).

Wattenberg, Ben. *Fewer: How the New Demography of Depopulation Will Shape our Future* (Ivan R. Dee, 2004).

TREND FIVE: EXPANDING LAY ROLES

DeLambo, David. *Lay Parish Ministers: A Study of Emerging Leadership.* A Study Conducted for the Committee on the Laity of the United States Conference of Catholic Bishops (National Pastoral Life Center, 2005).

Grisez, Germain, and Russell Shaw. *Personal Vocation: God Calls Everyone By Name* (Our Sunday Visitor, 2003).

Lubich, Chiara. *Essential Writings: Spirituality, Dialogue, Culture* (New City Press, 2007).

Murrow, David. *Why Men Hate Going to Church* (Nelson Books, 2004).

Podles, Leon. *The Church Impotent: The Feminization of Christianity* (Spence Publishing Company, July 1999).

Pope, Stephen J., ed. *Common Calling: The Laity and Governance of the Catholic Church* (Georgetown University Press, 2004).

Riccardi, Andrea. *Sant'Egidio: Rome and the World* (St. Paul's Books, 1996).

Second Vatican Council. *Apostolicam Actuositatem.* The Decree on the Laity. Promulgated on November 18, 1965. Available at: http://www.vatican.va/archive/hist _councils/ii_vatican_council/documents/vat-ii_decree_19651118_apostolicam -actuositatem_en.html.

Shaw, Russell. *Ministry or Apostolate: What Should the Catholic Laity Be Doing?* (Our Sunday Visitor, 2002).

United States Conference of Catholic Bishops. *Co-Workers in the Vineyard of the Lord: A Resource for Guiding the Development of Lay Ecclesial Ministry* (USCCB, 2005).

Urquhart, Gordon. *The Pope's Armada: Unlocking the Secrets of Mysterious and Powerful New Sects in the Church* (Bantam Press, 1995).

Vanier, Jean. *The Heart of L'Arche: A Spirituality for Every Day* (Crossroads Publishing Company, 1995).

TREND SIX: THE BIOTECH REVOLUTION

Andrews, Lori B. *The Clone Age: Adventures in the New World of Reproductive Technology* (Henry Holt and Company, 2000).

———, and Dorothy Nelkin. *Body Bazaar: The Market for Human Tissue in the Biotechnology Age* (Crown Publishers, 2001).

Avise, John C. *The Hope, Hype and Reality of Genetic Engineering: Remarkable Stories from Agriculture, Industry, Medicine, and the Environment* (Oxford University Press, 2004).

Bailey, Ronald. *Liberation Biology: The Scientific and Moral Case for the Biotech Revolution* (Prometheus Books, 2005).

Congregation for the Doctrine of the Faith. "Donum Vitae: Instruction on Respect for Human Life in its Origin and on the Dignity of Procreation. Replies to Certain Questions of the Day." Instruction issued February 22, 1987, and available online at http://www.vatican.va/roman_curia/congregations/cfaith/documents/rc_con _cfaith_doc_19870222_respect-for-human-life_en.html.

McKibben, Bill. *Enough: Staying Human in an Engineered Age* (Times Books, 2003).

Sowle Cahill, Lisa. *Theological Bioethics: Participation, Justice, and Change* (Georgetown University Press, 2003).

Walter, James J., and Thomas Shannon. *Contemporary Issues in Bioethics: A Catholic Perspective* (Sheed and Ward, 2005).

TREND SEVEN: GLOBALIZATION

Bhagwati, Jagdish. *In Defense of Globalization* (Oxford University Press, 2004).

Blundo, Giorgio, and Jean-Pierre Oliver de Sardan, eds. *Everyday Corruption and the State: Citizens and Public Officials in Africa* (Zed Books, 2006).

Burrows, Gideon. *The No-Nonsense Guide to the Arms Trade* (Verso, 2002).

Coleman, John, ed. *Globalization and Catholic Social Thought: Present Crisis, Future Hope* (Novartis Press, 2005).

King, Gilbert, with foreword by Eleanor Clift. *Woman, Child for Sale: The New Slave Trade in the 21st Century* (Chamberlain Brothers, 2004).

Novak, Michael. *The Spirit of Democratic Capitalism* (Madison Books, 1991).

Pontifical Council for Justice and Peace. *Compendium of the Social Doctrine of the Church* (United States Conference of Catholic Bishops Publishing, 2005).

Schroeder, Matthew, Rachel Stohl, and Colonel Dan Smith. *The Small Arms Trade: A Beginner's Guide* (Oneworld Publications, 2007).

United Nations. *The Millennium Development Goals Report*, 2007 (United Nations, 2007).

United Nations High Commissioner for Refugees. *UNHCR Global Report 2006* (United Nations, 2007).

Woods Jr., Thomas E. *The Church and the Free Market: A Catholic Defense of the Free Economy* (Lexington Books, 2005).

TREND EIGHT: ECOLOGY

Berry, Thomas. *The Dream of the Earth* (Sierra Club Books, 1988).

Cascioli, Riccardo, and Antonio Gaspari. *Le Bugie degli Ambientalisti* ["The Lies of the Environmentalists"] (Piemme, 2004 and 2006).

Catholic Bishops of the Watershed Region. "The Columbia River Watershed: Caring for Creation and the Common Good." An International Pastoral Letter. Available at: http://www.columbiariver.org/.

Christiansen, Drew, and Walter Grazer, eds. *And God Saw That It Was Good: Catholic Theology and the Environment* (United States Catholic Conference, 1996).

Guhlin, Jeffrey. "Where Are the Catholic Environmentalists?" *America*, February 13, 2006.

Hart, John. *What Are They Saying About Environmental Theology?* (Paulist Press, 2004).

Intergovernmental Panel on Climate Change. *Climate Change 2007* (Cambridge University Press, 2007).

Pope John Paul II. "The Ecological Crisis: A Common Responsibility." Message for the World Day of Peace (United States Catholic Conference, 1990).

Ruether, Rosemary Radford, ed. *Women Healing Earth: Third World Women on Ecology, Feminism, and Religion* (Orbis Books, 1994).

Shoumatoff, Alex. "The Gasping Forest." *Vanity Fair*, May 2007, pp. 272–285.

Snitow, Alan, Deborah Kaufman, and Michael Fox. *Thirst: Fighting the Corporate Theft of Our Water* (Jossey-Bass, 2007).

United States Conference of Catholic Bishops Committees on Domestic Policy and International Policy. *Faithful Stewards of God's Creation: A Catholic Resource for Environmental Justice and Climate Change* (USCCB, 2007).

TREND NINE: MULTIPOLARISM

Aikman, David. *Jesus in Beijing: How Christianity Is Changing the Global Balance of Power* (Regnery Publishing, 2003).

Clooney, Francis X. *Hindu Wisdom for All God's Children* (Wipf & Stock Publishers, 2005).

Eakin, Marshall C. *Brazil: The Once and Future Country* (Palgrave Macmillan, 1997).

Friedman, Thomas. *The World Is Flat: A Brief History of the 21st Century* (Farrar, Straus and Giroux, 2005).

Kejia, Yan. *Catholic Church in China* (China Intercontinental Press, 2004).

Meredith, Robyn. *The Elephant and the Dragon: The Rise of India and China and What It Means for All of Us* (W.W. Norton, 2007).

National Intelligence Council. *Mapping the Global Future: Report of the National Intelligence Council's 2020 Project* (United States Government Printing Office, 2004).

Politkovskaya, Anna. *Putin's Russia: Life in a Failing Democracy* (Metropolitan Books, 2005).

Pope Benedict XVI. "Letter of the Holy Father to the Bishops, Priests, Consecrated Persons and Lay Faithful of the Catholic Church in the People's Republic of China." Issued May 27, 2007, and available at: http://www.vatican.va/holy_father/benedict _xvi/letters/2007/documents/hf_ben-xvi_let_20070527_china_en.html.

Vardy, Nicholas. *Profit from Fast-Growth BRIC Economies: Brazil, Russia, India and China* (Eagle Financial Publications, 2006).

Wilson, Dominic, and Roopa Purushothaman. *Dreaming with BRICs: The Path to 2050* (Goldman Sachs, 2003).

TREND TEN: PENTECOSTALISM

Anderson, Allan. *An Introduction to Pentecostalism* (Cambridge University Press, 2004).

Cantalamessa, Raniero. *Sober Intoxication of the Spirit: Filled with the Fullness of God* (Servant Publications, 2005).

Cleary, Edward, and Hannah Stewart-Gambino, eds. *Power, Politics and Pentecostals in Latin America* (Westview Press, 1997).

Corten, Andre, and Ruth Marshall-Fratani, eds. *Between Babel and Pentecost: Transnational Pentecostalism in Africa and Latin America* (Indiana University Press, 2001).

Cox, Harvey. *Fire from Heaven: The Rise of Pentecostal Spirituality and the Reshaping of Religion in the 21st Century* (Addison-Wesley/Perseus Books, 1994).

Csordas, Thomas J. *Language, Charisma and Creativity: Ritual Life in the Catholic Charismatic Renewal* (Palgrave Macmillan, 2001).

Gifford, Paul. *Ghana's New Christianity: Pentecostalism in a Globalizing African Economy* (Indiana University Press, 2004).

Hallum, Anne Motley. "Taking Stock and Building Bridges: Feminism, Women's Movements, and Pentecostalism in Latin America." *Latin American Research Review* 38:1, 2003, pp. 169–86.

Miller, Donald E., and Tetsunao Yamamori. *Global Pentecostalism: The New Face of Christian Social Engagement* (University of California Press, 2007).

Pew Forum on Religion and Public Life. *Spirit and Power: A Ten-Country Survey of Pentecostals* (Pew Research Center, 2006).

Staff. "Christianity Reborn: Pentecostals." *The Economist*, December 23, 2006.

Steigenga, Timothy, and Edward Cleary, eds. *Conversion of a Continent: Contemporary Religious Change in Latin America* (Rutgers University Press, 2008).

Wiegele, Katharine L. *Investing in Miracles: El Shaddai and the Transformation of Popular Catholicism in the Philippines* (University of Hawaii Press, 2004).

INDEX